Behold the Pattern

by Goebel Music

BEHOLD THE PATTERN

5114 Montclair
Colleyville, TX 76034

Printed in the United States of America

First Printing — 3,000 — December 1991
Second Printing — 3,500 — January 1992
Third Printing — 3,500 — March 1992
Fourth Printing — 10,000 — May 1992
Fifth Printing — 5,000 — June 1992

Manufactured for Goebel Music Publications by:
Austin McGary & Company
P.O. Box 37552 Pensacola, FL 32526
(904) 944-7883

DEDICATION
TO

William S. Cline
A brother in the faith
Who, regarding this book,
Was a Barnabas personified.
He truly encouraged and
Inspired its writing.
His persistence
In this pursuit
Resulted
In this book's fruition.
Therefore to him
Is this book
Genuinely and Gratefully
Dedicated.

PREFACE

Behold The Pattern is a book that stresses the Bible pattern for the New Testament Church. There was a time in the "restoration movement" when the New Testament pattern was stressed with much more emphasis than it is being stressed, brotherhood-wide, today. There is a pressing need for brethren to review and/or reemphasize "the pattern" for New Testament Christianity. This book, **Behold The Pattern**, is quite replete in its emphasis on the pattern and/or doctrine of the **New Testament Church**. The title for this book reflects the need together with the content necessary to encourage and assist brethren who desire and choose to follow the pattern in a day when so many tend to drift with the tide of the ongoing religious world.

The book is interestingly written in **live** first, second, and third persons, as the circumstances and/or subject matter materials warrant. Thus, as one reads, the author is present all the way, and the applications and implications are very clearly set forth. This book has real merit. It has a very real place in the college and/or university classroom; in the teaching program of the local church, and on the desk of every minister of the gospel, as well as in every home.

The time is at hand when brethren of the churches of Christ very much need to take on a renewed and/or in-depth look at the Bible pattern for the New Testament Church. The purpose of the book is to meet and/or accommodate that pressing need.

Four chapters in the book - chapters V, VI, VII, VIII - are devoted to "strange and uncertain sounds from some brethren." To read about these matters tend to leave one faint and/or sick at heart, but those "uncertain sounds" are heard from time to time, and brethren need to be informed and/or forewarned. The New Testament writers were careful to forewarn and expose the errorist within the ranks of the church. Chief among the inspired writers who exposed the errorists during that early period of the church were Paul, Peter, Jude and John.

Rex A. Turner, Sr.
Chancellor
Alabama Christian School of Religion

FOREWORD

It was the first of February, 1987, when brother William S. Cline, editor of *Firm Foundation*, called me to see if I would be willing to speak on the Firm Foundation Lectureship in Seagoville, Texas, September 9-13, 1987. The subject was "Conquest By Faith," and the book of Joshua would be our text for the entire series. This was the Firm Foundation's Fourth Annual Lectureship and it was a part of covering another book in the Old Testament, and part of our plan to have each book in both the Old and New Testaments covered by a series of such lectures.

We discussed some of the topics to be covered in those twenty-four chapters. I told brother Cline of a thought I had from the book that had not been as thoroughly, exhaustively and extensively, covered as I felt the impact of it demanded. He asked me about it specifically, and I then quoted this verse to him:

> *"Therefore said we, It shall be, when they so say to us or to our generations in time to come, that we shall say, BEHOLD THE PATTERN of the altar of Jehovah, which our fathers made, not for burnt-offering, not for sacrifice; but it is a witness between us and you" (Josh. 22:28,* ***ASV****, emp. GM).*

When I explained about those three words, BEHOLD THE PATTERN, his encouragement to me began immediately, and he said: "Brother Music, you need to write a book on this subject, as it would make a great and most useful book for The Cause!" He was truly excited over such.

On February 9, 1987, brother Cline wrote me and said: "Please prepare a manuscript on BEHOLD THE

PATTERN (Chapter 22:28). This is the material that you will deliver for your sermon at the lectureship." I never once, not once, talked to him on the phone, at the lectureship, or at any other lectureship, etc., except he said to me, "Be sure and write a book on, BEHOLD THE PATTERN."

Our lectureship series on the book of Joshua, was, I felt, one of the very best done by the Firm Foundation series up to that point. The book was (is) 551 pages long and 28 men participated by writing the manuscripts and delivering the messages contained therein. The lecture I gave on "Behold The Pattern" is found on pages 454-467, most of which is now found "somewhere" in this book.

Even though much time has transpired since that February back in 1987, I never forgot about this subject, and I could not forget about brother Cline's emboldening, enheartening and exciting encouragement. I traveled extensively into the Far East in both 1988 and 1989, saw again the value of books and printed materials, observed the hunger of such by many, the need that was so very evident (I already knew of the urgent need in the States relative to the "pattern" concept that so many were rejecting), therefore, before I left to return home, in December of 1989, I announced that, the Lord willing, I would write a book entitled, "Behold The Pattern."

I had no earthly idea, when I landed at the D/FW Air Terminal on January 5, 1990, that so much would occur in my life, and the plans to write the book in those next three months would have to wait. Not only did we bury my father on March 17, 1990, but on May 17th I took ill and from that day until now has been one more experience. Not only was this book delayed, but the plans to write the one I was going to write during the winter had to be pushed aside.

I commenced this book on December 10, 1990, although still under the doctor's careful attention and having to rest at least two times per day. As I again read the Bible, did the research in the language, read what others were writing and their total rejection of "the pattern," listened to an unbelievable number of taped lectures and spent an incredible sum of hours and days both listening again and transcribing those tapes, as well as listening and proofing others, I made a commitment and a resolution. I resolved in my heart, as my soul was so burdened with the inundating and overwhelming error that I was both reading and hearing, that even if this book, with its stress and strain, finished my earthly pilgrimage, it would be well worth it for THE CAUSE that many of us love more than life itself.

On March 2, 1991, I mailed copies of the manuscript to some of our brotherhood's finest, including our beloved Bill Jackson, who, at the time of his death had not only read but proofed the first 209 pages. He had written me a letter the very day he died enroute home. I am so grateful to have his notes and comments, as well as those of many others, as they have truly been a source of inspiration. Brother Roy C. Deaver drove from Austin and spent some time with me and told me of his estimate of the book, stating it was a book, "whose time had come." Just let me hasten to say that I am deeply in debt for all the men who have taken the time and read either part of or the whole manuscript.

Even though 15 chapters in this book are very positive, instructive and informative, educational and edifying, many will say it is negative because of the 4 chapters (5-8) that quote 10 of our men in the very rank liberalism they set forth. Be it clearly understood that I have had no joy nor thrill in doing this. I have absolutely nothing personal against these men, as they are our brothers in Christ, but I firmly believe them to be brothers who teach and set forth error. I further believe we have an obligation to God, stemming from the book divine, that mandates us in these areas. Relative to these men, and the things I have written, I have taken every precautionary and preventative step I could to be exactly accurate, faithful, truthful and factual. If I have made any mistakes, it has been because of my own human frailty, my fallibility, certainly not purposeful, preplotted, or precontrived. That would be most unChristian and contrary to the Book's authorization.

This book has been written and produced with one and only one thought in mind, that being, to spread the Word of God. That has been my only motive, my only incentive and intention. This is the reason that I've done what I could, in the financial realm, to make sure that it gets to as many elders, preachers, both in our schools and out, missionaries, etc., as possible. To God, Christ and the Blood-Purchased Cause we love so much goes all the credit or glory, if there be any such that is gained by its production.

My prayer, aim and ambition, is that it will make, **even these 10 men herein named**, return to, never sway from, but always teach and practice the eternal thoughts found in the concept of "BEHOLD THE PATTERN."

Goebel Music

BEHOLD THE PATTERN

Table Of Contents

CHAPTER

Chapter One

THE PATTERN - AND THE TITLE FROM JOSHUA 22:28

THE PATTERN - AND THE TITLE FROM JOSHUA 22:28

There are many chapters in the Bible to which I could turn and strive to focus our awareness and alertness upon the unity desired by God for his people. Perhaps we could delve into and search out in minute detail Genesis chapter six and the instructions God gave Noah for the ark (vss. 14-22, esp.). It could be that Exodus chapters twenty-five and forty might be the areas of our investigation as we trace microscopically the tabernacle God instructed Moses to build. We might desire to probe and penetrate 1 Chronicles chapter twenty-eight and keenly observe the meticulous details of that grand and glorious temple that David charged his son Solomon to erect. Then again, while thinking and contemplating the idea of "unity with God" based upon following his every dictate and decree, we might explore 1 Chronicles chapters thirteen through fifteen and hear about the ark of God and how even the ones carrying it were vastly important and even that point could not change. The divine anger of God was manifested because "...we sought him not according to the ordinance" (*K.J.* has "due order," 1 Chron. 15:13). Finally, however, they did "...as Moses commanded according to the word of Jehovah" (vs. 15).

In addition to the Old Testament, the New Testament could also be examined; for herein we find the word "unity" two of the three times it is used in the entire Bible (cf. Eph. 4:1ff). It not only is just "in chapters" that we find the unity so desired by God, but also in words such as "tempered together," "builded together," "fitly framed together," "pattern," "example," "figure," and the lists goes on and on as we clearly come to grips in seeing that there is a "model," "rule," "canon," and a "type" to be followed. These things are just a bare beginning of the many ideas and thoughts presented to our minds about that which God has so craved for his people.

However, we must have a genesis for this book. I have chosen one chapter from the Old Testament, a chapter that presents unity by all the tribes like no other chapter I know. The chapter I have in mind is Joshua chapter twenty-two. Realizing that Paul said, "For whatsoever things were written aforetime were written for our learning, that through patience and through comfort of the scriptures we might have hope" (Rom. 15:4), I hope that we can learn just some of the lessons relative to this subject that can be found within those thirty-four verses. It is, indeed, a rare jewel when unity becomes our aim and ambition. This diamond-studded chapter is marked by prominent and precious objects that must be studied.

Just before, in our reading of the book of Joshua, we come to the chapter of our beginning, we hear these words:

> *"So Jehovah gave unto Israel all the land which he sware to give unto their fathers; and they possessed it, and dwelt therein. And Jehovah gave them rest round about, according to all that he sware unto their fathers: and there stood not a man of all their enemies before them; Jehovah delivered all their enemies into their hand. There failed not aught of any good thing which Jehovah had spoken unto the house of Israel; all came to pass" (21:43-45).*

The point of the faithfulness to God, as well as the faithfulness of God, needs to be emphasized. God has not changed. As God was with and blessed his people then, so will God be with and bless those today who do his bidding.

Moses warned that it would be "sin" to neglect God's every command (cf. Num. 32:20-24). Faithfulness to the Almighty is based on one thing (not on any man or group of men), and that is "the keeping of his commandments." There is a statement we find time and again throughout the Bible: "...as the Lord commanded...so did they" (cf. Gen. 6:22; Exod. 12:50; 40:16; 2 Kings 5:14; etc.).

I am keenly aware that we are not as familiar with the Old Testament as we are the New, therefore, with this in mind, but to a greater degree the precious pearls of this chapter, I am going to give it in its entirety, something, especially this long, I have not done before in my writing.

> *"Then Joshua called the Reubenites, and the Gadites, and the half-tribe of Manasseh, and said unto them,* ***Ye have kept all that Moses*** *the servant of Jehovah* ***commanded you,*** *and* ***have hearkened unto my voice in all that I commanded you: ye have not left your brethren*** *these many days unto this day, but* ***have kept the charge of the commandment of Jehovah*** *your God. And now Jehovah your God hath given rest unto your brethren, as he spake unto them: therefore now turn ye, and get you unto your tents, unto the land of your possession, which Moses the servant of Jehovah gave you beyond the Jordan. Only* ***take diligent heed to do the commandment and the law*** *which Moses the servant of Jehovah* ***commanded you, to love Jehovah your God****, and* ***to walk in all his ways****, and* ***to keep his commandments****, and* ***to cleave unto him****, and* ***to serve him with all your heart and with all your soul****. So Joshua blessed them, and sent them away; and they went unto their tents.*

"Now to the one half-tribe of Manasseh Moses had given inheritance in Bashan; but unto the other half gave Joshua among their brethren beyond the Jordan westward. Moreover when Joshua sent them away unto their tents, he blessed them, and spake unto them, saying, Return with much wealth unto your tents, and with very much cattle, with silver, and with gold, and with brass, and with iron, and with very much raiment: divide the spoil of your enemies with your brethren. And the children of Reuben and the children of Gad and the half-tribe of Manasseh returned, and departed from the children of Israel out of Shiloh, which is in the land of Canaan, to go unto the land of Gilead, to the land of their possession, whereof they were possessed, ***according to the commandment of Jehovah by Moses.***

"And when they came unto the region about the Jordan, that is in the land of Canaan, the children of Reuben and the children of Gad and the half-tribe of Manasseh ***built there an altar*** *by the Jordan,* ***a great altar to look upon****. And the children of Israel heard say,* ***Behold*** *the children of Reuben and the children of Gad and the half-tribe of Manasseh have* ***built an altar*** *in the forefront of the land of Canaan, in the region about the Jordan, on the side that pertaineth to the children of Israel. And* ***when the children of Israel heard of it, the whole congregation*** *of the children of Israel* ***gathered themselves together*** *at Shiloh, to go up against them* ***to war****.*

"And ***the children of Israel*** *sent unto the*

children of Reuben, and to the children of Gad, and to the half-tribe of Manasseh, into the land of Gilead, ***Phinehas*** *the son of Eleazar the priest, and* ***with him ten princes,*** *one prince of a fathers' house for each of the tribes of Israel; and they were every one of them head of their fathers' houses among the thousands of Israel. And* ***they came unto*** *the children of Reuben, and to the children of Gad, and to the half-tribe of Manasseh, unto the land of Gilead,* ***and they spake*** *with them,* ***saying, Thus saith the whole congregation of Jehovah, What trespass is this that ye have committed against the God of Israel, to turn away this day from following Jehovah, in that ye have builded you an altar, to rebel this day against Jehovah? Is the iniquity of Peor too little for us,*** *from which we have not cleansed ourselves unto this day, although* ***there came a plague*** *upon the congregation of Jehovah,* ***that ye must turn away*** *this day* ***from following Jehovah****? and it will be,* ***seeing ye rebel*** *today* ***against Jehovah,*** *that tomorrow* ***he will be wroth*** *with the whole congregation of Israel. Howbeit, if the land of your possession be* ***unclean,*** *then pass ye over unto the land of the possession of Jehovah, wherein* ***Jehovah's tabernacle*** *dwelleth, and take possession among us: but* ***rebel not against Jehovah, nor rebel against us, in building you an altar besides the altar of Jehovah our God. Did not Achan*** *the son of Zerah* ***commit a trespass*** *in the devoted thing,* ***and wrath fell upon all*** *the congregation of Israel? and* ***that man perished not alone*** *in his iniquity.*

"Then the children of Reuben and the children

of Gad and the half-tribe of Manasseh answered, and spake unto the heads of the thousands of Israel, The Mighty One, God, Jehovah, the Mighty One, God, Jehovah, **he knoweth; and Israel he shall know: if it be in rebellion, or if in trespass against Jehovah** (save thou us not this day,) **that we have built us an altar to turn away from following Jehovah;** or if to offer thereon burnt-offering or meal-offering, or if to offer sacrifices of peace-offerings thereon, **let Jehovah himself require it;** and if **we have** not **rather out of carefulness done this, and of purpose, saying, In time to come your children might speak unto our children,** saying, What have ye to do with Jehovah, the God of Israel? for Jehovah hath made the Jordan a border between us and you, ye children of Reuben and children of Gad; ye have no portion in Jehovah: **so might your children make our children cease from fearing Jehovah. Therefore** we said, **Let us now prepare to build us an altar,** not for burnt-offering, nor for sacrifice: but **it shall be a witness** between us and you, and between our generations after us, that we may do the **service of Jehovah** before him with our burnt-offerings, and with our sacrifices, and with our peace-offerings; **that your children may not say to our children in time to come, Ye have no portion in Jehovah.** Therefore said we, It shall be, when they so say to us or to our generations in time to come, that we shall say, **Behold the pattern of the altar of Jehovah,** which our fathers made, **not for** burnt-offering, nor for sacrifice; but **it is a witness** between us *and you.* ***Far be it from us that we should rebel against Jehovah,*** *and turn away this day from following Jehovah,* ***to build an altar*** *for burnt-offering, for meal-offering, or for sacrifice,* ***besides the altar of Jehovah our God that is before his tabernacle.***

"And when Phinehas the priest, and the princes of the congregation, even the heads of the thousands of Israel that were with him, ***heard the words*** *that the children of Reuben and the children of Gad and the children of Manasseh spake,* ***it pleased them well.*** *And Phinehas the son of Eleazar the priest said unto the children of Reuben, and to the children of Gad, and to the children of Manasseh,* ***This day we know that Jehovah is in the midst of us, because ye have not committed this trespass against Jehovah:*** *now have ye delivered the children of Israel out of the hand of Jehovah. And Phinehas the son of Eleazar the priest, and the princes, returned from the children of Reuben, and from the children of Gad, out of the land of Gilead, unto the land of Canaan, to the children of Israel, and brought them word again.* ***And the thing pleased the children of Israel;*** *and the children of Israel* ***blessed God,*** *and* ***spake no more of going up against them to war, to destroy*** *the land wherein the children of Reuben and the children of Gad dwelt. And the children of Reuben and the children of Gad called* ***the altar Ed:*** *For, said they,* ***it is a witness between us that Jehovah is God."*** *(ASV, emp., GM).*

I do not believe anyone can read the above chapter

without being touched by "their single cry to please Jehovah God." Actually, this was a cry "for unity among all the tribes," regardless of which side of the Jordan they lived. A few salient points are necessary.

1. **The charge of Joshua** to the Reubenites, the Gadites, and the half-tribe of Manasseh, after stating in verse two that they had kept all that Moses had commanded them and also those that Joshua had commanded them, as well as the charge of the commandment of Jehovah, is found in verse five. "Only take diligent heed to do the commandment and the law which Moses the servant of Jehovah commanded you, to love... to walk... to keep... to cleave... to serve him with all your heart and with all your soul." Jehovah God has been proven to be their very focal point. To him and to no other do they owe their allegiance. This is proven by the fact they kept "all the commandments and walked in all his ways." This is nothing less than total submission.

2. **With the blessings of Joshua upon them,** the children of Reuben, the children of Gad, and the half-tribe of Manasseh left "from the children of Israel out of Shiloh, which is in the land of Canaan, to go unto the land of Gilead,..." (vs. 9). Shiloh is the place where they had set up "the tent of meeting" (the tabernacle), as revealed in 18:1. This was where God placed his name and spoke of it as "my place" (Jer. 7:12). Here "in the land of Canaan" these two and one-half tribes "built an altar!" We know where this altar is built because of verses 10-11. The word "behold," as found in verse eleven, shows its importance and significance to the children of Israel. They knew this was a transgression of the law, as no sacrifices were to be made on any altar other than the one before the tabernacle (cf. Deut. 12:13-14).

3. **The whole congregation gathers together** and an

investigation is made relative to this altar. To have such unity among so many is most significant, as well as their gathering place, Shiloh. They were all united in their thoughts that this altar was "a trespass against the God of Israel," as they had "evidently" turned away from following God and had "rebelled by the building of this altar" (vss. 12-16). This was placed in the form of a question.

4. **The questioning encounter continues**, being based on two examples for the past (cf. Deut. 13:12-15 relative to their questions). They ask a question about "the iniquity of Peor," from which they had not been cleansed (vs. 17), and they asked one about "the trespass of Achan," with the thought that he did not perish alone in his iniquity (vs. 20). They plead with the fear of Jehovah when they said, "If the land of your possession be unclean, then pass ye over unto the land of the possession of Jehovah, wherein Jehovah's tabernacle dwelleth" (vs. 19). Note again the statement about "God's tabernacle" and "where it is."

5. **The horror of these two and a half tribes at the sin** of which they are supposed guilty (vss. 21-29) is easily detected in their double appeal to **El, Elomim, Yahweh;** God, The Mighty One, Jehovah. We observe the following defense of their actions.

a. God, The Mighty One, Jehovah, he knoweth; and Israel shall know: if it be in rebellion, or if in trespass against Jehovah.

b. Let Jehovah himself require it.

c. If we have not rather out of carefulness done this, and out of purpose, saying, In time to come your children might speak unto our children, saying, What have ye to do with Jehovah, the God of Israel?

d. It shall be a witness between us and you, and between our generations after us, that we may do the service of Jehovah.

e. Therefore said we, It shall be, when they so say to us or to our generations in time to come, that we shall say, **Behold the pattern** of the altar of Jehovah, which our fathers made...it is a witness between us and you.

f. Far be it from us that we should rebel against Jehovah, and turn away this day from following Jehovah.

6. **The words of truth in the appeal made** "pleased them well" (vs. 30). We now read: "This day we know that Jehovah is in the midst of us, because ye have not committed this trespass against Jehovah" (vs. 31). When word was brought (vs. 32) to the children of Israel, we read again, as we did in verse thirty, "the thing pleased the children of Israel" (vs. 33). Therefore, the altar was called **Ed**, for they said "it is a **witness** between us that Jehovah is God" (vs. 34, emp., GM).

This chapter twenty-two of Joshua is precious, priceless, and preeminent in a study on "the pattern," and I very seriously doubt if many have given serious thought to it. It is simply overflowing and bursting forth with words, thoughts, attitudes, phrases, and a desire for unity based on pleasing God that is perhaps found nowhere else. If studied honestly and accurately, that is, having a desire like these tribes in their earnest endeavors to please God, it will be dynamic and most productive for us today. It is replete and well-supplied with the kind of love for God and man that needs to be held in high esteem today. The reason is they are held in proper perspective. They not only were concerned about the present tribes, but also about "their children in time to come."

We skimmed through the chapter by giving some striking and significant thoughts. Now let us tabulate some words and thoughts if one truly desires to know more of this extensive chapter.

1. **Note these words:** kept (vs. 2), the charge (vs. 3), take diligent heed (vs. 5), love, walk, keep, cleave, serve (vs. 5), and blessed (vs. 6).

2. **Observe that they did** "all" that was commanded (vss. 2-5).

3. **Register the fact of** the "faithfulness of God" to them (vss. 2-6), the very foundation of their blessings/ possessions.

4. **Mark down that their love for** their families was secondary to their love for God (vs. 3). His was pre-eminent with them.

5. **Docket their loyalty to** complete subjection to Moses and to Joshua, but only as they were servants of God (vss. 2-5).

6. **Chronicle that all the heart and** all the soul shows us that the commandment and the law took priority over all things (vs. 5, cf. Deut. 11:1, 13, 22-23; 23:11; etc.).

7. **Record one half-tribe of Manasseh in** Bashan with the other half-tribe beyond the Jordan (vs. 7). Then be alert to the ten princes, and if war, it would be family against family (vss. 12-16). The importance is the value they placed on God being supreme! It was total loyalty.

8. **Notice specifically** "the tabernacle" and how that it served as "a pattern," and this was in Shiloh where God had put his name (vss. 19, 9, 28). Yes, the one in Shiloh followed "the pattern" (cf. Heb. 8:5).

9. **Pay attention to** this altar, a great altar, one patterned after the one in Shiloh, but it was "to look upon" (vs. 10).

10. **Commit to memory** that "there was only one place" where they were to offer sacrifices (vs. 11, cf. Deut. 12:13-14).

11. **Appreciate the fact** of the unity of the whole congregation and the concern over violating God's law (vss. 12ff), and if it took war then it would just have to be.

12. **Be aware of** "first hand knowledge," the desire to secure it, and the fact they did not "move to war" on "hearsay" (vss. 11-20; cf. Deut. 13:12-15).

13. **Point to** verse sixteen and catalogue a fact needed today for unity. When Phinehas and the ten princes met with these two and one-half tribes, they said, "thus saith the whole congregation of Jehovah" (vs. 16). All knew this could be rebellion against God's order of how to follow him.

14. **Study the destructive and devastating effects of sin.** It is to be seen as "trespass," "rebellion," "iniquity," etc. (vss. 16-20), against God and God's wrath is poured on man because of it. Sin destroys any hope for true unity and fellowship with God and his people.

15. **Give thought** that there is a time "to return to the true place and pattern in worshiping God" (vs. 19). Indeed, we, like they, can use examples of those "before us" to quicken our senses!

16. **Regard an honest,** sincere and God-fearing plea by those who love God and have proven it by their actions (vss. 21ff). Then be honest and sincere enough (cf. Heb. 4:12-13) to do that which is right.

17. **Apply oneself to** an attitude for unity among God's people, and, without rationalization, imitate Paul when he said, "If I be an offender, or have committed any thing worthy of death, I refuse not to die..." (cf. Acts 25:11). Rule out everything but pleasing God by doing exactly as God has prescribed (vss. 22-28).

18. **Be conscious of** the "all-seeing eye of God" (cf. Prov. 15:3; Jer. 23:23-24; Psm. 139:7ff; etc.), and remember that God has spoken as to the worship that pleases him (vss. 22:24; cf. John 4:21-24).

19. **Visualize the future** and the need to do that which will help keep anything or anyone from making our children "cease from fearing Jehovah" (vss. 24-27).

20. **Detect the word** "us" in verse twenty-six and take note that "this altar" was not to be used in "their worship of Jehovah." This altar served as a "sign" or a "symbol" of a common faith and desire to please only God.

21. **Contemplate** that this altar was made "after the fashion" of the one in Shiloh, the pattern given by God, therefore, it signified to them God's plan and that only it was authoritative (vss. 27-29).

22. **Rejection of** "the pattern" was rejection of God. This is one thought gleaned throughout the Bible (cf. 1 Sam. 13-15; vss. 28-29).

23. **Make it known** that unity can be and will be achieved if all parties involved do exactly as God says, for the reason that God says and with that kind of faith that "takes God at his word" (vss. 30ff).

24. **Catalogue** the gratitude and the attitude that caused the children of Israel to "bless God," and also the two and one-half tribes, when they declared, "it is a witness between us that Jehovah is God" (vss. 32-34).

I can only hope, trust, and pray that the little written, indeed, far less than trying to be exhaustive for I doubt that one could be with such a chapter, will serve us as both a "reminder" and a "blessing" as we strive also to please God. From the thoughts expressed and with the proper attitude requested, may we truly BEHOLD THE PATTERN as we read and study the chapters that lie ahead.

Chapter Two

THE PATTERN - AND A NEW TESTAMENT WORD STUDY

THE PATTERN - AND A NEW TESTAMENT WORD STUDY

It seems to me a good question to ask is, "Does the New Testament employ the use of this idea?" Better yet, "Does the New Testament, inspired by the Holy Spirit of God (2 Tim. 3:16-17; 2 Pet. 1:19-21; 1 Cor. 2:9-13), utilize and put to work the very word we are discussing, the word 'pattern'?" If it does not, then why are we to believe there is a pattern? If it does not, does that by force of circumstance, rule out the idea of a pattern? If it does, then why is it used if there is no pattern? If it does, then why do we have to rebuttal the idea of a pattern? Many such questions could be asked, but let us take a look into the New Testament and locate, if possible, where this word is exercised, the way it is used, as well as noting the various words chosen by the Holy Spirit to convey the idea and also observe the Greek words and their meanings. I do not mean to say that these items will be discussed in this particular order, but in the totality of what will be given.

The majority of the people in the world depend upon having the New Testament translated into their tongue. The remarks we hear about the use of the Greek New Testament are manifold; many being extremely critical. However, we need to understand that, for the most part, what we have in English today is because of the translation from Greek to English. For the most part, be it recognized or not, we are dependent upon a translation that has been made into our tongue, our language. The Greek words are vastly important and need to be studied. However, let me be quick to say that just looking at a lexicon is only a small part of a good Bible student's research. Very few matters can be settled by lexicography alone. The true Biblical scholar relies upon a total exegesis wherein he considers the Biblical teaching on the matter - lexically, grammatically, contextually, historically, etc. Regardless of the employment of the word in a Greek lexicon (a dictionary), the context is never to be overlooked, as it is therein we find the meaning, that is, how the word is used.

As far as I have studied, and as it is always true in my own particular study I may have overlooked something, there are three words in the Greek New Testament translated as "pattern." Perhaps the word that most will recognize is the word *tupos*. That is the one that is most frequently found, being given some sixteen times in the Greek New Testament.

Let us now observe those sixteen wordings, by way of quotation as found in the *King James*, with the change in the English word, as we have eight different English words used in translating *tupos*. Also, we will note the difference as found in the *American Standard*, that is, the 1901 edition. I list these according to order of the New Testament books, but when a different word in English is used, I will take it through the various scriptures where it is found.

1. **Print:**

> "The other disciples therefore said unto him, We have seen the Lord. But he said unto them, Except I shall see in his hands the print of the nails, and put my finger into the print of the nails, and thrust my hand into his side, I will not believe" (John 20:25, used twice).

2. **Figure:**

"Yea, ye took up the tabernacle of Moloch, and the star of your god Remphan, figures which ye made to worship them: and I will carry you away beyond Babylon" (Acts 7:43).

"Nevertheless death reigned from Adam to Moses, even over them that had not sinned after the similitude of Adam's transgression, who is the figure of him that was to come" (Rom. 5:14).

3. **Fashion:**

"Our fathers had the tabernacle of witness in the wilderness, as he had appointed, speaking unto Moses, that he should make it according to the fashion that he had seen" (Acts 7:44; *ASV* has "figure").

4. **Manner:**

"And he wrote a letter after this manner:" (Acts 23:25; *ASV* has "form").

5. **Form:**

"But God be thanked, that ye were the servants of sin, but ye have obeyed from the heart that form of doctrine which was delivered you" (Rom. 6:17; *ASV* has a footnote on the word "form" and says "or pattern").

6. **Example:**

"Now these things were our examples, to the intent we should not lust after evil things, as they also lusted" (1 Cor. 10:6; *K.J.* has marginal note "figures").

"Let no man despise thy youth; but be thou an

example of the believers, in word, in conversation, in charity, in spirit, in faith, in purity" (1 Tim. 4:12; *ASV* has "ensample").

7. **Ensample:**

   "Now all these things happened unto them for ensamples: and they are written for our admonition, upon whom the ends of the world are come" (1 Cor. 10:11; *K.J.* has "or types" in the marginal note; *ASV* has "example" with the footnote, "by way of figure").

   "Brethren, be followers together of me, and mark them which walk so as ye have us for an ensample" (Phil. 3:17).

   "So that ye were ensamples to all that believe in Macedonia and Achaia" (1 Thess. 1:7).

   "Not because we have not power, but to make ourselves an ensample unto you to follow us" (2 Thess. 3:9).

   "Neither as being lords over God's heritage, but being ensamples to the flock" (1 Pet. 5:3).

8. **Pattern:**

   "In all things shewing thyself a pattern of good works: in doctrine shewing uncorruptness, gravity, sincerity" (Tit. 2:7; *ASV* has "ensample").

   "Who serve unto the example and shadow of heavenly things, as Moses was admonished of God when he was about to make the tabernacle: for, See, saith he, that thou make all things according to the pattern shewed to thee in the mount" (Heb. 8:5).

Another word that is translated as "pattern" is the

koine Greek word *hupodeigma.* This word is found about six times in the New Testament, but is given as "pattern" in only one scripture. "It was necessary that the patterns of things in the heavens should be purified with these; but the heavenly things themselves with better sacrifices than these" (Heb. 9:23; *ASV* has "the copies"). This word is given as "example" (John 13:15; Heb. 4:11; 8:5; James 5:10; *ASV* has "a copy" in Heb. 8:5) and also as "ensample" (2 Pet. 2:6; *ASV* gives it as "example").

The word *hupotuposis* is used in 1 Timothy 1:16: "Howbeit for this cause I obtained mercy, that in me first Jesus Christ might shew forth all longsuffering, for a pattern to them which should hereafter believe on him to life everlasting" (*ASV* has "ensample;" 2 Tim. 1:13 is "form" in the *K.J.* and "pattern" in *ASV*). (It might help also to mention that the word *antitupos* is found in Hebrews 9:24; 1 Peter 3:21; "figure" in *K.J.* and "pattern" and "true likeness" in the *ASV* respectively given, with the *ASV* having a footnote on 1 Peter 3:21 as "in the antitype").

Basically, what I have done thus far is to take a brief look at the word *tupos* and to see "where" it is used, "how" it is translated and "how many" words are translated as "pattern." We found that we have eight English words translated from *tupos* (*King James*) and an additional word, "copy," given by comparing the *American Standard Version.* Also, we have two other words added to the list when we note the other three words from which the word "pattern" is translated, "antitype" and "true likeness." Therefore, from the three nouns and one adjective listed from the Greek words above, we have found the words in the *King James* and the *American Standard* to be: print, figure, fashion, manner, form, example, ensample, pattern, copy, antitype, type and true likeness (the word "type" is given in the margin in the *King James* on 1 Cor. 10:11). These words are all to be found in the twenty-four different passages that are mentioned above, wherein are used the four Greek words listed.

Finding the word "pattern," noting wherein it is used, as well as observing the New Testament Greek words, we now want to discern the various meanings that those skilled in the Greek language have attributed, assigned, and associated with this word. With this stated, we now turn and focus our earnest and sincere attention, first of all, to some of the lexicographers, listed at random.

1. ***Joseph Henry Thayer:***

> *"The mark of a stroke or blow; print:...John 20:25."*
>
> *"A figure formed by a blow or impression; hence univ. a figure, image:...Acts 7:43."*
>
> *"Form:* ***didaches****, i.e. the teaching which embodies the sum and substance of religion and represents it to the mind, Rom. 6:17; i.q. manner of writing, the contents and form of a letter, Acts 23:25."*
>
> *"An example; a. in the technical sense, viz. the pattern in conformity to which a thing must be made: Acts 7:44; Heb. 8:5, (Ex. 25:40). b. in an ethical sense, a dissuasive example, pattern of warning:...1 Cor. 10:6,...; an example to be imitated: of men worthy of imitation, Phil. 3:17; with a gen. of the pers. to whom the example is offered, 1 Tim. 4:12; 1 Pet. 5:3;... 2 Th. 3:9;...1 Th. 1:7;...Tit. 2:7..." (****A Greek-English Lexicon of the New Testament****, p. 632).*

2. ***William F. Arndt and F. Wilbur Gingrich:***

"...4. Form, figure, pattern...pattern of teaching, Rom. 6:17..."

*"5. (arche) type, pattern, model...a. technically, model, pattern, Acts 7:44; Hb. 8:5 (cf. on both Ex. 25:40). b. in the moral life, example, pattern...1 Ti. 4:12; Phil. 3:17; 1 Th. 1:7; 2 Th. 3:9; Tit. 2:7; 1 Pt. 5:3..." (**A Greek-English Lexicon of the New Testament and Other Early Literature**, p. 837).*

3. ***Ethelbert W. Bullinger:***

*"A mark or impress made by a hard substance on a softer one; then, model, pattern, exemplar in the widest sense" (**A Critical Lexicon and Concordance to the English and Greek New Testament**, p. 575).*

4. ***Harold K. Moulton:***

*"A blow; an impress; a print, mark, of a wound inflicted, Jno. 20:25; a delineation; an image,...a formula, scheme, Ro. 6:17; form, purport, Ac. 23:25;...a model, pattern, Ac. 7:44; He. 8:5; a moral pattern, Phil. 3:17; 1 Thes. 1:7; 2 Thes. 3:9; 1 Ti. 4:12; 1 Pe. 5:3" (**The Analytical Greek Lexicon Revised**, p. 411).*

5. ***George V. Wigram:***

"A blow; an impress; a print, mark,...a formula, scheme, Ro. 6:17; form,...a figure,...an anticipative figure, type, Ro. 5:14; 1 Co. 10:11; a model pattern, Ac. 7:44; He. 8:5; a moral pattern, Phil. 3:17; 1 Thes. 1:7; 2 Thes. 3:9;

*1 Ti. 4:12; 1 Pe. 5:3" (**The Analytical Greek Lexicon of the New Testament**, p. 411).*

6. ***G. Abbott-Smith:***

"...3. form: Ro. 6:17; the sense or substance of a letter...Ac. 23:25."

*"4. An example, pattern. Ac. 7:44; He. 8:5 (LXX); in ethical sense, 1 Co. 10:6; Phl. 3:17; 1 Th. 1:7; 2 Th. 3:9; 1 Ti. 4:12; Tit. 2:7; 1 Pe. 5:3; in doctrinal sense, type...Ro. 5:14" (**A Manual Greek Lexicon of the New Testament**, p. 452).*

7. ***Harper & Brothers:***

*(This is not repeated, as the wording and even the page number is the same as that of Moulton and Wigram, GM. **The Analytical Greek Lexicon**, p. 411).*

8. ***Liddell and Scott:***

*"...the impress of a seal, the stamp of a coin, a print,...2. figures or impressions wrought in metal or stone: simply, a figure, image,...3. an outline, sketch,...4. the original pattern, model, mould, type, metaph. a type, figure. 5. a system, form of doctrine..." (**A Lexicon Abridged From Liddell and Scott's Greek-English Lexicon**, p. 721).*

In addition to these Greek Lexicons, I also checked *The New Englishman's Greek Concordance And Lexicon* by Wigram-Green, *A Concordance to the Greek Testament* by W. F. Moulton, A. S. Geden, and H. K. Moulton (which is according to the texts of Westcott and Hort, Tischendorf and the English Revisers), and *Greek-English Concordance*

To The New Testament by J. B. Smith. However, since there were no different meanings listed, I did not list them (this is good information for the astute student and so I list it). Then, too, let me be quick to say that I tried to list, on the whole, the various different thoughts, but, of course, not all of what any one lexicon gave.

We now further our investigation and inspection, exploration and examination of those who can enlighten us relative to the meaning and message found in the Greek word *tupos* (English, pattern).

1. ***W. E. Vine:***

   "...c. a form or mould, Rom. 6:17...an ensample, pattern, Acts 7:44; Heb. 8:5, 'pattern;' in an ethical sense, 1 Cor. 10:6; Phil. 3:17; 1 Thess. 1:7;...'pattern;' 1 Pet. 5:3; in a doctrinal sense, a type, Rom. 5:14..."

   *"The representation or pattern of anything... 'form' in Rom. 6:17, 'that form (or mould) of teaching whereunto ye were delivered,' ...The Gospel is the mould; those who are obedient to its teachings become conformed to Christ, whom it presents..." (**An Expository Dictionary of New Testament Words**, pp. 33, 124).*

2. ***A. T. Robertson:***

   "The pattern...The very word used in Ex. 25:40 and quoted by Stephen in Acts 7:44... The tabernacle was to be patterned after the heavenly model."

   *"Moses was shown a **tupos** (model) of the heavenly realities and he made an **antitupon** on that model, 'answering to the type' (Dods) or model."*

"The singular looks at the church as a whole, the plural, as individuals... ***Tupos*** *as an old word from* ***tupto****, to strike...Then the figure formed by the blow, image as in Acts 7:43. Then the mould or form (Rom. 6:17; Acts 23:25). Then an example or pattern as in Acts 7:44, to be imitated as here, Phil. 3:17, etc. It was a great compliment for the church in Thessalonica to be already a model for believers in Macedonia and Achaia. Our word type for printers is this same word with one of its meanings."*

*"...and finally a type in a doctrinal sense (Rom. 5:14; Heb. 9:24)." (****Word Pictures in the New Testament****, Vol. V, pp. 390, 403; Vol. IV, pp. 12, 152).*

3. ***W. Robertson Nicoll:***

"The gen. is that of apposition: a pattern, sc. of faith, expressed in sound words."

*"****Tupos*** *is followed by the genitive of the person for whose edification the* ***tupos*** *exists in 1 Cor. 10:6; 1 Pet. 5:3."*

"According to 8:5 a ***tupos*** *of the heavenly realities was shown to Moses, and what he constructed from that model was an* ***antitupon****, answering to the type...that which corresponds to and prefigures." (****The Expositor's Greek Testament****, Vol. 4, pp. 158, 126, 338).*

4. ***Fritz Rienecker and Cleon Rogers:***

*"****Tupos****, type. The word means a visible mark left by some object. Then the mark left in history or nature by the antitype."*

*"**Tupos**, type. Incorporation of the antecedant into the rel. clause, 'to which form of doctrine ye were delivered.'"*

*"**Tupos**, example, type...a pattern of conduct, but more usually, as here, of an example to be followed." (**Linguistic Key To The Greek New Testament**, pp. 360, 362, 587; cf. pp. 418, 639, 654, 691).*

5. ***M. R. Vincent:***

*"Examples (**tupoi**). Peter uses three different terms for a pattern or model, **hupogrammos**, a writing-copy...**hupodeigma**,...an architect's plan or a sculptor's or painter's model (2 Pet. 2:6), **tupos**...of which our word type is nearly a transcript. The word primarily means the impression left by a stroke (**tupto**, to strike)... Generally, an image or form, always with a statement of the object; and hence the kindred meaning of a pattern or model. See Acts 23:25; Rom. 5:14; Philip. 3:17; Heb. 8:5."*

*"Form of doctrine (**tupon didaches**)...form of teaching...The Pauline type of teaching as contrasted with the Judaistic forms...Compare my gospel, 2:16; 16:25. Others explain as the ideal or pattern presented by the gospel. Form of teaching, however, seems to point to a special and precisely defined type of Christian instruction."*

*"Examples (**tupoi**). The word may mean either an example, as 1 Tim. 4:12, or a type of a fact or of a spritual truth, Heb. 9:24; Rom. 5:14." (**Word Studies in the New Testament**, pp. 318, 698, 783).*

6. ***Gerhard Kittel and Gerhard Friedrich:***

"In Paul, the Pastorals and 1 Pt. it is used 6 times for the determinative 'example' of the obedience of faith, also in R. 6:17 for Christian teaching as a mould and norm."

"As the term indicates and the context says, it is the model which makes an impress because it is moulded by God. 2 Th. 3:9 refers to the example of the apostle along with binding tradition (3:6) and authoritative direction (3:10ff). The example, then, represents what the word says and, like the word, it is effective only through faith... According to 1 Th. 1:7 the community, by receiving the word, has become an imitator of Paul and hence also of the Lord,..."

*"**Tupos** is rather the impress which makes an impress, so that in context the teaching can be described as the mould and norm which shapes the whole personal conduct of the one who is delivered up to it and has become obedient thereto." (**Theological Dictionary of the New Testament**, Vol. VIII, pp. 248, 249-250).*

7. ***Samuel Fallows, Andrew C. Zenos and Herbert L. Willett:***

*"Gr. **Tupos**, the mark of a stroke, print. In Tit. 2:7 it means example to be copied; while it has the meaning (Heb. 8:5) of type, pattern." (**The Popular and Critical Bible Encyclopaedia and Scriptural Dictionary**, p. 1294).*

I have not perused - read thoroughly - every Greek book I have in my library, but think the preceding number of lexicons and other scholarly works in that language should suffice for our study. Now I want to notice just a few comments from various authors who have written on one or more scriptures using the word "pattern."

1. ***W. J. Conybeare and J. S. Howson:***

   "But God be thanked that you, who were once the slaves of sin, obeyed from your hearts the teaching whereby you were moulded anew; and when you were freed from the slavery of sin, you became the bondsmen of righteousness... Literally, the mould of teaching into which you were transmitted. The metaphor is from the casting of metals."

   *"Hold fast the pattern of sound words which thou hath heard from me, in the faith and love which is in Christ Jesus... Sound words. The want of the article shows that this expression had become almost a technical expression at the date of the Pastoral Epistles." (**The Life and Epistles of St. Paul**, pp. 512, 773).*

2. ***Adam Clarke:***

   "Hold fast the form of sound words... No man was left to invent a religion for his own use, and after his own mind. God alone knows that with which God can be pleased. If God did not give a revelation of himself, the inventions of man, in religious things, would be endless error, involving itself in contortions of unlimited confusions. God gives, in his mercy to man, a form of sound words or doctrines; a perfect plan and sketch of the original building; fair and well defined outlines of every thing which concerns the present and eternal welfare

*of man, and his own glory." (**Clarke's Commentary**, Vol. VI, pp. 626-627; cf. p. 868 for his thoughts on 1 Peter 5:3, the perfect pattern).*

3. ***Alexander Maclaren:***

"...a kind of mould into which they were thrown, a pattern to which they were to be conformed...First, Paul's Gospel was a definite body of teaching; secondly, that teaching is a mould for conduct and character; lastly, that teaching therefore demands obedience."

*"It is no use having a perfect Pattern unless you have a motive to copy it." (**Expositions of Holy Scriptures**, Vol. XIII, pp. 114-115, 119).*

4. ***Matthew Henry:***

*"You have obeyed from the heart that form of doctrine which was delivered to you, v. 17. This describes conversion, what it is; it is our conformity to, and compliance with, the gospel which was delivered to us by Christ and his ministers...And so observe, First, The rule of grace, that form of doctrine - **tupon didaches.** The gospel is the great rule of truth and holiness;...The gospel is a doctrine not only to be believed, but to be obeyed,...To be a Christian indeed is to be transformed into the likeness and similitude of the gospel, our souls answering to it, complying with it, conformed by it - ..."*

"...by the form of sound words I understand the holy scriptures themselves...Adhere to it in opposition to all heresies and false doctrine,

*which corrupt the Christian faith... The Christian doctrine is a trust committed to us." (**Matthew Henry's Commentary On The Whole Bible**, Vol. VI, pp. 406, 836).*

5. ***J. W. McGarvey and Philip Y. Pendleton:***

*"But thanks be to God that these principles are not mere matters of speculation with you, but have been tested and applied by you in your actual experience, for whereas ye were once the slaves of sin, ye of your own free will and heart's choice, changed your masters, and became, by your obedience to it, the servants or slaves of the principles set down in the Christian or gospel form of teaching..." (**The Standard Bible Commentary**, on "Thessalonians, Corinthians, Galatians and Romans, p. 347).*

6. ***R. C. H. Lenski:***

*"The opposite is: 'being **tupoi** to the flock,' models for the flock to pattern after; as a die is struck, and its impress made by a blow so the die makes the counterstamp and impress on the material." (**The Interpretation of The Epistles of St. Peter, St. John and St. Jude**, p. 220).*

7. ***Roy H. Lanier, Sr.:***

*"To that form of doctrine. a. Pattern of sound words (2 Tim. 1:13), b. Sound doctrine, the gospel (1 Tim. 1:10,11), c. Sound in the faith (Titus 1:13,14)." (**Class Notes On Romans**, p. 42).*

8. ***David Lipscomb:***

*"To that form of teaching - ...Obedience to the form of teaching includes the quickening through faith, the death to sin, the burial and resurrection through baptism into a new life in Christ. This binds us to an obedience to all the laws and regulations of the Christian religion that fit us for enjoying the blessings of heaven." (**A Commentary on the New Testament Epistles**, Vol. 1, pp. 123-124).*

9. ***William Hendriksen:***

*"So, in the third paragraph (verses 13,14) of this section (verses 8-14) the author turns once to the matter of Timothy's duty. Says Paul: As a pattern of sound words hold on to those which you have heard from me...As an artist has his sketch,...so Timothy also had his model to go by. This sketch, model, or pattern consisted of the words which he had heard from Paul. Let him hold on to these, ever using them as his example, never departing from them...And it is exactly the necessity of remaining sound and of transmitting sound doctrine that is stressed throughout the epistle...The slogan, so popular today, 'It does not matter what you believe, just so you are serious in whatever you believe,' is flatly contradicted in the Pastorals!" (**New Testament Commentary**, I and II Timothy and Titus, pp. 236-237).*

Even though many more statements could be given, neither time nor space allows such for this particular chapter. However, there is yet one more word (at least one) in the Greek language which must be covered. From the English text, one would suppose, surmise, suspect and take a shot in the dark that the word is the very word, *tupos*, that we have been studying. Let us note this passage from the pen of Peter. "For hereunto were ye called: because Christ also suffered for you, leaving you an example, that ye should follow his steps" (1 Pet. 2:21, *ASV; King James* also has "example.") Whereas *tupos* is the "regular" word for example, this is not the regular word. It is the Greek *hupogrammos*. (Earlier, while listing a few authors of various Greek word study books, I had mentioned this word in a quote from M. R. Vincent).

Let us now contemplate and consider just what some of the scholars in the Greek language had to say about this word.

1. ***Joseph H. Thayer:***

   "1. a writing - copy, including all the letters of the alphabet, given to beginners as an aid in learning to draw them:... 2. an example set before one: 1 Pet. 2:21." (p. 642).

2. ***W. F. Arndt and F. W. Gingrich:***

   "model, pattern to be copied in writing or drawing, then example... Mostly of Christ, 1 Pe. 2:21." (p. 851).

3. ***E. W. Bullinger:***

   "a writing - copy, hence, a pattern, etc., for imitation." (p. 265).

4. ***H. K. Moulton:***

   "A copy to write after; met. an example for imitation, pattern..." (p. 417).

5. ***G. Abbott-Smith:***

"(... (a) to write under; (b) to trace letters for copying),... 1. a writing-copy, hence, 2. an example:..." (p. 460).

6. ***W. E. Vine:***

*"lit., an under-writing (from **hupographo**, to write under, to trace letters for copying by scholars); hence, a writing-copy, an example, 1 Pet. 2:21, said of what Christ left for believers, by His sufferings (not expiatory, but exemplary), that they might 'follow His steps.'" (p. 54).*

*"Note: Cp. **hupogrammos** (**hupo**, under, **grapho**, to write), an under-writing, a writing copy, an example..." (p. 240).*

7. ***F. Rienecker and C. Rogers:***

"Copy, example. The word is used in 2 Maccabees 2:28 of the 'outlines' of a sketch which the artist fills in w. details. It is also used as the model of handwriting to be copied by the school boy, then fig. of a model of conduct for imitation (Bigg; Beare)." (p. 755).

8. ***M. R. Vincent:***

*"An example (**hupogrammon**). Only here in the New Testament. A graphic word, meaning a copy set by writing-masters for their pupils. Some explain it as a copy of characters over which the student is to trace the lines." (p. 308).*

9. ***G. Kittel and G. Friedrich:***

*"**hupogrammos** is very rare... The earliest known instance is certainly 2 Macc. 2:28, where the epitomist says that he will leave the minuter detail to the author and simply give an abridgment of the books of Jason. This abridgment, however, will deserve the name of **hupogrammoi**:... There is little doubt that what is in the mind is a model or example,... where for the purposes of instruction a word is purposed (several examples are given) which contains all the letters of the alphabet in a form in which children can remember them, so that a model is given which is called **hupogrammos paidikos**." (Vol. 1, p. 772).*

Even though I have only listed nine out of the fifteen sources of Greek lexicons and study books, I want you to know that I have looked this word up in each of those fifteen books. I only listed from these nine some of the "different" wordings found in reference to this word. I saw no need to reiterate, rehearse and recapitulate the same thing time and again. I only state this as in your research some time it will save you from traveling through all of these works. For an example, the only difference I found in *The Expositor's Greek Testament* by W. Robertson Nicoll was the use of the term "copy-head, pattern, to be traced over by writing-pupils" (Vol. V, p. 61). This was so similar that I did not list it while giving all the different sources that I studied.

I do want to mention that the most thorough item I found on this word was in Kittel's *Theological Dictionary of the New Testament*. In this work, if you are interested in seeing the connections of such words as *grapho, graphe, gramma, engrapho, prographo* and *hupogrammos* then you will find a section of over thirty pages to study (*Ibid.*, pp. 742-773). He takes the word we are presently studying through its academic use, from the original pedagogic sense, right down and through the only time the word is found in our New Testament. In his last paragraph, he says, "Worth noting is the constant interrelating of ***hupo-grammos*** and - ***tupos***" (p. 773).

I not only went through those Greek sources, but I also followed, as closely as I could, this word through the writings of various men but found they could add little to what I gave in the nine authors noted above. If, for example, you happened to be honored by having the *Biblical Notes* by Roy C. Deaver, you will now understand why, and even perhaps know of the source, for his writing:

> *"The Lord is our 'example.' This is not the word **tupos**,... Rather, this is **hupogrammos**. This word means underwriting. The Lord is our underwriting. Consider: A stencil; The letters of the English alphabet, posted over the chalk-board, which the child is to strive to imitate; The letters of the Greek alphabet, which the little Greek boy was obligated to strive to imitate.*
>
> *Research on this word suggested the thought that if and when the student would do the very best that he could to imitate the posted letters, that the teacher would take the student by the hand and help him or her to do a better job in writing the letters." (Vol. XV, May, 1981, pp. 1-2).*

Possibly there are other words and terms that should be included in this section, but I have covered the ones I wanted to discuss. The reason is obvious, distinct and discernible, as the caption of the book informs us. From these words, their definitions and scriptures wherein they are used, we can note some very urgent, especially for our day and time, crucial and critical thoughts that must never be forgotten when studying the New Testament, the one and only standard, rule, model, norm, law, and doctrine that we are to follow.

1. The word ***tupos***, form, example, pattern, etc., is found sixteen times in fifteen verses in the New Testament.

2. In the *King James* and *American Standard Versions*, this word is translated by eight different English words, such as mentioned above.

3. Two other words, ***hupodeigma*** and ***hupotuposis,*** are also given and each one is translated, among other words, as "pattern."

4. We have learned that "the context" informs us of how the word is used, and some of these times refer most explicitly to "doctrine" (teaching), "example," "ensample," "pattern of sound words," or that God has had a "pattern" by which things were to be made in the past (cf. Heb. 8:5), therefore, it should be no shock for us today to realize that God has a "pattern" for us to follow.

5. By laborious, painstaking and persistent efforts, we have seen what some of the scholars of the world (in Greek) have written about the word ***tupos***.

> a. The teaching which embodies the sum and substance of religion and represents it to the mind.
>
> b. The pattern in conformity to which a thing must be made.

c. Pattern of teaching.

d. An example to be imitated, a model, a pattern.

e. A formula, a scheme, a form and a pattern.

f. It is used both "in a moral sense," and "in a doctrinal sense."

g. The original pattern, model, mould, type, figure, a system, a form of doctrine.

h. The gospel is the mould; those who are obedient to its teachings become conformed to Christ.

i. The singular looks at the church as a whole, the plural as individuals.

j. A pattern, of faith, expressed in sound words.

k. The ideal or pattern presented by the gospel.

l. A fact of spiritual truth.

m. Christian teaching as a mould and norm.

n. Both the term and the context says it is a model which makes an impress because it is moulded by God.

o. Form of doctrine, form of teaching.

p. In context, the teaching can be described as the mould and norm which shapes the whole personal conduct of the one who is delivered up to it and has become obedient thereto.

q. An example to be copied.

In examining the writings of some studied men (and they, as well as Greek lexicographers, are not our standard), we checked to investigate their thinking along these lines.

a. The mould of teaching into which you were transmitted.

b. Sound words... almost a technical expression.

c. No man was left to invent a religion of his own use.

d. Only God knows that with which God is pleased.

e. God gives, in his mercy to man, a form of sound words or doctrines, a perfect plan.

f. Paul's gospel was a definite body of teaching.

g. Paul's teaching is a mould and demands obedience.

h. The gospel is the great rule of truth and holiness.

i. The gospel is a doctrine not only to be believed, but to be obeyed.

j. The form of sound words is the holy scriptures themselves.

k. Adhere to sound words in opposition to all heresies and false doctrine which corrupt the faith.

l. These principles are not mere matters of speculation but set down in the gospel form of teaching.

m. The form of doctrine is sound words, the faith, the gospel.

n. The form of teaching binds us to an obedience to all laws and regulations of the Christian religion.

o. The pattern of sound words is what Timothy heard from the apostle Paul.

p. Paul emphasizes the necessity of remaining sound and of transmitting sound doctrine.

q. It does matter what you believe. Just being serious is not sufficient and is contradicted by Paul.

7. We noted the word in 1 Peter 2:21 is not ***tupos***, but ***hupogrammos.***

a. This declares to us that Christ is our example, our under-writing.

b. Christ is a pattern, a model, to be copied.

c. This is what Christ left for all believers.

d. All believers are to "follow in his steps."

e. An example, a copy, a graphic word the action of a student toward the original.

f. The words "pattern" (*tupos*) and "under-writing," "copy," "example" (*hupogrammos*) interrelate.

g. The Lord is our example, our under-writing, our "perfect example."

In speaking of Christ as our example, in whose steps we are to follow, I read:

> *"The life of Jesus Christ forms the most beautiful example the Christian can imitate. Unlike all others, it was absolutely* **perfect** *and uniform, and every way accommodated to our present state. In him we behold all light without a shade, all beauty without a spot, all the purity of the law, and the excellency of the gospel. Here we see piety without superstition and morality without ostentation; humility without meanness, and fortitude without temerity; patience without apathy, and compassion without weakness; zeal without rashness, and beneficence without prodigality. The obligation*

we are under to imitate this example arises from duty, relationship, engagement, interest and gratitude" (Fallows, Zenos and Willett, ***op. cit.****, p. 629).*

Roy C. Deaver, whose *Biblical Notes* I referred to earlier discussed the Lord, Our Perfect Example, as being perfect: (1) In Character (cf. Phil. 2:5-8), (2) In His Teaching (cf. John 7:17; Rev. 22:17; John 20:30-31; Matt. 7:12; etc., never an unsound argument, gave not a single false statement, condemned every false way, etc., etc.), and (3) As Our Model:

1. In recognizing **truth** as being **absolute**;

2. In being willing to **suffer any pain** in order to act in harmony with the truth;

3. In teaching and in practicing love for all men...;

4. In emphasizing that one's **mission in life** is to do God's will...;

5. In fighting the devil and dealing with temptation (cf. Matt. 4:1-11);

6. In dealing with persecution and false charges (cf. 1 Pet. 1:22, 23; John 15:19, 20);

7. As the Master Controversialist (cf. Alexander Campbell said about the Lord: 'He unsheathed His sword at the Jordan River, and threw away the scabbard' - *Millennial Harbinger*, Vol. 1, 'Controversy,' p. 41). (*Op. Cit.*, pp. 2-5. Brother Deaver had fourteen points, but I felt, for this section, I would just list six of them. GM).

I fully understand that this is not the easiest chapter in the book to read, especially for many. In fact, it was not "a piece of cake" to study through all the books from which I quoted, but one that was necessary. However, I do believe the summation, the recapitulation and realization, the consummation and culmination, has been well worth the effort expended in trying to get this particular material out of the books from my library and into an exclusive, distinct and detached chapter all by itself. If this is the case, and I pray that it is, then the effort and energy that has been expended has given me the dividend for which I wrote it.

Chapter Three

THE PATTERN - AND GOD HAS ALWAYS HAD ONE

THE PATTERN - AND GOD HAS ALWAYS HAD ONE

In our world today, there are as many different, diverse, discrepant and distinct ideas about the Bible, what it means, and how man is to use it, as I have ever observed. Some of these ideas are prevalent among us today, that is, the Body of Christ is not exempt from these multifarious and mixed thoughts. In the world today there are some who hold that the Bible is not for man, that is, it is not a revelation from God, therefore, there is no model for us today. Then there are those who believe the Bible is from God, but only as a historical record and has no real bearing, relationship, to what man is to do today. These would have us to believe that we must uplift, update and ugrade our teachings and make them "fit us" today. There are also some who again teach the Bible is from God, but that the essentials in it are very few. Yes, they would perhaps agree to the "gospel facts" (cf. 1 Cor. 15:1-3), but would deny a blueprint in such things as worship, baptism, teachings, organization, and so forth.

For the most part, we all realize that there is contained in the Bible evidence of three different periods, ages or systems of religion. It is a "must" that people today understand this if they intend to fully understand the Bible. I speak of the Patriarchal, the Mosaical and Christian time periods. These three systems of religion come within the borders of what is termed the Old and the New Testaments (Covenants). In the thirty-nine books of the Old Testament we find both the Patriarchal and Mosaical time periods. In the twenty-seven books of the New Testament, we find the Mosaic law being nailed to the cross and the New Law coming into effect. This New Law, New Testament (Covenant), is the rule, or guideline for people who desire to please God today. It ought to be clear enough, without any explanation, by observing a few passages where the words "new covenant" are found, such as in Hebrews 8:8, 13: "Behold, the days come, saith the Lord, That I will make a new covenant with the house of Israel and with the house of Judah;...In that he saith, A new covenant, he hath made the first old" (cf. Jer. 31:31ff; Matt. 26:28; Heb. 9:15).

The above paragraph is written, not in any way trying to be exhaustive about the systems of religion or the covenants, but to help us understand the divisions and outlined thoughts of this particular section. Now we want to focus, unite and unify, pivot and pole, our minds on some of the contents, relative to some of the "patterns" found in that first covenant.

GOD HAD A PATTERN IN THE OLD TESTAMENT

Let us begin by noticing a certain terminology used throughout the Old Testament. This will show us that authority, power and pattern by which things were to be done.

1. ***"According To"*** *Was The Pattern.*

a. Noah did "**according to** all that God commanded him" (Gen. 6:22; 7:5).

b. Israel did "**according to** the word of Moses" (Exod. 12:35; 12:50; 17:1; 39:42; etc.).

c. Aaron, and to his sons, "**according to** all that I have commanded thee" (Exod. 29:35).

d. Jehovah spoke unto Moses, saying,... "**according to** all that I have commanded thee" (Exod. 31:1,

11; 40:16; Lev. 10:7; etc.).

e. The sons of Levi did "**according to** the word of Moses" (Exod. 32:28).

f. Bezalel and Oholiab shall work,... "**according to** all that Jehovah hath commanded" (Exod. 36:1).

g. The passover was kept "**according to** all that Jehovah commanded" (Num. 9:5, 12).

h. The children of Israel remained encamped or journeyed, "**according to** the commandment of Jehovah" (Num. 9:20).

i. Moses spake unto all the children of Israel, "**according to** all that Jehovah hath given him in commandment unto them" (Deut. 1:3).

j. Jehovah spake unto Joshua, "This book of the law shall not depart out of thy mouth,... to do **according to** all that is written there:..." (Josh. 1:8; 4:10, "memorial stones").

k. Before Jehovah, with the elders of Gilead at Mizpah, Jephthah spoke "**according to** all his words" (Judg. 11:10).

l. Hiel built Jericho "**according to** the word of Jehovah,..." (1 Kings 16:34).

m. Elijah the Tishbite did "**according to** the word of Jehovah" (1 Kings 17:1, 5, 15, 16).

n. Elisha said, Give the people, that they may eat; for thus saith Jehovah,... and they did eat,... "**according to** the word of Jehovah" (2 Kings 4:38, 42-44).

o. Naaman did "**according to** the saying of the man of God" (2 Kings 5:14).

p. Josiah burned the altar at Bethel, and the high place as built by Jeroboam the son of Nebat, who made Israel to sin, "**according to** the word of Jehovah" (2 Kings 23:15-16; cf. v. 25).

q. David was anointed king over Israel, "**according to** the word of Jehovah by Samuel" (1 Chron. 11:3; cf. v. 10; etc.).

r. The children of the Levites bare the ark of God upon their shoulders with the staves thereon, as Moses commanded "**according to** the word of Jehovah" (1 Chron. 15:15).

s. During the reign of Hezekiah, the temple was cleansed, "**according to** the commandment of the king by words of Jehovah" (2 Chron. 29:15).

t. In the days of Darius, the elders of the Jews builded and prospered, through the prophesying of Haggai the prophet and...And they builded the temple "**according to** the commandment of the God of Israel" (Ezra 6:14).

u. During the time of "mixed marriages" in Ezra's day, when the people had married "foreign women" and had trespassed against God, a covenant with God was made and they put away all the wives and children "**according to** the counsel of the Lord, and of those that tremble at the commandment of our God; and let it be done **according to** the law" (Ezra 10:2-3).

v. It is found in Isaiah where we read, "To the law and to the testimony! if they speak not **according to** this word, surely there is no morning for them" (8:20).

w. It was Baruch who wrote from the mouth of

Jeremiah all the words of Jehovah, which he had spoken unto him, upon a roll of a book...And Baruch...did "**according to** all that Jeremiah the prophet commanded him, reading in the book the words of Jehovah in Jehovah's house" (Jer. 36:1-3, esp. vss. 4, 8).

x. So Jonah arose, and went into Nineveh, "**according to** the word of Jehovah" (Jonah 3:3).

y. It was the word of God by Haggai the prophet to Zerubbabel, and to Joshua, in which Jehovah said, "For I am with you,...**according to** the word that I covenanted with you when ye came up out of Egypt, and my Spirit abode among you: fear ye not" (Hag. 2:1-2, esp. vss. 4-5).

Being deeply impressed with various statements in the Old Testament, such as "it is written," "thus saith the Lord," etc., etc., I was greatly intrigued, captivated and carried away by "according to," and years ago commenced a book (which, like others, have been logged in my files until the time comes, if and when it does...). However, for this section of thoughts, I have gone through all the times and places where I found it listed. I cannot say that I personally found every one of them, but I did find 661 usages and every book of the Old Testament had, at least one, except Song of Solomon, Joel, Amos, Obadiah, Nahum and Zephaniah. So you can readily see that the listing above only touches a very few of them.

It isn't *how many* times this *wording* is found, but the *punch it packs* when speaking about *how* God wants things done, *how* He has acted by the instructions given and *how* very careful man has been and *must be* to be pleasing unto God. Note some further implications, if you will, in the following:

a. *Recall the "man of God," the prophet* who lied by saying "an angel spake unto me by the word of Jehovah, saying,..."? He was "disobedient unto the mouth of Jehovah, and kept not the commandment." It was just a "little bread" and a "little water" he had taken, so what could be so bad about such a small thing? On the way back, a lion slew the man, his body was cast in the way and both the ass and the lion stood by it. Then we find this most sobering statement: "It is the man of God, who was disobedient (the footnote says, "rebelled against the word of") unto the mouth of Jehovah" (1 Kings 13:11-26, esp. vss. 18, 21, 24, 26).

b. *Remember Baasha*, who in the third year of Asa king of Judah, in Gibbethon slew Nadab, son of Jeroboam, who had done evil in the sight of Jehovah, and made Israel to sin. The text says that as soon as he was king, "he smote all the house of Jeroboam; he left not to Jeroboam any that breathed,...**according unto the saying of Jehovah**,..." (1 Kings 15:25-29, esp. vs. 29; cf. Zimri in 16:5-12, esp. vs. 12).

c. *Reflect on the death of Ahab* and his body being brought to Samaria...and the dogs licking up the blood that had been washed off the chariot, **"according unto the word of Jehovah which he spake"** (1 Kings 22:37-38; cf. 21:17-19).

d. *Recollect the great famine in Samaria,* and then when Elisha, after hearing of such sad conditions (2 Kings 6:29-30), foretold of a measure of fine flour...two measures of barley being sold? "And the people went out,...So a measure of fine flour was sold for a shekel, and two measures of barley for a shekel, '**according to** the word of

Jehovah'" (2 Kings 7:16).

e. *Meditate on Joash* and the people still sacrificing and burning incense in the high places. Joash slew them...but the children of the murderers he put not to death; "**according to** that which is written in the book of the law of Moses, as Jehovah commanded, saying,...but every man shall die for his own sin" (2 Kings 14:6).

f. *Contemplate Job and his friends*, Eliphaz, Bildad and Zophar. Do you recall why they had to offer seven bullocks and seven rams for a burnt-offering? Jehovah said it was "because ye have not spoken of me the thing that is right,..." So these men did "**according as Jehovah commanded them**" (Job 42:7-9, esp. vs. 9).

What could be so important about "who" should carry the ark? Why be concerned about "how" it should be carried? Why not ask both David and Uzza (cf. 1 Chron. 13:9-11). Find the answer in 15:13: "For because ye bare it not at the first, Jehovah our God made a breach upon us, for that we sought him not **according to** the ordinance" (emp. GM). Now read verse fifteen: "And the children of the Levites bare the ark of God upon their shoulders with the staves thereon, as Moses commanded **according to** the word of Jehovah" (emp. GM, cf. Num. 4:15).

Was it really necessary "to offer burnt-offerings unto Jehovah upon 'the altar'" (cf. 1 Chron. 16:40)? Read where it says, "Then Solomon offered burnt-offerings unto Jehovah on the altar of Jehovah,...offering **according to** the commandment of Moses,..." (2 Chron. 8:13-14; cf. Deut. 12:13-14).

Did it make any difference about "where" anyone stood? What about the priests and the Levites? Let us read: "And they stood in their place after their order, **according to** the law of Moses the man of God:" (2 Chron. 30:13-16; cf. 35:10; cf. "watch next to watch" in Neh. 12:24).

Is it imperative, I mean is it obligatory, mandatory and magisterial that "I" do exactly, precisely, to the letter, word for word, line for line, yea, perfectly, **according to** what "is written"? *Note:* "The word that came to Jeremiah from Jehovah, saying, Hear ye the words of this covenant, and speak unto the men of Judah,...and say unto them, Thus saith Jehovah, the God of Israel: Cursed be the man that heareth not the words of this covenant, which I commanded...Obey my voice, and do them, **according to** all which I command you: so shall ye be my people, and I will be your God" (Jer. 11:1-4). Again, it was said by those who had dealt deceitfully against their own souls as they had said, "...**according unto all** that Jehovah our God shall say, so declare unto us, and we will do it." The answer was swift and certain: "...ye shall die by the sword, by the famine, and by the pestilence." But why? "Ye have not obeyed the voice of Jehovah your God..." (Jer. 42:20-22).

You may not believe it, obey it, teach it and practice it, but as for me, and for all faithful soldiers of the cross, may we never forget, but always practice the words of Micaiah when he said: "As Jehovah liveth, what Jehovah saith unto me, that will I speak" (1 Kings 22:14). No finer epitaph could any man have on the marker of his tombstone than: "...**died living and worshiping according to all Jehovah hath spoken**."

2. *It Was **"According To"** That Noah's Ark Was Built.*

a. In a day when the wickedness of man was great upon the earth, one man found favor in the eyes of

Jehovah. Noah was the man and it was upon him that God laid the obligation to build an ark (Gen. 6:5, 8, 13-14).

b. Noah was not left "without a pattern" by which to construct, form, fashion and frame the ark. God specified rooms, the wood out of which it was to be made, the length, the breadth, the height, the number of stories, and many such explicit instructions were given to Noah. The bottom line and the last word is "Thus did Noah: **according to** all that God commanded him, so did he" (Gen. 6:22).

c. A man would find himself all right in the eyes of God who fails to see that "there was a pattern" given to Noah by which he was to erect the ark! Which item would not be of consequence or concern? Would a change be all right in the wood, the rooms, the number of stories? How about in the length, the breadth or the height? To be right, Noah just observed, did, what was included!

3. *It Was "**According To**" That Moses Molded The Tabernacle.*

a. It is in the twenty-fifth chapter of Exodus that we find Jehovah speaking to Moses, saying, "And let them make me a sanctuary, that I may dwell among them" (vs. 8). In this chapter, before God spoke to Moses of the wood, the length of an ark, with the mercy-seat above upon the ark, and of all things "which I will give thee in commandment unto the children of Israel, God said it plainly: "**According to** all that I show thee, *the pattern* of the tabernacle, and *the pattern* of all the furniture thereof, even so shall ye make it" (vs. 9, emp. GM). When this chapter comes to a conclusion, God has finished the many details about the candlesticks, therefore, he says: "And see that thou *make them after their pattern*, which hath been showed thee in the mount" (vs. 40).

b. Talk about details, fine points and particulars, you can read of them beginning in Exodus 25. Regardless of the multitude of minute specifications, we find this statement in Exodus 40:16: "Thus did Moses: **according to** all that Jehovah commanded him, so did he" (sounds a little like what was said of Noah, doesn't it?).

c. In the New Testament, in a chapter in which God is about to, through the Hebrews writer, speak of "a New Testament," I find the warning God gave to Moses listed again: "...even as Moses is warned of God when he is about to make the tabernacle: for, See, saith he, that thou make all things **according to** *the pattern* that was showed thee in the mount" (8:5, emp. GM). It would be in the face of total ignorance if a man denied that God had a pattern for the tabernacle and that it was to be followed.

4. *It Was **"According To"** That The Temple Was Modeled.*

a. *"Then David gave to Solomon his son* ***the pattern of the*** *porch of the temple,* ***and of the*** *houses thereof,* ***and of the*** *treasuries thereof,* ***and of the*** *upper rooms thereof,* ***and of the*** *inner chambers thereof,* ***and of the*** *place of the mercy-seat;* ***and the pattern of all*** *that he had by the Spirit,* ***for the*** *courts of the house of Jehovah,* ***and for all..., for the...and for the...; also for***

the... *" (1 Chron. 28:11-12, 13-18, emp. GM).*

b. *"**All this,** said David, have I been made to understand **in writing** from the hand of Jehovah, even **all the works of this pattern**" (1 Chron. 28:18, emp. GM; note the word "pattern" in verse 18 as well).*

c. *"And David said to Solomon his son, Be strong and of good courage, **and do it:** ...until **all the work** for the service of the house of Jehovah **be finished**" (1 Chron. 28:20, emp. GM).*

d. If it were "**according to**" in reference to the use of every candlestick (vs. 15), would it be anything less when the pattern was of the...and of the...and of the...and the pattern of all...for the...also for the...and for all...for all...also for...for the...for every...etc., etc.? (vss. 13-18). When the father of Solomon said, "and do it," to what did he have or make reference? Later, when it was finished, and Solomon addressed all the assembly of Israel, he said: "Blessed be Jehovah, the God of Israel, who spake with his mouth unto David my father,...I have chosen Jerusalem, that my name might be there, and...thy son shall build...I am risen up... and have built the house of the name of Jehovah, the God of Israel" (2 Chron. 6:1-11). How did Solomon build the house of Jehovah? Was it by the pattern? Was it **according to** all things that David had been made to understand "in writing" from the hand of Jehovah, **even all the works of this pattern**?

5. *According To A Pattern "Of Action" Jericho Fell.*

a. Beginning in Joshua 6:3, God gave the instructions for the wall of the city of Jericho to fall. These directions were simple, as seen by the following items:

(1) All the men of war were to compass the city.

(2) These men were to compass the city once a day for six days.

(3) Seven priests were to bear seven trumpets of rams' horns before the ark.

(4) On the seventh day they were to compass the city seven times.

(5) After this, the priests were to blow the trumpets.

(6) Then all of the people were to shout.

b. In the New Testament, the Hebrew writer makes this statement: "By faith the walls of Jericho fell down, *after* they had been compassed about for seven days" (Heb. 11:30, emp. GM). What is the meaning of "by faith" in that verse? Did not these people have faith when God said, "See, I have given into thy hand Jericho"? Is it not clear that they had faith the very first day they compassed the city? The real question is, "When did they receive the city?" The answer is obvious. It was when they had obeyed every single item (note the six things mentioned above) that God had given unto them to do, and that included the very "last command," as the city was not theirs when they had compassed it those thirteen times in those seven days! Is it not true that faith is "taking God at His Word?"

6. *According To A Pattern "Of Action" Naaman Was*

Cleansed. This is clearly set forth in 2 Kings 5:1-14. It basically involved the very short statement: "Go and wash in the Jordan seven times, and thy flesh shall come again to thee, and thou shalt be clean" (vs. 10). Here a man being cleansed from leprosy was almost ruined by a statement so often heard today: "Behold, I thought" (vs. 11). I call this, "Reasoning Without God!" The Bible is full of such ideas and feelings, and so is our world today. After all, are not the rivers "of Damascus, Abanah and Pharpar (make the application to the things said/done today), better than all the waters of Israel"? It was only when Naaman, as the text says, "Then went he down, and dipped himself seven times in the Jordan, **according to** the saying of the man of God; and his flesh came again like unto the flesh of a little child, and he was clean" that his leprosy was healed. It is absolutely amazing how many people think Naaman was six-sevenths cleansed when he had dipped six times! I wonder what would have happened, after his dipping six times and seeing that his flesh was cleansed, if he had said, "Man, this is great! I think I'll dip five more times to make sure, to make it an even dozen!"? Again we need always to note, *What Does The Command Include?* The answer, of course, is seven times! There is no authority or power for any number but seven. Having "no authority" then is the excluding factor.

I have not touched on many examples, yea, many patterns, found within the pages of the Old Testament (cf. Num. 21:4-9). How true it is that God even had a pattern toward His Word (cf. Deut. 4:1ff, esp. vs. 2; 12:32; 18:20; Deut. 29:29; Prov. 30:5-6). We could yet have many thoughts on the "statutes," and this goes way back to the book of Genesis (26:5), "commandments" (Gen. 26:5), "laws" (Gen. 26:5, again I used this verse in Genesis to show how far such items go back in God's Old Testament), "ordinances" (Exod. 12:14, 24, 43; 18:20), "charge" (Gen.

26:5), "order" (1 Chron. 15:13), "precepts" (Isa. 28:10,13), "decree" (Dan. 4:24), etc.

Men today do not see **the value of the Old Testament**, therefore, I want us, at this precious and particular time, to note what the apostle Paul wrote: "For whatsoever things were written aforetime were written for our learning, that through patience and through comfort of the scriptures we might have hope" (Rom. 15:4). If this sacred verse does not help us to learn the nature, yea, the value of the Old Testament, then I doubt I could give another that would. Take notice of these things found in this scripture:

1. *Things written aforetime* certainly does refer to the Old Testament (cf. 2 Tim. 3:14-17; 2 Pet. 1:19-21; Luke 24:27, 44ff; John 5:39, 46; etc.). The Old Testament is called "scripture."

2. *Things written aforetime were for our learning,* and the Old Testament gives us our most vivid examples (cf. 1 Cor. 10:1-12, esp. vss. 6, 11). I seriously doubt that a man can fully understand the New Testament without knowledge of the Old Testament. It is an absolute necessity that we understand its relation to the New Testament. Consider type and antitype (1 Cor. 10:6, 11; 1 Pet. 3:21), shadow and substance (Heb. 10:1), copy and actual (Heb. 9:23).

3. *Things written aforetime give us hope.* Hope is a great New Testament word, thought (cf. Heb. 11:1; 6:18-19; Rom. 8:24; Titus 1:2). Read again that great chapter of faith (Heb. 11) and see if the faithfulness of those Old Testament characters do not give you hope. Read, and read again, such verses as 1 Kings 8:56 and Joshua 23:14 and see if your faith is not strengthened in God's promises (cf. Isa. 41:10-13).

4. *Things written aforetime teach us.* This perhaps might be somewhat "out of place" as seen in Romans 15:4, but I have, as I love to do, checked my Greek New Testament by Nestle (p. 420). I was amazed (perhaps I should not have been) that the word for "learning" is the Greek *didaskalian*, from the Greek *didaskalia* (*Vine's Expository Dictionary of Biblical Words*, p. 361). This word "is akin to the Greek *didasko*, to teach, and means teaching, instruction," and (p. 180) may refer, at times, to doctrine.

5. *Things written aforetime,* the Old Testament scriptures, written for our learning, giving us patience and comfort, should give us hope, which is the anchor of the soul. We need fully to understand that God pledged to us, in the Old Testament, such things as (1) the gospel, Romans 1:1-2, (2) the kingdom, which is the church, Daniel 2:31-45, esp. vs. 44; 7:13-14, and (3) according to the apostle Peter, salvation in Christ, 1 Peter 1:10-12.

It is no wonder then that we thank God for the Old Testament and also despise how some talk about it and also how they treat it. We need to read again Romans 7:7-14 and realize that the Old Testament law was "holy," "righteous," "good" and "spiritual" (vss. 12, 14). Yes, there was faith, mercy, and grace in the Old Testament. May we never forget that the principles of God never change, and many are there in the Old Testament that we desperately need to see, realize and comprehend. Indeed, God had a pattern in the Old Testament, and it very vividly relates to our salvation today. Remember, if all else is forgotten, Galatians 3:19-29, as the Old Testament did fulfill this as "it brought us to Christ" and to "the faith."

GOD HAS A PATTERN IN THE NEW TESTAMENT

As we began our study of the first section, "God *Had* A Pattern In The Old Testament," we now proceed with the thought, "God *Has* A Pattern In The New Testament." We also noticed a certain type language used, a vocabulary, a wording and a phraseology as to that pattern. I believe, and for many reasons, this can also be said of the New Testament. Therefore, we begin "now" where we began "then" with the Old Testament.

1. ***"According To"* Was The Pattern.** I have found this to be utilized all the way through the New Testament. In fact, it is listed about 127 times. Too, I found such an expression used in all of the New Testament books with the exception of 1 Thessalonians. I now repeat that perhaps I have missed some or even miscounted, but I do know that I have found it throughout the New Testament. Plus, it is interesting to observe that in the New Testament we find various references of "that" wording as found in the Old Testament. I deem it wise that we take note of the following:

a. "**According to**" the law of Moses (Luke 2:22; Lev. 12:2-6).

b. "**According to**" the law of the Lord (Luke 2:39).

c. "**According to**" the commandment (Luke 23:56).

d. "**According to**" your law (John 18:31).

e. "**According to**" the fashion that he had seen (Acts 7:44; *ASV* has "figure," it is the Greek *tupos*, regular word for "pattern." The statement here refers to the "tabernacle," that is, the "pattern" that Moses had seen).

f. "**According to**" the strict manner of the law (Acts 22:3).

g. "**According to**" the law (Acts 22:12, referring to the devout man, Ananias).

h. "**According to**" our law (Acts 24:6; read footnote in *ASV*).

i. "**According to**" the commandment of the eternal God (Rom. 16:26; statement prior to this said, "...by the scriptures of the prophets,...").

j. "**According to**" that which is written (2 Cor. 4:13; he then quotes Psm. 116:10).

k. "**According to**" the will of God (Gal. 1:4, a statement referring to Christ "giving himself for our sins").

l. "**According to**" the law (Heb. 7:5; 8:4; 9:19).

m. "**According to**" the pattern (Heb. 8:5).

It seems self-evident, doesn't it, that the New Testament men, the writers, inspired by the Holy Spirit of God (cf. 1 Cor. 2:9-13; 2 Pet. 1:19-21; 2 Tim. 3:16-17) understood and appreciated the locution, the expression, choice of words, the language as well as the deep and established reason for its use. They very well knew the law, its promised blessings, as well as its serious warnings. When God spoke and said, "...according to,"...then that settled any and every question, for "the pattern" was given.

2. ***"According to"* Is Still The Pattern.** Following the same line of study and meditation, I now want us to concentrate, hub our attention, on how this wording also penetrates the pages of the New Testament.

a. "**According to**" all things whatsoever he shall

speak unto you (Acts 3:22; referring to Moses and his statement about God raising up a prophet to whom every soul is to hearken or be destroyed, Deut. 18:15; *Englishman's Greek Concordance And Lexicon,* p. 467).

b. "**According to**" his promise God brought forth a Saviour in Jesus (Acts 13:23; 1 Kings 8:56; Josh. 23:14).

c. "**According to**" the spirit of holiness Jesus was declared to be the Son of God with power (Rom. 1:1-4, Paul speaks about the gospel of Christ promised afore through the prophets, etc.).

d. "**According to**" truth the judgment of God is declared to be (Rom. 2:2).

e. "**According to**" my gospel in the day when God shall judge the secrets of men (Rom. 2:16).

f. "**According to**" the will of God intercession is made for the saints (Rom. 8:27).

g. "**According to**" God's purpose to them that are called, all things work together for good, if they love the Lord (Rom. 8:28).

h. "**According to**" a lack of knowledge, even though they have a zeal for God, many are ignorant of God's righteousness (Rom. 10:2).

i. "**According to**" Christ Jesus (Rom. 15:5).

j. "**According to**" my gospel and the preaching of Jesus Christ (Rom. 16:25; 2 Tim. 2:8).

k. "**According to**" the revelation of the mystery... kept in silence through times eternal, but now is manifested... (Rom. 16:25).

l. "**According to**" the commandment of the eternal God is made known unto all the nations unto obedience of faith (Rom. 16:26; footnote in the *ASV*, obedience of "the faith").

m. "**According to**" the grace of God (1 Cor. 3:10; 2 Thess. 1:12).

n. "**According to**" the scriptures, said Paul, Christ died for our sins, was buried and was raised "**according to**" the gospel he preached, the word he preached (1 Cor. 15:3-4).

o. "**According to**" the authority the Lord gave me, said Paul (2 Cor. 13:10).

p. "**According to**" whether or not we are Christ's, but if so, we are Abraham's seed, and heirs to the promise (Gal. 3:29).

q. "**According to**" God's eternal purpose which he purposed in Christ, his manifold wisdom was made known through the church (Eph. 3:10-11).

r. "**According to**" the power that worketh in us, God is able to do exceeding abundantly above all that we ask or think (Eph. 3:20).

s. "**According to**" the dispensation of God Paul was made a minister to fulfill the word of God (Col. 1:25).

t. "**According to**" the gospel of the glory of the blessed God (1 Tim. 1:11).

u. "**According to**" sound words, even the words of our Lord Jesus Christ, and to the doctrine... if man consents not to such the great apostle Paul says he is puffed up (1 Tim. 6:3).

v. "**According to**" the power of God (2 Tim. 1:8).

w. "**According to**" the commandment of God our Saviour, Paul was intrusted with God's word in the message (Tit. 1:1-3).

x. "**According to**" the scripture there is a royal law which says to love thy neighbor as thyself (James 2:8).

y. "**According to**" his own works, every man is to be judged (1 Pet. 1:17; Rev. 2:23; 18:6; 20:12-13).

z. "**According to**" his will, if we so ask, God heareth us, and we know that he heareth us (1 John 5:14-15).

If these were the only ones found in the New Testament, we would need no others to prove our point. If the Old Testament (cf. Rom. 15:4) instructs us, then we need to learn that God means what he says and his authority is always found in the "according to." Here in these few listings from the New Testament, we can learn:

1. We must obey Jesus or be destroyed.

2. The judgment will be according to the gospel, His truth.

3. Christ is, indeed, the Son of God and with power.

4. Men are to submit to sound words, the doctrine, the words of Jesus Christ.

5. Paul's gospel was by the commandment of God.

6. If men are ignorant, have not knowledge of God's will, they will seek to establish a righteousness of their own.

7. If intercession is made for us, it will be by the will of God.

8. It is essential that a man love God if he is to be blessed by all things working for his good.

9. The gospel and the preaching of Jesus Christ are the same and this is made known unto all the nations unto obedience of the faith.

10. God's dispensation of the mystery, from times eternal, has now been made known.

11. It was according to the scriptures that Christ died, was buried and rose on the third day.

12. The authority by which Paul spoke was given unto him by the Lord.

13. If a man has been baptized into Christ, has put on Christ, is Christ's, then he is Abraham's seed and heir of the promise.

14. God made known through the church his manifold wisdom.

15. The power of God, the word of power, works in the believer.

16. The gospel is of and to the glory of our blessed God.

17. The words of Christ are sound words, doctrine, and to these men are to consent.

18. The gospel is the power of God.

19. God's word is the message that is for today.

20. Every man will be judged by his works and according to what is written.

21. If any man wants God to hear his petitions, that man must ask according to God's will.

THE NEW TESTAMENT IS THE PATTERN

It certainly would be most difficult for me to understand that God gave the people in Old Testament times so many patterns (Noah was given a pattern for the ark, Moses was given a pattern for the tabernacle, David and Solomon were given a pattern for the temple, etc.), yea, and instructed them in so many and variegated items, but when it came to us who live in New Testament times that He just left us to be "on our own." Can anyone truly believe that today, the people of God, are completely "patternless!" Thanks be to God that He did not do any such thing. Cry if you like, but we do have a divine design. Whether you call or term it a figure, a form, model, plan, order, criterion, blueprint, yardstick, rule book, guide, mold, measure, example, etc., etc., that is precisely what it is. Indeed, the New Testament is "the" pattern. We MUST be absolutely diligent in "walking in the footsteps of the Master" (1 Peter 2:21). If we do not emulate the New Testament pattern, we will be just like those we read about in Judges 17:6; 21:25, that is, we, too, can just "do that which is right in our own eyes." We know today that is exactly what is happening among us, as so many are dead set against a norm, a standard, yea, against rule and regulations. Does not God Almighty have the right to rule? *Note*, if you will, the following:

1. **Is there a way to walk?** Anyone who has read much of the Bible, the New Testament, knows that man is "to walk by faith" (2 Cor. 5:7). This faith, by which we are to walk, comes from one and only one place, "the hearing of the word of God (Christ)" (Rom. 10:17). To say that faith comes from the hearing of the word is to inform us that it is the result, the effect, the product of the word of God. Our knowledge then is the outcome and echo of our faith. Without this faith, which comes from the word of

God, there is not a man on earth (meaning, of course, accountable man) who can please God, else the Bible is false (Heb. 11:1, 6). And, it is just as definite, as true, solid and sound, that where there is no word of God there cannot be any faith, Biblical faith, and that is what it takes to please God. Yea, the very way that we are to walk.

2. **Is there that which we are not to go beyond?** Again, I want to list just three scriptures. To the Corinthians, Paul emphatically, explicitly, stated: "Now these things, brethren, I have in a figure transferred to myself and Apollos for your sakes; that in us ye might learn not to go beyond the things which are written;..." (1 Cor. 4:6). It is clear, from this one verse, that *whatever it is that* "is written," that is the thing that *I must learn* "not to go beyond." I know that "the dead" will be judged "by what is written" (Rev. 20:11-15), and Jesus said, "He that rejecteth me, and receiveth not my sayings, hath one that judgeth him: the word that I spake, the same shall judge him in the last day" (John 12:48). If a man cannot understand the reason why we are not to "go beyond" the written, that by which we are to be judged, it being our safeguard, and why it is not a concern as to "what is not written," as that is not going to judge us (and we have the word of Christ for it), then perhaps that man is safe anyway. Then, too, we are not left to "a guess" as to the standard, the norm, the rule, the book by which we will be, in that great day, judged. It is the "my sayings," and "the word that I spake," said Jesus, so we have HIS WORD ON IT!

3. **Has God given us a warning about the written?** Once again, I want us to magnet our minds on just three scriptures. It was the beloved John who wrote: "Whosoever goeth onward and abideth not in the teaching of Christ, hath not God: he that abideth in the teaching, the same

hath both the Father and the Son" (2 John 9). It seems so simple to say, but if a man "wants to have both the Father and the Son," then all he has to do is "to abide in the teaching." If this teaching is not brought, then a man is neither to be welcomed nor greeted, lest one becomes a partaker in his "evil works" (vss. 10-11). To the Galatians, Paul said, "I marvel that ye are so quickly removing from him that called you in the grace of Christ unto a different gospel; which is not another gospel: only there are some that trouble you, and would pervert the gospel of Christ. But though we, or an angel from heaven, should preach unto you any gospel other than that which we preached unto you, let him be anathema" (Gal. 1:6-8). Like those in the Old Tesament, we cannot afford to "add to it" or "take from it," lest plagues be added to us and lest God takes from us our part from the "tree of life and out of the holy city" (Rev. 22:18-19). God has plainly instructed us that man can "go beyond the teaching," fail "to abide in the teaching," "pervert the teaching," "add to" the teaching, "take from" the teaching, as well as being accused of "preaching another gospel," and "partaking in a man's evil works" if he welcomes and greets those who do not bring "this teaching."

4. **Is it true we have a New Testament?** Jesus said, "For this is my blood of the new covenant, which is poured out for many for remission of sins" (Matt. 26:28). The Hebrew writer made this statement: "And for this cause he is the mediator of a new covenant, that a death having taken place for the redemption of the transgressions that were under the first covenant..." (Heb. 9:15). He continues by saying, "For where a testament is, there must of necessity be the death of him that made it. For a testament is of force where there hath been death: for it doth never avail while he that made it liveth" (Heb. 9:16-17). Prior to this he quoted Jeremiah saying, "Behold the

days come, saith the Lord, That I will make a new covenant with the house of Israel and with the house of Judah;...In that he saith, A new covenant, he hath made the first old" (Heb. 8:8,13; cf. Jer. 31:31ff). It is serious, yea, dangerous for a man, any man regardless of who he is or how qualified he might be, to tamper with, disregard, change, set aside or try and in some way to change a man's testament. But this is the Lord's Testament and changing it has eternal consequences.

5. **Does "the written" speak of false teachers?** "Now I beseech you, brethren, mark them that are causing the divisions and occasions of stumbling, contrary to the doctrine (teaching) which ye learned: and turn away from them" (Rom. 16:17). "Beloved, believe not every spirit, but prove the spirits, whether they are of God; because many false prophets are gone out into the world" (1 John 4:1). Yea, there are some with whom we are to have no fellowship (cf. Eph. 5:11; 2 John 10-11; Titus 3:10-11; etc.). If there is no norm, and no standard, then how on earth could anyone be known as or be proven to be "a false teacher"?

6. **Can I prove what I do is right?** Certainly, we have in mind matters religious. It was Paul, who spake by the Spirit and said, "And whatsoever ye do, in word or in deed, do all in the name of the Lord Jesus, giving thanks to God the Father through him" (Col. 3:17). And Paul spoke with authority (cf. 1 Cor. 14:37; Gal. 1:11-12) and taught the same in every church (1 Cor. 4:17). To do something "in the name of Jesus" is to do it by his authority, by his power (cf. Acts 4:7-10). We are to teach what he commanded (Matt. 28:20) and we are to transmit "the same thing" to faithful men who are able to teach others (2 Tim. 2:2). If we build "by the pattern" we will do that which is right. Noah did, Moses did, David and

Solomon did, and man today can do the same. If not, then why not? In fact, man is under a divine obligation to "build according to the" **pattern**, as that is the only way he can be acceptable, that is, be pleasing unto God (cf. Heb. 11:1-7; John 8:29; 1 John 3:22).

7. **Does the New Testament teach there is but one way?** I want to bring to our attention, first of all, two verses in the Old Testament. "Thus saith Jehovah, Stand ye in the ways and see, and ask for the old paths, where is the good way; and walk therein, and ye shall find rest for your souls..." (Jer. 6:16). Isaiah said: "And a highway shall be there, and a way, and it shall be called The way of holiness; the unclean shall not pass over it; but it shall be for the redeemed: the wayfaring men, yea fools, shall not err therein...the redeemed shall walk there..." (35:8-9). Unless this is a case of Hebrew parallelism, we have two ways. That is the same thing taught by the Master, the Lord Jesus, in Matthew 7:13-14: "Enter ye in by the narrow gate: for wide is the gate, and broad is the way, that leadeth to destruction, and many are they that enter in thereby. For narrow is the gate, and straitened the way, that leadeth unto life, and few are they that find it." There are two ways, one broad and one narrow, but when Jesus spoke, as recorded by John, he narrowed that down to ONE WAY. "Jesus saith unto him (speaking to Thomas), I am the way, and the truth. and the life: no one cometh unto the Father, but by me" (John 14:6). If I know anything at all, then I know when the Bible speaks about a man called John the Baptist, he was the one and only one. When I hear Jesus speaking and saying, "I am the way," then there is one and only one way. He is THE WAY, just like He is THE TRUTH, and just like He is THE LIFE (cf. 1 John 2:25; 5:11-12). Man cannot be the director of his own steps (Jer. 10:23; Prov. 14:12; 16:26; 19:21; 21:2; Psm. 119:9). There is but one way as there is

but one Jesus, and He said, "I am the way."

Since there is but one way to walk, *since* that way comes to us by faith, *since* that faith comes by the hearing of the word of the Lord, *since* there can be no Biblical faith where there is no word, *since* we have the word written down, *since* we are not in any way to change it (go beyond it), *since* it has been once and for all delivered, *since* we cannot please God without the faith and without faith, *since* we must have Bible authority, *since* we have only one New Testament, *since* man has been warned about teaching any other doctrine (teaching), *since* we can prove what is right, *since* some do teach contrary to the Master's teaching, *since* only the narrow way leads to heaven, *since* Jesus has spoken, *since* the word that Jesus spake will judge us in the last day, *since* Jesus said he was THE WAY, THE TRUTH AND THE LIFE, and *since* we do have a pattern to follow and God does not lie (Titus 1:2; Heb. 6:16-18), pardon me then if I am too bold, brazen, barefaced, brassy, and brash when I make the assertion and the averment, the promise and the pledge that THERE IS ONLY ONE WAY. There is "no other" way for a man to come to God (cf. John 14:6; 6:44-45, notice should be given the Greek word *oudeis*, "no one" that is herein used). It was Christ, not Goebel Music, who said, "I am the way,...and the life: *no one* cometh unto the Father, but by me." Did He really mean it? Isn't that being just a little bit narrow? Do you truly think that would involve His teaching, and following the pattern? If this is true, where is His grace? (Just let me add, no one would even know the word "grace" without the Bible, our blueprint and pattern. Can we not see that there is no "mercy" or "grace," outside the gospel of Christ? Does grace nullify obedience?) But what about...? And so it goes on and on, but the facts are given and the truth has been stated. Therefore, I ask you to remember the definition of faith, which is, TAKING GOD AT HIS WORD. It is still written: "If ye love me, ye will keep my commandments" (John 14:15; cf. vss. 21, 23; 1 John 2:3-6; 5:3; John 15:14).

Chapter Four

THE PATTERN - AND IT STANDS ONCE AND FOR ALL

THE PATTERN - AND IT STANDS ONCE AND FOR ALL

In our world of rapid change, it is hard for most people to believe that there is something that "changes not." For many years, I have been hearing the idea of "change," and that we must "make a reversal of..." if we intend to keep up with each generation. In fact, in this regard we have one of those statements that I personally refer to as a "pronouncement of paralysis." Anytime a person makes a statement in relation to what they see as a problem, and then closes it with, "Yes, I believe in the gospel (or God), *but I believe that we must...*," well, that is powerlessness, it is impotence, like perhaps a paralytic stroke. If, on the other hand, a person views our world, with all of its perplexities, its variegated and vacillating, checkered and changing ways, ideas, thought-patterns, its new creations and updated methods, and says, "Yes, *but God* (or the gospel) *is, can* or *says* ...," then that is a proclamation of power! It is a rather simple way of saying it, yet it all depends where you place - station - the word "but." When it comes "after" the gospel or God, it is paralyzation, but when it comes "before" God or the gospel, it is potency and powerfulness.

How true it is that in this world of "uncertainty," of "change," and of "the changing;" we hear that the gospel has to be "adapted" to meet "the needs" facing us today. What does this "adaptability," this idea of "changeability" and "flexibility" tell us relative to what a man believes about the God of heaven and the Bible's message? Whether you can see it or not, it bespeaks, demonstrates, declares, and displays a lack of understanding of the Book that we hold so very dear, the Bible. I say this, as it is in direct contradiction to the announcement by the Holy Spirit of

God through God-inspired men, such as described by Peter (2 Pet. 1:19-21) and Paul (1 Cor. 2:9-13), that the Bible is "inspired of God" (cf. 2 Tim. 3:16-17). Please do yourself a blessing and find out what the meaning is of "inspired of God" (Greek, *theopneustos*, and you do not have to study the Greek to know what it means) and how that relates directly toward man's own special and precious needs. Let me hasten to say it is like talking about "an approved example." Reader, if it is approved, it is an example, and, in like manner, if the Bible is inspired of God, and if we can correctly talk of inspiration, then *the Bible is adapted*! How else would God be God, the author of the Bible, and be omnipotent (almighty, absolute, unlimited in power), *omniscient* (all-knowing, all-wise, all-seeing, all-perceiving), and have eternally purposed what is revealed to us, without having it meet "the needs" of man today?? Then, too, did the gospel **ever meet the needs of man?** If so, who is intelligent (should say "smart") enough to tell us **when the gospel stopped meeting the needs of man?**

SEARCH THE SCRIPTURE FOR THE STATEMENT

It may be enlightening to some to know that there is just a verse that states, and clearly so, the caption of this particular chapter. "Beloved, while I was giving all diligence to write unto you of our common salvation, I was constrained to write unto you exhorting you to contend earnestly for *the faith* which *was once for all delivered* unto the saints" (Jude 3, emp. GM). Even though there is much to write about in this verse, I want to list just a few precious and eternal thoughts from this magnificient scripture.

1. **Jude Felt A Necessity.** The literal rendering of the New Testament Greek, from the words, *anagken eschon*,

is "necessity I had." The word for "necessity" (*anagke*) is found eighteen times in the New Testament. Sometimes it is translated as "must needs" (Rom. 13:5), at times it is "distress" (1 Cor. 7:26), we have it translated also as "needeth" and "needful" (Heb. 7:27; Jude 3, *K.J.*), it is "necessary" (Heb. 9:35), "necessities" (2 Cor. 6:4; 12:10), and the rest of the time it is "necessity" (seven times if I have accurately counted them). One of those seven times is when Paul says, "For if I preach the gospel, I have nothing to glory of; for *necessity* is laid upon me; for woe is unto me, if I preach not the gospel" (1 Cor. 9:16). Another time we find it used when the Hebrew writer says, "For the priesthood being changed, there is made of necessity a change also of the law" (Heb. 7:12). Again, "For where a testament is, there must of *necessity* be the death of him that made it" (Heb. 9:16). It is also (*and can you even imagine this!*) used in Hebrews 9:23 when the author uses it in reference to "the patterns" (*K.J.*) or, as it is in the *ASV*, "the copies" of "the things in the heavens..." The Bible is its own best commentary! However, like Jude, I, too, felt a "necessity I had" to write these things. This entire book is an urgent matter, whether one can see it or not.

2. **The Necessity Was To Exhort.** The form of the Greek word here is *parakalon* (this is a present active participle from *parakaleo*), and it is found in most of the New Testament books, that is, it is found in twenty of them. Although this word is translated various ways, such as "desired" (Acts 8:31), "prayed" (Acts 16:9), "comfort" (2 Cor. 1:4; three times), "intreat" (1 Tim. 5:1), etc., I can safely and accurately say that it is "beseech," "beseeching," and "besought" (being so translated forty-two times) more than any other. It is given as "exhort," as per our text, twenty-two times. This is what Peter did on Pentecost (Acts 2:40, cf. 11:23; 15:32; 20:2), it is the same thing that

Paul did (1 Thess. 4:1; 5:14; 2 Thess. 3:12), as well as the Hebrew writer (Heb. 3:13; 10:25), and others.

The word in our text, Jude 3, is a verb form, but the word is also used in the noun form (this form is *parakletos* and is translated, in John 14:16,26; 15:26; 16:7, as "comforter"). This noun form has reference to a mediator, an advocate, an intercessor (Wigram-Green, p. 675), and Thayer gives it as "a pleader, one who pleads another's cause before a judge, counsel for defence, legal assistance,..." (p. 483). With this meaning, it is, therefore, not surprising to find it as "advocate" in 1 John 2:1. Jude actually "calls to his side" his (*para*, beside, and *kaleo*, to call) beloved brethren for the purpose, the aim, of instructing them, encouraging them, yea, warning them.

3. **The Exhortation Was To Contend Earnestly.** The word here is an outstanding one, being *epagonidzesthai* (present middle infinitive), and as far as I know, used only here in the New Testament. Arndt and Gingrich give it as "fight," "contend" (p. 281), Thayer as "to contend," (p. 227), Vine says "to contend about a thing, as a combatant (*epi*, "upon or about," intensive, *agon*, "a contest") (*Expository Dictionary of Biblical Words*, p. 125), and Moulton says it is "to contend strenuously in defence of" (*The Analytical Greek Lexicon Revised*, p. 149).

When either hearing this word pronounced, or seeing it written, a person can easily recognize the word "agonize." This is the word in our New Testament that is usually given as "strive" (Greek is *agonidzomai*, cf. John 18:36; Luke 13:24; 1 Cor. 9:25; Col. 1:29; 4:12; 1 Tim. 6:12 and 2 Tim. 4:7), "struggle," or "strain." This informs me of "the force" with which I protect that which is attacked. That is, I firmly stand upon (Greek, *epi*) the teaching and I am never to stop defending, fighting, striving (this is the force of the present tense) as a combatant in the Lord's army (cf. 2 Tim. 2:3-4). There will always be a battle, as there will always be those who are set against destroying the Lord's church, the Lord's doctrine (His teaching), yea, the Lord's Pattern (cf. Rom. 16:17-18; 2 Pet. 2:1-2; 2 John 9-11).

4. **Contend Earnestly Was For The Faith.** There are, perhaps, a heap more uses of "the faith" in the New Testament than some suppose. I say this, as the total number that I found is about seventy-seven, but in about thirty-five of these (in the Greek), for one reason or another, we do not have the "article" in the English rendering (translation). As an example, "purifying their hearts by faith," as given in Acts 15:9, is "purifying their hearts by *the faith*" in the Greek. One of the best known examples, and one that has very often gotten me into trouble, is the one that says, "For ye are all sons of God, through faith, in Christ Jesus," whereas it should be, "...sons of God, through *the faith*, in Christ Jesus" (Gal. 3:26). In fact, one of the most amazing times is the one that says, "for by grace have ye been saved through faith..." and there is abundant evidence it should read, "for by grace have ye been saved through *the faith*..." (Eph. 2:8, many of the Greek texts have *dia tes pisteos* such as *The Greek New Testament According To The Majority Text, The Greek Text Underlying The English Authorized Version Of 1611, The Interlinear Greek-English New Testament*, etc., and there is a footnote for it in *Nestle's Greek New Testament*).

It is crystal clear that Jude was speaking about something very specific when he used the term "the faith." Indeed, the article is tremendously significant, as reference is here to THE FAITH. He is speaking about that which "the priests were obedient to" (Acts 6:7, says they were obedient to "the faith"), "obedience of the faith among all the nations" (Rom. 1:5; 16:26), "preached by Paul after his conversion" (Gal. 1:23), that which people were "shut up unto"... "but now has come" (Gal. 3:23-25), that which "unifies us" (Eph. 4:5, 13), from which people have "erred" (1 Tim. 6:10, 21), that which Paul kept (2 Tim. 4:7), etc. This is that by which people become the sons of God (Gal. 3:26), therefore, it is the gospel of the risen Lord (1 Cor. 15:1-4; Rom. 6:3-4) and there is no other scheme, plan or pattern for a man's obedience. This system is to be defended against all counterfeit plans, and, believe me, the world (and the church has its share of them today) is full of the forged, the faked and the fraudulent. That there are charlatans with their pseudo, phony and spurious schemes no one can deny. God help us to fight for that for which the Son of God shed His blood.

5. **The Faith Was Once For All Delivered.** The Greek *hapax*, which we have in English as "once" (*K.J.*), "once for all" (*ASV*), "once for all been" (*Twentieth Century New Testament*) needs to be examined. W. E. Vine says, "it denotes once, one time...once for all, of what is of perpetual validity, not requiring repetition... Jude 3" (p. 137). Moulton says, "once for all...knowing once for ever, unfailing, constantly, Jude 3, 5," (p. 36). Arndt and Gingrich gives it as "once for all" (p. 80). Thayer has it "once, one time, once for all" (p. 80). Wigram-Green lists it as "once, once for all" (p. 66). Rienecker and Rogers has it "once for all" (p. 803). In *The Expositor's Greek Testament*, Nicoll has "used here in its classical sense 'once for all,'...This excludes the novelties of the Libertines, cf. Gal. 1:9," (p. 255). Bullinger gives it as "once, one time, once for all" (p. 552).

One of the best ways to ascertain its meaning is to let the Bible itself show us how it is used, therefore, its meaning. This word in the Greek language is found fifteen times, counting both Jude verses 3 and 5. In 1 Peter 3:18, we have this word: "Because Christ also suffered for sins once (*hapax*), the righteous for the unrighteous, that he might bring us to God; being put to death in the flesh, but made alive in the spirit." In Hebrews 9:28, it is written: "So Christ also, having been once offered to bear the sins of many, shall appear a second time, apart from sin, to them that wait for him, unto savlation." How many times did Christ suffer for sins? How many times was Christ offered? Could this possibly mean that Christ suffered (was offered) "once for all," "once and for all," or "once and for all time"? If *the faith* has been delivered *once*, would that not mean "once and for all time"? If it is "once," "once for all," and "once for all time," does that not mean that "the pattern set forth, the rule, goal, design, model, type, figure, example, gospel, plan, etc., is a once and for all time item"? Pray tell me what else does it mean or could it mean? How many times did the high priest, and I refer to "the day of the year," go into the second place, the holy of holies (cf. Heb. 9:7)? Indeed, the word *hapax* is herein used.

This is something that man did not think up, dream up, make up, conjure up, cook up or get up, as it was revealed by God through the holy men inspired by God (cf. 2 Pet. 1:19-21; 1 Cor. 2:9-13). It is written down for us in the very words of the Spirit, as Paul stated: "...we speak, not in words which man's wisdom teacheth, but which the Spirit teacheth; combining spiritual things with spiritual words" (1 Cor. 2:13). This was the same man who said: "...as touching the gospel which was preached by me, that it is not after man. For neither did I receive it from man, nor was I taught it, but it came to me through revelation of Jesus Christ" (Gal. 1:11-12). Therefore, like Jude, we, today, have a very sacred and solemn charge, yea, a divine mandate, to keep and to guard (cf. 1 Tim. 6:20-

21) that which once and for all time has been delivered. *The Greek New Testament* has it in this exact order, I mean word for word: "...necessity I had to write to you exhorting (you) to contend earnestly for the once delivered (or, as we noted the term, once and for all) to the saints faith" (Nestle, mine, p. 610). This is why I chose this most explicit verse for the division in this chapter, "SEARCH THE SCRIPTURE FOR THE STATEMENT." I speak, therefore, of this verse as having adequacy, completeness, extensiveness, sufficiency and that which serves to answer, satisfy, fulfill, saturate and quench the thirst of any man who hungers for a "once and for all pattern."

PONDER THESE POWERFUL PROCLAMATIONS

The scriptures are, indeed, powerful (cf. Rom. 1:16; 1 Cor. 1:18 as well as James 1:21, as all use the Greek *dunamis* which manifests "God's power"), they are certainly proclamations, as that was the task, the high calling, of the evangelists (*kerusso*, Acts 8:5; *euangelidzo*, Rom. 10:15f; *parrhesiadzomai*, Acts 9:27; etc.), and they are to be studied (2 Tim. 2:15), searched (Acts 17:10-11), heeded (1 Tim. 4:11-16) and obeyed (John 14:15,21,23; 1 John 2:3-5; 5:1-3). The power in these scriptural proclamations are to be observed with all diligence, and "the same things" (2 Tim. 2:2) are to be committed to faithful men for the ongoing of the gospel, its teachings. There are several passages that directly relate to the subject of this chapter, therefore, I list a few of these for our examination.

1. "But though we, or an angel from heaven, should preach unto you any gospel other than that which we preached unto you, let him be anathema" (Gal. 1:6-9, esp. vs. 8). When did the changing, twisting and perverting the gospel of Christ change from being wrong to being right? The fact is, it never has. They could not do it then, and no

man can do it today and please God. If a man has the capability of preaching, he must preach it just as God gave it, yes, first century or now.

2. Jesus said, "He that rejecteth me, and receiveth not my sayings, hath one that judgeth him: the word that I spake, the same shall judge him in the last day" (John 12:48). Note carefully, it is the "word that Jesus spake" that is going to judge us. When did Jesus deliver such? Has He given any word since the first century by which man is to be judged? Either this is a true statement, or it is a false statement? Either I will be or I will not be judged by the word He spake, now which is it? It cannot be a "changed or altered" word, as this verse says it is the word Jesus spoke.

3. Paul said, "in the day when God shall judge the secrets of men, according to my gospel, by Jesus Christ" (Rom. 2:16). Is the idea of "the day" still with us? Is the fact of God judging still correct? Is it true that the secrets of men will be made known (cf. Matt. 10:26; Luke 12:2; Rom. 14:10-12; 2 Cor. 5:10; cf. Eccl. 12:14). If these things are true, and they are, then will it be by what Paul preached that this will be done? How can any man even conceive the idea that the pattern, the faith, the word, the gospel, etc., has changed or that we need to "adapt" it for today?

4. Peter said, "seeing that his divine power hath granted unto all things that pertain unto life and godliness, through the knowledge of him that called us by his own glory and virtue" (2 Pet. 1:3). If, as Peter stated, we have "all things," and "all things as pertaining to life," and "all things as pertaining to godliness," I just need to ask, "What else do we need to meet 'the needs' of human beings today?" Was this just for those living when Peter lived or did it stop in the next century or just what

happened to "the all things" that his divine power hath granted unto us?

5. When inspiration through Paul said, "...not to go beyond the things which are written" (1 Cor. 4:6), was that just for the Corinthians? How is it that a man is to walk "by faith," "faith which comes by the hearing of the Word," and "without which no man can be pleasing to God," and yet, we hear talk/discussion today about the fact that we need a gospel that will answer the needs of man (2 Cor. 5:7; Rom. 10:17; Heb. 11:6). There can be no faith where there is no word of God! Neither can there be faith where the word of God has been changed. When a man rejects God's word, that man rejects God (cf. 1 Sam. 15:21-29).

6. John said, "Whosoever goeth onward and abideth not in the teaching of Christ, hath not God: he that abideth in the teaching, the same hath both the Father and the Son" (2 John 9, read vss. 10-11 also). Nothing could be as clear-cut, unconfused and unconditional, as the fact, from this verse, that God is going to condemn anyone who goes beyond the teaching, the doctrine, the written.

7. It was also John who wrote: "I testify unto every man that heareth the words of the prophecy of this book, If any man shall add unto them, God shall add unto him the plagues which are written in this book: and if any man shall take away from the words...God shall take away his part from the tree of life,...which are written in this book" (Rev. 22:18-19). How far would one have to go before he "added to" or "took from" that which is written? Would just a "little thought" here and a "little idea" there be wrong? Surely a God of love would be more tolerant than some say today! What saith the scriptures? (cf. Rom. 2:4-9; 2 Thess. 1:7-9; Eph. 2:11-12; 1 Pet. 4:12-19).

8. It was Jesus who said, "Ye do err, not knowing the scriptures, nor the power of God" (Matt. 22:29). Can a man "know" the truth of God (cf. John 8:31-32; 17:17; 7:17)? Can a man know the power of God (Rom. 1:16; 1 Cor. 1:18)? How could a man err, if the gospel is a gospel of "change"? After all, we must adapt it for today! It is, as the Book says, necessary to take heed "how" we hear, "what" we hear, and we are to "give heed" to what we hear (Mark 4:24; Luke 8:18; Heb. 2:1-4), therefore, let us heed and hold to the pattern.

9. Paul told Timothy, "Hold the pattern of sound words which thou hast heard from me, in faith and love which is in Christ Jesus" (2 Tim. 1:13). How can a man "hold to a pattern that is constantly changing, as it will mean one thing for this age, another for the next, etc?" Is it right to say that "the gospel" is to be preached to all creation, that God "desires the salvation of all men," that Jesus is the author of those who "obey him," and that there is such a thing as a "common faith/salvation" (Mark 16:15-16; Matt. 28:18-20; 2 Pet. 3:9; Heb. 5:8-9; Jude 3; Titus 1:3; etc.)?

10. If it is true, and it is, that God is no respecter of persons, and that "in every nation he that feareth God, and worketh righteousness, is acceptable to him," how can a man, in any or every nation be sure he is working righteousness? (Rom. 2:11; Acts 10:34-35). This is asked, because it is possible for man to be "ignorant of God's ways and establish his own," thus not submitting himself to "the righteousness of God" (cf. Rom. 10:1-3). How can a man be classified as being "ignorant," if this gospel changes unto a "new" gospel for our modern and most affluent world? How can such verses as Ephesians 3:4; 5:17 and 2 Timothy 2:7 be true, when what we read is really not what we need. That is, what we read does not

really mean what it is saying to us or what is written in the Book? Confusing, you better believe it is!

Let me hasten to say that an entire galaxy of thoughts could here be given, but perhaps these will help us as we seek to understand we have that today which changes not, which has been "once and for all time" delivered and by which we shall be judged (Heb. 13:8; John 12:48; 2 Cor. 5:10; Rev. 20:10-15; 22:18-19; Jude 3; Rom. 2:16; etc.). I gladly make the pristine, the original, primitive, initial, first, simple, uncomplicated and uncorrupted plea that THE GOSPEL OF THE FIRST CENTURY IS THE GOSPEL FOR THE CENTURY IN WHICH WE NOW LIVE!! Indeed, the message then is the message for today. The plan for them is the plan for us. It was God's pattern for those of early Christianity and it is still God's pattern for those of present day Christianity. It is a fact that God fully intended, and there is nothing plainer if a man can read and has the ability to understand, that "the faith delivered unto the saints" in the first century **be that for every century**. The whole truth must be preached, nothing more and nothing less (cf. Acts 20:27).

DETECT AND DISCERN THESE DEFINITE DECLARATIONS

In this section, I just want to call our attention to one of the great facts of the New Testament. A fact that is presented so very distinctly, that it would be most difficult for the student who has the trait of nobility of the Beroeans to overlook. As per the caption above, there are definite declarations revealed as we read the New Testament. These, as listed below, refer to that body of absolute, objective, attainable and unchangeable truth of God. I have already, in this treatise, made reference to such, but now we note some of those specific wordings.

1. *The faith* (Acts 6:7; 13:8; 14:22; 15:9; 16:5; 24:24; Gal. 1:23; 3:23, 26; Eph. 4:13; Phil. 1:27; Col. 1:23; 2:7, 12; 1 Tim. 3:9; 4:1; 5:8; 6:10, 21; 2 Tim. 2:18; 3:8; 4:7; Tit. 1:13; James 2:1; 1 Pet. 5:9; Jude 3; Rev. 13:10; 14:12).

2. *The word of the truth* (Col. 1:5).

3. *The teaching, doctrine* (2 John 9-11).

4. *The word of the cross* (1 Cor. 1:18).

5. *The word of the message* (1 Thess. 2:13).

6. *The word of God* (1 Thess. 2:13).

7. *The truth of the gospel* (Gal. 2:5, 14).

8. *The truth* (John 8:32; 2 Tim. 3:8; 4:4; Tit. 1:14; 1 Pet. 1:22; James 3:14; 5:19).

9. *The word* (John 12:48; Acts 17:11; 20:32; Eph. 5:26; Gal. 6:6; Phil. 1:14; 2:16; Col. 3:16; James 1:22; 1 Pet. 3:1).

10. *The word of reconciliation* (2 Cor. 5:19).

11. *The faithful word* (Tit. 1:9).

12. *The word of his power* (Heb. 1:3).

13. *The engrafted word* (James 1:21).

14. *The gospel* (Rom. 1:16; 2:16; 10:16; 1 Cor. 15:1; Acts 14:7; Gal. 1:6-7; 1 Thess. 2:4, 8; 2 Thess. 1:8; 1 Pet. 4:17).

15. *The word of prophecy* (2 Pet. 1:19).

16. *The gospel of the grace of God* (Acts 20:24).

This, as I have written before, is what a man is to preach (2 Tim. 4:1-5), it is what an elder is to hold faithfully (Tit. 1:9ff), it is what deacons are to keep in a pure conscience (1 Tim. 3:9), so they may have boldness in the faith (1 Tim. 3:13) and it is what we are to commit to faithful men to teach others (2 Tim. 2:2). If these things are not proclaimed, we betray the blood that was shed on the cross of calvary (Eph. 1:7; Col. 1:14; Rev. 1:5). Each of us needs again and again to be put in remembrance (2 Pet. 1:12-13, 15; 3:1) as there is always the possibility, and it just takes one generation to do it, to go astray, forsake God and to even turn unto idols (cf. Judg. 2:6-14).

CHALLENGE OF THE CHANGELESS

We live in a world "of the changing." It was Edmund Spencer who once referred to "the living, whirling wheel of change, to which all mortal things doth sway." Tennyson wrote, "the old order changeth, yielding place to the new..." It was a new word, SPUTNIK, that introduced us to "the space age" back on October 4, 1957, at 6:30 p.m. Talk about change! On May 15-16, 1963, Major L. Gordon Cooper, in FAITH 7, orbited the earth 22 times in 34 hours and 20 minutes, yet back in 1519 it took Magellan 1,080 days to circle the globe. It was not until 1850 that we had the first billion people on this earth, but then by 1976 we had in excess of three billion and today we have 5.2 billion and it is estimated that by 2000 there will be in excess of 6 billion people on earth. Today, just in a matter of minutes (perhaps even seconds) news travels all over the globe, and we can even watch the happenings around the world almost instantaneously.

Indeed, man's manner and method of living, war, transportation, communication, farming, household tasks, prepared foods, medicine, surgery, sources of power, theology, church creeds, concept of morality, etc., etc. have changed. And yet, with all the variegated, diversified and diverse, manifold and mixed changes that we witness from day to day, there are some things that never change. It is to some of these that I now wish to direct our attention.

1. **Human nature has not changed** (cf. Gal. 5:17, Greek, *sarx*). It will never change until it is brought under the power of God's divine nature (cf. 2 Pet. 1:3-4).

Men still have the greed of Lot and of Balaam, the love of preeminence and power of Diotrephes, the love of money and the lust of the flesh (Gen. 13; Num. 22; 2 John 9; 1 Tim. 6:10; 1 John 2:15-17; etc.). Men still have need of guidance (Jer. 10:23; Prov. 14:12; 16:25; 19:21; 21:2; Judg. 17:6; 21:25), salvation because of sin (Rom. 3:23; 6:23), encouragement and strengthening because of their weakness (Gal. 6:1-2), sympathy because of sorrow (Rom. 12:15; 2 Cor. 1:3-6) and hope because of death (1 Thess. 4:13-18).

2. **Sin has not changed.** Sin is still the "transgression of the law" (1 John 3:4), it is still "unrighteousness" (1 John 5:17), it is still doing that which violates our conscience (Rom. 14:23), it still separates from God (Isa. 59:1-2), it still has a sting (cf. 1 Cor. 15:56), it still causes misery (2 Sam. 12:7-23), there are still sins of omission (James 4:17), and it will still keep a man out of heaven (Rev. 21:27). Indeed, each man shall pay for his own sins (cf. Rom. 14:10-12; 2 Cor. 5:10; Eccl. 12:14; Rom. 2:16), as "the soul that sinneth it shall surely die" (Ezek. 18:4, 20; cf. 1 Kings 8:46; 2 Chron. 6:36; 25:4).

3. **Satan has not changed.** From the time of Genesis chapter three, until the present hour, Satan has not changed. He may still be described by every term that has ever been written in the Bible, as he is still "a liar" (John 8:44), he is still "walking about as a lion trying to devour" (1 Pet. 5:8), he is still the "destroyer" (Rev. 9:11), "the accuser of our brethren" (Rev. 12:10), "angel of the

bottomless pit" (Rev. 9:11, Abaddon and Apollyon), "Beelzebub" (Matt. 12:24; Mark 3:22; Luke 11:15), "Belial" (2 Cor. 6:15), "the devil" (Matt. 4:1; Luke 4:2,6; Rev. 20:2), "the enemy" (Matt. 13:39), "murderer" (John 8:44), "old serpent" (Rev. 12:9; 20:2), "prince of this world" (John 12:31; 14:30; 16:11), "prince of devils" (Matt. 12:24) and of "this world" (Eph. 2:2), "ruler of darkness" (Eph. 6:12), "the god of this world" (2 Cor. 4:4), "tempter" (Matt. 4:3), etc. His goal, his ambition, has never changed, yea, he is changeless and unchanging.

4. **Christ has not changed** (Heb. 1:8; Psm. 90:2; 93:2; Heb. 13:8; Matt. 28:18-20; Rev. 17:14; etc.). Jesus is still the "only begotten Son of God" (John 1:14,18; 3:16,18; 1 John 4:9). He is still the "head of the church and the Saviour of the body" (Col. 1:18,24; Eph. 5:23; 1:22-23), he is still "the founder" of the Church (Matt. 16:18), "the foundation of the Church" (1 Cor. 3:11; Isa. 28:16), the one of whom God said, "hear ye him" (Matt. 17:5), the one "in whom God said he was well pleased" (Matt. 3:17), the one who has "all authority" (Matt. 28:18), the one who told us to "preach the gospel" (Matt. 28:18-20; Mark 16:15-16), the one who will be with us "to the end" (Matt. 28:20; John 13:1), he who is our "advocate" (1 John 2:1), who lives to "make intercession for us" (Heb. 7:25; 9:24), etc. Whatever else one might find written IN THE BOOK about the Son of God has never changed one iota! Thank God He is changeless!

5. **Death and judgment have not changed.** Man is still going to die unless, of course, he is living when the Master returns (Heb. 9:27; 1 Thess. 4:13-18; John 5:28-29; Rom. 6:23) and man is still going to be judged (Rom. 14:10-12; 2 Cor. 5:10). Nothing has changed that tells us man will not die, will not face God in the judgment and will not be judged (cf. Matt. 25:31-46). That which is

called "the judgment bar of God and of Christ" has never yet been cancelled. This is why it is so necessary to preach repentance, as God "has appointed a day in which he will judge man" (Acts 17:30). There is going to be a day when God will judge "the secrets of men by the gospel" (Rom. 2:16). I know this is "certain" as the Bible so frequently speaks about "the day" (cf. Rom. 2:5), "that day" (Matt. 7:22), "the day of judgment " (Matt. 10:15), "the last day" (John 12:48; cf. 5:22), "a day" (Acts 17:30), "the day of wrath" (Rom. 2:5), "the great day" (Rev. 6:17), etc. If death and judgment have changed, who changed them? To what were they changed? What changes were made about them? Is it not true "the living know they shall die"? (Eccl. 9:5; cf. 3:2, 19-21; 7:2; 8:8; 12:7).

6. **Hell has not changed.** Hell is still the place where "the worm dieth not and the fire is not quenched" (Mark 9:43-49), "the place of darkness, weeping, wailing and gnashing of teeth" (Matt. 13:42-50), "the place of everlasting destruction from the presence of God" (2 Thess. 1:8-9), the place prepared "for the devil and his angels, eternal fire" (Matt. 25:41), "a place where the soul is destroyed" as written in Matthew 10:28, a place of "unquenchable fire" (Matt. 3:12), "a place of outer darkness" (Matt. 22:13), "a place of continual torment" (Rev. 14:10-11), a place called a "lake of fire" (Rev. 20:15) and a place called "the second death" (Rev. 21:8). If it is a fact that hell has changed, who changed it? What has changed about it? Has the length of it changed, the purpose of it changed, the intensity of the heat changed, has it changed relative to who it is that will go there, etc.? You might as well preach "NO SON OF GOD" as to preach "no hell" or to change what the Bible says "about hell."

7. **Heaven has not changed.** Heaven is still "God's dwelling place" (cf. Deut. 26:15; 1 Kings 8:30; 1 Chron.

21:27; 2 Chron. 7:14; Job 22:12,14; Psm. 11:4; 33:13; 102:19; Eccl. 5:2; Isa. 66:1), and we can still pray, "Our Father, which art in heaven" (Matt. 6:9). When we confess Christ, we have the assurance he will "confess us before our Father who is in heaven" (Matt. 10:32). It it still "the house of many mansions" (John 14:1). Indeed, it is a land "that is fairer than day" (cf. Rev. 21:22-27), and one where all tears "shall be wiped away" (Rev. 21:4). Heaven is a place of rest (Heb. 4:9; Rev. 14:13), it is a heavenly country (Heb. 11:16), and it is God's paradise (2 Cor. 12:2-4; Rev. 2:7). It is the "great city, the holy Jerusalem" (Rev. 21:10) and the place where the righteous will reign for ever and for ever (Rev. 22:4-5). I'd hate to think that heaven has changed! Yet, if the gospel has changed, the pattern has changed, the church, the bride of Christ has changed, why hasn't heaven also changed? After all, it is obedience to the gospel, according to the pattern, that one has the privilege of being with God (Matt. 25:31-46; 2 Thess. 1:7-9; 1 Pet. 4:16-19; etc.). I know this, as the Master said, "I AM THE WAY, THE TRUTH AND THE LIFE" (John 14:6) and He said, "NO MAN (ONE) CAN COME TO THE FATHER except through me" (John 6:44-45; 14:6).

Yes, there is "the changing," but there is also "the changeless and the unchanging." The only thing in the world that can fulfill the need of these things that have not changed is that which is unchangeable. Some things change, but those things that are of eternal consequence, that deal with eternity, never change.

MAN HAS NO MOTIVE TO MOVE THE MODEL

When God gives the pattern, the model, no man has a motive, the ground to move, that is, change it in any shape or fashion. Man cannot just assume that right. Certainly God never gave that right to man. Therefore, it cannot be right for any man to change it. We can note just here only a very few items for our meditation.

1. **Would changing it just "a little" hurt anything?** This might be settled by seeing how God dealt with such in the past. Did it matter about "strange fire," as in the case of Nadab and Abihu? Did it matter about "Cain's offering," as in Genesis 4:1-8? What if a king were to be the one who changed things, surely it would be all right for someone as a king to do it? Why not ask Saul, as recorded in 1 Samuel 15:1-23. But let's just go back as far as we can go back. Let's start with Adam and Eve. What would be wrong with eating of just "one" tree, that of the knowledge of good and evil? God would not surely cast us out of the garden of Eden for just one violation (cf. Gen. 3:22-24). Moses was told to "s-p-e-a-k" to the rock, but he chose to "s-m-i-t-e" the rock. What is the difference? You will note there is the same number of letters in these two words. However, though it seem but "a little" thing, God had told Moses "to speak" to the rock (Num. 20:8). Why wasn't Moses justified in this, after all, God did tell him to "s-m-i-t-e" the rock in Exodus 17:1-7, so why couldn't he do it again? Even idolatrous people, as those in 2 Kings 16:10-11, knew what it was to "build according to all the workmanship, the pattern."

2. **What about "the passing of time," as surely this would make it all right?** Of course, anyone can understand that things need to be updated. Right? How long after the pattern for "the people" who carried the ark and "how" they were to carry it was it when the man Uzzah "thought" he could "touch" the ark? Let's say about 450 years. It did not change God's pattern (Num. 4:15; 1 Chron. 13:1-10). God unleashed his anger for the simple reason "that we sought him not according to the ordinance" (1 Chron. 15:13-15).

We need to observe, and do it very carefully, that the passing of time had nothing to do with making it all right to change God's pattern. About 500 years after the pattern, you can read of Proverbs 14:12; 16:25; 19:21; 21:2. About 800 years later you can read what Isaiah said (55:8-9). Go 900 years later and you can read about the thinking of Jeremiah (10:23; cf. 6:16). Over 1,500 years later, you can read of what Jesus had to say (cf. Matt. 5:17-20; 15:3-14).

It needs to be established in the heart and soul of everyone who claims to believe in the Bible as God's eternal word that it cannot, by man or angel, be changed (no man has that right, that authority). Only God had that right, and God informed man by revelation when the change was made (cf. Heb. 7:12; 9:15-17; Col. 2:14-16) from the Old Testament to the New Testament. The New Testament will never be changed (Jude 3), as it is a "once and for all" message.

3. **Does God care if His pattern is changed?** If we are to learn the lessons that God has intended for us to learn from the Old Testament, indeed, God cares (cf. Rom. 15:4; Lev. 10:1-2; Gen. 4:1-8; etc.). If we learn anything from the New Testament, it is the fact that God does not allow the pattern to be changed (cf. Matt. 28:18-20). Just recall where we began in this chapter, with Jude 3, and study again the meaning of the Greek *hapax*, "once and for all," and observe how the New Testament uses that word (cf. 1 Pet. 3:18). This is why men are so severely warned not to change the gospel, the preaching, the pattern of sound words, etc. (cf. Gal. 1:6-9; 2 Tim. 1:13; 2:2; 2 John 9-11; Rev. 22:18-19; 1 Cor. 4:6; etc.), as it is the very thing that is going to judge us some day (John 12:48; Rom. 2:16; Rev. 20:10-15). Man can avoid having to face his sins (cf. 2 Chron. 7:14; Eph. 1:7; Col. 1:13-14; Rev. 1:5; Rom. 6:3-4; Acts 2:38).

If a person will only "look carefully" into God's word (cf. James 1:25, Greek *parakupto*), then that person can see, grasp and appreciate the very distinctive fact of the exclusiveness of the pattern of God. This will, if practiced, solve the problem of unity, and there will be no more a cry for what some term "unity in diversity" (this is a contradiction in terms). Man will know what to preach, how to preach it and the hearers will know what to do to be saved. The New Testament church will be recognized for what it is, the body of Christ, and it will be exalted to the place where it should be in the minds of all people. The pattern for unity is set, it is "once and for all," and it only needs to be heeded by the workmen of today (Matt. 28:18-20; John 7:17; 8:31-32; 17:11, 17, 20-23; Rom. 1:5; 10:17; 16:17-18, 25-26; 1 Cor. 1:10; 4:6; 12:13; 2 Cor. 5:7; Gal. 3:26-29; Eph. 2:11-22; 3:20-21; 4:1-6; 2 Tim. 2:15; Heb. 11:6; 2 John 9-11).

LESSONS TO BE LEARNED

It is now imperative, with this chapter having been written, as well as the first three, that we learn some of the lessons from the caption of the book, *Behold The Pattern*, as it pertains to Joshua 22:28, with the thought running through these chapters and now concluding with "Once And For All."

1. *In a positive way we note:*

   a. We must strive to keep alive the memory of what God wants for his people (cf. Mark 8:18; 1 Cor. 11:26).

   b. We must aspire to preserve the unity of the people of God.

   c. We must avoid the appearance of evil by always following, imitating, what we have learned from

God.

d. We must maintain the faith, regardless of where we are in this life, that is, we are to always be faithful.

e. We must remember "who" we are, "what" we are, "whose" we are, no matter "where" we are, as this is more imperative than all the silver, gold, lands, flocks and crops a man might own.

f. We must labor and toil for those who will follow later, our children and our grandchildren, etc. We must build for the future (cf. Josh. 22:25).

2. *In a negative way we note:*

a. We must have a zeal for the truth of God and act immediately when we believe dishonor might be brought to the very name of God.

b. We must be cautious in being zealous for the truth of God and make sure we know wherein our concern lies.

c. We must never let our gratitude blind us to the derelictions of our friends.

d. We must learn the truth, "Attack the disease at its commencement or it will defy all treatment."

e. We must recall the lessons of sacred history and how God has dealt with his children in order to handle the many situations that might arise.

f. We must forever remember that in one sermon we learn two lessons: "Judge not that ye be not judged," and "By their fruits ye shall know them."

Chapter Five

THE PATTERN - AND "STRANGE" AND "UNCERTAIN" SOUNDS FROM SOME BRETHREN (Part I)

THE PATTERN - AND "STRANGE" AND "UNCERTAIN" SOUNDS FROM SOME BRETHREN

(Part I)

There are two Biblical words that perhaps need to be brought to our attention for the thoughts of this particular section. Those words, upon which we want to introduce this area of our study, are found both in the Hebrew and in the Greek. Therefore, we magnet our attention on the word "strange" (Hebrew, *zar, zuwr*; Greek, *Xenos*) and "uncertain" (Greek, *adelos*).

Let us first notice the word "strange." This word, in the Old Testament Hebrew has the meaning, basically, "to turn aside," therefore, to be "a foreigner, a stranger, profane," and as you follow its meaning, as per the context in which it is used, it can even mean "to commit adultery." The word strange is found some seventy-six times, and I can safely say that the majority of uses refer to "strange gods" or to "strange women" (of gods, fourteen times; of woman or women, twenty-one times). In the New Testament, the word (Greek) "strange" is found only eleven times, and is only found in Luke, Acts, Hebrews, 1 Peter and Jude. It also has the meaning of "foreign, alien, unusual, unfamiliar, that which is without, on the outside and contrary to received thought."

The word "uncertain" is the New Testament Greek word *adelos*, an adjective. Let me hasten to say that this word has the negating alpha on it, as it comes from the word *delos*, which means "clear, manifest, certain, and evident." However, with the negative it means "uncertain," "indistinct," and perhaps "hidden." It is kin to the verb, *deloo*, which means "to make plain," "to reveal," etc.

EXAMINING THE WORD "STRANGE"

> *"And Nadab and Abihu, the sons of Aaron, took each of them his censer, and put fire therein, and laid incense thereon, and offered* ***strange fire*** *before Jehovah, which he had not commanded them" (Lev. 10:1, emp. GM).*

> *"Be not carried away by divers and strange teachings* (Greek, ***didachais****, dative plural of* ***didache****): for it is good that the heart be established by grace; not by meats wherein they that occupied themselves were not profited" (Heb. 13:9, emp. GM).*

> *"Even as Sodom and Gomorrah, and the cities about them, having in like manner with these given themselves over to fornication and gone after* ***strange flesh****, are set forth as an example, suffering the punishment of eternal fire" (Jude 7, emp. GM).*

Why is it that some things are classified as "strange" to God? What makes an item "strange"? For an example, why was the fire that Nadab and Abihu offered before God considered as "strange fire"? Let us take note of these thoughts.

1. Would you say this was a sin of presumption? (cf. Deut. 18:20).

2. Was what they did unsanctioned and unauthorized by God?

3. Why was no fault found with the censer and incense? (cf. Exod. 30:34ff; 25:9, 40; 40:16).

4. Is a counterfeit fire as good as what God requested?

(cf. Lev. 16:12-13).

5. May a man come to God in a way of his own devising?

6. Does this teach and make it clear that God only accepts what He himself has spoken?

7. Can a profession of desire to honor God excuse the wilful neglect of His injunctions?

8. Could it be said that "strange fire" was punished with "hallowed fire"? (cf. Lev. 9:24).

9. Consider the fact that even those openly dedicated to the service of God can be unmindful of His precepts. These had previously been consecrated as priests.

10. Relationships do not matter when it comes to serving God, as we have here the sons of Aaron and nephews of Moses. The most exalted at times forget that their position does not alter divine obedience.

11. How true it is that a brother may be mutually helpful or injurious.

12. They acted without direction as seen in the words, "which he had not commanded them." *Note:* Their crime was not in doing what was forbidden, but in doing what was not enjoined, included. Again, the excluding factor is "no authority" (cf. Deut. 4:2; 12:32; Prov. 30:5-6).

13. The sin of human judgment of God's purposes, self-will, the substitution of human inventions for divine legislation, thoughtless action, despising the authority of God and pure disobedience will cause one to suffer punishment from the same God he desires to serve.

14. What does the statement mean, "And Aaron held his peace"? (cf. Lev. 10:3).

15. Relative to the written Word, does it matter whether a person thinks a thing is small and insignificant or not? Can an item be seemingly small in the sight of man, yet great and vital in the sight of God?

16. Even though the intentions are good, can human device, self-assertion, self-will, human talent or a man's conscience (thinking a thing to be right, justifiable) take the place of obedience to God's instructions?

17. In summary, could Nadab and Abihu have offered any fire as good as the fire from the altar of burnt offering? What made the fire from the altar of burnt offering so special? Had God spoken? When God speaks does man have the right of altering those words?

What I have written about the case of Nadab and Abihu and the fire that was "strange," could be applied to the other verses I gave. The "strange teachings" of Hebrews 13:9 are any of a great number we find today to be contrary to the teachings (doctrine) of the New Testament. Some perhaps may be "twisted" or "perverted," and if so are "strange" when compared to "the teaching of Christ" (2 John 9-11; cf. Gal. 1:6-9). Any teaching that "adds to," "takes from," "abides not in the truth," "perverts," "goes beyond the written," etc., is, indeed, "strange" to God (Rev. 22:18-19; John 8:31-32; Gal. 1:7-9; 1 Cor. 4:6; John 12:48; Jude 3; etc.), as we are "to commit the same thing" we have received to faithful men so others can also be taught (cf. 2 Tim. 2:2). Whatever is "foreign," "alien," and "contrary" to that which is revealed is "strange" to God. God had said, "I am Jehovah thy God,... Thou shalt have no other gods before me" (Exod. 20:2-3; cf. Gen. 1:1; Exod. 3:14; Psm. 90:2; Isa. 44:6; 45:5, 18, 22; 47:8, 13-15). It is no wonder then that so very often the Old Testament speaks about "strange gods" (cf. Gen. 35:2; Deut. 32:16; Josh. 24:20; 1 Sam. 7:3; 2 Chron.

14:3; Mal. 2:11). Just as surely, explicitly, clearly, and distinctly as God said, "I am God and besides me there is no other," God revealed "the teaching," or "the doctrine," and "there is no other!" Indeed, anything else is "a strange teaching" to God. When any preacher says, "Let us learn to love each other *overlooking disagreements in doctrine*, overlooking those things of the flesh, and only observe the inner man" (quote from a newspaper from a preacher who entitled his article "Our Traditions," emp. GM), he needs to know if one can "forget doctrine," he can "forget God!" Error has, and error will always, send people to a devil's hell (cf. John 8:31-32; Matt. 16:12; 2 John 9-11).

When I read about "Sodom and Gomorrah, and the cities about them, having in like manner with these given themselves over to fornication and gone after *strange flesh,...*" (Jude 7), I wonder just what it is that is "strange flesh"? It doesn't take very much common sense for a man to understand just two scriptures, Genesis 2:18-25 and Matthew 19:3-12. God had formed every beast of the field and every bird of the heavens and Adam had given name to them all, but there was not found a help meet for him (Gen. 2:20). God took one of his ribs, made for him a "woman," brought her unto the man and the record says, "...bone of my bones, and flesh of my flesh: she shall be called Woman... Therefore shall a man leave his father and his mother, and shall cleave unto his wife: and they shall be one flesh" (Gen. 2:22-24). In Matthew 19:4-5, Jesus recalls this divinely inspired writing from Genesis and said, "So that they are no more two, but one flesh. What therefore God hath joined together, let not man put asunder" (Matt. 19:6). Indeed, God made them "male" and "female," and anything else to serve as a companion for a man but a woman, or for a woman but a man, is *strange flesh*! Jude 7 refers to Sodom and Gomorrah and their grievous, atrocious, appalling, and acute sins. There are a few things we absolutely know about this: (1) we know the sins of Sodom and Gomorrah, as they are revealed to us in Genesis 13:13; 18:20-33; 19:1-11, (2) we know then of the cities about them, as they, too, "having in like manner with these given themselves over to fornication," (3) we know the term "fornication" (Greek is *ekporneusasai*, 1st aroist active participle of *ekporneuo*, an intensified and strengthened form meaning "to be utterly unchaste, to give oneself over to" and implies excessive indulgence) can refer to relations of man to man, man to woman, woman to woman and human to animals (Arndt and Gingrich, pp. 244, 700; Thayer, pp. 199, 532; Kittel, Vol. 6, p. 579), (4) we know that these went after what is called "strange flesh," (5) we know why in this reference it is called "strange flesh," (6) we know they were "set forth" as an example, and (7) we know their end, "suffering the punishment of eternal fire."

Just in case one would like to read of this sin in the Old Testament, let me list, in addition to the verses I listed in Genesis, Leviticus 18:22; 20:13; Deuteronomy 23:17; 1 Kings 14:24; 15:12; 22:46; 2 Kings 23:7. Also, in the New Testament we have such passages as Romans 1:27; 1 Corinthians 6:9 and 1 Timothy 1:10 (cf. Matt. 15:19; 2 Pet. 2:6-8). There are three Greek words that should be studied: (1) *orexis* as in the Roman passage, (2) *arsenokoites* as found in 1 Corinthians and 1 Timothy 1:10, and (3) *malakos*, also in 1 Corinthians. In these three words we have: (1) men burning in their lust one for another (women also, v. 26), (2) a male who submits his body to unnatural lewdness, a catamite, a boy kept for sexual perversion, and (3) a man who lies with a male as with a female, a sodomite, a male bed partner. Is there any known reason why the God of heaven, who made them male and female, made the two to become one flesh, should not look upon such and say when such is done that they have gone after "strange flesh"? Is there any reason, in harmony with Romans 15:4, why this should not be "set forth" as an example? Is it unreasonable to state and declare of such that they will "suffer the punishment of eternal fire"?

CONTEMPLATING THE WORD "UNCERTAIN"

> *"But now, brethren, if I come unto you speaking with tongues, what shall I profit you, unless I speak to you either by way of revelation, or of knowledge, or of prophesying, or of teaching? Even things without life,* ***giving a voice,*** *whether pipe or harp,* ***if they give not a distinction in the sounds,*** *how shall it be known what is piped or harped? For if the trumpet give an* ***uncertain voice,*** *who shall prepare himself for war? So also ye, unless ye utter by the tongue* ***speech easy to be understood,*** *how shall it be known what is spoken? for ye will be speaking into the air...* ***If*** *then* ***I know not the meaning of the voice,*** *I shall be to him that speaketh a barbarian, and he that speaketh will be a barbarian unto me" (1 Corinthians 14:6-11, esp. vs. 8, emp. GM).*

As far as I am able to ascertain, the word "uncertain" is just used here and in Luke 11:44. I am speaking about the Greek word *adelos*, the meaning of which is "vague," "indistinct," or "uncertain." We do have the adverb used in 1 Corinthians 9:26 (the only time it is used). The noun form of the word is *adelotes*, "uncertainty," and is used in 1 Timothy 6:17: "Charge them that are rich in this present world, that they be not highminded, nor have their hopes set on the uncertainty of riches, but on God, who giveth us richly all things to enjoy." Again, that is the only time it is used. Moulton gives the meaning of *adelos* as being "not apparent or obvious," "uncertain," and "not distinct" (p. 6). Bullinger says, "to the ear, not distinct, indistinct" (p. 828). Arndt and Gingrich gives it as "give out an indistinct sound, so that the signal cannot be recognized, 1 Cor. 14:8" (p. 16). Thayer states it is "indistinct, uncertain, obscure: 1 Cor. 14:8" (p. 11).

It might be well to note the word "distinction" as used by Paul in reference to the things without life, giving a voice, "if they give not a distinction in the sounds,..." (vs. 7). This is the Greek *diastole* and means "variation, distinction, difference." It is from *dia*, asunder, and *stello*, to set, place or arrange, therefore, a setting asunder, a distinction, difference. It is found three times, Romans 3:22; 10:12; 1 Corinthians 14:7 (cf. Arndt Gingrich, p. 118; Thayer, p. 142). Also, the word for "sound" and the word for "voice" is the same Greek word (*phone*) and is so used this way throughout the New Testament. This word is found in our text four times (vss. 7, the first usage, 8, 10, 11), and by metonomy it is "speech," or "language." However, the most frequent translation of the Greek word is "voice" (cf. Matt. 3:17; 17:5; John 10:3-5, 27; 11:43; Acts 2:6; 9:4; 12:14; Heb. 3:7, 15; 4:7; Rev. 3:20; etc.).

The voice, be it of a musical instrument, one without life, or be it man's voice, if used according to the laws of either, will convey a distinct message. If not, then it is both meaningless and pointless. Both have a message and both can sound forth a charge, a retreat, or other signals can be given. If not, then one might as well be "speaking into the air." Indeed, our world is full of many sounds, but they only become a discernible language when the rules are obeyed. McGarvey said, "If you use your voice to speak a foreign, and hence a meaningless, language, you degrade it, so that to your hearer it becomes a mere profitless sound. This you should not do" (*Thessalonians, Corin-*

thians, Galatians and Romans, p. 137). "To speak words that have no significancy to those who hear them is to leave them ignorant of what is spoken; it is speaking to the air" (*Matthew Henry's Commentary*, Vol. VI, p. 579). "...trumpet...varied signals can be given by its simple note, provided there is an understanding between trumpeter and hearers;...Without such agreement, or with a wavering, indistinct sound, the loudest blast utters nothing to purpose:...How disastrous, at the critical moment, to doubt whether the trumpet sounds Advance or Retreat!" (Nicoll, Vol. 2, p. 904). "If ye do not speak in the church so as to be understood, your labour is useless...your speech will be lost and dissipated in the air, without conveying any meaning to any person: there will be a noise or sound, but nothing else" (*Clarke's Commentary*, Vol. 6, p. 275).

I mention, in the chapter on "preaching," the Greek term *parrhesia*, which is "boldness." However, this word is used adverbially in its dative case and translated "plainly." In John 10:24, we find the Jews round about Christ and they ask him, "How long dost thou hold us in suspense? If thou art the Christ, tell us plainly." Christ replied that he had told them, but they believed him not. In the next chapter of John, we have the record of the death of Lazarus. It was in the eleventh verse that Jesus said, "Our friend Lazarus is fallen asleep." However, since the disciples took it that he was resting in his sleep, the record states: "Then Jesus therefore said unto them plainly, Lazarus is dead" (11:14). The plainness with which Christ spoke was understood! Let us note some "plain," not "uncertain" things, in the New Testament. You can scrutinize and analyze, inspect and investigate, cross-examine and cross-question, but you will find no uncertain, obscure, vague, indistinct, not apparent and unrecognizable truth in the following, which are given in no certain order.

1. "Ye shall know the truth, and the truth shall make you free" (John 8:32).

2. "Upon this rock I will build my church" (Matt. 16:18).

3. "I tell you, Nay: but, except ye repent, ye shall all likewise perish" (Luke 13:3, 5).

4. "For we walk by faith, and not by sight" (2 Cor. 5:7).

5. "So belief cometh of hearing, and hearing by the word of Christ" (Rom. 10:17).

6. "And without faith it is impossible to be well-pleasing unto him; for he that cometh to God must believe that he is, ... " (Heb. 11:6).

7. "... that in us ye might learn not to go beyond the things which are written" (1 Cor. 4:6).

8. "Speaking one to another in psalms and hymns and spiritual songs, singing and making melody with your heart to the Lord" (Eph. 5:19; cf. Col. 3:16).

9. "What therefore God hath joined together, let not man put asunder" (Matt. 19:6).

10. "Whosoever shall put away his wife, except for fornication, and shall marry another, committeth adultery: and he that marrieth her when she is put away committeth adultery" (Matt. 19:9).

11. "There is one body, and one Spirit, even as ye also were called in one hope of your calling; one Lord, one faith, one baptism, one God and Father of all, who is over all, and through all, and in all" (Eph. 4:4-6).

12. "And gave him to be head over all things to the church, which is his body, the fulness of him that filleth all in all" (Eph. 1:22-23).

13. "For the husband is the head of the wife, as Christ also is the head of the church, being himself the saviour of the body" (Eph. 5:23).

14. "All the churches of Christ salute you" (Rom. 16:16).

15. "Jesus answered, "Verily, verily, I say unto thee, Except one be born of water and the Spirit, he cannot enter into the kingdom of God" (John 3:5).

16. "He that believeth and is baptized shall be saved; but he that disbelieveth shall be condemned" (Mark 16:16).

17. "Every scripture inspired of God is also profitable for teaching, for reproof, for correction, for instruction which is in righteousness; that the man of God may be complete, furnished completely unto every good work" (2 Tim. 3:16-17; cf. 2 Pet. 1:19-21).

18. "For I am not ashamed of the gospel: for it is the power of God unto salvation to every one that believeth; to the Jew first, and also to the Greek" (Rom. 1:16).

19. "Seeing that his divine power hath granted unto us all things that pertain unto life and godliness, through the knowledge of him..." (2 Pet. 1:3).

20. "Mark them that are causing the divisions and occasions of stumbling, contrary to the doctrine which ye learned: and turn away from them" (Rom. 16:17).

21. "Whosoever goeth onward and abideth not in the teaching of Christ, hath not God: he that abideth in the teaching, the same hath both the Father and the Son"

(2 John 9).

22. "And having been made perfect, he became unto all them that obey him the author of eternal salvation" (Heb. 5:9).

23. "And even as they refused to have God in their knowledge, God gave them up unto a reprobate mind, to do those things which are not fitting" (Rom. 1:28).

24. "For in one Spirit were we all baptized into one body, whether Jews or Greeks, whether bond or free; and were all made to drink of one Spirit" (1 Cor. 12:13).

The above twenty-four quotations from the God-breathed and God-inspired Scriptures are distinct, clear, certain, sure, obvious, apparent, recognizable and beyond them no man dare to go. It makes me want to quote Paul, when he said, "Wherefore be ye not foolish, but understand what the will of the Lord is," and "Whereby, when ye read, ye can perceive my understanding in the mystery of Christ" (Eph. 5:17; 3:4; cf. 2 Tim. 2:7). I just typed off a few of the hundreds of scriptures that could have been given, but did list those that today many of our brethren find hard to believe and accept, and, evidently, they think are too fuzzy to be understood. Therefore, they must explain them to embrace ideas of such foolishness as "one cannot know the truth," to "mechanical instrumental music," to "divorce for any cause," to "the Bible is not an infallible guide," to "doctrine does not truly matter," and on and on. Once again we need to read, study and meditate on such verses as, "If any man willeth to do his will, he shall know of the teaching, whether it is of God, or whether I speak from myself" (John 7:17). When I observe the language that is being employed today, instead of a "thus saith the Lord," or an "it is written," and because some are trying to be also "married to the world and the language of denominationalism," I think of both Judges 12:6 and Nehemiah 13:23-24. Indeed, some are speaking according to the language of the people. But the voice of the people is not the voice of God. God has spoken, and we are to speak His Oracles!

OBSERVING SOME STRANGE AND UNCERTAIN SOUNDS

There are many things today that cause both the heart and the soul to most sincerely ache with spiritual pain. Indeed, like Paul, many brethren can state: "Besides those things that are without, there is that which presseth upon me daily, anxiety for all the churches" (2 Cor. 11:28). Some things in life are most disagreeable and distasteful, unpleasant and unpleasing, yet they, too, must be handled if one is to be true to the Book of God and its eternal message for all of us. There is such an item as "contending for" and "defending" the faith. It is not herein my object to be dishonorable, disgraceful, despicable and detestable, no, never, publicly or privately. However, because I deeply believe when a man picks up his pen to write or lifts up his voice to speak he owes his allegiance, fidelity and faithfulness, to Almighty God, to Him and to no other, I list some (only a few in comparison to the many that could be) of the "strange and uncertain" sounds permeating our beloved brotherhood today.

I want it clearly understood that these are not listed in any particular order, that these men from whom I quote are our brethren, brethren precious to the great family of God, but brethren who are issuing forth "strange and uncertain" sounds and these are helping further to destroy the church, the beautiful bride of Christ, its purpose and influence in the world today. I love these men, but despise, detest and feel disgust and distaste for these "strange and uncertain" sounds. Also, it is not mine in this chapter to rebuttal each thought, as my intent primarily is to make known, inform, as to some of those things being said/taught, and these all have been publicly proclaimed. Indeed, they were not done in private. However, I reserve the right to make some comments along the way. Then, too, the book itself has been written for the purpose of trying to set forth Biblical instruction in these areas. This is one reason I have done so much research on various words, etc., and have not resorted to and relied upon "quotes from our brothers." It was my desire, my hope and prayer, to stay with "the pattern" as found ACCORDING TO the written, and mainly on the pages of the New Testament. After all, that is what is going to be our standard of judgment (John 12:48).

1. **Strange And Uncertain Sounds From Max Lucado.** Carolyn Jenkins, who is the World Religion Editor of *Tulsa World*, wrote an article about brother Lucado. It appeared in the "Religion" section on Sunday, March 12, 1989, and was entitled: "Minister Teaches Simplicity in Faith." I have the article before me and now quote from it.

> *"The Rev. Max Lucado - minister of Oak Hills Church of Christ in San Antonio, Texas - has taken a different approach to help 'people redefine God.'*
>
> *Lucado...will speak in Tulsa during the 14th annual International Soul Winning Workshop, which runs March 23 to 25...*
>
> *He credits author Chuck Swindoll of Fullerton, Calif., for much of the success of his book sales. Lucado called Swindoll the 'voice of insight for living,' and one of the most prolific Christian writers today. Swindoll endorsed Lucado's books,*

'and sales took off,' the Texan said.

Lucado also feels strongly about ecumenicity. 'There are fresh winds blowing in the church of Christ denomination,' he said. 'Alexander Campbell's intent was not to create a sectarian church.'...

'The thrust of the Restoration Movement was to build bridges, not walls; to agree, not disagree; to find a common ground as opposed to pointing out differences. I see a strong desire to recapture that spirit.'

He said, 'I have a gut feeling that we (the Church of Christ) have approached the Bible as engineers, looking for a certain design or architectural code. And I think we find that everyone finds a different code. As a result, we split into 27-28 splinters or factions.

There is no secret code. The Bible is a love letter as opposed to a blueprint. You don't read a love letter the same way you read a blueprint.'

Lucado admitted that 'for me, for years, Christianity was a moral code. It is now becoming a love affair. For years there were rules and regulations, now, it's a relationship,' he said.

'First we need to realize that we are a movement, not a monument. We're a group of people in covered wagons going to the promised land, looking to the future.

And we need to realize that if somebody from another 'stripe' believes in Jesus Christ, we immediately have much more in common than we have in opposition.'"

In an undated letter on the stationery labeled: Oak Hills Church of Christ, 8308 Fredericksburg, San Antonio, Texas 78229, (512) 696-0582, brother Lucado wrote the following entitled: Reflections on TULSA WORLD Article.

> *"My interview with Carolyn Jenkins of the* ***Tulsa World*** *has spawned significant reactions--some extremely positive and some extremely negative. I wish I had time to address each letter individually, but since I don't, here are some general observations.*
>
> *The article contains several errors:*
>
> *—I'm not a reverend.*
> *—I'm not thirty-nine.*
> *—I didn't refer to the "Church of Christ denomination."*
> *—I didn't call Chuck Swindoll 'the voice of insight for living.' (He is the speaker on the radio program, 'Insight for Living'.)*
>
> *Several concepts in the article have been misinterpreted. Perhaps it would be helpful to affirm:*
>
> *—I love our fellowship and am thrilled about the future.*
> *—I feel the teaching of the wrath of God is certainly part of the Gospel presentation.*
> *—We are a movement and the health of a movement depends on its flexibility and honesty.*
>
> *I hope this clarifies what was stated and quietens at least some of your concerns. Warmly, Max Lucado. ML/ms."*

I would be less than honest to know these "general observations" existed from brother Lucado, and fail to give them following the article by Carolyn Jenkins of TULSA WORLD. I also must be honest enough to state that if it were a reply or response to the article, it should have covered other points. I mention this, as there are other "strange and uncertain" sounds that the article contained. I mention a few.

a. Did he or did he not call Chuck Swindoll "one of the most prolific *Christian* writers of today"? I refer to the word that is emphasized, "Christian."

b. What is his feeling about "ecumenicity"? What does he mean by it? Is it the unity of Ephesians 4:4-6; John 17:11, 20-23?

c. He needs to document fully, in context, his statement about the "thrust of the Restoration Movement," and especially, about "...a common ground as opposed to *pointing out differences*." What about their "pointing out differences"? Did they do that?

d. Even though he called it "a gut feeling," is there anything wrong about "looking for a certain design" in the Bible? Is this the true reason for the splinters? (Does baptism have a design?)

e. Can a "love letter" be a "blueprint"? Does it follow they have to be "in opposition" one to the other?

f. If you are seeking to please God, and God alone, knowing of God's "severity and goodness" (Rom. 11:22) as well as His "love" and "wrath" (Rom. 5:8-9; 2:4-9; 1 John 4:7-11; Heb. 10:31; 12:29; Deut. 32:35-36; etc.), why can you not read the Bible "as a love letter and also as a blueprint"?

g. Max, did you mean to imply that the Bible is not

"a moral code"? Does a "true love affair" have any restrictions?

h. Again, Max, are you conveying to us that there are no "rules and regulations"? Is it just "a relationship" without any "rules and regulations"? (As I said, I mention "a few" of these "uncertain sounds," but there were others).

My questions and thoughts may to some whose hearts are overflowing with what they term "love," be harsh and unkind, but nothing is further from my heart than such nonsense. After all, even if I were rebuking, etc.; "love does rebuke" (cf. Rev. 3:19; Heb. 12:5-11)...

If this were a "one time" slip it would be serious enough for one who is said to be a gospel preacher. But let it be noted, and from the following documented information, this is not just a single occurrence in the life and ministry of brother Lucado. The San Antonio EXPRESS-NEWS, Saturday, December 2, 1989, carried an ad with his name at the very top in large print, MAX LUCADO, Pulpit Minister, Oak Hills Church of Christ... WILL SPEAK AT St. John Neumann Church (this is a Roman Catholic group, GM), 7:00 P.M. Monday, Dec. 4th, "Getting To Know Jesus Personally." Then it said, "Please join us for an evening of inspiration and fellowship. Refreshments will be served afterward in our Family Center and you will have an opportunity to meet and talk with Max. 6680 Crestway, 654-1643."

You might still be doubting me. In fact, you may be saying, "But this surely did not occur, did it?" "The ad was wrong, wasn't it?" *Reader*, not only do I have the "ad" before me, I also have before me a copy of the brochure of the scheduled event (in full). On the front of the brochure we have only three things: (1) ST. JOHN NEUMANN

CHURCH, (2) MAX LUCADO, and (3) "GETTING TO KNOW JESUS PERSONALLY." The inside pages (two) had the order of their service:

Opening Solo	"Emanuel"
Welcome & Opening Prayer	Father Tony Cummins
All Sing	"Silent Night"
Reflection Reading	"Christmas Night"
Duet	"Sweet Little Jesus Boy"
Guest Speaker	Max Lucado
Solo	"O' Holy Night"
All Sing	"Away In The Manger"
	"O Come All Ye Faithful"
All Sing	"The Lord's Prayer"
Fellowship & Refreshments	Family Center

(Verses from "Silent Night," "O Come All Ye Faithful," and "Away in a Manger" were typed out on these pages, GM).

I could not believe this myself, and I am certainly not in the habit of printing, speaking, etc., what I cannot document. Therefore I called San Antonio to verify this. It not only happened on Monday, December 4th, but we have two brethren present who observed it all. Here are some things that perhaps might astonish you. Max called the priest, "Father," he sang with guitars during the "all sing" parts, held hands and sang with the priest during the last song: "The Lord's Prayer."

I am just guessing, but since there are "no rules and regulations," since the Bible is "not a blueprint," has "no design," and since it is just "a relationship," then it does not matter about the Master saying, "And call no man your father on the earth: for one is your Father, even he who is in heaven" (Matt. 23:9). If such is true, then Paul's statement: "and have no fellowship with the unfruitful works of darkness, but rather even reprove them" (Eph. 5:11), has no meaning for us and such "fellowship" (?) is all right. Since this happened, and evidently approved by the Oak Hills' elders (at least there has been no rebuking of Max about it as far as I know, certainly no discipline), when will the Oak Hills' elders have the priest to speak at their worship or fellowship? Also, when will they allow the use of the mechanical instruments (guitar, piano, or organ)? (I am glad the back page of the brochure was just blank, GM). If Max was concerned about being called "The Rev. Max Lucado" in the TULSA WORLD and stated in his letter of "general observations," as "The article contains several errors: 'I'm not a reverend,'" why be so concerned if you can call a priest, "Father"? It makes me also wonder, so I ask, "Is St. John Neumann Church (remember it is a Roman Catholic group) to be considered as 'somebody from another stripe'?" After all, they believe in Jesus Christ, don't they? If this is true, is it true that "we immediately have much more in common than we have in opposition" with this group of another 'stripe'"?

In addition to the above, and these two events are certainly not an end to such associations, there was then the "ad" captioned as follows: **Lucado guest at Trinity Church Family Center.** This particular one stated: "Trinity Church Family Center, 8750 Fourwinds Drive, will feature guest speaker Max Lucado at 7:30 p.m. April 6. Lucado, author of 'God Came Near' and 'On the Anvil,' is currently a pastor at Oak Hills Church of Christ." This was April 6, 1990. I did not know too much about this group, but in the San Antonio telephone book, page 302 in the yellow pages, it is listed under the heading: Churches - Charismatic. This told me about what I thought, but wanted to find out for sure. Even though inspiration says for us to "believe not every spirit, but prove the spirits, whether they are of God: because many false prophets are gone out into the world" (1 John 4:1), and "Whosoever goeth onward and abideth not in the doctrine (teaching) of Christ, hath not God: he that abideth in the teaching (doctrine), the same hath both the Father and the Son" (2 John 9), yet, since there are no "rules," "regulations," "design," blueprint" or "code," these things can be dismissed as they have no real meaning or message for us today. Then, too, they just might be one more "stripe" of somebody "believing in Jesus Christ" and we have so much in common with them that we need not be "in opposition" to them. Nor do we have to be concerned about our "fellowship" (the Greek word for "partaketh" in 2 John 11 is *koinonei*, 3rd person singular, present active indicative of *koinoneo*) with such causing us to partake "in his evil ways." If such is the case, which it certainly is not, the floodgate is open for full-fledged fellowship with any and every group in the world and there are no boundary lines. Who can believe such in view of Matthew 7:13-14, 21-23, 24-29; Luke 6:46; 8:19-21; 11:27-28; John 14:1-6; 6:44-45; Galatians 1:6-9; 2 Thessalonians 1:6-9; Ephesians 1:22-23; 4:4-6; 5:23; Colossians 1:18, 24; 2 John 10; Romans 16:17-18; Ephesians 5:11; etc., etc.? According to another book, page 293, Allen R. Randolph is "Pastor." I just wonder, do you also, does this violate (I'm not talking about trying to "teach" this man the gospel and make known the New Testament Church) any scripture at all?

Brother Gene Kile, an elder for the Southside Church of Christ, in Fort Worth, Texas (dated August 29, 1990), wrote a letter for the elders of Southside and stated: "Brother Lucado, who begins a gospel meeting at the Midtown Church of Christ...is one of the most qualified and best known ministers in our brotherhood." This letter was an invitation for the September 16, 1990 Tarrant County Convention Center meeting, an annual gathering as evidenced by articles in both the August and September issues of *Christian Journal* (Vol. XXXI, No. 8 and No. 9, both front page articles).

It was on September 19, that brother Lucado delivered his closing lesson at the Midtown effort, which had begun on the morning of the 16th. He spoke on "When Your Options Are Gone." If you love stories and illustrations, you'll love this sermon. He begins it with the famous "Christ the Redeemer Statue" and gives some twelve or more in the course of the lesson. One such was by one of "my favorite authors" by the name of Tony Campolo (his book is: *Twenty Hot Potatoes That Christians Are Afraid To Touch*). Out of a 13 page, single spaced transcription, this took an entire page.

a. It is strange that "one of the most qualified" preachers that is among us today uses so little scripture. After reading the text (Matt. 15:29-39) and making sure of the three points, "God hurts when we hurt," "God hears when we praise," and "God gives when we give," about the only other scripture given is when he is close to closing (Rev. 21:1-5b, *NIV*).

b. It is strange that he calls Karl Barth one of the greatest theologians that ever lived. No doubt about Karl Barth being well known, but I guess I had enough of him while in Vanderbilt University to last me a lifetime. But what is it that truly makes a man a "great" theologian?

c. It is strange that he "indirectly" (?) hits at "the pattern" concept: "Don't listen to the way that we...go back to the original plan," "I doubt seriously if they formed a worship and praise committee," "I doubt seriously if they got real serious and solemn, and were very careful to do everything in just the right way, in the right manner and were very quite. I doubt...if they wrote a liturgical book or a doctrinal book...," "We've kind of made a science out of this thing called worship." "You can't make a system out of worship," "Next time somebody tries to get religion too complicated for you, you tell them the Eddie Rickenbacher story," etc.

d. It is strange to hear of the invitation he extended. Listen to it and see if "it is strange" to you:

> *"...stand and sing a song now. And the purpose of this song is to give anyone here an opportunity to make a request of this church. You can make any request you want, friend, any request. If you have a friend, who needs prayers, come down here and tell us and we'll pray for him tonight. If you have something you're thankful for, come down here and share it with us and we'll all thank God together. If you have somebody in your life that really, that really needs encouragement come down here and tell us and we'll pray that God would encourage him and we'll try to help you find ways to encourage him or her. Maybe your life is in need of encouragement. Fact is folks, we're all in this boat together. If you're perfect, you blow our curve, none of the rest of us are. We're all messed up and if you just need some special encouragement and prayers of a thousand people, this is the time to ask for it, okay? If we can help you in any way, as we stand and sing together, just come to the front and we'll help you. Let's stand." (Song: "Sing to Me of Heaven").*

It was Jesus who gave us the commission (Mark 16:15-16, as one example of it) and we are to invite people to come to Him (cf. Matt. 11:28-30). We should tell them "what" to do (cf. Acts 2:36-41; 3:19; 8:4-5, 12-13; 22:16; 1 Pet. 3:21) and "when" to do it (cf. 22:16;

2 Cor. 6:2; Heb. 3:7; 4:7). It is one thing to sing "of Heaven" and another to tell someone how to "get to Heaven." But, of course, if there is "no pattern," what would you tell a person?

I know full well, from reading, from hearing, from listening, etc., that often speakers do a number of things "to get attention," and so it may well be that brother Lucado called his text Matthew chapter fourteen (instead of fifteen, but he mentioned it this way three times, and said, "I think I did this last night, too"). The only other place they were asked to read along was Revelation 21:1-5b, but twice he called it "twenty-two," and said, "I keep messing up." Then he said, "Listen to how he describes it beginning in verse twenty-one" (he started reading at verse one) and read as per the listing above. Maybe that was on purpose, but if it were not done on purpose, maybe brother Lucado (remember, as far as I know he only had these two sections to read, just two) needs to spend more time "with the Book" (cf. 2 Tim. 2:15; 1 Tim. 4:6-16; Rev. 1:3; Isa. 34:16; 5:13; Hos. 4:6; 2 Tim. 4:1-5; Psm. 119:11, 97, 99; 1:2; etc., etc., etc.) and less time with Robert Fulgum, Tony Campolo, Karl Barth, etc. Perhaps he does not care about being "very careful to do everything in just the right way," or maybe "that would make it too complicated."

Remember, Jesus is our example (1 Pet. 2:21) and Peter described him as "a man approved of God" (Acts 2:22). Paul tells us how that we, too, can be "approved unto God" (cf. 2 Tim. 2:15), and we need to be approved of God *by studying* as we have been "approved of God to be intrusted with the gospel" (cf. 1 Thess. 2:4). Do you want a challenge? Then study the Greek words for "approved," and "prove" (2 Tim. 2:15; 1 Thess. 2:4; James 1:12; 1 John 4:1; Rom. 1:28; etc., words like *apodeiknumi, dokimos*, and *dokimazo*, and note the negative *ouk* in Rom. 1:28). Indeed, we only have "the divine approval" after "the proving."

It was "a woman elder" who informed us that brother Max Lucado was going to speak for them. However, she could have been mistaken. So, the office was called where she worships. She was not mistaken. If the plans do not change, etc., brother Max Lucado will be speaking on March 20, 1991, which is not long before "Easter Sunday," (?) for them. Who is it, you say? It is the First Presbyterian Church, located at 404 N. Alamo, in downtown San Antonio, Texas (and this will be at 7:00 p.m. and it is "from their own church office"). They may have their "normal dinner" at 6:00 p.m. and this would make their "fellowship" (?) complete. Could it be, as per the letter we noted earlier that this is why brother Lucado is "one of the best known ministers in our brotherhood"? Now we sure do not want to act like there is anything in "a doctrinal book" that would prevent such fellowship, but, just in case you might want to ponder the words of the Holy Spirit through Paul and John, you might read Ephesians 5:11; Romans 16:17-18; 1 John 4:1; 2 John 9-11. But then again, there really are no "rules and regulations" for us.

Somehow it does not surprise me any more when I read of all that so many of our preachers are both "doing" and "saying." No, I cannot, in all good conscience say that. I am, still yet, stunned and shocked, jarred and jolted by such happenings and by what so many are today both speaking and writing. I guess when it comes to the Family of God, the New Testament Church, and all gospel preachers, that I am just too naive, void of suspicion, overtrusting, overconfiding, etc. It aches my soul to know that we have "the written Word of God" and that we are to "know the truth" (cf. 1 Cor. 4:6; John 12:48; 17:17; 7:17; 1 Pet. 4:11; 2 Tim. 4:1-5; 1 Tim. 4:6-16), study to show ourselves approved unto God (2 Tim. 2:15), being ready to give an answer (1 Pet. 3:15), have the trait of the nobility (Acts 17:11) in examining the Word daily, and then for God's own speakers (cf. 2 Cor. 4:7) to fail "to commit the same thing" to others (2 Tim. 2:2). I know "for a fact" that God's servants have "gone far away from book, chapter and verse preaching," and that some have termed such as the death of the church, but what better way is there to do what Paul said in 2 Timothy 4:1-5 than "to preach the Word"? Indeed, studying is very hard work. It is only by hard work, which some evidently fail to enjoy and like (one preacher said he "hated" to read, said this to me while I was preaching in Little Rock, Arkansas years ago), that one comes "to know the Book." This may give us some "insight" as to why some quote so few verses, and perhaps even why they speak about the men who do know the Book well enough to quote it. Yes, you would not even know the word "grace," without the blueprint, the rule Book, the instruction manual, the Bible.

Now here is the latest thing and the last thing that I am going to give about brother Lucado, at least latest as far as I know. I say this, as our own dear brothers, gospel preachers, are today changing so fast that it is most difficult to state that "anything" is the "latest" as to "where" they will be worshipping, "what" they will be saying, and "the thoughts" they will be writing and also for "whom" they will be writing.

I ask you to please note the following:

> *"CHRIST IN EASTER A Family Celebration Of Holy Week by Charles Colson, Billy Graham, Max Lucado, Joni Eareckson Tada" (this is the title of the book, along with the four*

authors, and is A NavPress publication, GM).

The Publisher has written the following:

"Easter should be a day of unsurpassed joy and celebration. Without the Resurrection there is no Christianity. From the Cross, Jesus cried, 'It is finished!' On the following Sunday this was confirmed with the resounding 'Amen!' of the Resurrection. The price has been paid for our sins and the sacrifice had been accepted. Jesus conquered death and sin. In Him we, too, are victorious.

This book will enable your family to experience this Easter joy in a new way. Through devotional and Scripture readings, hymns, poems, family discussions, and activities, your family will come to a better understanding of the events surrounding the death and resurrection of Jesus Christ. In the process, family bonds will be strengthened as you see how the stories of Holy Week are relevant to all of life.

Covering the eight days from Palm Sunday to Easter, ***Christ in Easter*** *provides a way for your family to prepare for Easter with worship and fun times together.*

The four main sections of study are Palm Sunday, the Last Supper, Good Friday, and Easter. There are also four shorter lessons for the other days of Holy Week. ...It will be helpful if one family member looks ahead at the activity suggestions and gathers the things needed for the activities your family is most likely to enjoy...

*As you see the events of Holy Week unfold day by day, you will get a fresher sense of the mystery and meaning of Easter and how it can change your life. May the Resurrection life of the Lord fill you as you as you draw closer to Him this Easter. Happy Celebration!" (The Publisher). (**Evangelical Book Club Bulletin,** 1000 E. Huron, Milford, MI 48381, February 1991).*

If brother Lucado is not "one of the best known ministers," he is sure headed that way, wouldn't you say? But again, fellowship and doctrine are not to be "a bother" for anyone today, right?

2. **Strange And Uncertain Sounds From Stephen Taylor.** You may not recognize the name of Stephen Taylor, and you may not know where he has been teaching and preaching, recently or otherwise. Also, you may not know where he has gone nor the purpose for which he went. Since I believe in documenting what I write, and as thoroughly as I possibly can, I now give the following for your meditation, contemplation and cogitation.

I have on my desk, right before me, a copy of *The Abilene Reporter News*, dated May 26, 1990, pp. 11A-12A. Right under his picture, and the picture is taken on the campus of Abilene Christian University, are these words: "The Rev. Stephen Taylor, a former Abilene Christian University instructor, will pastor three congregations of the United Reform Church in the United Kingdom." The caption of this article (by Roy A. Jones II, Religion Editor; the picture was taken by Don Blakley of the *Reporter-News*) is: Pastor leaving Abilene, heading for England.

The article begins by saying the distance separating

Abilene and London (it says 5,000 miles) is "symbolic of the long way the Rev. Baker Stephen Covington Taylor has come, theologically, in seeking his first fulltime pastorate." It speaks of him being "reared in the Church of Christ," being a "former instructor of church history and American history at Abilene Christian University," and having "graduated from ACU and from a Presbyterian seminary." It also says "he's preached for the Church of Christ, United Church of Christ, Presbyterian Church (USA), Christian Church (Disciples of Christ), Christian Methodist Episcopal Church and several community churches."

The article is most lengthy, having in excess of twenty-four paragraphs, therefore, I am not going to give all of it. I am, however, going to give several quotes from it and/or Stephen Taylor. I want you to keep in mind that he is leaving Abilene "to be ordained a 'minister of the word and sacrament,' as well as 'teaching elder,' in the United Reformed Church in the United Kingdom." Also, "The United Reformed Church was formed by the union of the Congregational Church in England and Wales, the Presbyterian Church in England, and the Reformed Association of Churches of Christ, the later of which is linked to the Church of Christ and Christian Church (Disciples of Christ) in the United States" (the reporter then saying, Taylor explained).

> *"The first two groups united in 1972, with the Church of Christ joining in 1981. The URC comprises about 2,000 congregations with 1,400 ministers, both men and women.*
>
> *'Since it is out of the reformed tradition it in many ways is very similar to the Presbyterian church in theology,' Taylor said.*

Whether he baptizes infants by immersion or sprinkling 'will be the option of the parents,' Taylor said.

Use of musical instruments is up to the individual congregation, but all three he will serve use them in worship, he added.

Taylor said his father, H. I. Taylor of Houston, a Church of Christ minister for more than 50 years, has been supportive of his decision. 'He would have liked to have seen me stay in the Church of Christ, of course, but he realizes that's just not where I should be,' he said.

'I feel like, in a sense, I am leaving the Church of Christ denomination, but not the Church of Christ,' he said.

...didn't seriously consider the ministry as a career until his senior year at the University of Texas...He also considered the Peace Corps. He'd already been accepted for law school when he felt the Lord's call.

First, he earned a bachelor's degree in biblical science from ACU,...Taylor said he elected to attend Austin Presbyterian Theological Seminary because it had 'a very structured, sound course of study,'...and because of a good scholarship program. He earned his master's degree in divinity in 1985.

During his three years of seminary, he did pulpit supply in the Austin area for various congregations. A three-month interim pastorate for a United Church of Christ congregation in Austin was particularly meaningful.

Taylor came to ACU to work on another master's degree and work as a graduate assistant in the Center for Restoration Studies in 1986, and wound up teaching church history and American history in 1988-89. Last summer, he accompanied a group of ACU and Hardin-Simmons University students on archaeological digs in Israel,...detoured by London on his way home to visit with a former seminary professor...

Out of that friendship...resulted in Taylor being called to pastor the three London churches...Each has its own distinctive history...'But they're trying desperately not to give up their identity - they even sponsor a Brownie Troop,' Taylor said...

I have no earthly way of knowing if you think this is a "strange and uncertain" sound or not, but it aches my soul to think he taught students on the campus of ACU, accompanied them on an archaeological dig and could go from ACU to "being an ordained minister of the word and sacrament," and a "teaching elder" in "the United Reformed Church," and I do not care where it is located. Let me ask you:

a. Isn't it rather "strange" to have had such a person on the teaching staff at ACU?

b. How do you think godly parents feel, godly parents who sent their children to ACU, having known of its purpose and goals since it was first founded? Did they get "their value's worth"?

c. Did you note that the ministers of the URC are "both men and women"? Strange indeed! Just recall the "New Hermeneutic" (?).

d. To think that "his baptizing infants either by immersion or by sprinkling is the option of the parents," leads me to ask, "Does it not matter what THE BOOK teaches?" Of course, it doesn't, as we today see on every hand where people are guided by PURE SUBJECTIVISM. There is no body of absolute and objective truth, no, not in "The Movement" we are facing today, that of the new hermeneutic.

e. Yes, it is "strange" to leave where they had no mechanical instrumental music and go to where it is used in worship in each of the three (one would be sufficient) churches he will serve. When did he start believing like this? I wonder if he believed it while at ACU, and if so, did he share his thoughts with the students?

f. I also wonder if he had some "partners in theology" at ACU, and if so, when will they leave "on their mission"?

g. It bothers me, as being truly "strange," regarding his being hired at ACU. Just think! A graduate assistant in the Center for Restoration Studies! It is rather brassy, brazen and bold, don't you think to have his picture made where he did (was it really in the chapel?)? Is it true that no one on the ACU administration knew of his deep liberalism?

3. **Strange And Uncertain Sounds From Larry James.** It was in 1985 when I read a copy of *CARE* (Vol. V, April 24, 1985, No. 16), wherein Larry James, preacher for the Richardson East Church of Christ in Plano, Texas, wrote relative to a meeting of some brethren on the campus of Dallas Christian College. Those "strange and uncertain" sounds in his article I list as follows:

a. The division over the use of instrumental music "is truly ridiculous."

b. That "our division in the past has been over an issue of opinion and not of revelation."

c. You spoke of standing in the camp of "weaker brethren..."

Yes, indeed, I contacted Larry James, a brother in Christ, and a preacher for the Church. It was on May 8, 1985 that I wrote brother James about the article. In that letter I also challenged him for a debate, wrote the two propositions, signed my name in the denial of one and the affirmative of the other. Nothing ever happened.

However, the article from his pen this time that we notice is the one entitled: "Tradition or Truth?"

> *"More often than we would like to admit, tradition assumes for us the role '**Most-Authentic, Only-Authorized, Truly-Autonomous Interpreter of Scripture.**'*
>
> *What in the world does that mean? **Simply** this: Often what I **bring** to the Bible determines what I receive from it in terms of meaning, direction, and practical application.*
>
> ***Hans Kung** refers to this tendency as '**quarry-exegesis.**' The student in Kung's image comes to the text like a miner. He 'discovers' isolated jewels. Carefully seeking the precious stones he needs for the work of art **he already has in mind**, he digs them out of their 'context,' disregarding the damage done to the equally precious material surrounding the chosen stones. Precise selection pays off in a finished product perfectly in keeping with the miner's*

__predetermined__ vision, decision, and understanding.

'__Give me an example__,' you say? Music in worship of Churches of Christ. Only a carefully refined '__quarry-exegesis__,' having nothing to do with the heart and essence of the Gospel, can argue for __a cappella__ music only, while insisting that instrumental music is in fact sinful. True exegesis will not support our long-held tradition. The outcome of our ingenious 'mining' creates a host of problems for us.

Among them the worst and most obvious include: __needless division__ in the body of Jesus Christ...an unfortunate __squelching of gifted people__ in the church, who find no outlet for their God-given abilities to minister...an unbearable __pseudo-spirituality__ before other Christians who do not employ our 'pick and shovel' methods of interpretation.

God help us to grow. God help us to be brave enough to change. God help us to discover truth, even when the price will be many 'sacred' traditions. Above all oh Lord, may we in the process come to know you. Amen."

Below this article there was one entitled: 1989 Thanksgiving Praise Service Set for Sunday, November 19 - 7:00 p.m. It is listed below.

"Once again this year RE will join with the __First Christian Church__ in a special service of praise and thanksgiving. Our celebration will expand as we invite our brothers and sisters at __Central Christian Church, Community Christian Church__ to join in our adoration and praise.

*RE will host the special unity service on Sunday, November 19 beginning at 7:00 p.m. Members of each congregation will be involved in the activities of the evening. Following our time of praise, we will enjoy refreshments together. Plan now to join in this historic gathering of Christians who share common roots in the Stone-Campbell movement of the early 19th century. Our prayer is that the gathering would be an annual event rotating among the various congregations with a different church serving as host each Thanksgiving" (**Careline**, A Monthly Newsletter For Family & Friends Of Christians At Richardson East Church of Christ, Vol. 1, October 25, 1989, No. 4, all emp. Larry James).*

Let us take note of just a few of the "strange and uncertain" sounds in these two articles.

a. Please observe the use of the word "tradition." Have we forgotten that what "is written" in the Word of God is "sacred tradition" and is "truth"? I suggest a good study of the Greek *paradosis* needs to be made by Larry James.

b. In case you do not recognize the name of Hans Kung, he is a German Catholic theologian, and a liberal one at that. This, to me is a good reason to study Thayer, p. 481 and Arndt and Gingrich on p. 621. This will be a good dose against the Catholic's use of the word "tradition." After all, the title of the article could well be "Tradition Is Truth," instead of "Tradition or Truth" (cf. 1 Cor. 11:2; 2 Thess. 2:15; 3:6; 1 Cor. 14:37; 4:17).

c. What does the word "sing" or "singing" mean as

used by Paul in Ephesians 5:19; Colossians 3:16; etc.?

d. Could it be that Larry James has some "insight" into a person's heart by stating how he comes "to the text"?

e. Ask Larry James what he means by "the Gospel," and your answer will certainly not be the totality of the twenty-seven books of the New Testament.

f. Take note that his article is purely subjective. There is no proof given in it for his own personal statements, yet they are stated "as a fact." Let him prove that *a cappella* music can only be argued for by a carefully refined "quarry-exegesis." Let him prove that our exegesis of Ephesians 5:19; Colossians 3:16 is wrong (cf. 1 Thess. 5:21; 1 Pet. 3:15). Let him prove that solid and sound exegesis has nothing to do with the heart and essence of the gospel.

g. Ask him to study such words as *dokimazo*, *dialegomai*, *apologia*, *suzeteo*, etc., and then tell us explicitly that he is under no obligation to "set forth argumentation" and "to clear one's self."

h. How do you feel when he says that "True exegesis will not support our long-held tradition"?

i. Let us ask Larry James to prove to us that *a cappella* music in worship to God is just "tradition," as well as proving that instrumental music (his words) in worship is not sinful.

j. Evidently, from what he wrote, he believes that which is not explicitly forbidden is not sinful.

k. Again, let him prove that we use a "pick and

shovel" method of interpretation.

Yes, I wrote brother James again, told him he did not answer my first letter (he later informed me he never received it, so I sent another copy to him - no debate then either), wrote him three full pages, challenged him for a debate, wrote the two propositions, and signed my name in the proper places. Once again, no debate.

In addition to the first article, how did you like the article about the "1989 Thanksgiving Praise Service"? Yes, the "joining" up or with (his word) the First Christian Church, and "our brothers and sisters" at Central Christian Church and the Community Christian Church? How do you like the term "unity" service? Would that be a true "unity" service, one based on the Word, or is it just another "union" attempt and one of the "agreeing to disagree" gatherings? Remember, here is one of the men like those who attended the Joplin Summit meeting (those four brethren who met with him at Dallas Christian College, which is a First Christian College, are all of the same persuasion). This so-called "unity service" is not based on the prayer of Jesus in John 17:11, 20-23, or on Ephesians 1:4-6; 1 Corinthians 1:10; etc., as it is not in harmony with the Word of God, that is, based on God's Word.

Indeed, it is so "strange" today that men calling themselves gospel preachers can write such, promote such, but never do they have to defend it. They can write and promote such and not too many get very alarmed about it. But to anyone who knows what is going on in our beloved brotherhood knows from whence it is all stemming. There is no pattern, no rules, no regulations, no norm, no standard, no blueprint and no design. It is high time for "a new hermeneutic" as our "picks and shovels" have worn out the old hermeneutic. There is no such item as THE

TRUTH being absolute and objective, attainable and unchangeable, just pure subjectivism.

I do not know about "you," but I do not like to be charged by such brethren as causing "needless division" in the body of Jesus Christ. That is one more serious statement and I do not sit idly by and let people spew and spout such without a challenge. To say that we are guilty of "squelching gifted people" in the church is just to make a very foolish argument when carried to its logical conclusion. To make the charge of "pseudo-spirituality" (cf. Matt. 7:1-5), preceded by the word "unbearable," and "before other Christians..." is one that is not strange by these ever-so-loving, positive preaching, unfounded argument-making brethren. How do you like the charge of being false (the word *pseudo*, a Greek term, means "to deceive by lies, a liar, false"), in your spirituality? Yea, in essence it is a "strange source charge."

I had ordered the tape of his lesson that he gave on February 26, 1989, but failed to receive the same. However, I would like to give this quote from the very knowledgeable and studious Wayne Jackson:

> *"Meanwhile, in the Dallas-Fort Worth metroplex, Larry James of the Richardson East congregation, has boldly blasted churches of Christ for their opposition to the use of instruments of music in worship. In a sermon delivered on February 26th of last year, James caustically attacked our position on worship innovations. He made no attempt, of course, to answer the major arguments employed to sustain our stand; rather, he chose simply to ridicule those who contend for the primitive pattern of worship" (Christian Courier*, Volume XXV, No. 10, February, 1990, p. 39).

I am sorry that our beloved brotherhood, that is, for the most part, does not study and read about what is happening today among us. In the issue of the *Christian Courier* (3906 East Main Street, Stockton, CA 95205; mailing address being P.O. Box 55265), which issue's theme was "The Church In A State Of Crisis," there were some very fine thoughts on "An Era Of Uncertainty," "Theological Liberalism," "The New Denominationalism," "The Silent Majority," and, the one under which I quoted the thought relative to brother James' sermon was entitled, "Is Unity-In-DIVERSITY The Only Game In Town?"

As brother Jackson closed these particular thoughts, he gave this: "*Editor's Note:* We truly regret that this edition of the *Christian Courier* has been dominated by brotherhood controversy. This is not our normal policy. However, sometimes the issues are so crucial and the danger so imminent that this sort of discussion is justified" (*Ibid.*).

He closed his personal letter to me on February 15, 1991, by saying, "We are living in perilous times indeed." Indeed, we are and that is perhaps putting it mildly.

Chapter Six

THE PATTERN - AND "STRANGE" AND "UNCERTAIN" SOUNDS FROM SOME BRETHREN (Part II)

THE PATTERN - AND "STRANGE" AND "UNCERTAIN" SOUNDS FROM SOME BRETHREN

(Part II)

4. Strange And Uncertain Sounds From Rick Atchley. On October the 14th, 1990, at the 8:00 a.m. assembly of the Church of Christ meeting at 6300 N.E. Loop 820, Fort Worth, Texas, the Richland Hills Church of Christ, brother Rick Atchley delivered a sermon entitled, "Don't Bother Your Brother." I have heard the tape different times. I also at this writing have before me the transcription that I personally made of the tape. I transcribed the sermon on January 16-17, 1991, as I have done my best to make sure just exactly what it was that brother Atchley said. This reproduction, with my typewriter set on a space and a half, is nine and one-half pages long, therefore, there is no way that I am able to duplicate it in this chapter. However, I can list numerous quotes from it. I ask you to please keep in mind that it is not mine to give all the examples, etc., he gives, as I just cannot do that, but right after the introduction, a story about "the knight who came to report to the king," relative to the "enemies" he had caused the king to now have, he began with the words, "And I'm afraid too often like that knight, disciples of Jesus have fought unnecessary battles and have made enemies out of peaceful neighbors. Maybe that's one reason why you don't hear very many sermons on Mark chapter 9:38-41. You're going to hear one this morning, and I must confess I'm a little bit nervous about it."

In explaining this "nervous" thought, he gave a couple of reasons and the second one was: "I am not going to say anything this morning that I haven't said throughout my career in preaching. But you haven't known me for ten years like my friends in Abilene did. You've only known me one, and so I'm just going to ask you to believe this morning before I start that I have a great love for scripture, and for the church. And I hope you'll hear every thing I say through that filter. But I want us to think today about what our King has to tell us about where we draw battle lines."

"I want you to read with me, starting in verse thirty-eight":

> *"Teacher," said John, "we saw a man driving out demons in your name and we told him to stop, because he was not one of us." "Do not stop him," Jesus said, "No one who does a miracle in my name can in the next moment say anything bad about me, for whoever is not against us is for us. I tell you the truth, anyone who gives a cup of water in my name because you belong to Christ will certainly not lose his reward" (although not given, this is the reading of the* ***NIV****, GM).*

Now, with the text of the sermon set before us, *let us notice first* some thoughts given about the text, Mark 9:38-41.

> a. *"Earlier in Mark 9 when...the disciples themselves were trying to cast out a demon and unable to do so. So the ones who could not cast out demons feel it's their place to tell those who can cast out demons that they shouldn't be doing that. And the fact that John says 'we' shows all of the disciples concurred with this decision. It was twelve to zero vote that they should tell that man to stop." (This is what Rick calls "what is ironic" about*

Mark 9).

b. "*...that Jesus is the Son of God and he is casting out demons based on this faith in the name of Jesus...He really does believe in Jesus...you didn't cast out demons just because you knew how to spell Jesus. But only because of your deep sincere faith in who he was."*

c. "*The issue here is not that he is not following Jesus, but is instead he is not following the twelve. And that is what bothers them...Jesus did not have as restrictive view of who could legitimately participate in his mission as the disciples did...The disciples looked too much like the Pharisees...Now how are the disciples different from the Pharisees, if they cannot see the obvious work of the Holy Spirit in this man?"*

d. "*Now what is your attitude about good deeds done by people who don't belong to your camp? ....Secondly, are these deeds being done in the name of Jesus for his glory and not for the glory of the one who does it? Now hear me church. If the answer to both questions is yes...then those deeds and the doers of them deserve our endorsement."*

e. "*...talk about how this particular lesson specifically concerns we who make up what we call the churches of Christ."*

Now, *let us notice the second thought*, as brother Atchley says: "I'd like to share with you three implications."

a. "*The first is let's learn not to limit God to what we can do (statement repeated). The view of some of God's tremendous work in the world is needlessly narrow... Now when you find someone in whom God has been working... (1) you can deny the good they're doing, (2) you can say that the good they are doing is prompted by the devil, or (3) you can give God the glory.... God was around before we are, as hard as that is to believe."*

b. *"Second, let's not limit the kingdom of God to the size of our brotherhood... my history and heritage is churches of Christ. I was raised in churches of Christ... maybe this wasn't said, but this is what I heard... the only people that could go to heaven were in churches of Christ... I'm going to suggest to you not only is that not Biblical, but it is in fact a violation of the very restoration plea to which we are heirs."*

c. *"I believe that where there is faith and repentance and new birth of water and the Spirit there is a Christian... 'Well, are you saying that there are Christians in the denominations?' Let me read you a quote from old brother F. D. Srygley, an early preacher in our movement..."*

d. *"Let me say this clearly. A Christian is determined by his affiliation with Christ, not with any particular group. Its time to say two things clearly: When I accept someone who has believed and repented and been born again of water and the Spirit that does not necessarily mean I endorse everything he says or does. And let me say this clearly, I have brothers and sisters in Christ who may be in churches where I couldn't worship... But if grace will cover moral error, why are we so afraid to let it cover doctrinal error?..."*

e. *"... number three. Let's not limit our plea by a*

sectarian spirit... Maybe this little poem explains it better than anything I could say. 'Believe as I believe, no more no less, that I am right no one else confess, feel as I feel, think as I think, eat what I eat, drink what I drink, look as I look, do always as I do, then and only then I'll fellowship you.' ... Tolerance... is based on the fact that truth is magnitudal and grace is magnificient. And I don't think we have to give up anything we deeply believe."

Brother Atchley now adds three additional thoughts to his second major point.

a. *"First, about our past... 'If we're the only Christians, and we've only been around since the early 1800's, where were all the Christians the first 1800 years of the church?..."*

b. *"... a little bit about the present... We live in a culture that has no interest in sectarian religion, none. Researchers have shown that in the last 20 years people are showing less loyalty to their denominations than ever before... the people on your street are not worried about which church is the best,... drugs... crime... AIDS... materialism... to raise kids... I met... who planted... a Baptist church... he polled people... he asked, 'Would you be open to an invitation to the brand new Southlake Community Church?' Nine out of ten said 'I would consider visiting your new church.' He asked those nine, 'And would you also be open to an invitation to the brand new Southlake Baptist church?' Seven out of nine said, 'No.' Our world has no interest in simply supporting institutions against other institutions. None."*

c. *"And let me talk about our future quickly...I would like to keep my children in this fellowship, but I have grave concerns about that...I suggest to you our future will depend on giving our children a vision of a battle worth fighting."*

At this point, brother Atchley was ready to close his lesson. He made it clear "I've only spoken for myself this morning." Just here he listed three things.

a. *"I will be supportive of the good done by others in the name of Jesus. I will be supportive of the good done by others in the name of Jesus...I will endorse any work by any body if it is in fact pushing back the kingdom of darkness and giving more people a chance to learn about Jesus."*

b. *"I will be open to any opportunity to teach and be taught more fully the way of Jesus. I'll be open to any chance, any place, any where with any body to teach and to be taught more fully."*

c. *"I will be content to be a Christian only...This church is in a war, evil is destroying our community...Real battles...crime...against immorality, against drugs, against materialism, and we need help fighting those battles."*

To help you understand more fully and clearly this sermon on "Don't Bother Your Brother," and to make it positively, undeniably and unquestionably, crystal clear that I have not misrepresented it in any way, I now give the outline distributed at Richland Hills relative to this sermon (this is as honest as I can be, as I would not misquote, misread, misreport, misstate or mislead a single soul. That is never my intent. Nor is it mine to be ugly, arrogant or haughty, just as he stated in his sermon about himself and the lesson he taught at A T & T. I had not seen the outline until this very day, the 23rd of January, 1991).

Gospel of Mark #32 *Mark 9:38-41*
10-14-90 A.M.

DON'T BOTHER YOUR BROTHER

I. AS FAR AS HE'S CONCERNED
  A. The spirit of John -
  B. The spirit of Jesus -

II. AS FAR AS WE'RE CONCERNED
  A. Three implications -
    1. Let's not limit ______________________.
    2. Let's not limit ______________________.
    3. Let's not limit ______________________.

  B. Additional thoughts -
    1. Concerning our past -
    2. Concerning our present -
    3. Concerning our future -

III. AS FAR AS I'M CONCERNED
    1) I will be ______________________.
    2) I will be ______________________.
    3) I will be ______________________.

I must make some comments about such a lesson as this one entitled: "Don't Bother Your Brother." I ask you again to please keep in mind I cannot either "answer" or "ask" all that could be on this lesson. However, I can touch on a few of those "strange and uncertain" sounds and make some comments along the way.

a. After reading the excerpts that I gave, to whom do you personally think the word "brother" refers to in the caption? (Surely, a preacher should know the indepth meaning of the word for brother, *adelphos*, its root meaning and its spiritual application, cf. Luke 8:21, brotherhood, *adelphotes*, 1 Peter 5:9). Does God really have children outside His family? Remember, the church is the family of God (cf. 1 Tim. 3:14-15).

b. Rick is right about one thing, we sure do not hear many sermons on Mark 9:38-41, that is, not like his. And I, for one, will continue to hope that he is "nervous" about it and his influence. I just wonder what he will be preaching when he has been there for as long, ten years, as he was in Abilene. Just think, as he said, they had only known him for one year.

c. No one will deny that people do good deeds who do not belong to Jesus, but good deeds does not mean "an endorsement" (cf. 2 John 9-11). If this is the case men like Billy Graham, Oral Roberts and a host of others "who do not belong to our camp" (as he says and it sounds strange to make such a statement) deserve our endorsement. I say just ask them if they work in the name of Jesus. If you do you will have your answer, along with those whom you are to endorse.

d. How do you like the statement, "we who make up what we call the churches of Christ"? I thought that name was a divine name.

e. What work done in harmony with the Word is "needlessly narrow"? Is it narrow to say that Jesus is "the Way"? How many "ways" go to heaven? (Matt. 7:13-14; John 6:44-45; 14:6; cf. the meaning of the words "no one" or "no man" in those last two verses).

f. What about his statement: "Let's not limit the

kingdom of God to the size of our brotherhood"? Let me ask, "Does anyone belong to the kingdom of God who is not subject, in submission, to the laws or commandments (rules, if you please) of the King? (cf. 1 Tim. 6:13-16; Rev. 17:14).

g. I wonder why he never, no, not once, in speaking about becoming a Christian mentioned "confession" (cf. Luke 12:8-9; Rom. 10:9-10).

h. If a person can be a Christian without being a member of the New Testament Church, please inform me on it. His statement was: "A Christian is determined by his affiliation with Christ, not with any particular group." That means one can be "affiliated" with the *Jesus Only Group* and be a Christian. Such logic (?) must be seen for what it is. Listen to him: "But if grace will cover moral error, why are we so afraid to let it cover doctrinal error?" I am here to tell you there is "no grace" apart from or outside of the gospel of Jesus Christ! (cf. 2 Tim. 2:1, as grace is located "in Christ" and obedience to the gospel puts us there as seen by Galatians 3:26-27; Romans 1:5; 16:26).

i. His little poem (?) shows a failure to understand such marvelous chapters like Romans chapter fourteen. However, when it comes to some things, we are "to speak" the same thing (cf. 1 Cor. 1:10; Phil. 1:27; 2:1-2; John 17:11, 20-23; 1 Pet. 4:11; Col. 3:17; 2 Cor. 13:11; Acts 2:42; 2 John 9-11; etc.).

j. I want you to observe his use of the word "exclusive" as he gave from Robert Frost as being the ugliest English word. I ask you, "Was Jesus being exclusive when he said, 'I am the way'?" Also what about "my church," "the body," "the faith," "the Holy Spirit," "one Lord," "one baptism," "one hope," "one God," a man is to have "one wife," that Christ is "the head of the church being himself the saviour of the body," etc., etc. What was Rick trying to get the people to see? Is the "family of God" not an exclusive family? (cf. Eph. 3:14-15; 1 Tim. 3:14-15).

k. I want to repeat his emphasis: "I will be supportive of the good done by others in the name of Jesus. I will be supportive of the good done by others in the name of Jesus...I will endorse any work by any body if it is in fact pushing back the kingdom of darkness and giving more people a chance to learn about Jesus." What all do you think might be involved in the words "supportive," "endorse any work," etc.? Can one be a Christian and not "prove the spirits" (1 John 4:1), fail to follow 2 John 9-11, refuse to obey Ephesians 5:11 or Romans 16:17-18?

These are just a few of the "strange" and "uncertain" sounds in brother Atchley's message. However, I noticed some other "strange" and "uncertain" items and I name just a few of these.

a. There was a total, 100% absence, of any quoted or read statements of scripture (he did mention Mark 9:38-41 following some verses, spoke of earlier in Mark 9, chapter three and "over in the ninteenth chapter of Acts," but that is it!) in his entire lesson.

b. I want YOU to observe how he answered the question on the subject of "Christians in the denominations." He began, in a specific way, by quoting, commenting or telling about Lynn Anderson, his own grandparents, and his own great grandparents, his uncle Waymon Morgan, F. D. Srygley, Reuel Lemmons, N. B. Hardeman, Alexander Campbell, M. C. Kurfees, G. C. Brewer, J. C. McQuiddy, Max Lucado, etc. I'll tell you right now, and it won't take me as much time as it would a snowflake to melt in hot water, brother, that is not on the same par as quoting Jesus (like in John 3:5), Paul as in Ephesians 5:23; Colossians 1:18; 1 Timothy 3:14-15; Romans 6:3-5, 17-18; Colossians 2:12, Peter in 1 Peter 3:20-21; Acts 2:38, 47 or any of the other men "inspired of God" (cf. 2 Pet. 1:19-21; 2 Tim. 3:16-17). Where is his scriptural authority? It seems to be in the answer of men, but even if men have declared, promoted and promised it, in explicit terms, that is not the way to answer (cf. 1 Pet. 3:15) such, as it is faulty and false. Man is not now and never has been the standard (cf. John 12:48; Jer. 6:16; 10:23; Prov. 19:21; 21:2). One of the troubles today is "man quoting men" in trying to prove his statements instead of giving "a thus saith the Lord" (cf. John 8:32; 17:17; 7:17).

c. It makes me smile to hear a preacher say, "I want to go on record" and relate that to the fact that Jesus "said" Mark 9:38-41 and that Jesus "meant" Mark 9:38-41. Of course, he said it and He meant it, but that does not say he gave it so we could include the denominational world as "brothers in Christ." Pure subjectivism will never be our authority, nor can it prove that His statement was "given to mean" what brother Atchley made its message to be.

For anyone to use this as a text, or to even hint at it being a text to prove there are Christians in denominations and that these became Christians by getting into a denomination, is in conflict with John 3:5 (observe that it contains the word "except," and surely one should know what an exceptive thought is); Galatians 3:26-27; Romans 6:3-4; Matthew 16:18-19; Colossians 1:18; Ephesians 5:23; Acts 2:38-47 and other verses. Only those in the kingdom of God are Christians, the New Testament Church is the kingdom of God, people are baptized into Christ, are added to the New Testament Church, Christ is the head and saviour of the New Testament Church, which is his body, the family of God, the house of God and God does not have any children outside his family!

We are not discussing the fact that man can obey the gospel of Christ, become a member of the New Testament Church and then leave and go into denominational error. If such happens, it does not change the fact that this person is a child of God. However, it does mean that he is a child of God IN ERROR! If a child of God dies in sin he is lost (cf. Rom. 3:23; 6:23; Rev. 21:27; James 5:19-20; etc.). This is a far cry from saying that a person can be a Christian by getting into a man-made institution or by being content and staying in such. This person must repent and return to the King of the Kingdom into which he had been called (cf. 1 Thess. 2:12; 1 Cor. 1:9; Col. 1:13; 2 Thess. 2:14; 1 Pet. 2:9; Col. 3:15; 2 Tim. 1:7-9; Rom. 1:7). Indeed, the Lord's Supper is in the Kingdom (cf. Luke 22:29-30).

Would it be contrary to the text of Mark 9:38-41 to state that the one forbidden to "cast out demons" was a true and faithful believer? I challenge you to prove it would be. This man was casting out demons **in the name of the Lord**. That phrase is bound to be in harmony with its usage in the New Testament. Then, too, did not Jesus say, "he that is not against us is for us"? Does not this tell us that "this man" was not "against Christ and his mission and men," but "for Christ and his mission and men"? Did not Jesus say the man belonged to Him when he gave the statement about the drink "because ye are Christ's"? This man must have done that which he was authorized to do (cf. Col. 3:17; Acts 4:7-10). Just because the man "was not known by them" does that warrant the conclusion that he was not a true believer? The statement of "in thy name" and the statement "in my name" must be in harmony with the Book! Was the power to cast out demons limited to the apostles? Could the problem be that they had hindered an authorized work by forbidding that which was being done "in the name of Jesus"?

d. It is a sad day when our preachers quote statements and slogans from men in the restoration period, and later, and act like these are divine concepts, inspired concepts, scriptural concepts, and are a "basis" for our thinking. Then, too, I challenge anyone who knew N. B. Hardeman to prove he thought, believed, taught and or practiced that a person could become a member of a denomination and that he was a Christian in so becoming such and if he stayed there he could "be" a Christian. I am not discussing the slogan, no one ever said it was scriptural, that is, inspired, and even the fact brother Hardeman said it did not make it right or prove it to be right.

Brother Atchley quoted from N. B. Hardeman,

mentioned Ryman Auditorium, the tabernacle sermons, etc., but he did not give the location as to where the statement could be found. I remember so very vividly when I secured my set of those lessons, and I challenge a person to read through them and see if N. B. Hardeman taught that there were Christians in denominations. In fact, go get Volume III and turn to his sermon entitled "Unity" (No. 1), pp. 124-136 (the quotation given by brother Atchley is on page 125) and see why the paragraph just before it was not given and the one following it. Consider the battle he was fighting about "unity among God's people," "the church of our Lord" (he gave it in the singular!) and what he thought about those who "wear the name of Christ" being in a divided state. Then read through "Unity" (No. 2), pp. 137-150, but don't stop there. Read on through "Unity" (No. 3), pp. 151-163. See if he does not speak about "professed Christians." Now, if you are honest, what does that tell you thus far? He very explicitly stated he was speaking about "unity" and (not about that which our brethren today are concerned, GM) not "union." Yea, be sure to read of him and his usage of the names of Martin Luther, John Wesley, John Calvin...and those who wear human names. Read of him talk about "There is one body...Jesus Christ established one church...I am against denominations...they are of human origin and God knows nothing about such." Read of him refer to the Methodists, Baptists, Presbyterians, Episcopalians, and to be honest and fair, Alexander Campbell, etc. Hear him say that denominationalism is a useless thing in the sight of heaven. Is this sufficient, or shall I continue? To any person who "wants to know what N. B. Hardeman -

himself and no other - said, let him read 'in context' the *Tabernacle Sermons*" (if not all of them, then please read the three lessons on Unity! You owe it to yourself before you swallow without knowing what you swallowed!). He fought the digressives.

Brother Atchley said, "Now hear me church," so let me say, "Now hear me, preacher," go back and study it all the way through. Then write a public apology for being unjust, unfair, unbalanced, uneven and unequal and for being totally unfair to all that brother N. B. Hardeman taught. Have both the grit and the grace to correct an implication that brother Hardeman taught one could become a member of a denomination and be a Christian. Anything less than this is unacceptable to those who know the truth about this matter.

There is something yet that I MUST give, as someone will surely accuse me of "taking things out of context," "hearing only one sermon," "not knowing what I am speaking about," being "partisan, partial, and prepossessed," etc., but I can assure you that is not the case. Let me further prove some "strange and uncertain" sounds.

a. Under his caption, "Looking Ahead," by Rick Atchley, he wrote, in speaking of the last Sunday as "a marvelous day," "Old natures were transformed into new, as eight precious souls sealed their decision for Christ with baptism" (*Rejoice*, Vol. 14, Number 29, July 18, 1990, front page, 6th sentence). I do not know what he means, and I wonder if the members did. Could it be "an outward sign of an inward grace," or perhaps it was just an "unclassifiable" and "obscure" term. Reader, what do you think about people "sealing their decision for Christ with baptism"? Strange, indeed, when one stops using Bible terms, names, definitions, etc. (cf. 1 Pet. 4:11). One thing for sure, the language needs some amelioration.

b. Not long after the October 14th sermon on "Don't Bother Your Brother," this statement was made about their responses: "Also dozens have come to be one of us and were accepted because of a genuine, biblical conversion experience in another fellowship" (*Ibid.*, Vol. 14, Number 44, October 31, 1990, inside left page, third sentence, Don Phillips on "Sharing Jesus"). Please note four items in that sentence: (1) "...come to be one with us," (2) "and were accepted," (3) "because of a genuine, biblical conversion experience" and (4) "in another fellowship." Those four things should settle any doubt, if you still have any, about how they feel toward other religious bodies, accepting them, being united with them and on what is termed "a genuine, biblical conversion experience."

Since brother Atchley introduced a quote from N. B. Hardeman, one great brother in Christ, let me in conjunction with the above statement quote brother Hardeman:

> *"I charge, candidly and respectfully, however, that* ***my digressive friends*** *have gone so far that they* ***have become as much a denomination as any other*** *on this earth.* ***They have forsaken the principles of the Bible;*** *they have fled the Restoration movement; and they are divided among themselves over matters once considered fundamental.*
>
> *...* ***Some of them have gone back upon the doctrine of baptism*** *- immersion - as an act*

> *of obedience to God, and as a condition of pardon. Hence, on foreign fields, and even in this land,* ***they have become so sweet-spirited and so anxious to be one among their sister denominations, that they will receive members into their fellowship who have not been buried with the Lord Jesus in baptism. They will blend in with almost any religious body*** *- even those whose doctrines they do not believe" (Hardeman,* ***op. cit.****, p. 162, all emp. GM).*

I do not believe that we will have to "wonder" why brother Atchley did not quote this from brother Hardeman. Look at it. It is in the **same** book, the **same** volume, by the **same** speaker, on the **same** subject, at the **same** location, during the **same** series and it was to the **same** general gathering. Indeed, when quoting brother Hardeman along these very lines, one ought to pay particular attention as to how he used the word "Christian," that is, in reference "to whom" he used it. If not, you will have brother Hardeman saying something that he did not say.

> c. Have you ever deliberated and cogitated as to where some of these men got their thoughts about Mark 9:38-41? Yea, I have also, and I just speculate (and I surely do not know if Rick got this from brother Shelly, brother Shelly from Rick, or both secured it from somewhere else) that one place might have been from a book that I am now going to quote.

> *"I have been appalled by the degree of* ***party spirit within my church. Like John in Mark*** *9, we seek too often to* ***build a fence around a clique*** *and* ***leave on the outside*** *all the* ***people who do not possess our special know-***

ledge. ***Like John, we have yet to learn that the Kingdom of God has God's dimensions,*** *and that* ***those who truly do the works of Christ, and bear fruit of the Spirit, belong to Him.***

John was looking for labels. *He wanted to be sure that the man doing good belonged to* ***the right party and wore the right name. Jesus said,*** *in effect,* ***'Look,*** *instead,* ***for actions, attitudes, and dispositions.*** *When you find the things which delight me - mercy, justice, faith - welcome them. Do not meet them sourly.' How desperately my people need to learn this lesson. We often find it hard to be glad about* ***work done by those who do not share our interpretations.*** *We talk of...then we went in with what we were pleased to call the 'real truth' and sought to* ***convert them to our own particular set of dogmas****...*

Christ...said of the man, 'I have not found so great faith,...' 'If Christ were to make this statement about some religious group,...' 'If the man has so much faith, ***why is he not a member of the right church?'***

One of our greatest needs is to realize to what degree most of us are ***prisoners of our heredity and environment****...*

...the general rise in levels of formal education, and a wider knowledge of different religious parties, is slowly but surely ***changing us****...*

The time is ripe for the beginning of a slow,

*massive turnover. I have no doubt that it is underway...that God will lead us, together with **all** Christians, into fields of greater Christian service than we have yet known."*

In the above quote all emphasis is mine, except the word "all," which is found in the closing sentence. When you read about "party spirit," "like John in Mark 9," "building fences around a clique," "our special knowledge," "the Kingdom of God has God's dimensions," "those... works of Christ, and bear fruit of the Spirit, belong to Him," "labels," "right party and right name," "look for attitudes, and dispositions," "our interpretation," "convert them to our own particular set of dogmas," "the right church," "prisoners of our heredity," and "all Christians," who does that sound like? Does it have a familiar ring? Well I took that from the book entitled, ***"VOICES OF CONCERN"*** (subtitle: "Critical Studies in Church of Christism"), which was edited by Robert Meyers and he was the one who wrote what I gave (pp. 258-263). Yes, indeed, it was produced by none other than "Mission Messenger" (1966). The writers were Logan J. Fox, Thomas P. Hardeman, Ralph V. Graham, Margaret Edson O'Dowd, Ralph Milton Stolz, David Darnell, Robert Myers, etc. Do you want a sample of what was written in the very opening chapter? Listen to this: "Our biggest problem, I think, is our stand on immersion. Our hearts and minds tell us that people baptized by sprinkling are Christians,... Next to our position on baptism, I am convinced that our view of the Bible is the biggest barrier to spiritual growth among us" (pp. 29, 19). Tell you what, just keep some of these things in mind as you read through this book and certain things will absolutely amaze, not just astound and astonish, but dumbfound, flabbergast, shock, jolt and jar you.

d. Evidently, more than we think, believe we must have started in the 1800's with Alexander Campbell: "If... and we've only been around since the early 1800's,..." Let me give you the wording of this road marker: CHURCH OF CHRIST - 1710. MEETINGHOUSE OF THE CHURCH OF CHRIST IN RUMNEY MARSH, ERECTED IN 1710. THOMAS CHEEVER, THE FIRST SETTLED MINISTER, DIED DECEMBER 27, 1749, AGED NINETY ONE YEARS. Massachusetts Bay Colony Tercentenary Commission. Was this not about 53 years before Thomas Campbell was born? 62 years before B. W. Stone? 78 years before Alexander and 86 before Scott?

If this is not sufficient, note the following:

"Among the fells of Furness was founded the first ***Christian*** *Church in England.* ***By Christian*** *I mean here not congregational, not Presbyterian, not Episcopal,* ***not Baptist****, but simply Christian in its unrestricted sense...a church of people acknowledged as Christians and nothing else.*

The old minute book of Tottlebank Church is still preserved and bears the inscription - 'This booke is for the use of that Church of Christ in Broughton, ffurnessfells and Cartmell...is Elder.'

The first entry stands thus: -

The 18th day of ye sixth month, called ***August 1669, A Church of Christ was formed*** *in order and sate down together an the ffellowship and order of ye Gospel of Jesus Christ.*

> *In the records of Quarter Sessions held at Lancaster there is a entry dated 1663... This was six years before the formation of the Tottlebank Church and four out of five were present when the Church was founded" (**A Brief History of Tottlebank Baptist Church**, Greenodd Ulverston, Founded 1669, pp. 3, 5 emp. is the book's).*

Take note that there had been a faithful congregation of the Church of Christ; when it went into apostasy, became Baptist! Now we have a notice of 1710, one before that of 1663 and there are others that we could also name. But, forget about all of them and just remind yourself of "the seed being the Word of God" (cf. Luke 8:11) and that was the rule of God Himself in Genesis 1:11-12. If anyone is half as intellectual as he seems to be, then that person ought to know that seed, when uncorrupted, will produce as per God's instructions. This means anywhere, anytime and by anyone, if the heart is honest, that is, good soil (cf. Luke 8:15). (I wish I had the space to tell you of a conversation that took place recently relative to the Tottlebank Baptist Church and that a man actually said the property was ours, etc., as well as many other things relative to dates and the seed).

e. Brother Atchley said: "I will be open to any opportunity to teach and be taught more fully the way of Jesus. I'll be open to any chance, any place, any where with any body to teach and to be taught more fully... I will seek any chance... or to be taught because a disciple is, by definition, folks, a learner." What makes this "strange," you say, well, hear me out. First, however, I want you to understand he said "any opportunity," "any chance," "any place," "with any body," "to teach and be taught," and "I will seek any chance..." *If* that is not comprehensive, extensive, all-embracing, all-encompassing, a real umbrella, across-the-board and compendious statement, pray tell me what it is. Yet, on July 25, 1989 he was sent a letter of only four paragraphs, was asked two questions, *but did not respond*. On August 18, 1989, he was sent a reminder of the July 25th letter and it gave him the respect of perhaps being busy or maybe the letter did not even reach him. Therefore, this one was sent RESTRICTED DELIVERY. Can you guess or even have the slightest idea of what happened to that one? Remember the man who said "I will be open" and then gave all the various "any" statements? Well, this man, REFUSED THE LETTER and it was dated 8-21-89. Yes, I do KNOW THIS. It was stamped RETURNED TO SENDER and it was returned, "refused." I do not know about you, but it sure makes one wonder. You see, I understand this, as I had the identical experience with the preacher there before Rick Atchley. I have the files to prove it, too. What do I mean? My first letter was received and then there came a REFUSED on the restricted delivery letter. These fellows may not believe in "the pattern," but it does seem they "follow a pattern." How would you feel about me since I put an "open to anyone" DIVORCE DEBATE CHALLENGE!, wrote the propositions, signed my name, placed it in the June issue of the *Christian Journal* (I did this in 1985, and it is on page 11), if a man responded and I would not acknowledge his letter, if he sent me a "restricted delivery" one and I just simply refused it and sent it back? Regardless of my "ifs," "ands," "buts," "ors," "neithers and nors," and all my subjectivistic statements, the fact is I did not keep my word. I am not very "open to any..." after all, am I? Since he gave the definition of a disciple as "a learner," maybe he is not a true disciple. Now the best way to handle this is simply to say, "My own attitude and disposition is right," but "your attitude and disposition is wrong," and this way you will not have to answer "any one," at "any place," "any where," at "any opportunity or chance," or even "seek any chance," with "any body." Case closed.

f. It is "strange," but yet, considering the movement among us, it is not so strange that this particular sermon would have sales up to 700 (orders) and that made it "the most popular tape" (*Rejoice*, Vol. 14, Number 46, November 14, 1990, inside right page in the article by Pat Riddle "Angels At Home"). There is no way to tell why this tape was so popular, it would, for all of us, be a matter of pure subjectivism, but it is not a matter of subjectivism that it was Rick's "most popular tape."

g. Isn't it rather "strange" for a preacher to say, "Let's not limit the kingdom of God to the size of our brotherhood" and try to prove all such differences are normal? After all, "If you do, beloved (that is, have "to believe every single thing correctly to be saved") most of this church is in big trouble." Out of the five items he mentioned (and he said, "I could go on and on and on with the list..."), the first, among them was "different views on marriage and divorce." Really, this is "not strange" for those who know, as one of their elders said, "scriptural divorce is a variable, depending on which church you are in. So, that is a significant factor...Our church does not have a set policy." And the question is, "would you place this subject in the same category as the length of days in Genesis?" Is that not like comparing apples and oranges?

h. Remember the example that brother Atchley gave about the man he met who planted a Baptist church, "just north of our building," and who had "polled people all over Westlake, and Southlake, and Keller." Now this "young man" that Rick met asked: "Would you be open to an invitation to the brand new Southlake Community Church?" Unless you know what is happening and the plea for "Community Churches," those to "meet the needs of drugs, AIDS, evil, materialism, etc., etc." then you will not understand his question since he had "planted a Baptist church already." Indeed, a Baptist is now asking if people would attend "a brand new community church!" He said "seven out of nine unchurched people said I would consider visiting..." However, of those nine, when asked, "And would you also be open to an invitation to the brand new Southlake Baptist Church?" that only two said "yes" (seven out of nine had said "No.") Now why would I give this? Perhaps, but I do not know it for a fact (remember the sermon was preached on October 14th, the tape orders went up to 700, dozens became one with them, were accepted as they had had a genuine biblical conversion experience in another fellowship, etc., and you can find those dates listed above), it might have influenced SOMEONE (yes, the one who had the authority to do so), to prepare their marquee as the following so very clearly shows (after the sermon, and not long, came the sign).

I do not know about you, but, to me, this is a "strange" saying to be placed on the church's marquee. Indeed, it may leave "the wrong impression," wouldn't you agree? To say the least, and that is perhaps the reason for it being a question and the phone number listed, it would have to be explained. I'm sure, if you called 281-0773 they could explain the reason for it, if not, and if they did not so expect such, why the phone listed and why the question anyway? It is strange to me, as I cannot, "for the soul," of me, dream, envision, opine, visualize, fancy, or theorize such.

I am not as studied and learned as some, but I do understand something of the "nature" of the New Testament Church. The church is a "purified people," therefore, it is called a "Bride" (cf. Tit. 2:11-14; Rom. 7:4; Rev. 21:9;

Eph. 5:25-27; see the thought in 2 Cor. 11:2-3). Christ wants His bride to be pure, as seen from Ephesians 5:25-27 and 2 Corinthians 11:2-3. I believe this, among other things, relates to purity in name (cf. Acts 4:12; 1 Pet. 4:14-16), in doctrine (1 Tim. 6:3-5; 2 John 9-11; 2 Tim. 1:13), in worship (cf. John 4:21-24; Matt. 15:7-9; Col. 2:23; etc.) and in life (cf. 1 John 3:1-3; Rom. 6:3-5, 17-18; Eph. 4:17-24; James 1:27; 4:4; 2 Cor. 5:17; etc.).

I further state that the purity of the Lord's New Testament Body, His Church, can (and is) be seen in its "exclusiveness" and in its "universality." *Note*: (1) It is "methodist" in that it endeavors to follow the method of Christ (2 John 9-11). (2) It is "adventist" in that it is looking for the second coming of Christ (Acts 1:9-11). (3) It is "Baptist," in that it baptizes (Matt. 28:18-20; 1 Cor. 12:13; Gal. 3:26-27; Rom. 6:3-4). (4) It is "presbyterian," or "episcopalian" in that it has elders; bishops or overseers, in the church (1 Tim. 3:1-7; Tit. 1:5-9; Acts 20:17, 28). (5) It is "protestant" in that it protests against any head of the church (or some other things) but Christ (Matt. 16:18; Eph. 1:22-23; 5:23; Col. 1:18, 24). (6) It is "catholic" in that it is for all men (Mark 16:15-16; Heb. 2:9; 1 Tim. 2:6; cf. Matt. 20:28). (7) It is "holiness" in that its members have the gift of the Holy Spirit (cf. 1 Cor. 3:16-17; Eph. 2:19-22; Acts 2:38; 5:32; Gal. 4:4ff). Enough.

I personally think that I would be somewhat less than honest if I were to place on the church's marquee: (1) "Are you looking for an Independent Methodist Church?" (2) "Are you looking for an Independent Adventist Church?" (3) "Are you looking for an Independent Baptist Church?" (4) "Are you looking for an Independent Presbyterian or Episcopalian Church?" (5) "Are you looking for an Independent Protestant Church?" (6) "Are you looking for an Independent Catholic Church?" (7) "Are you looking for an Independent Holiness church?" You can choose any or all, list your phone number and then "explain away" some things and explain other things about the sign's question. And so it is with the words "Independent Community Church." I think that I can understand the words, "Independent," "Community," and "Church," but back forty years ago there were eight Independent Baptist Churches, about 354 Independent Churches and some 650 Independent Fundamental Churches of America, etc. Check today and you will find how that list has grown. Today, in our own area we have "Allied Communities of Tarrant," "Bethel Community Church," "Bethesda Community Church," "First Community Missionary Baptist," "Forest Hill Community Church," "St. Joseph's Catholic Community Church," "Arlington Community Church," "Community Christian Church," "Metropolitan Community Church," "Agape Community Church," "Salvation Army Corps Community Church," and, as Rick said about a certain list, I could "go on and on and on." But, now we have the Richland Hills Church of Christ marquee asking: "Are You Looking for an Independent Community Church?" It makes me wonder when we will hear them using the words "Memorial," "Compassionate," "Restoration," "Fellowship of Love," "Progressive," or better yet, "Greater Progressive," "Ecumenical," etc. I guess their sign goes along with their "Richland Hills Church of Christ Christian Community Center." It is listed "Community Care" and also referred to as "Community Enrichment Center." Recently, over fifty groups helped in their program and among them was St. John's Christian School and First Baptist Church.

Many perhaps would not accept this sign's question if I just wrote of it, therefore, I thought the picture would be better. After all, it was "public," wasn't it? I guess I am just helping them to advertise it. I cannot imagine the New Testament statements to read:

> *"Upon this rock, I will build my Independent Community Church" (Jesus, Matt. 16:18).*
>
> *"Take heed...feed the Independent Community Church which he purchased with his own blood" (Paul, Acts 20:28).*
>
> *"Unto the Independent Community Church of God which is at Corinth" (Paul, 1 Cor. 1:2).*
>
> *"All the Independent Community Churches salute you" (Paul, Rom. 16:16).*
>
> *"And he put all things in subjection under his feet, and gave him to be head over all things to the Independent Community Church" (Paul, Eph. 1:22).*
>
> *"And he is the head of the body, the Independent Community Church" (Paul, Col. 1:18).*
>
> *"...that thou mayest know how men ought to behave themselves in the house of God, which is the Independent Community Church" (Paul, 1 Tim. 3:15).*

Whether we want to admit it or not, there is "something" in a name. Indeed, something very precious! If we speak as the Bible speaks, but that is kinda "old fashioned" (1 Pet. 4:11; 1 Cor. 4:6), we will find and use those designations that are found in the scripture. It is referred to in enough ways to use that I do not have to add that which is normally given to "gain members."

I am not amazed that brother Atchley, the very next Sunday night, October 21st, began his sermon entitled, "Caring For The Erring," with "...I want to talk about baptism...the discussions I have had this past week over last Sunday morning's message." His sermon on "Apollos" was given on how one should treat a preacher when he makes "an inaccurate statement," "teaches something that you do not believe the scriptures teach," "makes a mistake," etc. Of course, he took the time during the lesson to speak about, "being a recipient of a variety of responses," how he had sat at the feet of men "very educated, but sometimes you wonder if their heart ever burned," "hearing talk about the text, working with the text...almost as if this was not a living word that was to burn in our hearts, but it was an old piece of literature that was to be dissected and analyzed to death." And, he included such things as, when a preacher is wrong, "getting a hold of the nearest editor," "the favorite pastime of some - they love intramural battling more than reaching the world," "writing brothers up," "impossible to please everybody," etc. He even threw in "I don't think there's anything that's hurt the image of our fellowship more than the perception that we are the only ones who know anything." He did say, "It's been my experience that most people like to try to follow scripture as best they can like I do." Apollos is a great example in so many marvelous ways, and to this there is agreement. But keep in mind what we have today is the Book of God with the instructions "to study" (2 Tim. 2:15), "being ready to give an answer" (1 Pet. 3:15), etc., and there is no excuse for a gospel preacher to stand up and talk about "Christians in the denominations" when we have the entire Book of God written, and in our own precious language. In his lesson he talked about "others," but now don't "you" be arrogant and talk about him. He mentioned how Apollos was taught "in private" and that is how we need to handle things, but before he was through with Apollos he gave where he (and this is his own quote) "vigorously refuted the Jews in public debate."

Maybe Eldred Echols came to the defense of the marquee's question "Are You Looking For An Independent Community Church?," as he wrote a short article entitled: "Richland Hills Church of Christ: An Independent Community Fellowship" (the last three words are identical to the last three words on the marquee, except he used "fellowship" instead of "church"). (I do not have space to give it, but you can mark it down as being in Vol. 15, Number 1, January 2, 1991, inside right page under the article "Sharing Jesus" by Don Phillips). I do think you just might need to read about "If anything can be defended according to churches of Christ guidelines, it is congregational autonomy" (that is about like "church of Christ preachers"), "This says to Joe Blow that he is not becoming a subject of some conference, synod or... who will determine... whether or not he can remarry, or how many times a year he must take communion" (sounds kinda like there is no pattern in the Book for marriage or communion), and "It suggests warm neighborliness and a group of people who share and care about each other, rather than a cold cathedral or chapel where professionals intone the ritual and the individual worshipper has no communion with others" (without the New Testament Church, there would be no "fellowship" and the assembly of God's people, with the Lord's Supper, etc., "is not a cold item"). I have given one quote from each of the three words "Independent," "Community," and "Fellowship," respectively.

I know this has been lengthy (and even yet it has not all been as thorough as it could have been), but I'm weary of preachers saying anything they desire, yea, publicly, and then no one can say anything in rebuttal. If you do, even when they've given it publicly, the first thing you'll hear is

Matthew 18:15-17. Talk about something being ludicrous, farcical and absurd, it is to so apply Matthew 18:15-17 to something that has been done "publicly." God help us to have the intestinal fortitude to get the right Book and then get right with the Book and not to go beyond its teachings (cf. 1 Cor. 4:6; Gal. 1:6-9; 1 Tim. 4:6-16; 2 Tim. 2:2; 2 Pet. 1:12-15; 3:1; 2 John 9-11; Rev. 22:18-19; 1 Pet. 4:11; Rom. 1:16; 1 Cor. 1:18-25; etc.), doing anything else might well be termed "boondoggling." You judge my attitude and my disposition if you like, say nothing of the preacher's attitude and disposition, but we have a charge to "contend" and "defend" the faith (cf. note *dialegomai*, "to contend," "to be a contender for the faith," Acts 17:2; 18:19; 17:17; 19:8-9; 24:2; Jude 9; *apologia*, "to give an answer," "defense," "to clear one's self," Acts 25:16; 1 Pet. 3:15; 2 Cor. 7:11; Phil. 1:7, 16; *suzeteo*, "to dispute," "to reason," "to question," Acts 6:9; 9:29; Luke 24:15; Mark 8:11; 9:14; *elencho*, "to reprove," "to rebuke," "to convict," Eph. 5:11, 13; 2 Tim. 4:2; 1 Tim. 5:20; Titus 1:13; Rev. 3:19; *sumbibazo*, "to prove," Acts 9:22). Elders are told to "stop the mouths" of some (cf. Tit. 1:9-11), so it appears that "some mouths ought to be stopped." If not, then there is no meaning to the scripture just given. God help us to "buy the truth, and sell it not" (cf. Prov. 23:23), and regardless of the cost we must pay. I can tell you this, it does cost when a man preaches error, such as "Christians in the denominations." Indeed, one cost is that he does not get away with it, that is, he is challenged and answered, as God only knows how many souls are at stake.

5. **Strange And Uncertain Sounds From Randy Fenter.** Brother Randy Fenter, who preaches for the MacArthur Park Church of Christ located at 1907 NE Loop 410 in San Antonio, Texas, spoke at the 39th Annual Lectureship at Oklahoma Christian College in

Oklahoma City, Oklahoma (January 22-25, 1989). His subject was, "Do Not Go Beyond What Is Written" and it was based on 1 Corinthians 4:1-7. It was, of course, publicly given, taped and made available. I have before me, at this writing, the tape and a transcription made from that tape, as well as his other materials given, written and relating to, his delivered lecture. To these I will make reference, but not at this point.

Again, let me be redundant, reiterate and restate, what I have at other times about these delivered lessons and the lengths of them. I can, in no wise, cover all he said and do not intend to, but do fully intend to make known some of what he said. The reason is simple. The transcription is sixteen pages, single spaced! He said, on page eleven, "I'll go over tonight," and he sure told the truth about that, as it was five pages later, about one third of the entire lesson, that he quit. Let me also say, if I have answered something within the realm of another's lesson, normally, I would not do it again. In this lecture, I just mainly want to point out some of his statements, therefore, they will be listed "in the course" as to the way the lecture was delivered. A few other things will be mentioned.

a. As he gets through with his introductory remarks, he makes sure that we understand the church has a lot of "flaws, imperfections, and failures," and that we also understand that he is a "biblicist who loves the word of God and believes there is no other rule of faith... Bible."

b. He mentions, and more than once that "silence means something is prohibited and that something is permitted." On this he quotes men like Alexander Campbell, referring to volumes 2 and 5 of the *Christian Baptist*, Woody Woodrow's article in *Restoration Quarterly*, where he quoted Benjamin

Franklin, J. W. McGarvey, David Lipscomb and G. C. Brewer.

c. Just here he mentions that he cannot say something that would please "all of you," and for them "not to hold OCC responsible..."

d. He explains about the issue of silence being a "great struggle," and gives as examples refusal of fellowship and salvation on issues like "how many cups...," "...Christian College or not," "instruments of music," "use of a church building," "if you can even have a building,..." "a coke machine, water fountain, or a bathroom." We fight, split, divide, cut each other to shreds and the basis for this, he said, is on "what silence does or does not say. Yet, from the beginning of our movement, we have never had uniformity on how do you determine when silence is prohibitive and when silence is permissive."

e. As we come to the Scriptures, we do so as biblicists, and it "colors everything we read." He mentions there are "questions about the Word of God...the canon, the way it was written, inspiration and inerrancy." This is the way we come to the Bible and others who do not, we "judge their motives" and "we sin, we sin,...but we sin."

f. He says that the way we view the Bible as "a constitution," or "a collection of letters" is an example of what he is speaking about. He says, "If the Bible is a constitution...that silence is necessarily prohibitive...because you can't do what you don't have the authority to do." But, he says, if this is true, then what are we going to do about "Christian colleges...about schools of preaching and ownership of church property, of which there is no authority, no command, no inference, no example in all of scripture. What are we going to do about radio and t.v. programs, microphones... buses and baptistries?"

g. At this point he mentions another view and says, "it is the view I share." So, there is the "constitutional" view and there is the "epistolary" view of scripture, which is a "collection of letters." He says the "textual evidence" from the Bible itself "seems to be a collection of letters rather than a gathered constitution." Then his statement declares "had God's intentions been the maintenance of a strictly adhered pattern...one would think...The New Testament was never intended to be viewed as a legal brief..." He says it is biblical suicide to come to Scripture with an example of presuppositions.

h. He speaks about "necessary inference" (a dangerous doctrine and filled with mines...profusion of rules and regulations) as an approach to "silence" that has resulted in splits, name calling and of sending people to hell on both left and right. Also, we have tried to solve "silence" by "approved example." His example here is the Lord's Supper and so he asks, "must the Lord's Supper always be taken in an upper room?...must the preacher preach to midnight...must someone fall out of a window?"

i. I have a question, he said: "Is there a better way to unravel this twisted gordian knot of silence than trying to pick it apart with the clumsy fingers of necessary inference and approved example? Or are we destined to forever be a unity movement creating disunity?" There is, he says, but it will require "a return to the old paths of our movement." By this he means a freedom from the codification of all beliefs. "The dream of our restoration fathers was not a new denomination. It wasn't an unwritten codification...silence for them meant freedom... freedom from ecclesiastical hierarchy...They were free to accept any man who gave honor to Jesus Christ and was baptized into his name."

j. "...I have the freedom to speak here tonight. I may never be able to speak here again...in our brotherhood we have freedom from ecclesiastical hierarchy" (Randy sure likes those last two words, as he used them seven times in the next few paragraphs). "I call you to serious Bible study...to to hear God both in His words and in His silences."

k. The second thing silence meant for them (the restoration fathers he mentioned earlier) was the "freedom to follow Christ only." Above the obligation to the church, it is an obligation only to Christ. Brother Fenter says if we take this principle ("do not go beyond what is written") and lift it out of its context, we make it say, "unless the Bible authorizes something it can't be done." In other words, he says, "the constitutional approach" to scripture. And if we do this, then we do "violence to this text." "This was not Paul's intent. He was not saying that. He didn't mean that at all. He meant...To build an entire hermeneutic on it would be a very dangerous thing." And here he mentioned the Greek being a very difficult phrase.

l. His answer is that Paul "is looking for the church to stop judging...stop judging brothers who are different from them...stop being arrogant...being prideful..." Here, he says, we discover the freedom "to be tolerant..." and then states, and it is to us, "many people neither know God, nor His mercy and kindness expressed in His great grace to us." This is a blunder, "a dangerous blunder that will destroy the churches of Christ." Just here he brings in 1 Corinthians 14 (he means Romans 14, GM, as he mentions one man eating meat and another not eating meat and both honoring God) and his thought is still on "judging," and "it is presumptuous of human beings to speak as if though they were God." "Only by respecting the silence of God's Scripture will we ever respect the force of His words" and he refers to Matthew 13:28-30 although the location is not given. "And the one who seeks to speak God's mind for Him today determining who is wheat and who is tares...root out everything to which he personally does not agree. The one who builds his case on necessary inference and approved example to tear apart the church of my Lord Jesus Christ, for which he died, is a person who respects neither the words of Jesus spoken nor the silence of Scripture." (Examples given of military and policemen, differing views and yet fellowship at MacArthur Park).

m. From Philippians 3:1-16, he makes the point that Paul says a difference can disappear with maturity, and that he will give the people time. Each person should live up to what he knows. He repeats that we can honor the Lord by eating or not eating vegetables, being in or not being in the military and this way we will not run over each other or run people out of the brotherhood. We will be honoring the Lord by not speaking where he has not spoken.

n. "I know of no doctrine, in my judgment, in any fellowship, any fellowship, that is more dangerous than the doctrine of necessary inference. Because it fills in the silences of God with its own voice. It presumes to speak for God. It gives license to people to construct their own theological temples and the arrogance to claim that those temples belong to God. And I call upon our brotherhood to stop going beyond what is written. To stop legislating where God has not." (January 23, Monday night lecture, 1989).

Let me hasten to say, before going any further, that brother Fenter (remember the OCC lecture was in January) later published three articles in *Image*. Part I was in Vol. 5, Num. 8, Aug. '89, pp. 9-10, 31; Part II was in Vol. 5, Num. 9, Sept. '89, pp. 8-11; Part III was in Vol. 5, Num. 10, Oct. '89, pp. 6-10. Note: Part I was mainly "introductory," speaking about biblicists, quoting men like William Willimon, M. Robert Mulholland, Jr., Alexander Campbell, Woody Woodrow, who had quoted Benjamin Franklin, J. W. McGarvey, David Lipscomb and G. C. Brewer, and he introduces the thoughts of "necessary inference" and "approved example." After some words of introduction and quoting men like Monroe Hawley and the authors of *"Discovering Our Roots: The Ancestry of Churches of Christ"* (by Leonard Allen and Richard Hughes), his article has three headings: "Is the New Testament a Constitution?" (quoting more men, Michael Armour, Larry James and Dr. Fred Craddock), "The Pilot of 'Necessary Inference'" (quoting Eddie Sharp), and "The Pilot of 'Approved Examples'" (quoting Milo Richard Hadwin). He completes Part II under the heading of "The Course of our two Pilots," discussing the results of these two thoughts. In Part III, he refers to Alexander Campbell, Barton W. Stone, the authors of *"The Responsibility of*

Hermeneutics" (Roger Lundin, Anthony Thiselton and C. Walhort), tells of some educators in New York City and the school yard fence, the dream of the Restoration Fathers, after which, we get to his major points. These are: "Silence Means Freedom from Hierarchy" (mentioning James O'Kelly, Rice Haggard, Elias Smith, Barton W. Stone and some examples), "Silence Means Freedom to Follow Christ Only" (gives 1 Cor. 4:1-7, the difficult Greek phrase, thoughts relative to judging, etc.), "Silence Means Freedom to Explore Courageously" (referring to Barton Stone, Acts 17:11, Thomas Campbell and the need to critically examine approved examples and necessary inferences), "Silence Means Freedom to be Our Best Selves" (Alexander Campbell noted again, Rom. 14 observed briefly and "Who gives me the right to makes laws from God?"), "Silence Means Freedom to be Patient" (John Locke, Thomas and Alexander Campbell) and then he gives his "Conclusion" (he repeats his judgment that no doctrine is more potentially dangerous in any fellowship than elevating necessary inference and approved examples to the status of God's commands. The hermeneutical principle of "the not beyond written" is our only hope of unity. He ends with Acts 20:32).

After his three part series, consisting of twelve pages and most of thirty-two columns, brother Fenter then wrote "A Hermeneutical Firestorm" ("Observations Since My OCC Speech") and it was published in Vol. 6, Num. 2, March/April 1990, pp. 18, 22. He began by saying "A hermeneutical firestorm is raging through our brotherhood" and compared it to the Yellowstone fires of 1988. However, he said this "maelstrom (confusion, chaos, turbulence, mess, GM) may offer greater benefits... Fresh, new growth in biblical studies is already sprouting from the singed earth as light streams onto seeds long hidden by a forest of traditions and comfortable conclusions."

Evidently, from the opening of the next paragraph, he takes some of the credit, as he says, "One of many sparks that lit the fire was an address I made at Oklahoma Christian College in January of 1989." He says that he began with the text and asked "logical" and "obvious" questions: "Why did Paul write this chapter to these people?" "What does it mean to us today?" "Does our traditional interpretation of this Scripture match with Paul's intent?" He also compared his particular study and found "that such a spirit was clearly evident in the early days of our movement." He then listed the response to his address in five groups with the "overwhelming response, 'I'm so glad someone finally said something'" listed first and the "least common response, 'I disagree with you, but I do not doubt your integrity,'" listed last.

Since listening to the tape, the tape and the transcription, and not just once either, reading through all three articles time and again, as well as the "Observations Since My OCC Speech," I decided, that for the most part, it would be best to leave it alone, as it perhaps will "self-destruct." On rethinking such, I do want to list some of the things that, to me, are "strange" sounds, indeed.

a. It is strange that a man will use the term biblicist so many times in reference to himself (the word itself was used as many as six times in a half page of transcription), talk about how he loves the Word and the church, yet, besides the text, give so very little of it in a lecture so important. As far as I was able to detect, he only gave two full exact quotations (and did not locate either of them). He did mention some locations in reference to a few items. He also used the names of some books, like Philemon, Jude, Ephesians, book of Corinthians. He made mention of some of the New Testament men, like Paul, John and Apollos. Let me also be quick to add that his three articles in *Image*, the first being in the seventh month after his lecture, are basically the lecture, but he adds both scripture and men's names, etc., to those articles that are not in his lecture and does give others verbatim that he only mentioned in the lecture (*examples*: M. Robert Mulholland, Jr., and Larry James for men; 2 Pet. 1:21; 3:15-18; Jer. 23:28-40 as scripture references; Rev. 22:18-19 as a verbatim scripture added, as well as others; Jas. 4:12; Acts 20:32 as locations for quotations; then there are other items).

b. It is strange that a man who believes that there is no other rule of faith other than the Bible will quote, refer to, mention by name, and give book titles, etc., as trying to prove his position. Yes, he did mention a few, at least eighteen men and various books. I pray to God that I do not have to prove what I believe by others who also are just human flesh. I do not call that "preaching the word" (cf. 2 Tim. 4:1-4). There is no substitute, I do not care if you can stack up all the early restoration men, every single one of them, for the Bible, as it is "the power" (cf. Rom. 1:16; 1 Cor. 1:18, 21).

c. It is strange that a man, who supposedly "knows" that "this" is wrong, but "this" is right, would place "a church building, a coke machine, a water fountain, a bathroom" on the same par as, his words, not mine, "instruments of music." Yea, even how many cups...

d. It is strange that he would talk about "the beginning of our movement," as if the New Testament Church commenced with men like the

Campbells, Stone, Smith, etc. He also spoke about "...a return to the old paths of our movement."

e. It is strange that a man would declare his belief in the Bible (and how he loves the Word of God) and state that he believes there "is no other rule of faith other than the Bible" and then declare it is not "a constitution," that there is "no pattern," "rigid patternism is not only divisive, it is directly contradictory to Scripture," etc. What in the world is his definition of "rule" (cf. Greek *kanon* in Gal. 6:16; Phil. 3:16), and "rule of faith" (cf. Jude 3; Acts 6:7; Rom. 1:5; 16:26; 2 Cor. 13:5; Gal. 1:23; Eph. 4:13; Phil. 1:27; Col. 1:23; 1 Tim. 3:9; 4:1; 5:8; 6:10; 2 Tim. 2:18; 3:8; 4:7; Tit. 1:13).

f. It is strange that a man would say, "If the Bible is a constitution...you can't do what you don't have the authority to do," and "if we take this principle, 'don't go beyond what is written,' and we lift it out of its context...we make it say that unless the Bible authorizes something that it can't be done." I always thought a man had to have authority for what he did in religion (cf. Col. 3:17 and compare it with Acts 4:7-10).

g. It is strange to hear a man say "there is no authority, no command, no inference, no example in all of Scripture" for "ownership of church property." Is there authority for "renting," "borrowing," or "using someone else's property"? What about "leasing," or "building" a building, or...? If God commands us to assemble, how can we fulfill the command without a place? There are only a few options, such as buy, build, rent or meet in a privately owned one. But then the Bible says nothing about that either (cf. Heb. 10:25; James 2:2, same basic Greek word in both, *synagoge*), but we cannot assemble without a place.

h. It is strange to hear how much subjectivism there is in this lesson, and such thoughts as "had God's intentions been the maintenance of a strictly adhered to pattern...one would think..." How smart does a man have to be to say, "Find me a case of someone being baptized in a baptistry in the Bible"?

i. It is strange to hear one speak of his faith, his love for the Bible, the church and then speak as though there was nothing, not a single truth, in "the seed promise" (cf. Gen. 1:11-12; Luke 8:11). I say this as he speaks about the church of my Lord as it were a denomination. "The dream of our restoration fathers was not a new denomination." (Or does one have "any right" to "infer" what is "implied" in a statement?). He goes on: "It wasn't an unwritten codification of every question,..." So he says, "I call you to serious Bible study...to hear God both in His words and in His silences." Guess he thinks that no one has done or is doing any "serious" study (cf. 2 Tim. 2:15; 1 Pet. 3:15).

j. It is strange that we all have been so wrong, yet he can say "It was not Paul's intent...He was not saying...He didn't mean...He meant..." I have a question, how does brother Fenter know? Did Paul use a "command" on him "somewhere" and so revealed it?

k. It is strange, that is, to me, for me to hear him say, "the Greek is a very difficult phrase" (he is referring to our English, "do not go beyond what is written," as found in 1 Cor. 4:6). In his third article, to which I have already referred, he makes the statement: "First, the phrase '*to me hyper* (this should be *huper*, not *hyper*) *ha gegraptai*' ('the not above what is written') is a difficult phrase that does not flow easily. It seems to be quoted material (I'm not for sure what on earth he means here) (being introduced by the neuter article '*to*'), but there is wide discussion as to what it refers." Then one sentence later he says, "Whatever the meaning of this obscure phrase, whether the Old Testament Scriptures or what Paul has written in chapters one through three (is that all to which it might refer?), it is incredibly dangerous to infer a firm doctrine of 'approved examples only' from this passage" (who has?). The next time he transliterates this (of course, I know printers make mistakes, but I thought that all galley sheets were proofed by the author and especially any material like a foreign language), it is *"two me hyper ha gegraptai,"* and the first and third words are incorrect. That is not any point but it is when he speaks "of the meaning is clouded" but the primary thrust of this passage is sparkling clear, and this "transparent intent..." Yes, it is strange to hear this as "a very difficult phrase," "does not flow easily" (that should not be strange, as a lot of Greek does not, try Jude 3), "seems to be quoted material," "wide discussion as to what it refers," "obscure phrase," and "the meaning is clouded." I checked several Greek texts that I personally have and saw nothing so very unusual. Beginning with the purpose clause, it is *hina en hemin mathete to me huper ha gegraptai* (the word giving him trouble might have been *phronein*, "to think," which is in the critical apparatus, but in no text of the verse, except perhaps some *Interlinear* one like George Ricker Berrys, at least no text that I personally have). Since I am not the best in Greek, I talked to one who is extremely schooled in it and he saw nothing more than what I have said. If I thought there was value in listing each word whether it was subjunctive, indicative, 1 aorist, 2 aorist, active or passive, plural or singular, first, second or third person and the root word, I would (all that I just listed is in 1 Cor. 4:6). I mentioned earlier Jude 3, and the last part, in the Greek order, says: "necessity I had to write to you exhorting to contend earnestly the once delivered to the saints faith." We would have to supply the "you" after "exhorting." Now, does that help to show some does not flow easily? However, regardless, brother Fenter knows what Paul's intent was and he also knows what it was not. In fact, he knows it both "coming" and "going."

l. It is strange to hear him say, with all that he has both said and written: "I call upon our brotherhood to stop going beyond what is written. To stop legislating where God has not." I simply ask, who has? Statements are made throughout this lecture about a number of things, yet no proof given. And that is strange, since he does try to prove what he says in his own particular beliefs and thought about various items. How does brother Fenter know Paul's intent? Who has elevated human reasoning to the level of God's command? What "system" or "human court" does he have in mind to which he thinks "we" must be proven faithful? What are the "new found decrees" he mentions? Has he done what he has accused others of doing? Does brother Fenter, in his "Conclusion" leave the impression

> that he is legislating for God? Read it and see. Also, if you want to know the real key, hear him: "I first went to the text..." "I asked the logical question: 'Why did Paul write this chapter to these people?'" "Then I asked: 'What does it mean to us today?'" "A third question was equally obvious: 'Does our traditional interpretation of this Scripture match with Paul's intent?'"

It is of interest to know that some opposition to brother Fenter's lecture, "Do Not Go Beyond What Is Written," came from the platform on the very night it was given. Also, the very next day, Tuesday, the 24th of January, at the forum, it was again "a subject" of discussion. To use his thought about the hermeneutical firestorm raging through our brotherhood (*Image*, Vol. 6, Num. 2, March/April 1990, p. 18), let me say, this "was the beginning of many sparks that lit the fire raging against such a lecture on the new hermeneutics" as many today are not convinced of "a forest of traditions and comfortable conclusions," as per brother Randy Fenter.

One of those "many sparks" might have caused "a hermeneutical firestorm" at MacArthur Park Church of Christ where brother Fenter is now laboring. Just to the right of their pictures, separate picture of each elder (Branch, Brown, Clements, Hutchinson, Stewart, Taylor) was this article entitled, **From the Elders:**

> *"We believe the scriptures teach the need for sensitivity to the feelings of all who gather for worship. Romans 14:19 provides excellent guidance. 'Let us therefore make every effort to do what leads to peace and mutual edification.' In our opinion, clapping in the assembly does not contribute to peace and mutual edification. Therefore, we request the congregation refrain*

*from clapping or applause during this time" (**The Reminder**, Vol. XXI, Num. 50, November 21, 1990, inside right page).*

Let me close this by thanking God that these elders (named above) have both made and "stuck with" this decision. I am sure that this was not pleasing to brother Fenter.

Chapter Seven

THE PATTERN - AND "STRANGE" AND "UNCERTAIN" SOUNDS FROM SOME BRETHREN (Part III)

THE PATTERN - AND "STRANGE" AND "UNCERTAIN" SOUNDS FROM SOME BRETHREN

(Part III)

6. Strange And Uncertain Sounds From Jim Hackney. Our brother Jim Hackney preaches for the Midtown Church of Christ, 1701 Oakhurst Scenic Drive, Fort Worth, Texas. Just this past week he wrote an article captioned, "Let's Change Our Emphasis!" That article is now given as a "strange" and "uncertain" sound.

> *"I have seen a lot of changes in my years of association with the church. In my opinion (which is no better than yours) some have been good and some not so good. We have quit having classes on Sunday evenings...put a kitchen in the church building...allowed projected images to be shown in the auditorium... quit putting a tablecloth over the Lord's Supper emblems...broke the routine of two songs and a prayer...allowed men to specialize in certain areas of ministry...accepted other translations of the Bible...built Family Centers with gymnasiums in them...and some other changes in the future, some of which we would find hard to believe right now.*
>
> *There is one change more than any other which I hope to see in my lifetime and it is a change in emphasis. I pray to see the time when churches of Christ change their emphasis from* ***'What We Should Do'*** *to* ***'What God Has***

__Done__' for our salvation. That involves a change in emphasis from __our part__ to __His part__. It will cause us to focus on the __grace__ of God. It is extremely important that every person be exposed to the grace of God.

__'See to it that no one misses the grace of God and that no bitter root grows up to cause trouble and defile many,'__ Heb. 12:15.

I spent too many years of my Christian life not knowing what __grace__ was. The only thing I knew for sure was that 'we' didn't believe in it. It seems as though we always had a way to explain away God's gift of salvation. We were very adapt at tying it back into something that 'I' do. It was an underwritten rule in preaching that you never mentioned grace without mentioning the works that must accompany it. The reverse of that was perfectly okay. Consequently, we caused a great many people to 'miss the grace of God.' God forgive us!

Some will say that I am disregarding man's responsibility. Such is not the case! I want to show man the real reason for doing anything the Lord would have him do. The motivation is not 'in order to be saved' but rather 'because we are saved.' Emphasizing man's part over and above God's grace is just plain wrong! The New Testament boldly proclaims this again and again. To do so robs God of the glory and man of his assurance. What do you think?" (__The Grapevine__, Vol. 22, Num. 4, Jan. 23, 1991, inside left page, all emp. his).

Now before listing some thoughts relative to the

above article, allow me to direct your minds to an earlier, and much longer, one by this same brother. Since it is almost two pages, with three columns each, I cannot take the space to give it in its entirety (the thoughts are in a sense similar to the first one, but much more in detail, so I may just give my response to them together), but I can list his major points, as well as some of his statements. The title of this article is, "THERE IS FREEDOM." After giving his first example, asking two questions about it, he then says, "But before we become too critical we might stop for a moment to examine our own philosophy." Then he gives this scripture from Paul: "Now the Lord is the Spirit, and where the Spirit of the Lord is, there is freedom" (2 Cor. 3:17). He now gives two more illustrations, and then writes, "In trying to analyze that question (about why we don't feel spiritually free), I have concluded that the reason we often don't feel our freedom is because we've been robbed of it." He speaks of the "freedom robbers" and explains them as "things that keep us from living everyday with a real sense of salvation. These are the things that fuel the philosophy of wishing we had died at baptism" (one of the three illustrations). Now I outline for you his four "freedom robbers."

> a. "First of all, We don't understand God's grace." From his own experience, he says "one of the most difficult concepts for us to understand is that God gives us salvation (Eph. 2:8 & 9). For some reason that doesn't make sense to us... Yet that is exactly what our salvation is (Rom. 6:23)." He declares that "we keep trying to earn it,... deserve it... or be worthy of it... I can never do enough to believe I deserve salvation... that God owes me eternal life (1 John 1:8). Its no wonder that we doubt our salvation. We've been robbed of freedom simply because we don't understand the grace of God."

b. "The second freedom robber is this: We don't believe the scriptures." He tried to head off an objection "that many have to being saved by grace," which is: "If I'm given my salvation and its not based on my performance, then I will live as I please." Brother Hackney's response to this is "that it's just not so! If you ever really understand the grace of God, you will do more and live closer to His will than ever before in your life. You'll do it because you are saved and not in order to be saved... and there's a big difference. I know because I have tried them both. The grace of God brings freedom." On this particular point we find him giving a few scriptures: John 8:32; James 1:25; 2:12; 1 John 5:13; 1 Thessalonians 5:9; Romans 10:13. He asked: "Can it be that we just don't believe scripture?"

c. "Our third problem is: We don't trust Jesus." Here he gives John 8:36; Ephesians 3:12; Galatians 5:21 and Hebrews 2:14-15. He simply on this point says, "Trust Jesus... Trust Jesus... Trust Him!... trust Him... trust Jesus."

d. "And Fourthly, We don't fight legalism." This is one of the "greatest robbers of all time... It's one of the most insidious false doctrines to ever strike the Christian movement (he is referring, of course, to meriting salvation, keeping commands and trying to earn salvation by performance)." He stated that "the brave are called upon today to join the apostle Paul in his fight for freedom... a fight that will move you from the position of earning salvation based on performance to the position of receiving salvation based on God's grace... then we will be free." He now returns to one of his three illustra-

> tions and says, "Friends, I for one am glad that I didn't die when I was baptized." Then to his second one, "I am glad that my children do not have to be murdered with a butcher knife to have security of salvation." He closes this particular thought with, "I'm tired of being robbed of my freedom because..." (*Image*, Vol. 2, Num. 12, June 15, 1986, pp. 9-10).

There is no doubt in my mind about "The Movement" that we began to hear about just a few years back, being, I personally believe, the movement of "The New Hermeneutic" bolstered by "the Scholarship Movement." This movement is being hosted on our college campuses (thus far one at Pepperdine, one at Abilene and the one for 1991 will be at David Lipscomb. Then the next one is to be at Harding, followed the following year at Oklahoma Christian College. Of course, these plans could change).

I have mentioned that found in the preceding paragraph, because it speaks of "one" of the many facets of the movement that is among us today, that of "grace." The kind of grace that would eliminate, take away, remove and abolish anything about "obedience" on the part of man. These brethren no longer emphasize and stress "the conditional" side of salvation, an active, live, responsive and obedient faith to the demands, commands, of God as clearly set forth in His Word. Basically it is "grace alone," and moves right into "once saved always saved." You see, no one is wrong, everyone is right, there is no pattern, no norm, blueprint or guideline, Christians are those who just believe in Jesus and all believers are brethren. Indeed, there are Christians in all denominations, doctrine does not matter and is not a real concern for discipline, our old way of interpretation must go, the new hermeneutic must be accepted, and this way we can soon have the mechanical instruments of music, women in official capacities, be one with our religious neighbors (all just be part of the ecumenical movement) and can have the unity for which Christ prayed (if you can take all of that in without getting a headache). One of their "keys" to this is their view on "grace," and that is why I took the time to state a few more thoughts just now. Brother Hackney is among those, to use one of their "famous" words, of this "stripe."

a. It is strange to hear of "the changes" that he has seen in his years of association with the church, and to mention them as perhaps they have all been approved and accepted. Liberalism is always "changing" some things, but I doubt they would be concerned about "the tablecloth over the Lord's Supper."

b. It is strange that he would speak about "the future changes," and then say, "some of which we would find hard to believe right now." The above paragraph may have aspects of that "change," yes, it would be hard to believe for a New Testament Christian, but if such comes, be it "here," "there," or "elsewhere," does not mean it is pleasing to God. Man's acceptance of "some change" does not automatically make it God-approved, God-authorized, that is.

c. It is strange, this emphasis about which brother Hackney is speaking, as we cannot change one iota about the grace of God. Regardless of what any man might say, we are saved by grace, but no one is saved without meeting God's conditions, therefore, we must inform man there is something he must do (cf. 1 John 2:29; 3:7; Acts 10:34-35; etc., etc.) There was something that was told Saul that he "must" do (cf. Acts 9:6; 22:10).

d. It is strange to place "one" side (God's) against another side (man's), when both are absolute "musts." Indeed, it is important for every person to be "exposed to the grace of God," but not to something that is a siamese twin to "grace only," or the doctrine of "once saved always saved."

e. It is strange that he would have to use (well, maybe it is not so strange after all) the *NIV* and give Hebrews 12:15 out of it (read again that quote, please) right after he said, "It is extremely important that every person be exposed to the grace of God." So he gives Hebrews 12:15, "See to it that no one misses the grace of God..." I would like to point out that this may be a twisting of the word "misses" the grace of God in connection with "exposed to" the grace of God. The Greek word is *hustereo*. It is found sixteen times in the New Testament (cf. Rom. 3:23; Heb. 4:1) and is translated as "lack," "to be in want," "come behind," "come short," "fail," etc. The word in Hebrews 12:15 is a present active participle, nominative singular masculine, and I would suggest that brother Hackney study Thayer, p. 646; Arndt Gingrich, p. 856; Kittell, Vol. 8, p. 592; etc., and note how it is given, is to be translated and, of course, the "meaning" of the word. To leave the impression that it is almost a synonym to "expose," "misses" the point and "misses" the "misses" of Hebrews 12:15! No wonder they like these "other translations."

f. It is strange to hear a gospel preacher speak of "too many years of my Christian life not knowing what grace was." Then to add to that thought: "The only thing I knew for sure was that 'we' didn't believe in it" (he can speak for himself, but not for the church, as it has always believed in the grace of God!). If a man wants to be saved, in the Bible way, he had best "tie" the grace of God to "man's acceptance of it by an active, living and working faith." No one is saved by grace (or faith, for that matter, without any further acts of obedience) and grace alone. I went to college for eight and a half years and I never heard of this "unwritten rule" for preachers. Thank God we had sense enough to know that grace brought the plan and faith caused man to obey it! (cf. Titus 2:11-12, grace teaches us!).

g. It is strange, this saying: "The motivation is not 'in order to be saved' but rather 'because we are saved.'" Say what you desire about that statement, but The Book says man's faith put him into this grace: "Being therefore justified by faith, we have peace with God through our Lord Jesus Christ; through whom also we have had our access by faith into this grace..." (Rom. 5:1-2). It is stated that "grace is in Christ" (2 Tim. 2:1), now how does a man get "into Christ"? (cf. Gal. 3:26-27; Rom. 6:3-4). Is it not "faith working through love" (cf. Gal. 5:6)? He ended this brief article with "What do you think?" Therefore, I have told him exactly what "I think" it is that is "in harmony" with the will of God, but "out of harmony" with the new hermeneutic.

h. It is strange that there are so many implications in the article, "There is Freedom."

(1) Is it implied that no Christian can be in any danger of ever losing his soul?

(2) Is it implied that he, brother Hackney, now understands, and knows, what most Christians do not know, the real truth?

(3) Is it implied that he, brother Hackney, understands grace but few others, if any, in the church understand grace?

(4) Is it implied that God gives salvation unconditionally?

(5) Is it implied that the majority of people in the church feel that we can earn, merit, deserve, etc., our salvation?

(6) Is it implied that if a person does understand the grace of God that he will always live closer to God's will? If so, is it implying the wrong thing about Demas, Peter and some of the seven churches of Asia, as evidently they did not understand, not in brother Hackney's viewpoint, the grace of God as they became indifferent to it.

(7) Is it implied then that the warnings of the Bible are of no value? I wrote a tract on "Falling From Grace" and the first thing I did was to list ninety verses that teach one can fall. I then listed thirty verses showing that the blessings of God are contingent upon our faithfulness (there are at least sixty such verses). I listed five major warnings just in Hebrews. The Bible declares that a man can "turn back," "draw back," "slide back," "shrink back," "fall back," and "look back." He implies that such will not be the case if you understand the grace of God as he now understands it. If he can answer all of the above, then I will gladly give

him the other seven pages of my tract. His implication is totally false.

(8) Is it implied that, regardless of a Christian's performance, he will still inherit heaven? (cf. Matt. 7:13-14; 2 Pet. 2:20-22; Rev. 3:14-15; 2:10; etc.).

(9) Is it implied, I believe it is, that he does not know what true legalism is? One thing for sure, obeying the commandments is an indication of love (cf. John 14:15, 21, 23; 1 John 2:3-6; 5:3), not being legalistic.

(10) Is Baptist doctrine implied in his article? "You will do it because you are saved and not in order to be saved," is his statement.

(11) Is it implied that for a thing to be wrong the Bible has to state it explicitly?

(12) Is the doctrine of "once saved always saved," "the great umbrella of grace," implied in his article? (I suggest that you read it extremely close and very thoroughly and digest it completely before you sound forth an "amen.").

This article is "a strange sound," to be from one so learned, one who "knows that he knows," and who "knows that others among us know not what we know." I've never yet heard any one in the church of my Lord teach, preach or practice that (1) salvation was not a gift, (2) that we are trying to earn, deserve, do enough, are worthy of it and that God owes it to us, (3) that we are not to believe Ephesians 2:8-9 (yet if we do understand it, we "will do more,") as we have been taught it, (4) that trusting Jesus is totally on the grace of God, and has nothing to do with anything else, no performance at all, etc. If "we do even more," won't someone else accuse us of trying to earn and merit salvation?

I have known a long time that (1) salvation is a gift of God, (2) it is by the grace of God that anyone will be saved, (3) grace is God's plan to save and that it came to us in the person of Jesus the Christ, (4) that it came "teaching us," (5) that it is doing for us what we cannot do, (6) that no one can earn, merit, be worthy of it, (7) God does not owe it to me (wouldn't it have been great if he had documented each thought? I mean thoughts like we didn't believe in grace, did not know what it was, was working to earn and merit salvation, felt we had no freedom, etc., etc., etc. and I do not mean his own life either! I mean full statements by men, women, children, and full quotations of each, verbatim from preachers, elders, teachers in the church. These subjective statements ought to be so documented and not just given as "I know" statements and expect the church to believe the same! Yea, and not just some woman somewhere who killed her own children... as a "proving example." I mean a Christian!), (8) that it (grace) is God's riches at Christ's expense and (9) it is something we "needed" but did not "deserve." Evidently, brother Hackney sure had a terrible teacher, unlearned elders and preachers, and perhaps even those of his own family who have taught him to work to earn his salvation. I am sorry that he was so raised, taught, instructed and then grew to a man, preached for years and just did not know any better. I am more sorrowful that he now believes as he has written, and surely, most assuredly, there is no reason for me to fully explain that in the light of what I have written.

7. **Strange And Uncertain Sounds From Jeff Walling.** Brother Jeff Walling is the preacher for the Mission Viejo Church of Christ, 26558 Marguerite Parkway, Mission

Viejo, CA 92692. Again, there is no way to list all such from brother Walling, but I do want to give some of his statements from the Fifteenth Annual Tulsa International Soul Winning Workshop (March 29-31, 1990) speech that he made on Friday night, 7:30 p.m., March 30, 1990. His assigned subject was, "That They All May Be One." Before I do, let me assure you that I have the tape, and also have my transcription right on my desk as I type this. It is not my aim, ambition or goal to misquote or misapply anything that a brother says, take it out of context, etc., and, as all the others, there is nothing personal against this or any brother, but there are some "strange" and "uncertain" sounds that need to be heard by many.

a. "And I really want you to get used to being with a lot of Christians, because in spite of what some of my brothers think, I think there's going to be a ton of folks that God's going to give grace and mercy to... I don't think... a small crowd."

b. "I'm afraid I have to share with you a weak thing within this lesson with regard to the church... good at singing... at amen-ing... we just have a problem with one minor issue, getting along with each other. Unity isn't our strong suit... If you know much about the churches of Christ, you know that we ain't good at this... I need to start this lesson by asking God, 'forgive us for being so crummy at getting along.' In that prayer he prayed in part, '... that I and many whom I love dearly have been no help when it comes to seeing Jesus' request answered... precious little on that which ought to draw us together... love and mercy and everlasting grace... forgive us, for we don't know what we're doing... fill us with your spirit that we might... learn to get along...'"

c. "There are two odd things about this request... that all of them may be one...say it with me, will you? *That we may be one*. One more time, *That we may be one.* The problem is...when you say the word 'we.' What if we were at a gathering where there were people sitting next to you who didn't go to a church of Christ? Now they believed in Jesus. They loved the Lord...they are not fellowshipping in a building that says 'church of Christ' on it. Now just free your mind up for that bizarre possibility."

d. "The first odd thing...Jesus doesn't say...the obedient might be one...that the 'church of Christers' might be one...He prays for those who will believe in me...put their faith and trust in me...the text says 'believers'...I'll tell you what, in order to preach the text, we can't get into this lesson without appreciating the fact that Jesus asked that we would throw the calfrope around all of those who just believe in Him, and pray and work for the unity of all believers."

e. "The second odd thing...He doesn't say that they be united...that they agree...be 'one.' Not just sing 'We are one in the Spirit, but I still hate your guts!' Take every one who believes in me...my first challenge tonight in preaching the text is convincing you that Jesus was right...is important..."

f. "Three quick reasons. Number one,...Jesus was sent by God...the power to get along in Christ...If there's anything that oughta awe people about Tulsa,...that we could all hug and talk...folks are hugging them..."

g. "Second, it's a symptom of what is happening to

us...I've gotta go through this stuff quickly...be like-minded is a symptom of real commitment to Christ...True commitment to Jesus will cause me to be out there rubbing shoulders with all believers... to love every human that comes across my path and causes me to work toward oneness with every believer in Jesus. Now that, folks, is the kind of commitment that we need to call ourselves to."

h. "And thirdly, it is the solution to the world's hurt. I wonder why the church is often so ineffective at meeting the needs of the world...we've got care groups and hug groups and...if you will be united you will become the solution to the world's problems. Imagine what all believers could do if we'd just start holding hands to work for God. But before I hold your hand, I've gotta check your hand out. Whose hand am I holding here?...Land's sakes, if we have to, let's pass out gloves, but let's HOLD HANDS! Whatever it takes!...I recognize that unity for you may mean at first reaching across the aisle to grasp the hand of the person who's across your aisle...but brothers and sisters, we've got to reach outside our doors...the hand of every believer in Jesus to seek some kind of oneness."

i. "...some practicalities...what oneness in Christ doesn't demand and what it does demand...from three scriptures...1 Corinthians 12:12-14...Paul tries in several verses to underline the fact that unity and oneness does not mean we all in the body have the same function...God's desire that we be ONE was not desiring that we be CLONED."

j. "Now, let's get down to where you stop amen-ing and start going 'Ooooo! That hurts'! We have almost homogenized the churches of Christ. We have worked so hard subtly and carefully to make all of our churches so cloned, do the same, that you could almost fall asleep in Nashville and wake up in Dallas and not know you'd changed. You could almost walk into a church in any city and go on automatic pilot and come out the other side and it's like a motel room, you'd never know you were in a different city... Oh! Call that fudge to repent!... at the world of believers and said, because you don't do it like we do it, we divorce ourselves from you!... Ahh! I ain't holdin' your hand..."

k. "... we take our suits and our own tradition and we wanna strap 'em on to every brother... cause them to cease to be eyes, or kidneys, or gallbladders, or whatever they are. Brothers and sisters, in your church you need those old gallbladders."

I most sincerely almost hesitate to say a single thing about such a lesson, one that would almost make any good student of the Bible ill, given as a lecture on the farewell prayer of our Master. If it doesn't mean any more than "holding hands," "hugging," "throwing a calfrope around all of those who just believe in Him," "learning to get along" (Jeff said he was thrilled to speak on "getting along"), "rubbing shoulders with all believers... every believer in Jesus," it doesn't mean much. Why did Jesus have to shed his precious blood to have this explanation preached? That is a high cost of "hugging."

It is strange for me to hear a man speaking about how many people *"I think"* that God's going to give grace and mercy to, when the Bible gives us the very words of Jesus on this subject in Matthew 7:13-14. *It is strange* to hear a man deliver a lesson on John seventeen and not emphasize "through their word" (vs. 21), "knowledge of the only true God and Jesus Christ being life eternal" (vs.

3), "an explanation of the 'these only' and 'them'" (vs. 20), "the context of the chapter in which verses 20-23 are given," "the sanctifying of himself and the others" (vss. 18-19), "a mention of verse eleven about 'that they may be one, even as we are one,'" "thy word" (vss. 6, 14, 17), "the words" (vs. 8), "the truth" (vss. 17, 19), "the distinction between those God gave Jesus and the world" (vss. 6, 8-9, 11-12), and "to whom is Jesus going to give eternal life" (vss. 2-3), etc. *It is strange* for me, even from someone whose sermons have been advertised to be chuck full of wit and humor, to hear a gospel preacher speak of "us being so crummy at getting along," "we don't know what we are doing (let brother Walling speak for himself, but not for the church), and have been no help when it comes to seeing Jesus' request answered" (sermons like this one surely aren't any help, but again, let him speak for himself only), "to use the words 'church of Christers'" (I just wonder how my precious Lord, the Christ, feels about his own men speaking of his beautiful bride in such a manner), "...I still hate your guts" (such talk from God's pulpit!), "referring to this 'stuff'" and "call that fudge to repent." *It is strange* what he implies about the New Testament Church, about "believers in Jesus," about "Jesus not saying they be united, not agreeing, but being one," "that Jesus did not say the obedient might be one" (Jeff, read verse 11, just as one verse on this and then repeat your statement. However, read again to find other verses that state the same), "that true commitment to Jesus is rubbing shoulders with all believers," "about homogenizing the church," and about "being cloned." I challenge any good logician to read (to hear) his entire lesson and come up with anything less than the fact that every person who "just believes in Jesus" is in the body, the church, the kingdom and that there are Christians in every denomination, as this is clearly the "implication." *It is not strange* that he uses the *NIV* on some of the passages, *but it is strange* about his reading of Philippians 2:1-3 (his words are "the first three verses"). He might say he was just paraphrasing, rephrasing, summarizing, interpreting, metaphrasing, rewording or rehashing the verses, but the fact remains he said: "Paul, in Philippians two, the first three verses, he says..." Having checked at least fifty versions, translations and paraphrases, I did not find his wording. I checked my Greek New Testaments and it is not even in a horseshoe game - being close - to the Greek text, for example, the word "grace" (Greek, *charis*) is not in the Greek text for those verses (meaning, of course, the texts that I personally have) neither is the word "good" (Greek, *agathos*). It may be he made fun of those who know Greek (he used iota, zeta, and theta..."that's one for the Greeks in here"). Maybe Jeff made his own translation, if so, maybe he thought *agapes* was *agathos* and *charan* was *charis*, but these are four different Greek words. Here is what he gave: "If God has done anything good for you, if you have any grace, if you have any comfort, if you have anything good, if God's been kind to you, then be one." Guess what? Even the word for God (Greek *theos*) is not in any of my Greek texts in verses one through three. (If you check this out, check out also his statement "that we may be one," from his text of John seventeen. The Greek text says, "that all may be one." The phrase "as we are one" is used at the closing of verse twenty-two in reference to God and Christ, but even it is not close to the one he gave. In verse twenty we have *auton* (their), in verse twenty-one we have *autoi* (they), *en hemin* (in us), in verse twenty-two we have *autois* (them), *kathos hemeis* (as we), and then in verse twenty-three we have *autois* (them) twice used. This is as far as I can determine from my own Greek texts that I have).

It use to be "a strange thing" when one of God's

preachers would go and participate with denominations by singing with them and preaching for them, but this "is not a strange thing" with brother Walling. I give the following from his Tulsa lecture that we just noticed.

> *"A few months back I spoke at a convention, a youth leaders' program at which there was a multiplicity of groups represented. And when I say groups, I'm saying people with different religious backgrounds and different traditions... opinions...beliefs about things. There were some folks there that you might describe as pentecostal, and there were there from different church groupings of the name that you can rattle off if you read through the yellow pages. And I had asked to speak on the topic of praise."*

Ozark Christian College (Christian Church) of Joplin, Missouri held their annual preaching and teaching convention and homecoming on February 22-28, 1987. You guessed it. Brother Walling was one of their speakers. In fact, in his tape he said, "It's been a lot of fun being here...I had four lectures today..." And, of course, the group known as *Acappella* was also there (as Jeff said, "I love being with those fellows...good friends...a lot of teen rallies all across the country with Acappella...And I am just 'proud as a papa' to stand up here tonight and share their message in song with you...The singers...very gifted...with the gift of intonation and all those other musical things that help 'em sound good.") with their "bar-um, bar-um, bop-bop a lu bop a lop bam boom" (imitating instruments with the voice). This was the 45th Anniversary of what was formerly the Ozark Bible College. During this convention, brother Walling spoke on "Lordship Is Relationship." I want us to observe some of the "strange" statements (strange for a New Testament Gospel preacher to make) he made in that speech.

a. "And you thought we didn't have instruments!" (laughter, applause).

b. "...getting to hear me today has been a rare experience to hear somebody from the non-instrumental group of our fellowship. Whatever, we haven't come up with good words for that. I hope we never do. I hope we lose the words we've got now that describe the division, but (clapping) whatever you want to call it...You see, we're all Christians here." He goes on to say that these to whom he was speaking is 'my family' and 'brothers, I love being here.'"

c. "It is a blessing for me to gather together and sing with you,...tomorrow night to sing with the members of my congregation."

d. "My commitment is to God's word and doing things as effectively and Biblically as I can. For that reason I don't go around the country preaching against instrumental music. I go around preaching 'for' praise and singing, and preaching and teaching...Some things really aren't very important but other things are extremely important."

e. "Real Lordship in life is knowing God. As some would say, you're talking about a better felt than told feeling, YEP!" He also says, "Knowing the Lord is not just rules and you can put slash legalism by that if you want to...We're not going to heaven because of the rules...A relationship with God, if you will, is based on, a real relationship, trust, trust. Do you trust the voice of Jesus?" He continues: "...doing all the right things,...punching all the right buttons,... following the rules,... is a miserable way to live. It's a pitiable way to live. And, besides, following all the rules is not why you're going to heaven."

I am not going, at this particular juncture, to say anything about the above quotations. I will, for the time being, let them stand as they are. I want, however, to continue with some of the things that transpired after the lecture at Joplin, Missouri (Ozark Christian College, Tuesday, February 24, 1987).

In the *Four State Gospel News*, edited by Bobby Key, with Don Deffenbaugh being the News editor, there appeared an item of news in that section, "News and Views" (Vol. 26, Num. 4, April 1987, p. 1), relative to the Ozark Christian College and its convention and home-coming. This news item was written by Don Deffenbaugh. It spoke of Jeff Walling's speech (the one from whence the quotes above came) and gave various items, statements, from it.

Brother Walling then wrote the following as pertaining to that news item (the one in the *Four State Gospel News*):

"The April issue of this paper quoted certain statements I had made in a speech at Ozark Christian College which prompted some questions and may have caused some confusion among your readers. In order to clarify, I have not, nor do I now, support, encourage or practice the use of instrumental music in the worship of the church. Further, I do not support any 'movement' which would introduce this practice into our worship. I am sorry that misunderstandings arose from the publishing

of my comments. For a longer response to this situation I refer interested readers to an article by me in the August issue of the ***Christian Chronicle*** *or to my office: Mission Viejo Church of Christ, 26558 Marguerite Parkway, Mission Viejo, CA 92692. May the Lord bless His Church and may Christ be seen in us" (July 16, 1987).*

This letter from brother Walling was printed in the *Four State Gospel News* (Vol. 26, Num. 9, September 1987, p. 1). First, let me state that brother Walling is wrong about the date of his "longer response," as it was in the July issue of the *Christian Chronicle* (Vol. 44, Num. 7, July, 1987, "Opinion" section, p. 23). Second, from some indication, such as silence to some questions asked, brother Walling may not answer if you write and ask him certain pin-pointed questions. He does say, "...or to my office" and gives the full address.

I would never want to be anything but open, fair, honest and most thorough in anything I quote (note how I document each item from which I quote these "strange" and "uncertain" sounds), therefore, it is only fair that I now take the time and the space and give that "longer response" of his in the *Christian Chronicle.*

"To the editor: Those who make their living by public teaching will always struggle with the problem of being misquoted, misunderstood or misrepresented. It's an occupational hazard.

Recently, an article in a publication has caused confusion with regard to my position and feelings on instrumental music in worship. The situation arose when selected sentences from a tape of lecture that I had given were published without the full context and without contacting me.

I had been invited as a 'non-instrumental' minister and some deference had been shown to my convictions by having an a cappella group sing before I spoke and some a cappella songs sung in the services in which I took part. Unfortunately, during the conclusion of one lecture, an organist began playing. Later those in charge apologized. But this apology was not noted in the article.

Since that time I've received numerous calls from those who were both curious and concerned. I felt compelled to contact the ***Christian Chronicle****, a publication that has done its best to avoid becoming an issue-oriented paper.*

In short: I do not endorse or advocate instrumental music in worship. It is my conviction that the church of Christ should worship through singing as God authorized and history shows the early church practiced. It is to this practice that I hold and that we call all worshipers of Jesus in a spirit of restoring New Testament Christianity. If any comments or quotations have appeared to suggest I feel differently, I am sorry this confusion has arisen.

One other comment may be appropriate. While situations like this are bound to occur, their frequency might be diminished if those who edit and publish such journals contacted the person about whom they write, especially when those comments may be understood in a confusing or controversial light.

If you have questions about the matter, please feel free to write or call me or my elders in Mission Viejo, Calif." (Jeff Walling, and I repeat, Vol. 44, Num. 7, July 1987, "opinion" section, p. 23).

After all of this, both Acappella and brother Walling were to appear at the Northeast Mississippi Youth Rally slated for August 20, 1988, in Booneville, Mississippi. Knowing of these things, these various happenings, and the fact that brother Walling had mentioned twice about having people to contact him (both are given above in his own statements), with one saying, "If you have questions about the matter please feel free to write or call me..." This is exactly what the very wise, knowledgeable and godly elders of the East Corinth Church of Christ in Corinth, Mississippi did (cf. 1 John 4:1; 1 Pet. 3:15; Acts 20:28-31; 2 John 9-11; Matt. 7:15-23; Gal. 2:4-5; 2 Pet. 1:12-15; 2:13; Rom. 16:17-18; Phil. 3:17-19; etc.). These men of vision, foresight, and men who care for the flock of God, watch over and warn the flock of approaching dangers, wrote brother Walling on June 23, 1988 (and I want you to note that this was from the elders, not the preacher, and that is the great way that such should be handled and I thank God for such). I now give their three paragraph letter, along with some of the questions they asked brother Walling. After the inside address and the proper saluation, their letter begins.

"We are writing to you to ask you a few Bible questions. We hope you will take a few minutes of your time and fill out this questionnaire. Every question is designed so you can give a yes or no answer. If you would like to include a passage of scripture or feel that further

explanation is necessary, feel free to include it.

We are asking these questions because we see you are scheduled to speak at the Northeast Mississippi Youth Rally on August 20, 1988. Since this is in our area and some of our young people may attend, we want to be assured of your faithfulness (soundness).

It is the policy of the church here at East Corinth to have all missionaries, preachers, and teachers fill this out. Do not feel that you are being singled out. The elders here, in keeping with our charge to 'guard' and 'feed the flock,' use this means to make sure all we do is in accordance with God's will.

Do you believe the Bible is the verbally, inerrant, plenary, inspired Word of God? yes ___ no ___

Do you believe a person can become a Christian without becoming a member of the Church of Christ? yes ___ no ___

Do you believe there are Christians scattered among the various denominations? yes ___ no___

Do you believe the use of mechanical instruments of music in worship is sinful and that one will be lost for using them? yes ___ no ___

Do you believe one can sing with a mechanical instrument of music and meet with God's approval? yes ___ no ___

Do you believe it is permissible to participate in any kind of joint activities with denominations? yes ___ no ___

Do you believe that women (girls) can pray or teach in the presence of men (whether in worship or not)? yes ___ no ___

Do you believe a person can divorce their mate and marry again with God's approval? yes ___ no ___

Do you believe a person who has been divorced (but not because of their mate's fornication) can remain in a second marriage with God's approval? yes ___ no ___

What version of the Bible do you use in teaching and/or preaching? ____________

Do you believe the elders have the final authority in making decisions that pertain to the optional matters of the local congregation? yes ___ no ___

Do you believe those who are 'disorderly' should be withdrawn from if they will not repent? yes ___ no ___

Would you be in favor of using films with denominational people as the speakers? yes ___ no ___

Do you believe individuals who teach contrary to New Testament doctrine should be publicly named (marked) and avoided? yes ___ no ___

Would you 'hedge' on any of the answers you have given? yes ___ no ___

I have, at random, typed off some of the questions these elders sent to brother Walling. They also included questions on the church, the second coming of Christ, the Holy Spirit, evolution, the Lord's supper, Christian living, benevolence, modern versions, fellowship, and Bible authority.

The next thing "in print," as far as I know, was the marvelous issue of "Light For Living" (the bulletin of the East Corinth Church of Christ) written by the beloved soldier of the cross, and their faithful local evangelist, Garland M. Robinson. The inside caption of the page read: "Jeff Walling's Ozark Speech." It included, in addition to that speech, thoughts about the April 1987 issue of *Four State Gospel News*, Jeff's letter of July 16, 1987 (gave it in full), and the fact the elders had written brother Walling asking him what he believes and teaches concerning the many doctrinal issues facing the Lord's church today. It closed with "A Note Of Explanation." Once again, brother Robinson assured all of the readers of the bulletin that he had nothing against brother Walling as a person, nothing of a personal nature but only was concerned about what he has said and done (he did this as he "opened" this issue of the bulletin and did it again as he "closed" it, and it seems nothing could be done in any finer way to forestall such comments as might arise). (Vol. 4, Num. 32, August 7, 1988, pp. 1-7).

The next item from brother Walling was entitled: "On The Use Of Instruments In Worship and Sin."

> *"The use of instruments in worship is never specifically addressed in the New Testament. Singing is commanded. Early church history and the apostles' practice are the strongest cases for excluding instruments from worship. During the lifetime of the apostles, and for the first few hundred years of the church thereafter, no instruments were used in worship. Their introduction caused a flurry of controversy and contention. It seems clear that the*

men who knew Jesus best chose not to use instruments in the worship of the church.

For these reasons, I have never chosen to serve at a church which uses instruments in worship. I believe that the scriptures call for, and history supports, accapella music in worship. This has always been my practice and teaching as a minister in the church of Christ. On occasion, when invited, I have spoken for groups that use the instrument. Some contend that this means I support all their practices and beliefs. This is not true. I have also spoken for the Kiwanis, but I do not agree with all they do or believe.

Others criticize because I do not make the instrumental question my theme every time I speak to these groups. Paul spoke before the Jews in the synagogue and the Greeks at the Acropolis, yet there were some issues of their differences he never addressed. I imitate the apostle Paul and try to use my allotted time to speak about the center of Christianity: Christ and Him crucified. I always share about Jesus in every lecture I give to every group. I also address the instrumental issue at some point when with those who use the instrument...but not in every speech in every session. Not mentioning the instrumental issue each time I speak, betrays only that I feel Jesus Christ is by far the more important topic.

Finally, if one believes that instrumental music in worship is wrong, yet does so anyway, he is committing sin. If one substitutes God's command to sing with a command to play, he is committing sin. But in my opinion, I must not judge the state of a fellow Christian who, in good conscience, approves singing with an instrument. To do so would place myself in jeopardy of grievous sin indeed: Judging a brother by my opinion.

May Jesus be glorified by all we do, and may He be our most talked about topic" (Jeff Walling, Minister, Mission Viejo Church of Christ, December 1, 1988).

a. *It is strange*, in view of Ephesians 5:11; Romans 16:17-18; 2 John 9-11 that brother Walling would participate with various denominational groups (remember the convention of youth leaders) and with those at Ozark Christian College. Actually, no other point has to be made, not if you believe the New Testament.

b. *It is strange,* that he would be so associated with the group called Acappella because of the tension and strife they have caused, yea, for more than one group, but especially for the church in Paris, Tennessee.

c. *It is strange,* to hear him speak of "...the non-instrumental group of 'our fellowship.'" To say "we're all Christians here." To call them "my family" and say "I'm offering an invitation just like I would any place I've preached up until now."

d. *It is strange,* to hear him speak of "singing with you," "Some things really aren't very important..." and "I don't go around the country preaching against instrumental music."

e. *It is strange*, to hear him say, "We're not going

to heaven because of the rules." Can a person go to heaven without the rules? Watch the attitude in "doing all the right things, punching all the right buttons, following the rules (I guess you can break them)."

f. *It is strange*, to hear him say "I have not, nor do I now support, encourage... the use of instrumental music... I do not support any 'movement' which would introduce this practice into our worship" (Jeff, you had best stay clear of the Christian Church, because if they get the chance, they'll do it). Any time we participate in denominational groups, etc., we are, to that extent, not only violating God's written instructions but also encouraging the practices of such. Unless, of course, we are there to truly, most explicitly, make known the New Testament pattern of things.

g. *It is strange*, that brother Walling would talk about someone writing an article publicly without "contacting me." When a man is in a public place and giving a public lesson and it is taped, etc., it is ridiculous that a preacher thinks he must be contacted personally for that which was done publicly (Matt. 18:20 does not apply! That deals with a private matter between two brethren.).

h. *It is strange*, what brother Walling DOES NOT SAY in all the articles he wrote. If it is his conviction that the church of Christ should worship through singing... is it also his conviction that the denominations should do the same? Is it just "a practice" with us, or is it "in harmony with the truth of God"? If he believes that God authorized singing, then can one do that which is not authorized or participate with those doing that which is not authorized without sinning?

i. *It is strange*, that brother Walling would encourage people to write or call him, and yet, when the elders of the East Corinth Church of Christ wrote him he refused to answer. That is right, *Jeff did not answer their questions* (like he referred to the August issue of the *Christian Chronicle* when it was the July issue, so he mentioned they asked him 47 questions, but they did not, it was 43. And like he said write or call...but then *he refused to answer their questions*, so they might as well not have written).

j. *It is strange*, that a man will participate with a denomination, give a public speech, it is taped and sent around the country, and yet when someone writes about it, he whines! They always cry, "you misquoted, misunderstood, misrepresented me or took it out of context, did not give the context, just lifted a thought here and one there, etc." I'll tell you what, I have the tapes, the articles, the letter, the papers, etc., and if you think I've taken things wrongly, you are sadly mistaken. It is the blanket truth that an explicit statement is hard to cover and rationalize away. It makes me wonder if he is not trying to hold on to being "a party" to both the denominational world and also to the New Testament Church.

k. *It is strange*, to have to write and try to clear up the confusion from his speeches. If he can speak as clearly as he ought to be able to, why would all this happen in the first place? If he will stop worshipping with denominations, those of different traditions, opinions, beliefs, like pentecostal, and from different church groupings, then he will not be making such statements and they will not be called into question.

l. *It is strange*, to hear him talk about "our tradition." Let it be known that "tradition" is not always a bad word (cf. 1 Cor. 11:2; 2 Thess. 2:15; 3:6; 1 Cor. 14:37; 4:17 and perhaps a study of the Greek *paradosis* would help).

m. *It is strange*, that in private conversation, at times, he makes sure that what he says is not "repeated," or "published."

n. *It is strange*, that brother Walling does not seemingly know or understand that what the Bible teaches it does so either explicitly or implicitly and that one is as binding as the other. I ask again that each reader read extremely careful his statements, observe his wording, what he says, how he says it and what he does not say. As an example, does "the use of instruments in worship" (his wording) have to be "specifically addressed in the New Testament" (his wording)? Is there "anything" that God condemns by "implication"? What does Jeff mean when he says (speaking about the apostles), "it seems clear (Jeff, does it just "seem" clear?) that the men who knew Jesus best chose (Jeff, why did they so choose, what made them choose, and was it just a matter of "personal choice"?) not to use instruments in the worship of the church"?

o. *It is strange*, to hear Jeff say, "On occasion (Jeff, is it just "on occasion" or is it "just a little bit more frequent than that"?) ... (I wouldn't think he would speak "unless invited," so I left his words "when invited" out). "I have spoken for groups (this is not a singular word) that use the instrument."

How many times does a person "fellowship"(?) darkness, works contrary to the doctrine of Christ, BEFORE it is a violation of 2 John 9-11? It seems to me the words of Paul are clearer than that, as he says, "HAVE NO FELLOWSHIP..." (Eph. 5:11), and "NO" DOES NOT MEAN "SOME" FELLOWSHIP, as brother H. A. (Buster) Dobbs said (*The Spiritual Sword*, Vol. 5, Num. 2, January, 1974, p. 29). By the way, the same passage, Jeff, says, "BUT RATHER EVEN REPROVE (footnote has "convict") THEM," and this is not to be overlooked, or is it? I just believe that "anything," yes, "anything" in God's Book is important.

p. *It is strange*, that brother Walling would make the statement "Some contend that this means I support all their practices and beliefs," and I wish he would "document" that statement about "the some" and "supporting all their practices and beliefs." What is it that Jeff "always shares about Jesus" in every lecture? Is it that only "a few" (cf. Matt. 7:13-14) will make it? Is it that "His Word" will judge us (cf. John 12:48)? Is it that he has a doctrine ("the doctrine of Christ," 2 John 9-10) that man is not "to go beyond"?

q. *It is strange*, after writing, "If one substitutes God's command to sing with a command to play, he is committing sin" to then say, "But in my opinion, I must not judge the state of a fellow Christian who, in good conscience, approves singing with an instrument." Brother, that is strange! Jeff, if it is, as you said, "committing a sin," and we know what sin is and what it does (surely we know 1 John 3:4; Isa. 59:1-2; Rom. 6:23; Rev. 21:27; 1 John 5:17; Rom. 6:1-2; 8:1-3; 1 John 1:7-10; 5:16;

James 5:16; Eph. 1:7; Col. 1:14; James 4:17; James 1:13-15; 1 Tim. 5:19-22; etc., etc.), as it is so declared by the Word of God, what does "your opinion" have to do with it? When you tell a man, by the Book, that he is committing a sin, are you judging (cf. John 7:24; Luke 7:43)? What is "the state" of one who, even if it is, as Jeff says, "in good conscience," that he "approves singing with an instrument" (cf. Acts 23:1; 1 Tim. 1:12-17)? What does "a good conscience" have to do with the violation of a "command of God," by which one commits sin, in relation to "his state"? Jeff, if a man so commits a sin, and remains with and in the doing of that sin, and dies doing that sin, would you be judging if you said "the man died in sin"? Would you also be judging if you said "sinners who die in sin are lost?" Jeff, in matters spiritual, of the Book, how do you form "your opinion"?

In the *Christian Chronicle* article by Jeff he spoke about "...it's an occupational hazard" (public teaching). I can sure tell you how to ease part of that. Stop speaking and worshipping with the denominations, stop calling them "Christians," "my family," calling them "brothers," "extending to them an invitation 'just like I would any place I've preached...,'" and be explicit in your statements, defend and contend for "the faith" (cf. Jude 3), stop associating with the men who are sending forth "uncertain sounds" when it comes to "the doctrine of Christ" (cf. 2 John 9-11), reprove and rebuke those who are teaching falsely on "marriage and divorce," "unity in diversity" (unity and diversity), "grace and no law," stop saying such on unity as you did in your lesson at the Tulsa workshop, use a standard, not a modern speech or paraphrase or... (version), translation, stop trying to be full of wit and humor in your lessons (such as cause people to clap, applause) and give speech as becoming God's speaker for the gospel, keep your word when you say that people can write you...write back and give them an answer, don't hedge, and let them know exactly and precisely what it is you truly believe and stop being so associated with the highly questionable Acappella, etc. These things might help to ease your "occupational hazard."

It is strange to me that brother Walling wants everything so very confidential and personal, contact me first, but when the elders of the East Corinth Church of Christ in Corinth, Mississippi wrote and addressed their letter to Jeff Walling (that would be personal, would it not?) that one of his elders took the questionnaire, answered the same and sent it back with his personal notes added. If that is the standard of being personal, then please know that I have full permission for the use of the material relative to their letter (February 4, 1991, Monday at 11:05 a.m.), as if he can share it, then so can they. Yet, please keep in mind that I did not publish that elder's answers, comments or his personal notes that he wrote on the front (above the first paragraph of the letter) or in relation to the last question asked. That is being fair, right? Wonder how that elder came to have Jeff's personal letter which was personally written to him as a distinct and individual person? Ah, consistency thou art a jewel!

I want to take just enough time and space to say that we all need to be very reverent (respectful, reverential, godly, God-fearing and heavenly-minded) when talking to, addressing, talking about, yea, and in the songs we sing, or in giving a compliment to the lyrics that are sung by others, such as Acappella, *if such would even intimate that one could speak to and address God as "daddy."* It is just as wrong to compliment a group that would sing such lyrics (such is encouragement to young people to believe and or do the same) as it is to do it yourself. Now if you think that has not been done, and if you think that it cannot be proven it was done, that is a mistake on your part. Such happened at the Northside Church of Christ, 3800 County Avenue, Texarkana, Arkansas 75502 during their Summer Youth Series and one of our very faithful gospel preachers, dedicated, loyal and true to the Book was there and witnessed, that is, he both heard and saw what was sung and said. Guess what his reaction was? He was so distraught, distracted and disturbed, yea, with righteousness in his soul (righteous indignation, I would imagine), that he walked out. Yes, he left the meeting. I have talked to him in the past about this, when I was in a gospel meeting in the area. However, I have just recently visited with him twice about it (January 30, 1991 at 5:30 p.m. and then on February 7, 1991 at 1:30 p.m.). To the very best of their remembrance (meaning he and his wife), it was in 1983 when this happened. Indeed, he gave me the permission to use his name, but I have personally decided not to give it at this time. This, however, goes to show just how far and long these "strange" and "uncertain" sounds have been issuing forth from brother Walling. Imagine calling God Almighty, our heavenly Father "daddy," or even hint that such is permissible, yea, even in those lyrics!

Brother Walling had this to say about *Image* magazine, which started with Volume 1 in June of 1985 with brother Reuel Lemmons as editor: "If choosing to read is the best choice a person can make...then choosing to read IMAGE is one of the wisest. How desperately we all need something positive and spiritually nourishing to read and enjoy! IMAGE provides me with refreshing thinking and a Christian approach to everyday challenges. This is a magazine for Christians who are looking for the good things in life. In short: Read IMAGE, your soul will thank you for it!" (Vol. 5, No. 9, September 1989, p. 30). I need not comment on such "a wise choice of words." He often has to explain what he says, or his actions ("The Three Questions That You May Want To Ask," April 18, 1987 was written relative to the Joplin Convention I earlier mentioned). I wonder what he wrote relative to the *Advanced Christian Training* book by the Central London Church.

8. **Strange And Uncertain Sounds From Randy Mayeux.** Brother Randy Mayeux preaches for the Preston Road Church of Christ, 6409 Preston Road, Dallas, Texas 75205. For some time now, we have heard some very "strange" and "uncertain" sounds coming from him. We certainly heard of these before he came to Preston Road, as before this he was with the church in Long Beach, California (37th and Atlantic, 3707 Atlantic Avenue, Church of Christ, Long Beach, CA 90807). He was here when he was one of the participants in the 1986 "Regional Church Growth Seminars" (May 16-17 in Tulsa, Oklahoma; June 6-7 in Rochester, Michigan). Others were Joe D. Schubert (president and founder), John W. Ellas (Associate director), Tim E. Matheny (executive director) and all were of the Center for Church Growth (P. O. Box 73362, Houston, Texas 77273; *Image*, Vol. 2, No. 8, April 15, 1986, inside cover).

And, yes, he was in California when he attended the "Restoration Summit" in Joplin, Missouri. Note what he said:

> *"Here at 37th and Atlantic, we have already made first steps. The First Christian Church met with us on a Wednesday evening last December. We are invited to their building for a Wednesday this December. (They will not use their piano that evening - a noble gesture,*

*consistent with the attitude and actions that I felt from all of our Christian Church brothers in Joplin)" (**One Body**, Vol. 1, No. 2, November 1984, p. 6; Don DeWelt, Publisher, P. O. Box 1132, Joplin, MO 64801; Victor Knowles, Editor, 2504 N. E. 102 Avenue, Portland, OR 97220).*

You can understand some of his "thinking" from this article in the *One Body* publication (remember this "Restoration Summit" was held August 7-9, 1984), as it was in this same article that he had made the statement: "But we each learned of the integrity, the sincerity, the true but honest 'difference' of opinion on the subject (*Ibid*, and please observe that word "opinion" as it was used in the context of the preceding sentence which dealt with "pianos," GM).

In helping us to get familiar with "the thinking" of brother Mayeux, I want us to observe an item or two from some things he has written. In this first article, entitled, "Needed: Champions of Unity," he set the stage by speaking about the city of Berlin and the intimidating Wall that divided the people. He said, "To attempt to cross the Wall is to risk your life. To tear it down is a dream." Now then, watch some of his statements, the transition, very closely.

"The powers that be have constructed the Wall and imposed it against the wishes of the people... The leaders have their doctrines to protect. No one is allowed to question the doctrines. They are afraid that the people would abandon their carefully constructed and carefully policed way of life... The parallels are uncomfortable.

"When a person decides to become a champion of unity, he is quickly labeled as 'dangerous,' 'a compromiser,' 'one who is leading us into apostasy.' ... Champions of unity are rare...

"We have had nearly a century of division... I have attended the meetings with the members of the Independent Christian churches at Joplin (summer, 1984) and at Malibu (summer, 1985). The people at these meetings want to usher in a new century of unity... There is a spirit brewing... It is a spirit created by the Spirit.

"For a number of years now, the North American Christian Convention has used speakers from our fellowship. Congregations all over the country are having combined assemblies with congregations of the Independent Christian churches. A few have exchanged preachers/pulpits.

*"And so, we will continue to meet with our brothers in the Christian churches. Relationships will be built" (**Image**, Vol. 2, Num. 7, April 1, 1986, p. 26).*

Now watch for the same "kind" of thought from his article which is headlined, "Let Us, Too, Lift Our Lamp!" Once again he sets the stage with his example. This time it is the "Mother of Exiles" on Liberty Island... "The promise of freedom is seen in her eyes... This July 4, she will be recommissioned... The offer is still the same. 'Liberty' - 'Freedom' - she calls people to a life with no shackles."

"Her offer is His offer... It is the nature of man to restrict. It is the nature of God to set man free. In our heritage we know the pain of

restriction.

"I love it when someone wants to study the Bible. And I mean 'study.' ...Whether it means to change doctrinal understanding or actual practice, to study is to be open to change.

"But there is a tendency, even within our fellowship, to be closed rather than open to such a desire to study and change. And this should come as no surprise. We are, like all generations and all religious movements, prone to reduce the doctrines to a creedal formula (whether written or unwritten). We hire our preachers, and then tell them what they can preach. And they dare not go beyond the limits.

*"...people sense an atmosphere of freedom, it drives them to the Word with joy and a sense of wonder. Freedom, real, genuine freedom, will create a true movement of Bible students... free of lives of empty of meaning, then Bible study becomes the channel through which God can give His gift of life" (**Op. Cit.**, Vol. 2, Num. 7, June 15, 1986, pp. 26-27).*

Concerning the magazine in which these quotations are listed, it is most interesting to read what brother Mayeux said about it (the items quoted above were when brother Reuel Lemmons was editor).

"'Ideas are weapons,' wrote Max Lerner. 'Ideas attain history in process,' wrote Ernest Wrage. This is an era of great change in Churches of Christ. With a solid, biblical heritage, it is now beginning a new chapter. Its history will be set

*and evaluated by the ideas shaping us as a movement. If you love this movement, you will seek to discern the ideas giving us rebirth. Read and listen, or you will be left behind. IMAGE is a key source of these ideas. I commend IMAGE to you as a loving chronicle of our heritage, a mirror of our present questioning and accomplishments, and a courageous shaper of our history" (**Op. Cit.**, Vol. 5, Num. 9, September, 1989, p. 30).*

It really is not surprising that brother Mayeux would write such a statement about *Image*, as he was listed as a staff writer back in 1985 when the first issue came off the press (June of 1985). He has been associated with the men of this particular persuasion for some time.

Let us note again, from his own pen, a statement that also will tell (inform) us as to some of his thoughts. However, to make it truly understandable, let us give the statement from the pen of the one that caused the pen of brother Mayeux to write what he did. Howard Norton, editor of the *Christian Chronicle*, wrote his "Editorial: A Plea to Critics Of The Church" and from it we now quote.

"Someone, instead of writing another book on how awful we are and how shabby our Restoration heritage is, needs to tell us that the path we are traveling is more nearly correct than that of any other religious group known to us. If we cannot make this assertion about the churches of Christ, we are in the wrong fellowship and have no right to exist as a group.

"At least one other thing needs to be said. I am convinced that a few men in our pulpits

today are out of step with what the Bible teaches and, therefore, with what churches of Christ stand for. Although well-intentioned and very committed, they appear to be in sympathy with that part of the Restoration Movement that went its separate way in the early 1900s. These preachers and teachers have adopted an approach to Scripture that the conservative Christian Church and the Disciples of Christ have long espoused. They would, I believe, be quite comfortable in Christian Church pulpits. Such men do a great disservice to the cause of our Lord by remaining with churches of Christ only because this is their religious heritage" (Vol. 46, Num. 4, April 1989, "Opinion," p. 18).

After reading the above, brother Mayeux wrote a brief letter "to the editor," and I now give the following from his letter.

"You wrote that 'the path we are traveling is more nearly correct than that of any other religious group known to us.' I am extremely uncomfortable with the self-righteousness of that claim.

"To claim that we are most nearly right ignores gaping deficiences... Your assessment that we are most nearly right only is true when we, somewhat arbitrarily and narrowly, define what constitutes the issues on which we need to be right.

"You clearly would have me resign from my pulpit and seek a position in the Christian church...the ideal discovered over a century

ago...beckons me to stay. We were built as a movement with genuine freedom:...I believe that you and others would have me sign your creed. I will not do so. I must not do so" (Vol. 46, Num. 6, June 1989, "Forum: Readers Respond to Coverage," p. 19).

Even though some "strange" and "uncertain" sounds have been coming from brother Mayeux for the past few years, there is nothing from him that truly compares to what he said in Lubbock, Texas. This event in Lubbock was advertised as "The 21st Annual Youth Minister's Seminar (National Youth Ministers Seminar, sponsored by Lubbock Christian University, 5601 19th Street, Lubbock, Texas 79407), October 16-19, 1989...keynote speakers are F. LaGard Smith and Randy Mayeux (Contact LCU at 806, 792-3221, extension 201 for more information)." The theme of this event was "The Church Of The 90's" (*Image*, Vol. 5, Num. 9, September 1989, p. 34, along with the cover and front page of the brochure advertising the same). Brother Mayeux's subject, "The Church Of The 90's Will Celebrate Genuine Diversity," was delivered in the Lubbock Civic Center. It is from this lesson we now quote. Please understand that I have the tape right with me on my desk, along with my own personal notes from it, as I type this (if you desire a tape, write to Paul Tuller, TULLSTAR, 504 Cosgrove, San Antonio, TX 78210).

"There are doctrinal differences...But whoever wrote this tract, 'Can We All Understand The Bible Alike?,' and the answer is, of course, we can. Forgive me, that's just an ignorant view. It's just ignorant.

"You want to talk about the issue in the 90's. There are Bible majors at Abilene Christian and Lubbock Christian who are female...The

bottom line is that in the 1990's diversity is the only game in town, folks...Can a woman lead prayer in a mixed group?...And the answer, of course, is yes she can, I mean, because it's happening (let me add just here that brother Mayeux had a class of his at ACU during a lectureship to stand, get into groups of four, hold hands, and each one, male and female, lead an audible prayer, so he is right about 'it's happening!' He should know, right? GM).

"...the split became official under the guise of the instrument and missionary society. David Edwin Harrell seems to imply it was really an economic split, a North - South Civil War split. The churches that could afford organs bought them. The churches that couldn't afford them condemned the groups that did. Now you check into that.

"I don't know many in our fellowship who are arguing that the New Testament doesn't teach baptism. It's what happens to the person who doesn't understand the teaching that way. And if we were to ask this question and take a little poll, and I'm not about to in this setting, in your opinion will Mother Teresa go to heaven? Now Mother Teresa hasn't been baptized by immersion for the forgiveness of sins. I think it would be a pretty interesting show of hands on that one.

"But if you ask me what happens to the person who loves their God, and loves Jesus Christ, and hasn't seen it that way, I defer to the view of Alexander Campbell in the Lunen-

burg Letter. I believe that view is accurate. That's where my heart stands. Campbell said in the Lunenburg Letter that when a person follows the will of God as far as they understand it God accepts that person.

"But there are people in our fellowship right now, good people, people that if I told you their name you would know them, and you would respect them, who are just not certain that our view on baptism is exactly correct. Now I want to just state it as bluntly as I can, whether you like it or not, whether you agree with those different positions or not. The fellowship of which you are a member in the 1900's is going to have that kind of diversity. And there is nothing that you can do to change that. Nothing. Nothing.

"I think it would have been just virtually unthinkable fifteen years ago that we would have people, and I'm not about to give you names, and for the record, just so you will know, and I really hesitate to do this on tape. Turn the tape off. I have preached and believed, I believe deeply that the New Testament teaches that salvation is a free gift of God period. You are saved by grace alone.

"...what is happening in our generation that has never happened before in any other generation of church of Christ people...We are listening to people like Swindoll on the radio, that's what...they are getting much good Bible exposition and teaching...But Charles Swindoll is an unashamed Calvinist... our people are reading Swindoll's books...

messages...end up thinking more and more like Swindoll.

"In Dallas, and in Lubbock, and in Los Angeles, we've got tons of our women going to something called 'Bible Study Fellowship.' It is a wonderful thing where...Hundreds and hundreds of church of Christ women across this country are getting into it. It is an unabashed, unashamed Calvinistic Bible study. That's the stance...philosophical doctrinal basis of that study. The day is over, whether you like it or not, the day is over when an eldership is going to be able to stand up and say you can't...The church that says if you only go to church of Christ stuff...that church is going to be down to nothing in the 1990's. Whether you like it or not that's the fact. That's the fact."

At this juncture, it is time for us to reflect on just a few items from the above quotations. There are, indeed, some very "strange" and "uncertain" sounds in some very "smooth and fair" speech. I repeat again that I want us to observe some of his "thinking."

a. *It is not strange*, but straightforward, penetrating and piercing, steady and steadfast, when he speaks of "the powers that be," "the leaders" and "doctrines to protect," "no one is allowed to question the doctrines," "carefully policed way of life," and then to state, "the parallels are uncomfortable." Indeed, *it is strange* for many an ear, but *it is not strange* to his readers and listeners, as the parallel is all too clear.

b. *It is strange* for a person to set himself up as a "champion," as this is evidently how he sees himself, that is, a "champion of unity," when he is causing so much unrest in the beloved brotherhood. (He must love the word "champion," as he used it no less than ten times in his article).

c. *It is strange* for him, at least to me, to talk about meeting with the Independent Christian Church members at Joplin and also at Malibu, and speak how they want to "usher in a new century of unity." Indeed, "a spirit created by the Spirit!" Let them remember who it was that "broke away," and "satisfied themselves" in having the mechanical instruments of music in worship. If they so desire unity, they "know" how to achieve it and it will be by the Book. No man-made rules, on God's inspired and inerrant Word.

d. *It is strange* that he gave no proof of "congregations all over the country having combined assemblies with congregations of the Independent Christian churches...exchanged preachers/pulpits."

e. *It is strange* to hear him speak about "loving it" when someone wants to study the Bible, as he adds, "and I mean 'study.'" My guess is that we haven't been doing that and brother Mayeux truly knows what real Bible study is. Let him prove that we have a tendency "to be closed" rather than "open" to such a study, and that we are prone to reduce "the doctrines to a creedal formula."

f. *It is strange* to hear him speak of "life with no shackles," a "true movement of Bible students," and people will be "free of lives of empty of meaning." Does brother Mayeux not realize that we are bond-servants of Christ (Greek *doulos*) but therein we find the only real freedom there is. This is perhaps (the word servant) the most frequently used word of our relation to Christ (at least one of the most frequent). Observe such in these passages: Matthew 20:27; 24:46; 25:14,21,23, esp. vss. 26, 30; Luke 17:10; John 13:16; 15:15; Romans 1:1; 6:16-17,20; 2 Corinthians 4:5; Galatians 1:10; Ephesians 6:6; Philippians 1:1; 2:7 (note how it is even applied to Christ); Titus 1:1; James 1:1; 1 Peter 2:16; 2 Peter 1:1 (how about a study, and "I mean a study," on the word servant which gives man his freedom?). I am sorry, but as a servant of Christ my life is full of meaning and I sure do not feel shackled, so I am sorry if I broke the shackles of such thinking. Sorry about your own life if it is "empty of meaning."

g. *It is strange* to hear him speak about the change in the Church and state "its history will be set and evaluated by the ideas shaping us as a movement." Wonder if he ever thought of being a member of the New Testament Church and not "some movement." The only "rebirth" needed is "the new birth." Brother Mayeux, please do not be too concerned about "leaving" us "behind." Who wants to go beyond "what is written" (cf. 1 Cor. 4:6; Rom. 10:17; 2 Cor. 5:7; John 12:48; Rev. 20:12; etc.).

h. *It is strange* (no, not really, since we kinda know of his own strange ideas) to hear him say "I am extremely uncomfortable with the self-righteousness of that claim" (meaning the statement, "the path we are traveling is more nearly correct than that of any other religious group known to us"), as it wasn't the strongest that one could make. If he keeps on going, it might just be that the Christian church would not even want him in their pulpit (note his statement in the quote relative to the Christian church, etc.).

There was absolutely so much to list from the speech at the Lubbock Civic Center that I could not list for lack of both space and time, that I wish every member of the Lord's New Testament Church could get the tape and hear it. I only listed some of the things that are real "attention getters." You must hear it for yourself. As I listened to it and made my notes, I listed the thoughts I quoted in the order of their deliverance in the tape (but there were repeated statements on some thoughts and interspersed in his lesson). Most of these do not need answering (they've already been answered), but focus your mental powers on the following.

a. *It is strange* about not being able to understand the Bible alike. Perhaps brother Mayeux ought to notify the author of the tract he had and tell him "that's just an ignorant view. It's just ignorant." If he is true, then the one writing this is surely ignorant as well as a whole host of brethren. There is a way, brother Mayeux, to speak the same thing, be of the same mind, having the same love, being of one accord, standing fast in one spirit, with one soul, etc., and "striving for **the faith of the gospel**" (2 Tim. 2:15; 1 Tim. 2:4).

b. *It is strange* that in the 1900's "diversity is the only game in town." To use a word that most of these fellows use so much, let me say, "*Folks*, I do not think brother Mayeux is an inspired prophet." I cannot believe that these preaching brothers do not realize that in "matters of obligation" there must be unity. It is in matters of option, those matters that are not obligatory, we can and will have our freedom and differ in love and respect. The differences in many matters that are optional does not mean there can be no unity in other matters (those of obligation). My own "I think," "I feel," "I believe," along with all of the rest of the "I's" that I hear from various other preachers (which is pure human judgment) should melt into nothingness when we have a "thus saith the Lord."

c. *It is so strange* to learn that all of the churches would have had organs if they could have only afforded them. It seems that the poor ones "condemned" the use of the mechanical instrument in worship only because they themselves could not have such (no money). If that is all the history (note the words "it seems" and "to imply" from his statement from David Edwin Harrell. That makes it 100% definite!) he knows, I believe I would not give any more history quotes. It makes me wonder why he did not quote some from Ben Franklin. It also makes me wonder why these men hunt so to find the "exception" in these men they quote and then set them up as an authority. It matters not what any man says, only the Book! Inspiration no longer exists, in fact, in case you may not know it, the men of the restoration were not "holy men inspired of God" (cf. 2 Pet. 1:19-21). We today can imitate only as Paul said (cf. 1 Cor. 11:1; Greek *mimetes*).

d. *It is strange* to give three paragraphical quotes on the subject of baptism, yea, from Mother (?) Teresa, to Alexander Campbell and his Lunenburg Letter to brother Mayeux who said, "I believe that view is accurate. That's where my heart stands," but that will give you more of "the thinking" from this brother. **Either the exceptive statement of**

John 3:5 means what it says, or we can just do away with all of the New Testament. Since the Bible does not contradict itself, we know that the new birth must comply with the Master's divine authority, be a burial and for remission of sins (cf. Matt. 28:18-20; Rom. 6:3-4; Col. 2:12; Acts 2:38; Matt. 26:28; check the phrase, *eis aphesin hamartion* in those last two passages, please. If it is not identical, then I will apologize). If there is another "door" into the kingdom, then John 3:5 is a false statement. If one must go through "that" one door and "she" did not, then you "take the cake" in saying you believe the Book. Baptism is a command (cf. Acts 10:33, 44-48, esp. vs. 48).

e. *It is not strange*, at this point, in "thinking" with brother Mayeux, that he would make the statement, "I deeply believe that the New Testament teaches that salvation is a free gift of God period." Not even when he adds, "You are saved by grace alone." How else could it be and get Mother (?) Teresa to where he thought she ought to be? And where is that but "to heaven." If, as he contends, that baptism is necessary for the one who believes it that way, then "grace alone" is for the person who does not believe baptism is a "must" ingredient. I would imagine that the majority today believe that salvation is a gift of God's grace, truly, we are saved by God's grace, but it is conditioned upon man's response. If not, everyone would be saved, as His grace is to all and He gave His Son for the whole world (cf. Titus 2:11-12; John 3:16; 1 John 4:7-11; 1 Tim. 4:10; etc.). When the people in the book of Acts, beginning with those on Pentecost, asked, "what shall we do?" (Acts 2:37), why didn't Peter say, "Nothing, for salvation is free, you are saved by grace alone"? Paul must have understood about baptism (remember, it is essential to you if you believe it that way but it is not a must if you do not see it in that light, way), as the voice said, "but arise, and enter into the city, and it shall be told thee *what thou must do*" (Acts 9:4; cf. 22:10; 22:16, the Greek *dei* is the word for "must" in 9:4). Otherwise, it would not have been "a must" for him. Therefore, the man who wrote Ephesians 2:8-9 was not one of those saved "by grace alone." Brother Mayeux said, "I have preached and believed... a free gift of God period." If it is a free gift of God, that is, saved by grace alone, I'm convinced it should not just be "period," but I would have said "exclamation mark!" *Let me remind brother Mayeux that these Ephesians had* "heard" (Eph. 1:13), "believed" (Eph. 1:13), "repented" (Acts 20:20-21), "confessed" (1 Tim. 6:20-21), "been baptized" (Acts 19:1-7; Eph. 5:25-27), "remission of sins" (Eph. 1:7) and "the Holy Spirit of promise" (Eph. 1:13; cf. these last two items imply baptism, cf. Acts 2:38), **before he made the statement in Ephesians 2:8-9, "For by grace are ye saved..."** Is there "grace" or "mercy" apart from the law of God? Again, without the "rule book" (the Bible) no one would even know of "God's grace."

f. *It is strange* for brother Mayeux to make such a play about the "tons of our women" (and others, "We" are listening, he said, referring to church of Christ "people") going to an "unabashed, unashamed Calvinistic Bible study" ("good Bible exposition and teaching," "a wonderful thing,") and then contrast it with "church of Christ stuff." This is another word that these brethren most frequently use. Yes, I am speaking about how they employ the word

> "stuff" to the Bible, and to its precious teachings, to the beautiful bride of Christ, to great sermons, etc. Following a multitude never did prove anything (Exod. 23:2; cf. "fear not 'little' flock," in Luke 12:32; Matt. 7;13-14). Brother Mayeux, "Is the voice of the people the voice of God?" Does "majority" action or rule make a thing scripturally right? Does not God and "one" make a majority (cf. Rom. 8:31). Even if the entire (that is, all but "one") church went astray, would that "out of necessity" take away the "responsibility" toward God of that "one"?

Brother Mayeux's speech has been critically criticized, and I am sure he has felt the impact of the same (I "know" these things as I have read of such and heard him speak on tape of the same). Therefore, this led him, from the pulpit of the Preston Road Church of Christ, in Dallas, Texas, to deliver his Sunday evening lesson on the subject, "Reflections On Questions Raised." This is "the tape" that I just mentioned as having "heard." Indeed, I would not write this if I had not heard what he said, made my notes on the same and have the tape on my desk and am even listening to it "once again" as this is written so I am trying to be as careful as a man can be. I absolutely have nothing against brother Mayeux as a person. He is outstanding in so many ways. However, if he can stand up and publicly state his declarations (they are taped and made available), then I have the privilege (and it does not violate Matthew 18:15-17, as the context of that passage is extremely crystal clear, bright as the sun), yea, the responsibility (cf. 1 John 4:1; 2 John 9-11; Jude 3; etc.), the charge, to do exactly as I am doing (notice the Greek words that I have given in this book relative to the kind of preaching that is pleasing to God), the charge to the evangelist of God.

From some viewpoints, if that is possible, I deem this lesson on the evening of February 25, 1990 ("Reflections On Questions Raised") to be more disturbing than the one given in Lubbock. Even though I did not cover various subjects in that former lesson, some may well be brought up in this one as his rebuttal to his criticism is absolutely amazing. I only wish, whether in preaching a lesson for the first time or as per this lesson, speech would be becoming to God's pulpit, yea, even in our illustration (*example*: the quote from Ira North, yea, even if it makes the people at Preston Road laugh).

a. *It is not strange* that he said, "If I had it to do over, I would not have made that third presentation the way that I did. I am sorry for the grief... the unrest..." *It is strange* that nothing has made an impression upon what he said, so he stated, "I do not disagree with what I said in the presentation." From what he said, not all of the elders or all of the deacons "agree with me," then he added, "My impression is that a large number... fed spiritually by what I say."

b. *It is strange* that he tried to even strengthen his statement about grace (recall, if you will, this quote: "I have preached and believed deeply that the New Testament teaches that salvation is a free gift of God, period. You are saved by grace alone."), as he said, "We do have people saying that and I am one of the ones saying it. So let me clarify what I believe about grace alone." He then takes the assembly to Romans 1:16-17; 3:20-26, 28; Hebrews 12:2; Galatians 2:21; 5:4, and after reading the first one he speaks of a translation (you can call it a "translation" if you like, but I suggest you study most precisely what the word "translation" means in relation to the Bible. Check to see if this one "measures up" to the standard of a translation) that renders Romans 1:17 as "...faith alone."

(1) He said he was reading verbatim from the transcript (that of the one who had written a critical review of the speech), but I've personally listened time and again to the tape and, if he had the transcript as it was written (and I do have a copy in front of me at this time), he just missed it by thirty-eight words and added, after a slight pause, two words, "who say," as this made the transition very smooth. I may not "know" why he did this, but one thing I do "know," he did it.

(2) I was preaching in Little Rock, Arkansas when a translation (?) came on the market that said "...faith alone." I tried my best to get my former professors interested in...and when that failed, I took it upon myself (yes, *much later* some professors did get interested and even met with those behind this so-called translation of the New Testament), examined this new (?) item, listed exactly one dozen Greek constructions, phrases, etc., etc., and on November 8, 1967 wrote the translator, Dr. Robert Bratcher.

(3) On November 20, 1967, I received a reply to my letter and it contained, after an almost full page of...a listing of my several questions, the scripture, the Greek, and then his comments. It was on page three of his letter that he discussed my seventh question; guess what passage it was on? You are dead right, as it was this one that brother Mayeux read about "faith alone" (Rom. 1:17).

(4) He wrote: "This is an attempt to give the meaning of the phrase *ek pisteos eis pistin.* I believe that Paul used this phrase to emphasize that it is faith, alone and completely, through which man is justified. Here and elsewhere he is concerned with eliminating altogether the role of 'works' in justification - it is by grace, through faith, as is said elsewhere. Now, it seems to me that 'from faith unto faith' doesn't mean much to the average and the not-so-average reader; and the language of translation should be natural and clear - and that is what the TEV attempts to be. The KING JAMES 'from faith to faith' and the RSV 'through faith for faith' are both equally obscure; these phrases will not, I am convinced, carry much meaning to the reader. So, one asks: what did Paul mean in using the phrase? And if the answer is what I believe it is, then one expresses the meaning clearly and unmistakably."

(5) *Note*: "This is an attempt," "to give the meaning" *(he did not say "translate")*, "I believe that Paul used this phrase to emphasize that it is faith, alone and completely, through which man is justified," "eliminating altogether the role of 'works' in justification," "Now, it seems to me," "the language should be natural and clear," "the King James...the RSV...equally obscure," "I am convinced," "what did Paul mean" (again, the translator is to do the work of a translator, which is "to translate." If he wants to "give the meaning" of words, why didn't he give "immersion" for the Greek *baptizo* instead of transliterating it?), and "if the answer is what I believe..." There you have it, brother

Mayeux, clear and simple and in the words from Dr. Robert Bratcher about the "faith alone" of Romans 1:17. (This may not be the one that you had in mind, but it clearly tells why it is given as "faith alone," and it is the one that came out in *the 60's*.).

(6) Since this was advertised as "a Greek text prepared by an international committee of New Testament scholars and published in 1966," I asked Dr. Bratcher to send me the Greek text, and to my amazement they sent far beyond my request and so I have two files filled on this subject. I have that Greek text on my desk right now as I write this. It reads exactly like *Nestle, Westcott and Hort, Berry's Interlinear, Lard's Commentary on Romans, Expositors' Greek Testament*, etc. These files contain letters that I wrote to a lot of our professors and others and they are most enlightening. I could give many names just here, but I choose rather to deal "with the text" and the "translator" than to "pit one brother either for or against it," as that is not the way to accurately prove or test the rendering. (Just so you will know, I took most of my Greek under J. W. Roberts and we were the very best of personal friends. Yes, I do have a letter from him, *I write not to defend him*, but his explanation needs to be heard as to why he said what he said lest it leave the wrong impression and the one giving it does a mis-service to him as he has long since died. He said, among other things, "The Greek has literally out of faith, unto faith. This translates a Hebraism very literally from the Septuagint... such passages as 1 Sam. 1:3, 25; 3:19..."

(November 20, 1967, p. 3 and signed JWR).

(7) *Brother Mayeux, guess what?* It was not long until they had made a listing of thirty-seven (37) pages of corrections and revisions and, yes, I also have that in my files.

(8) *Brother Mayeux, guess what?* My first copy was received on March 3, 1967, but by the time the third edition came out how do you think they rendered Romans 1:17. Here it is: "For the gospel reveals how God puts men right with himself: it is through faith, from beginning to end. As the scripture says, 'He who is put right with God through faith shall live.'" *Now Brother Mayeux*, where is the "by faith alone"? What happened to it? Why was it removed? What caused it to be changed? Did the Greek phrase *ek pisteos eis pistin* change from the first to the third edition? Yes, don't you doubt for a minute about me having the copy they sent me either!

(9) *Brother Mayeux*, if you want a "faith only" or "faith alone" wording you can find it at least twice in the New Testament. Here they are: "*monon pisteue*" (Mark 5:36) and "*pisteos monon*" (James 2:24) and both are translated correctly, "only believe," and "faith only." Take a good look now at *ek pisteos eis pistin* and see if you really think these are identical phrases (what is missing?) and should be translated the same way. Before you do, where is the word "alone" in Romans 1:17? Do you still insist on *faith alone*?

(10) *Brother Mayeux*, if you want to prove

something (?) by just any translation (?) how about: "washed/sprinkled/dry cleaned" for Acts 2:38 (yes, it has so been given in one), "only incest" as in Matthew 19:9, "on Saturday evening" and "fellowship meal" as that found in Acts 20:7, "young woman" for "virgin" in Isaiah 7:14; leaving out Mark 16:9-20; removing the words "only begotten" from the five places it is so given as from *monogenes* (John 1:14, 18; 3:16, 18; 1 John 4:9), the changing of flesh (Greek *sarx*) into the words "sinful nature," that people are "included in Christ" at the point of hearing as in Ephesians 1:13; the changing of "making melody" to "make music" in Ephesians 5:19 while omitting the word "spiritual" completely. Now if this is the way you prove some idea, some wording to be correct, then why not just use *The Reader's Digest Bible, The Cotton Patch Version, The Satanic Bible*, *The X-Rated Bible*, or *The Word Made Fresh*, etc., etc., etc.?

(11) People can laugh and mock those of us who studied the New Testament Greek and dealt with the text, but the fact is that we all depend upon a translation, therefore, since they are not inspired of God it behooves us to "know" if it is translated correctly! I perhaps was the first in our brotherhood to be concerned enough and to contact Dr. Robert Bratcher, but I thank God I did and that my files prove the same and that we can use such to handle such arguments as "A translation came out . . . 'by faith alone.'" Are you willing to commit yourself to just any translation, regardless? If so, why not take *The New World Translation*?

(12) *Brother Mayeux*, your Lubbock speech said "grace alone," so why did you come to a passage that said "faith alone"? If it is "grace alone," does that rule out "faith"? If it is "faith alone" does that rule out "grace"? Can you truthfully say that our salvation is "by anything 'alone'"? Does "saved by grace" as per the pen of Paul mean "grace alone"? Tell you what, your switching from "grace" to "faith" and perhaps using both with the word "alone," sure sounds a lot like E. T. Hiscox's *The Standard Manual For Baptist Churches* on pages 61-62 ("wholly of grace" and "solely through faith"). Why did you omit "the" before "law" in Galatians 5:4?

c. *It is strange*, in his defense of what he said about the preacher Billy Graham (which I did not list when I listed those nine other quotes, nine paragraphs as per earlier in this section), his praying for him to have responses, praying unashamedly and then saying that he is a "believer in Christ who doesn't quite understand baptism the way we do." If he does not understand it, then baptism to him is not essential, and he is just like Mother (?) Teresa, as per our brother Mayeux. Remember, it is essential if you understand it that way, but it is not essential if you do not undersatnd it that way. Whew! Know what? That makes it about the most subjective salvation that I've ever heard of, yes, about 100% subjective!

d. *It is strange* to hear him say, "If you put your trust in Christ that Christ's goodness will be imputed to you (2 Cor. 5:21). That Christ's righteousness is imputed to the believer and we are taken to heaven on the strength of the goodness of

Christ, not on the strength of our own law keeping regardless of the system of law (tape not clear but it sounded like it was as follows) that we try to keep (?). That's what the New Testament teaches. Do I believe that a person can do whatever he wants to - he cannot disown God... (quoted Ephesians 2:8-10). You are saved and then you work. You do not work and then get saved... Baptism is not a work... It is not something you do to earn salvation..." (cf. 1 John 3:7; 2:29; Acts 10:34-35; and then remember that faith is "a work," John 6:28-29 and note the Greek phrase, *ta erga tou theo* in Thayer, p. 248, "the works required and approved by God"). I do not know of anyone who believes that we earn our own salvation. This is not the point. Is salvation, the gift of the grace of God, conditioned upon man's response? If he is saying that we are "righteous" through "the righteousness of Christ alone" then that is Calvinism's imputed righteousness pure and simple. It is absolutely not on Christ's righteousness alone. Man's response (faith is a work, cf. thoughts on John 6:28-29 above) by faith into His grace is a must. We are not, as we often hear sung, "dressed in his righteousness alone."

e. *It is strange* that on Mother (?) Teresa, who hasn't been baptized by immersion for the forgiveness of sins, he said, at Lubbock, "I think it would be a pretty interesting show of hands on that one." At Preston Road he added: "I think it would be an interesting show of hands tonight." This does not need any comment, it only reminds me of what Jeremiah said ("...grown strong in the land, but not for truth," 9:3).

f. *It is strange* for him to use Alexander Campbell and the time period (eleven years after his immersion to understand it was for the remission of sins - a firm connection) from 1812 to 1823 before he understood it as we do. I guess the Lord should have made Acts 2:38 more explicit, because if a smart man like Alexander Campbell, very intelligent, could not understand it until eleven years after his baptism, well, what about us? Was that Alexander Campbell's own fault or the fault of the Bible being confusing? (cf. Eph. 3:5; 5:17; 2 Tim. 2:7). Evidently God made it so difficult to understand that if a person does not understand it that way, then to him it is not essential. Brother Mayeux asked Preston Road this question. "If a person who believes in God and trust in Christ has to be baptized by immersion for the forgiveness of sins in order to go to heaven...had Alexander Campbell died in 1811 before...would he have gone to hell? So, Mother (?) Teresa and her...and now a question in reference to Alexander Campbell and his...and he says "I don't have that view of God...my view is what Alexander Campbell wrote about in the Lunenburg Letter...1837." Why ask people such questions? Why not just give baptism as a command of God and the teaching of the New Testament on this subject? (cf. Acts 10:38, 44-48; Gal. 3:27; 1 Cor. 12:13; Rom. 6:3-4; Col. 2:12; 1 Pet. 3:21; Acts 22:16; Mark 16:15-16; Rom. 5:1-2; 2 Tim. 2:1; Eph. 1:3; 2 Cor. 5:17; John 3:1-7; etc., etc., etc.). God will do the judging (and it will be by the Word of Christ, John 12:48, so it is important to know what the Book says) as clearly taught and it is clearly taught that Christ is the author of salvation "to all who obey him" (cf. Heb. 5:8-9). Is it necessary for one to "obey the commands of Christ"? (cf. John 14:15,21,23; 1 John 2:3-5; 5:1-3; note that "love" and "commands" are connected and one but not the other makes a man "a liar." cf. Rev. 21:8; 22:15).

g. *It is not strange* that he now goes to the question asked to Alexander Campbell, "Are there any Christians among the protestant parties?" and then proceeded to give Alexander Campbell's statement. I want to say again, and to all of these brothers in this "movement" (?), spend more time with THE BOOK and less time with the men of the restoration movement, as they are not the standard and regardless of what they said, it will not be our judge in the day of judgment. Stop trying to look to them for the "proof" of your particular ideas. Prove it by the Book or stop trying, as there is nothing in this entire world that will or can compare with or to the New Testament. We need desperately to follow John's injunction (1 John 4:1), and we do have THE STANDARD by which to do it. However, to do it, we must **know** it. The number of quotes and the amount of time and the playing on the "people's being questioned," maybe intimidated, is not as taught by Paul in 2 Timothy 4:1-5. Do we really believe Luke 8:19-21; 11:27-28; 6:46; Matthew 7:21-23, 13-14; John 8:31-32; 7:17; 17:17; 6:44-45; 14:6; etc., etc.? And neither will our own brotherhood papers, even if the speaker shows their controversies, prove what will stand in the day of judgment, and it will not be our standard or the making a right wrong or a wrong right.

h. *It is not strange* under his thoughts about Calvinism to hear him say, relative to "our history," "...We asked Christians from all the sects, all the denominations, to come and unite in simple, pure New Testament Christianity. We did not say to them, come and become a Christian. We said you are a Christian, come, unite. And if you do not (don't) know our history you won't know that... Cane Ridge revival... 1809... Barton W. Stone..."

The last point he covered, if I have ascertained his thoughts in the order he gave them, was on "doctrinal differences." He emphasized again that "we cannot understand the Bible alike." He said he knew the Bible said that we are all to speak the same thing, but then he said, "But I think that is to speak the same thing about the Christ" (it seems his "I think" once again comes forth strongly and clearly). He returns, as per his natural course, to men, and this time mentions David Lipscomb about "voting" and "killing" to show our differences. Then he asked, "Do you want to run him out?" "Do you want to run me out?" After this he assured us again that "I believe that a woman can lead a prayer in a mixed group" and that in the 1990's we will face the question about "women in the church." He referred them to his former sermons (last fall) on this and mentioned 1 Corinthians eleven and said "I believe that was verbal" (reference to women praying and prophesying in a mixed group). He did not (and I had not given a quote on it when I first gave those various thoughts from his tape at Lubbock Civic Center) repeat about the Herald of Truth conference on the family (900 attended at Dallas, men and women) and the Ph.D. The one referred to was a woman and he said, "she preached. And she was dynamite! Do we want to drive these people away from us?... I will tell you that the churches of Christ cannot survive the resource drain if we drive people away like that in the 1990's. We cannot survive it. Literally can't survive it" (he never gave 1 Tim. 2:8ff).

At this point he said, "some conclusions." It did not take him long to get back to his example of Alexander Campbell, he makes his own distinction in the difference between "rebellion" and "ignorance" (cf. 2 Thess. 1:6-9; 1 Pet. 4:12-16; Eph. 2:11-12; 1 Thess. 4:13), and please note them carefully and even the words "no hope." Then look at what Paul taught about himself, Acts 23:1; 1 Tim. 1:12-17; Gal. 1:11-13, 23; Acts 26:9-11; Phil. 3:1-6; etc. and observe whether it was possible that Paul was both "ignorant" (Paul's word) and that he also "rebelled" (he persecuted the church and made havoc of the faith), and tells them "...I will never introduce practices that all of you object to with your consciences, because it would be divisive. I do not believe in dividing the church" (I wonder if he will introduce an item if "the majority," or "a sizeable percentage," would object to in his own conclusions?). Again he says we need "to learn our history" (mentions Leonard Allen and what he is writing about, especially right now), says "his views are the views that were held in our history, 120-150 years ago," "its the last 30-50 years we have become so exclusive and so rigid"... "saying there are no Christians in other groups" (referred evidently to the banner that Rick Atchley in his sermon also mentioned and which I have already covered), we must understand today's "hunger," "we've got to change some things about how we worship and praise our God," "we've got to understand the need for Bible study" and gives an example about the largest church in Lubbock with church of Christ people, raised in the church of Christ, the largest number of people raised in the church of Christ, of any church in Lubbock is a church that is not church of Christ; is an independent non-denominational." Then he says we must decide "how firm an unwritten creed has to be. If it is wrong for Randy to hold these views, then you write your creed and tell me what I have to believe." He then tells about sitting at the Y.M.C.A. in Dallas trying to decide (he read brother Brownlow's book on "Why I Am A Member Of The Church Of Christ") on the Baptist church or the church of Christ and he says, "I ended in the church of Christ." He says the year he was in downtown Dallas at the Y.M.C.A. was 1968. His fifth observation is that we need to decide "what saves a person." He says it is clear in my opinion that we ought to be immersed, but Barton W. Stone (and so he quotes this uninspired human being) as late as 1830, said you should not make your own peculiar view of immersion a term (?) of fellowship. He said that Stone, at another time and place said that we must not bind our opinion on people, teach baptism by immersion and let people draw their own conclusions. His sixth and last thought was that we "really do need to decide to be united and to feed all hunger in the name of Christ."

His last thoughts were "two personal reflections." Almost the last thing that I heard on the tape (it evidently ended before he completely finished) was him saying, "But I will tell you that I am very weary of the circles of criticism." As I have said before, in relation to other men, brother Mayeux, I can tell you how to ease "the circles of criticism." Stop preaching that salvation is by "grace alone," stop saying what you have been about Billy Graham (if salvation is by grace alone, you do not have to be concerned about him anyway), stop declaring that baptism is essential to the one who understands it but it is not to the one who fails to understand it, stop speaking like you have been relative to mechanical instrumental music, Charles Swindoll, that women can lead prayer in mixed assemblies, and that we cannot understand the Bible alike. Spend more time with the Book and give God's people His message and not what Alexander Campbell, Barton W. Stone, and many others have said and are saying (writing) about things. Stop talking about "our movement" and "our history," and talk about the New Testament Church and show how it was in the mind and the plans of God, came to fruition and that the "seed promise" is valid for mankind today and for all days (cf. Gen. 1:11-2; Luke 8:11-15). If you do not like the thought of division, stop being so "divisive" with the questions about Mother (?) Teresa, etc., and stay with an "it is written" and a "thus saith the Lord."

It seems that brother Mayeux is still perhaps laboring with some of the questions that have been raised about his Lubbock lesson, "The Church of the 90's Will Celebrate Genuine Diversity." I say this because not only did he deliver the lesson at Preston Road, "Reflections On Questions Raised" (February 25, 1990) in reference to the Lubbock lesson, but now he has written an article, "Saved by Christ" (*Image*, Vol. 7, No. 1, January/February 1991, pp. 5, 12). Just think, his lesson in Lubbock was in October of 1989, then he tried to answer questions about the questions and criticisms that came from that lesson. This he did, as previously mentioned, on February 25, 1990. Evidently, the questions have not been settled or brother Mayeux is having a rather hard time explaining what he actually believes. I say this, as his article in *Image* opens with this statement: "It's been over a year since I made a presentation to the youth ministers in Lubbock. As I look back over the questions this presentation raised, I would like to clarify some of my beliefs and offer some relections" (p. 5). Now maybe in 1991 he can settle "everything."

One of the most flapdoodling things I read about is for our brethren to keep on, keep on and keep on telling us about all of the many changes "in the world." Surely, they know we "live," "think," "read," "listen," "watch," "understand," "discuss," "talk," "visit," and use our senses relative to what is going on in the world. We do not walk around with all of our senses dulled, blinded or stamped out. I just wonder if we need to tell the world that "bathrooms" have gone "indoors," and that we now have "air-conditioning, television, medical advances" (*The Grapevine*, Vol. 22, Num. 8, Feb. 20, 1991, p. 2) and "countless numbers of other significant changes." On the inside of the cover of the book "*The Church in Transition*," I read: "If there is one word which more accurately than any other describes the mood of the times, it is the word 'change'...change is sweeping us with hurricane force into the third millennium. If the church remains aloof from the changes taking place today, it for all practical purposes, will have pulled the plug" (by James S. Woodroof, The Bible House, Inc., 901 South Main, Searcy, AR 72143, 1990). However, if it were not for them quoting "the observers of religious trends," I do not think they'd play this up so much. Religious groups have almost always "changed" things, yea, and that certainly does include the message of the Master. It is pure balderdash to think otherwise. If we're just concerned about numbers, social needs of the community, or about "being one (?) with the denominational world," then we can forget "the changeless message of the Master."

Brother Mayeux, in the Lubbock speech said "... salvation is a free gift of God period. You are saved by grace alone." In the lesson at Preston Road he said: "We do have people saying that and I am one of the ones saying it. So let me clarify what I believe about grace alone." However, he then used a translation of the passage in Romans 1:17 and gave it as "faith alone." Now which is it? What in the world does "grace alone" or "faith alone" mean, that is, what does the word "alone" mean, except "only, just, nothing but, unaided, unassisted, unhelped, by itself, exclusive," etc., etc.? If something is "alone" does it have room for "anything else"? Or did he take the position that "grace" and "faith" were the same thing? Now he comes in this article (the one mentioned above) and entitles it "Saved by Christ."

Here are some statements from that article:

> *"Though standing on the centrality of the authority of Scripture, these men believed and offered that followers of Christ should (and would be able to in these new churches) read the Bible and draw their own conclusions... the appeal struck a responsive chord in the hearts of men and women who were so very tired of being told what to believe by others.*
>
> *"That spirit is again alive and well in the America of the 1990's. In multitudes of situations, men are leaving their churches...to preach what they conclude from their own study of Scripture.*
>
> *"If our churches are going to be true - true to the ideals of the Restoration Movement, true to the call of God, and true to the needs of the age - ...But to do so, I believe, is the only road to renewal and health.*
>
> *"The problem, of course (speaking about the motto, 'In matters of faith, unity; in matters of opinion, liberty;...'), is that there are some who allow for very little latitude on what constitutes a matter of opinion.*
>
> *"At the heart of my own belief is the conviction that we are saved by grace. What do I mean by this statement?*
>
> *"I mean simply that we are saved by Christ,*

not by our own goodness. Salvation is a gift because we were lost without Christ and cannot stay saved without Christ...The New Testament makes it very clear that salvation is a gift of God, freely given to those that receive the gift with true faith/truth (cf. Eph. 2:1-9 and Rom. 6:23).

"There is no human part of salvation!

"I believe that the New Testament teaches that faith is the human responsibility in receiving this gift. Baptism is part of the response of faith...earns nothing.

"To be saved, a person must place his or her faith in the saving efficacy of Christ...What will happen to the honest believers in Christ who have not yet accepted this teaching about baptism? That decision is in the hands of God.

"...that we allow for diversity in matters of opinion. To do anything less is to spell doom for our movement."

There you have it, and now all of his beliefs are clarified and all reflections are crystaline. I feel there is no need for me to do anything but just call attention to that which is so very, very obvious, and I am just going to mention first of all that readers need to be aware of what he actually said, what was implied in some statements and what he did not say.

a. *It is not strange* for the article to include thoughts about "reading the Bible and drawing your own conclusion" (as that is what Philip told the eunuch to do, after the eunuch said, "...how can I, except some one shall guide me?" Yep, draw your own conclusions)... "men and women... so very tired of being told what to believe by others," and "... preach what they conclude from their own study of Scripture." (Wonder why Nehemiah read so distinctly, 8:1-8?). We have all, in one area or another "been told about the norm, and about instructions, what things mean," but when it comes to God's sacred Word, just draw your own conclusions. I could not do that in any field, as I always had an instructor, a text book, and rules to follow. I had it in Hebrew and I had it in Greek, yea, I had it in all of my Bible courses, etc. But there has come along a generation that feels CRAMPED if any of our faithful Bible teachers try to teach them or inform them of various... However, I can guarantee you that this is not the case when it comes to other men, men like brother Mayeux wrote: "My teachers spoke! For years, I've read the works of John Scott, Charles Swindoll, J. I. Parker, Dan Baumann, James Boice, Charles Colson, Os Guinness, and countless others" (Randy Mayeux, "Keeping the Dream Alive," *Contending For The Faith*, Vol. XVIII, No. 4, April 1987, p. 4). As far as I know, every one of these teachers of his that he named is a denominational preacher/teacher. Wonder if they have helped to shape any of his own conclusions and I also wonder if he is tired of what they have been and are telling him to believe?

b. *It is not strange* (at least anymore, it isn't) to hear him speak of being true "to the ideals of the Restoration Movement... and true to the needs of the age" as the "only road to renewal and health." Nor is it strange to hear him speak about "some who allow for very little latitude on what constitutes a matter of opinion." It would be most amazing to know just what he calls or labels as "opinion." Wonder if he thinks "instrumental music" is a "matter of opinion"? What about women preachers or praying with or in the presence of men?

c. *It is not strange* that in this article he said, "...of my own belief is the conviction that we are saved by grace," *but it is kinda strange* that he did not say "by grace alone" or even as he has said, "faith alone" (as the way he had read Romans 1:17).

d. *It is strange* (but it is getting less so after reading so much from some of these that I have covered in this book) to hear him say, "...saved by Christ, not by our own goodness." I do not know of any of our men who teach we are saved by our own goodness, by our own works of merit (as if we had any such), earning salvation and who deny we are saved by grace (grace alone is a horse of a different color). The blessings of God are conditional!

e. *It is strange* to hear him then say that, "There is no human part of salvation!" (the exclamatory point is his). This means then that salvation is by "...alone!" Does he not fully understand he is saying that this "rules out faith" (cf. John 6:28-29 and please note the meaning of *ta erga tou theo* and even check Thayer, p. 248, for "study"). Yet, he says, "I believe that the New Testament teaches that faith is the human responsibility..." If, as he says from his own heart, that there is a "human responsibility," and that human responsibility is "faith," then is it true that what he said about "there is no human part of salvation," true? Or will he come back and say he was speaking about "God's part"? If so, surely he knows that no man had a part in "God's...salvation" (please give me the courtesy to know that Jesus was born of Mary, etc.). Why did those on Pentecost, as well as others, ask, "what shall we do?" as revealed in Acts 2:37 (cf. Acts 9:6; 22:10; 16:30; Phil. 2:12; Tit. 2:11-12; Heb. 5:8-9; etc., etc.). If, as per his words, "there is no human part of salvation," then it is strictly, totally, solely, singly, only, distinctly, unhelped, independently, yea, it is by grace **alone!** by grace **period!** by grace **exclamation point!** It is by grace **without anything that man is to do, can do should do, or any others of the "do family!"** It sure makes me wonder about such passages as Matthew 7:21-23; Luke 6:46; 8:19-21; 11:27-28; Matthew 10:22; 24:13; 1 John 2:29; 3:7; Acts 10:34-35; Revelation 2:10; 22:14; etc., etc. If "baptism is part of the response of faith" (his own words), if "faith" is the part that man does, if "faith" is a work, as per John 6:28, if "faith" is what causes a man to be immersed, it just seems to me that "there is a human part of salvation" (I just changed his sentence a little, from a word of two letters to just a single word of one letter, from "no" to "a," but it sure makes the difference!). "There is no human part of salvation" is not in keeping with "a thus saith the scriptures."

f. *It is strange*, that on top of these two statements, he then says, "To be saved, a person must place his or her faith in the saving efficacy of Christ." Note the words, "must," "place," "his faith," "in," and "the saving efficacy of Christ," as that sure sounds like "a human part of salvation." Indeed, if it is "to be saved," that this "must" be done, then that response by man is something that man does and is "a human part of salvation." However, this is what happens when a man makes a statement contrary to Bible teaching (saved by grace alone) and then tries to explain it, clarify it, etc. Such statements would perhaps not be made if his "teachers" were not who he said they were. Indeed, brother Mayeux, there is a way to stay clear of being wearied by "the circles of criticism."

g. *It is strange*, no, not really, not in this "age of change" we hear so much about, that a man states: "What will happen to the honest believers in Christ who have not yet accepted this teaching about baptism? That decision is in the hands of God." That decision is found "in the Book of God" (if not, then one does not have to obey God to be saved, cf. Acts 10:33, 43-48; John 14:15, 21, 23; 1 John 2:2-5; etc., etc.)! If a person must love Jesus to be saved, if loving Jesus is, as Jesus said, 'keeping my commandments,' if baptism is a command, and it is, then a person who loves Jesus is a person who has kept the command to be immersed. Therefore, I ask a similar and a simple question: "What will happen to the honest believers in Christ (?) who have not obeyed the commandment of baptism? That decision is in the hands of God." I ask you simply and sensibly, is that all we can declare by the authority of the New Testament of Jesus? Read again Hebrews 5:8-9; Acts 10:33-35; 1 Peter 3:21; Galatians 3:26-27; Romans 6:3-5, 16-18; 2 Corinthians 12:13; 5:17; etc., etc. Does not a person have to be "in" Christ to be saved? Can a person be "in" Christ without first of all getting "into" Christ? How does a person get "into" Christ, or "into" the kingdom (cf. Gal. 3:26-27; John 3:3-7; etc.). I can tell you, as the Hebrew said, "For we know him that said, Vengeance belongeth unto me, I will recompense. And again, The Lord shall judge his people (cf. Deut. 32:35-36). It is a fearful thing to fall into the hands of the living God" (better watch out for those hands, cf. Rom. 11:22), as found in Hebrews 10:30-31.

I think I would have been disappointed had brother Mayeux not mentioned Alexander Campbell in this article, "Saved by Christ." He used him again: "It took Alexander Campbell many years to get from his beginning point of infant baptism to his end point, where he taught the need for immersion for the forgiveness of sins" (p. 12). He had mentioned him at Lubbock (in the Lunenburg Letter), but he truly did make use of him in his Preston Road speech and especially those eleven long years it took him (from his immersion, from 1812-1823) before he understood this "and he was such a smart man." So, how long do you think it will take people today to understand this? Remember how he provoked thinking by asking, "...had Alexander Campbell died in 1811 before...would he have gone to hell?" I guess the Pentecostians should have been given more time to really comprehend the answer to their question (cf. Acts 2:38). I guess those three thousand just kinda "took a chance on it" (reckon that was any harder to understand than Matthew 26:28?). I would like to suggest that brother Mayeux read more about Alexander Campbell (as if it made such a colossal, elephantine, dinosaurian, herculean, stupendous and skyscraping difference) and whether or not he understood the specific design of baptism. Why not commence with the *Memoirs*, 1, pp. 393-394, 398, 410, 438; J. R. Graves' (the Baptist writer contemporary with him) *Trilemma: By The Masterful Baptist*, p. 195 (he quotes Campbell saying, "Remission of sins cannot be enjoyed by any person before immersion... Belief of this testimony is what impelled us into the water." Campbell in *The Christian Baptist*). Also, read what Mrs. Alexander Campbell said (an interview in the

American Christian Review, Vol. XXII, Nov. 25, 1879, p. 379), as she spoke directly to this point and began by saying: "Some of the brethren say that because 'remission of sins' was not named at his baptism, he was not scripturally...Alexander Campbell was baptized into the full faith of the forgiveness of sins, when baptized into Christ's death...freed from the guilt and pollution of sin... with the pardon of all his past sins,..." (cf. Thompson, pp. 12-13).

I give the above for this reason. Some say that he was positively not baptized for such a reason, however, there seems to be confusion on this point and I doubt that any one can be so very positive as has been the case of some. Therefore, I raise the question: "Can it be, with full evidence shown, proof documented, that he did not fully understand baptism to be for remission of sins?"

But I want to make it clear to every reader that it does not matter "one whit" what Alexander Campbell (or any other man, past or present) thought or did, as God's sacred Word of Truth, the New Testament, the Word of the Master (cf. John 12:48) is really the guideline (the rule, the law, the pattern, the last word, the standard, etc.), and there is no other. To say it was so difficult to be understood, perhaps implies something about revealed truth that one might not desire with which to live. Think about that, please, good brother.

Chapter Eight

THE PATTERN - AND "STRANGE" AND "UNCERTAIN" SOUNDS FROM SOME BRETHREN (Part IV)

THE PATTERN - AND "STRANGE" AND "UNCERTAIN" SOUNDS FROM SOME BRETHREN

(Part IV)

9. Strange And Uncertain Sounds From Rubel Shelly. At the present time, brother Rubel Shelly preaches for the Woodmont Hills Church of Christ (2206 21st Avenue, South, Nashville, Tennessee 37212). It was in the latter part of 1982 when brother Shelly delivered a series of lessons on the subject, "Undenominational Christianity" (this was at the Ashwood Church of Christ, in Nashville, where Rubel was at that time preaching). It was perhaps the enormous requests for these lessons, along with his great popularity, that led him to speak in Centerville, Tennessee at the preachers' forum on March 21, 1983. He chose as his topic for this occasion, "Is Unity Possible?"

As far as I personally know, this was the first time he ever delivered a lecture (excepting perhaps that earlier series) where his doctrinal thoughts had "seemingly" changed (his tract, "Christians Only: A Plea For Unity In Christ," was basically the lesson of the forum, 20th Century Christian, 1983, 23 pages). However, brother Shelly assured his brethren that he had not changed on doctrine, only in his attitude. Since the dates we have just mentioned, brother Shelly has been a lot of places, delivered a number of speeches, lectures, been on a number of forums (like the one in Joplin, Missouri, August 7-9, 1984, first of that particular type and it was called "Restoration Summit"), and has written much. It won't be long until he will be speaking at the Northeastern Christian College (1860

Montgomery Avenue, Villanova, Pennsylvania 19805), where he will deliver three lessons on "The Second Incarnation" (March 24-27, 1991; Rubel's lessons are on the 25th, 26th and 27th from 2:30-3:15 p.m.) during their lectureship. By the time this book is off the press that series, as well as others, perhaps, also will be history. He has continued since late in 1982, and it seems crystal clear, that with the beginning point of such lessons as he gave at Ashwood and Centerville, that more than just his earlier attitude and disposition have changed. However, he continued to say that he was being misrepresented and misunderstood. Brothers Roy C. Deaver and Thomas B. Warren met with brother Shelly on Monday, August 8, 1983, and the following is what brother Deaver wrote about the "very fine visit" they had.

> *"Brother Shelly assures us that he believes now exactly what he wrote in the 1972 article (referring to "What About the Ecumenical Movement?" in* ***The Spiritual Sword****, Vol. 3, Num. 4, July, 1972, pp. 30-34, GM)...He emphatically declares that his 'doctrinal stance' is exactly what it has always been - that he* ***has not*** *changed doctrinally. With equal emphasis he stresses that he is fighting a 'bad attitude' among us, a 'sectarian spirit.' He says this 'bad spirit' is the* ***only thing*** *he is fighting, and that this alone is the area in which he has changed - that he himself has repented of a bad attitude, a sectarian spirit" (****Biblical Notes,*** *Vol. 17, October, 1983, pp. 74-75, emp. Roy Deaver).*

With brother Shelly's permission, brother Roy C. Deaver published that excellent article by brother Shelly (*Ibid*., pp. 65-74), and the comment above was "at the end" of that article.

In the same year of the Centerville speech, 1983, many brethren, being deeply concerned, began to write on various subjects relating to various thoughts of that speech. In the *Christian Light* (Vol. 3, Num. 12, September, 1983), the front page article was "Christians Only And The Only Christians" (Roy C. Deaver, pp. 136, 139-140). The editor of the paper, brother J. Noel Merideth, wrote his editorial on "The Centerville Speech" (Vol. 4, Num. 1, October, November, 1983, pp. 2-3, 9-10. The Paper was published at 2006 South Locust Ave., Lawrenceburg, TN 38464). Various other men wrote about the same, therefore, different papers, some earlier than the *Christian Light* (*Words of Truth, The Word Of Life, The Restorer*, etc.) and some later that very year (such as *The Gospel Advocate*), carried articles by men like Bobby Duncan, R. C. Oliver, Franklin Camp, Hugo McCord, Alan Highers, etc.

In 1984, the messages continued to flow through the pens and papers of men concerned with biblical unity and the way to achieve it. In all probability, one of the finest articles to compare "the former teachings" of brother Shelly, to "the present teachings" of brother Shelly, was the one produced by brother Alan E. Highers. If you have not read his article, "Smooth And Fair Speech," you need to read it. It can be found in the following papers:

a. The *Christian Light*, Vol. 4, Num. 4, February, 1984, pp. 43, 48-50, 52.

b. *Contending For The Faith* (ed. Ira Y. Rice, Jr.), Vol. 15, Num. 3, March, 1984, pp. 1, 3-5.

c. *Biblical Notes*, Vol. 17, March/April, 1984, pp. 121, 123-127.

d. *Firm Foundation* (ed. William S. Cline), Vol. 105, Num. 9, June, 1988, pp. 55-59. (Normally, I would not give all of these, but this article is of service to the Master, and so am I trying to be. Maybe you take one of these, maybe you do not, maybe you do not take a religious paper, but maybe you know of someone who does and you could read this article. It needs to be read and I trust this listing of these will only enhance its circulation, GM).

Also, in 1984, the *Christian Light* carried articles by Robert R. Taylor, Jr. (Vol. 4, Num. 9, July, pp. 97-98) and by J. Noel Merideth (Vol. 4, Num. 11, October, November, pp. 114, 117, 121). It was Ben F. Vick, Jr., who, in 1985, compared the teachings of brother Shelly to those of W. Carl Ketcherside (*Contending For The Faith*, Vol. 16, Num. 2, February, 1985, pp. 1, 3-5; #2, Vol. 18, Num. 4, April, 1987, pp. 8-10). Roy J. Hearn's front page article was "Differences Between the Church of Christ and the Christian Church" (*op. cit.*, pp. 1, 3-4). There were other articles in the same issue that were also revelant to the ideas promoted by brother Shelly.

Indeed, 1984 was one more busy year regarding various activities in the realms wherein we have been discussing various issues. *The Gospel Advocate* carried an article by Alan E. Highers on "Are We The Only Christians?" (January 5, 1984, pp. 17-18). *The Spiritual Sword* had an issue on "The Strategy For Victory" (Vol. 15, Num. 2, January, 1984), with various articles pertaining to unity, denominations, the only Christians, is the Church of Christ a denomination, instrumental music and other topics. It was this year that brother Shelly gave his speech in Memphis, Tennessee and explained his "two levels" of fellowship (one was spelled with a capital "F" and one was spelled with a lower case "f"), and it was also this year that he wrote his book, "*I Just Want To Be A Christian*" (20th Century Christian Foundation, 2809

Granny White Pike, Nashville, TN 37204). This was also the year that brother Bert Thompson published his booklet, *"Non-Denominational Christianity: Is Unity Possible?"* (Apologetics Press, Inc., 5251 Millwood Road, Montgomery, AL 36109-9990, 30 pages).

For more than one reason, I deem it now necessary to observe those two articles (by brethren Highers and Vick) and the specific points of comparison they made in their respective articles. Brother Highers listed: (1) the nature of the church, (2) passing judgment, (3) whether we can say anyone is lost, (4) on knowledgeable, devout Christians in all denominations, (5) on whether the use of instrumental music must be confessed as sin, (6) the Church, unity, and compromise, (7) contradiction and inconsistency, etc. The latter of the two listed: (1) fellowship with the Christian church, (2) crystallized into a religious sect, (3) confession of wrong, (4) no repudiation of basic beliefs, (5) encouraging unity of believers, (6) the one faith, (7) the one faith and instrumental music, (8) the argument on silence, (9) clinched fist versus clinched teeth, (10) holding to your opinion, and (11) passing judgment on sinners. (The word-for-word transcription of the Highers-Shelly confrontation on Thursday afternoon, February 9, 1984, needs to be read just here. *Contending For The Faith*, Vol. 15, Num. 3, March, 1984, pp. 5-12, "Open Forum," Freed-Hardeman College Lectureship. The following pages, 12-16 also needs to be read, GM).

One thing that made us truly look at what brother Shelly was saying and doing was the fact that men from the very liberal group were praising and lauding him and his new stance. In fact, the very first issue that I received of *The Reformer* had this to say about the tract that brother Shelly wrote on "Christians Only."

"Rubel Shelly has authored a fine pamphlet on

'Christians Only' (20th Century Christian Foundation, 2809 Granny White Pike, Nashville, TN 37204). It will be worth your time to obtain a copy. It sells for 75¢.

Some of us have been saying for 30 years what Rubel is saying so well now. But his saying them will probably have more of an impact for he is considered to be 'in fellowship' with the mainline churches. Those of us who have been saying what he is now saying have been labeled heretics. And heretics are not permitted to vote in the decision-making process!" ("Christians Only," Vol. 1, Num. 8, September, 1985, p. 3, by Bluff Scott, Jr., 1003 Pilot Ave., Cherokee, Iowa 51012).

Just before Buff Scott listed his thoughts about brother Shelly's tract, he stated: "I am convinced that the honest unimmersed who are seeking to serve the Lord but who die without coming to an adequate understanding of the new birth, will be eternally saved by God's grace and mercy" (p. 2). Just above the blocked caption of Shelly's tract, Buff Scott wrote: "Excellent Words From Restoration Review." He began by saying, "Our good brother Leroy Garrett" and then told about his editing the *Restoration Review* (p. 3) and gave a "choice wording" from him. Such men were welcoming brother Shelly with the finest of compliments and praise.

In 1985, we also had a year of major proportions. It might well be called the year of the "Unity (?) Meetings/ Forums." On March 18-20, there was one in Tulsa, Oklahoma (and like the one in Joplin it was a rather closely screened and a pretty closed meeting for all practical purposes). On its heels came the "mini-summit" (my term for it) in Dallas, Texas at Dallas Christian

School (Christian Church), on April 19, 1985. It, too, was certainly kept "from us." Next in line was the meeting on the campus of Pepperdine at Malibu, an "open meeting," on July 7-9, 1985. There was talk of one in Cuyahoga Falls, Ohio, but it did not develop. However, on August 14, 1985, some gathered at the Hillsboro Family Camp in Hillsboro, Ohio for a "Unity Forum" (many quotes have been given from brother Shelly's part in this particular meeting). *Of great significance this year* was the book that Alan E. Highers wrote, "HOW DO YOU SPELL (F) (f)ELLOWSHIP?" (a reply to the teachings of Rubel on "Fellowship and Unity"), which was published by him in Henderson, Tennessee 38340 (sixty-six pages).

I want to make an added statement just here about the book that I have just mentioned. *For those of our young men who are* throwing the names of F. D. Srygley, G. C. Brewer, N. B. Hardeman, as well as others, around trying to prove "Christians In Denominations," please read the quotes from these men in this book. *For those who have read* brother Shelly's "I Just Want To Be A Christian," read the quotes from the book that brother Highers gives (and he gives some sixteen or more, if I have discerned these accurately). *If you want to read* (maybe you do not have and have not heard some of the tapes from brother Shelly's speeches, like the Hillsboro Forum) some of the the things he has said, then read this book. *If you would like to read some of the questions* that have been asked of him, read those of Wayne Jackson that are found in this book. Yes, indeed, this book is "of great significance."

This year, 1985, was also the year when the Preachers' and Elders' Forum was held at Freed-Hardeman College in Henderson, Tennessee. The subject again related to the restoration movement and unity. It was on October 12,

1985 that brethren Alan E. Highers and William Woodson met with Rubel Shelly and Monroe Hawley.

In the years to come, there would be many more articles, books and various speeches by several men at the "Forums." As an example, it was on April 29-30, 1986, in Johnson City, Tennessee that one such was conducted at Milligan College. It had been earmarked as "Restoration Forum IV." The very next year, April 28-30, 1987, there was a "major meeting" with a resembling arrangement, formula, and this time it was to be held at the Cincinnati Bible College and Seminary in Cincinnati, Ohio. The Highers-Blakely Debate was conducted April 12-15, 1988 at the Hillcrest church of Christ building in Neosho, Missouri. In the April/May issue of the *Christian Light*, J. Noel Merideth had an editorial on the subject, "A Review Of Shelly's Book - I Just Want To Be A Christian" (pp. 2, 9; 1988, published at 125 Lawrence Street, Lawrenceburg, TN 38464). The Restoration Forum VI was conducted at Akron, Ohio, November 1-3, 1988. Indeed, articles on "instrumental music in worship," "unity," "grace," "liberalism," "translations," "the church," "fellowship," "restoration," "Mark 9:38-41," "authority," "Ephesians 4:4-6," etc., came at an ever increasing speed in various journals. Then, let me say, that we began to have some "new" books, like *The Worldly Church* (1988, authors Leonard Allen, Richard Hughes and Michael Weed), as only one example, along with the "Scholarship Movement," and "The New Hermeneutics." It appears that these men are using, as one of their vehicles of communication, the paper that Reuel Lemmons first edited, *Image,* but whose editor now is Denny Boultinghouse.

I do not mean to give brother Rubel Shelly all of the credit for all of the confusion that has been going on among us for the past several years, but I do credit him with igniting the spark that led to such. It seems to be a proven fact, especially if you take note and observe very carefully how he is so often quoted, where he is speaking, what his subjects are, what he is saying, and what he is writing. Evidently, from all indication, as per his first defense, he is still being misunderstood, misrepresented and misinterpreted. However, that is just a lot of fiddle-faddle, as I believe his own writings can show. Indeed, it is more than that of attitude and disposition.

The first single speech that I mentioned in this section was that of the preachers' forum in Centerville, Tennessee. I have that before me, that is, in transcript form. The tape ended before he answered the questions, but I have twenty-seven pages and it is from this transcript of his *March 21, 1983* speech on "Is Unity Possible?" that I now give the following.

> *"I am trying to think my way out of a sectarian spirit. I grew up in the context of one. I learned a sectarian spirit. I breathed a sectarian spirit. I exhibited a sectarian spirit and I taught a sectarian spirit. I am embarrassed. I am ashamed. I have repented. I am trying to outgrow it. And I'd like to encourage other people to rethink some attitudes and to rethink some matters that pertain to unity of believers" (p. 1).*

It wasn't long after this, that Rubel brought up Mark 9:38-42, a passage which he thought proved his point. He said that "John was practicing that day a spirit that has been nemesis (ruin, Waterloo, downfall) of those of us who try to wear the name of Christ, from that day to this" (p. 7). He turned his thoughts again to the spirit of arrogance, sectarianism, and that is what makes a person as sectarian as he can be. Then he said, "And the obvious modern day application of this text from Mark 9 has been avoided among us. I've never heard anybody ever preach on it in all the years that I have listened to our folks preach" (p. 7). He spoke of some "petty, trivial, little things that sever us from one another, divide us into various fragments." He finally, on page nine, reached (it seems to me) a pinnacle point in this lesson.

> *"Somehow those of us who make the plea for people to be Christians only have let that plea come out to the world something after this fashion: 'Come over to us, and be Christians only because after all we are the only Christians.' That is arrogant, that is wrong, that is self-righteous, that is sectarian... heal the breaches that we've created within our own fellowship" (p. 9).*

> *"...And anybody who has been born again of water and the spirit is a child of God, a member of the spiritual body of Christ, a Christian" (p. 10).*

> *"The Church of Christ is that total body of believers who have been obedient to the gospel" (**Ibid.**).*

> *"We don't come across quite so smug or defensive if we preach undenominational Christianity than when we're preaching church of Christism. Surely there are individuals in practically all the denominations known today who've learned of Jesus, looked to him in sincere faith, turned away from their conscience rebellion against his will and embraced him as savior through immersion in his name. And their unfortunate entanglement in some*

denominational error or some other in no way alters the fact that they are Christians. They have complied with the biblical terms of admission into the church. They're God's children. And to fail to recognize these people as members of Christ's church would make it proper to refuse recognition to any of us who are in error on any point, or to one of our brethren who has some moral problem or doctrinal misconception. And a posture like that would utterly destroy the New Testament concept of the church and make a mockery of divine grace. It would reduce salvation to a matter of human merit and knowing and doing every detail of the divine commandments and such an understanding would make us Old Testament Pharisees rather than New Testament Christians" (p. 12).

"...Sectarianism is an attitude that holds that only I or my friends and the people close to me can know or learn or teach the truth. It's a position of exclusivism that holds that we're the only ones who could possibly interpret the truth of God correctly and realize its significance for salvation" (p. 13).

"There are sincere, knowledgeable, devout Christians scattered among all the various denominations. Yet, they are separated from one another by credal formulations, human names, cumbersome organizational structures..." (p. 18).

"...let me ask that we rethink the biblical concept of the church. Let's not be flag waving partisans who demonstrate the sectarianism

we decry. We have exhibited a sectarian spirit through our attitudes and speeches and papers. Papers founded just to push one sectarian narrow view" (p. 19).

In 1984, brother Shelly wrote the book, *"I Just Want to Be a Christian"* (20th Century Christian, 2809 Granny White Pike, Nashville, TN 37204, 250 pp). Let us now observe some of the statements he made in this book.

"We must not narrow the base of fellowship beyond those fundamental teachings of the Word of God. Beyond the foundation matters which will be identified later in this volume from Ephesians 4, there is a broad ground where we can be charitable as brethren and hold our differing views (remember his speech in Memphis in 1984 of "F" and "f" fellowship, GM) without feeling a compulsion to coerce others to hold the same view. Hold to your opinion in good conscience, and explain or defend it when called upon to do so. Convince others of its truthfulness if you can, but don't force it upon others or make it a test of your fellowship with that person" (pp. 48-49).

"They have stoutly argued that the fellowship of American Christians known as the Church of Christ composes the total and exclusive (i.e., us all and us only) 'true church' in this age. No interpretation of the doctrine of the church could be more denominational" (p. 61).

"...if one's unfaithfulness relates to difficult ethical issues, church government, or worship (while not denying one of the foundational doctrines of Christianity), fellowship may be

maintained indefinitely for the sake of exhorting and encouraging in the truth" (p. 65).

"If one speaks of the church of Christ in its New Testament sense, then only those who are members of the church of Christ are saved - for the church of Christ is made up of all the saved... But if one speaks of identifiable modern-day fellowships of the Church of God or the Church of Christ and claims that only those who are members of one of those fellowships are saved, he has the immediate task of proving that the biblical sense and the modern-day sense are one and the same" (pp. 69-70).

"The 'one faith' has nothing to do with our methods and procedures of doing God's work; it has to do with the death, burial, and resurrection of Jesus and our response to that once-for-all act of atonement" (p. 82, note also his words of "... atonement..." p. 81, GM).

"My suggestion is that only such terms as pertain directly to the seven ones of Ephesians 4:4-6 are of such nature as to qualify as issues of faith (i.e. doctrinal tests of fellowship"), (p. 91).

"Adultery and lying are explicitly condemned in the Scripture; whatever else one can say about pianos and organs in worship, he cannot find their explicit condemnation in the Bible. Acceptance of their use certainly does not repudiate any of the seven essential items of Christian faith identified in Ephesians 4:4-6. At best, one comes to regard their use as wrong on the basis of a process of inferences

> *concerning biblical authority" (113).*
>
> *"The modern-day application I see for this episode relates to the way we treat people who are not members of the Church of Christ. Some of these people are our brethren in Christ whom I believe to be in error on certain points" (p. 138, cf. 121, 124, and remember this is in reference to Mark 9:38-42 that he also gave in his Centerville speech and with which he began his tract, "Christians Only," GM).*
>
> *"I see no reason to think one has to understand 'for the remission of sins' in order to be baptized scripturally, for I do not think there is* ***one*** *right reason for being baptized. I would say that one must be baptized for* ***a*** *right reason in order for his baptism to be acceptable..." (p. 144, emp. his).*

In a letter to Wayne Jackson, relative to the above point, brother Shelly said:

> *"I don't think one has to understand 'for the remission of sins' in order to be baptized scripturally, for I think there is ONE right reason for being baptized. I would say that one must be baptized for* ***a*** *right reason in order for his baptism to be acceptable - to obey God, to wash away sins, etc. (This means that I don't think that one receiving baptism 'to join the Baptist Church,' for example, has been scripturally baptized.) So long as one is baptized for a right reason, however, and is not consciously rejecting other clear teachings of the Word on that subject (e.g.: denying Acts 2:38,*

as one might well do if under a Baptist evangelist) his baptism seems to me to be proper" (p. 1, emp. in original, July 18, 1983, as given in the book mentioned earlier that Bert Thompson wrote, p. 15).

It was in February of 1984 that brother Shelly wrote:

*"Lately I have been bothered by two false teachings about baptism which are being circulated within our fellowship... Unless one expressly understands that baptism is 'for (i.e., unto) remission of sins,' he has not been baptized for the right reason, is still in his sins, and needs to be baptized again" (**The Ashwood Leaves**, "What Are They Saying About Baptism," February 1, 1984, Ashwood Church of Christ, 2206 21st Avenue So., Nashville, Tennessee 37212. Alan Highers, **op. cit.**, p. 30; Dub McClish, "**The Current 'Unity Movement' Its History, Status and Direction,"** Valid Publications, Inc., 312 Pearl Street, Denton, Texas 76201, p. 23, both refer to this and also give Shelly's example about the man he convinced to be baptized for the purpose "to obey Christ," GM).*

In March of 1985, brother Shelly said:

"From a biblical perspective, the letter of 1 Corinthians puts the matter to rest as to whether there are two levels of fellowship among believers" (Restoration Forum, March 18-20, Garnett Road Church of Christ, 12000 E. 31st St., Tulsa, Oklahoma 74146, a speech by Shelly, March 19th, unpublished ms.).

"If one adopts a policy of refusing to extend

*any measure of fellowship to brethren in Christ in whose beliefs and practices he cannot fully endorse, he will live in splendid isolation from everyone" (**Ibid.**).*

In August of 1985, brother Shelly said:

"I don't draw the line at the instrument. I don't think the Lord died over that. I'm not going to make that a test of fellowship with you in Christ...I don't want to be divisive over it. I refuse to be divisive over it. If I were in a congregation where the will of that congregation, the decision of the elders, was that the instrument was going to be used next week, I wouldn't mount the pulpit and condemn them and divide the church. I'd have a conscience question whether I could stay and worship with that church, but I would not stand up and say, 'Let the faithful of God step across the line and stand with me'" (Unity Forum, Hillsboro Family Camp, Hillsboro, Ohio, August 14, 1985, from a transcription of a tape by Shelly).

"Disfellowship of a believer is biblical under certain circumstances, but disfellowship of a believer ought to occur only when the error of belief he embraces denies the very heart of the gospel message (in this speech, brother Shelly also stated that this would be the sort of thing that John was talking about in 2 John 7-9, where some were denying that Jesus has really come in the flesh, Gnostic-type false teachers, GM), or an eror of conduct is flagrant and unrepented, or a divisive spirit is being exhibited that rides roughshod over others to bind

on them what God hasn't bound" (***Ibid.***).

"Brother DeWelt and I were in a forum...I would like to see, he would like to see, two congregations have enough vision - an instrumental/non-instrumental church...to send a single missionary team...individuals whose love for the Lord is uppermost, to work together in the real business of Christ - which is not promoting a certain sort of music... without it being made an issue or a bone of contention...some might be inclined to say, 'but they would have to...disavow it and say... it is evil, it is sinful and that anybody who does that is sinning.' Why? I don't believe that. When it is foregone simply as a matter of courtesy to the conscience of a brother or a group of brothers within the group,..." (***Ibid.***).

In February of 1988, brother Shelly delivered the first in a series of lessons on "The Sermon on the Mount." I take the following from the transcription of that lesson (given in the order of his presentation).

"The sermon that he must have preached many, many times. The sermon that Matthew from memory, maybe from some notes he jotted down hearing Jesus preach at various times. Maybe even written forms of this same sermon that others had pieced together and were circulating in written form (pp. 1-2).

"In Matthew's version of the sermon that he particularly links in memory to a particular day with crowds around him when he sat on an elevated place...the same sermon in content that over in the book of Luke is preached out

on the plain... Matthew's version, a composite put down for us... (p. 2).

"I'm not sure there is any sense in which the law of Moses is abrogated (p. 4).

"Obeying laws doesn't put a person into the kingdom of God (p. 8).

"The kingdom of God or the kingdom of heaven is neither the church nor the future state of the saved. It's an unfolding possibility in the life of every faithful disciple in the here and now...But the kingdom of heaven itself is the sovereign rule of God in the hearts and lives of the redeemed right now,...I hope we will be encouraged to pray your kingdom come...If there is any prayer the believing, existing, imperfect church of Christ needs to pray in this world today, it's precisely that petition. God, for this church, let your kingdom come (p. 11).

"I'm just beginning to understand some of the key principles but together with prayer and searching and openness I think...as we learn what it is to live in an evil age but to live with a new age pattern of the kingdom of heaven... (pp. 11-12).

"And having cleared the ground, I hope of a little bit of the idea that the sermon on the mount is some of those things that in the past we've thought or been told it is that really it obviously is not when you think about it" (p. 13, delivered at the Ashwood Church of Christ, February 7, 1988).

In March of 1988, brother Shelly delivered his seventh lesson in the series and it is from this transcription that I now give the following. Again, I give these quotes in the order of his presentation.

> *"...scripture for some of us, at times, has been the platform for fighting more than it has been the means of access into the heart of God...righteousness grows out of relationships, not out of battles over theology...a greater righteousness than the righteouness which is legalism and law keeping...And no where have we missed the interpretation of the Sermon on the Mount more grievously, consistently and damagingly to people than in hearing what Jesus said about divorce and remarriage... Verses thirty-one and thirty-two...These verses say, '...except for marital unfaithfulness...' (do you recognize this as being from the* **NIV?** *GM)...(pp. 1-2).*
>
> *"Adultery is not some later remarriage following a divorce. Adultery is the failing to keep covenant. Adultery is treating one's covenant companion with treachery. The basic reason God hates divorce is, it is a type of covenant breaking...I've begun to learn something about the Bible. God also deals with his creatures on the basis of reality as well as on the basis of the ideal. The ideal...The ideal is not only... The ideal is not only...(p. 3).*
>
> *"The one thing that the law specifically says defiles people before God is what we, under grace, have told people they have to do to honor the will of God...As with all the other commandments and rules of the Old Testa-*

ment, the historical interpretation has tended to miss the point of the rule though by a wide mark (p. 6).

"Jesus says, look, if you understand a court of law, just to get a divorce is to be guilty of adultery. Remember, adultery is not a sexual word. Fornication is the sexual word. The word adultery means covenant breaking. Adultery means disloyalty to pledges and covenants. So Jesus says don't get involved in divorce because divorce itself is adultery. Forget remarriage, remarriage is not what makes it adultery, it's divorce, that's covenant breaking. Remarriage is incidental if it does or doesn't occur (p. 7).

"If you get married and for whatever reason you get a divorce, you know what that makes you, it makes you a covenant breaker... Adultery is not just having an affair with somebody while you're still married. It can be failing to stay married when some effort might have changed things so you could have stayed married. The remarriage, I repeat, isn't adultery, but the failure to see through the original covenant, that's what adultery is (p. 8).

"I tell you the one thing I've decided I won't do. I'm not gonna ask anybody to try to cure a stituation by committing adultery, that is covenant breaking. I'm not gonna ask anybody to break up a covenant in order somehow to come in line with the will of God that says don't be a covenant breaker. At ten years ago, I could have given you every answer on every complex marriage and divorce question in a five minute sermon and given you time to sing

an extra song. But, I've lived long enough to come up against some real life situations that I don't believe fit any of the ideals which are stated in law and the law just doesn't tell you what to do when the ideal is left... The issue here is to not legalism's desire to fix case law for all situations, but the issue is new hearts for the basis for new relationships. I could work you out a book of case law, others already have and it's on sale... counsel them to throw themselves on the mercy of God for hope and salvation... the case, law judgment scenario and turn elders or congregations into courts of inquisitions into people's marriages (pp. 12-13).

"... but I tell you, whatever you've heard said by any body,... live in the certainities and not the ambiguities. Here's the certainty I have to offer you. I don't care what's in your past... At one level I can tell you I really don't care what's in your past, God's done something to fix that mess for you that you can never fix (p. 14, delivered at Ashwood, March 28, 1988).

In 1990, brother Shelly delivered a number of lectures and lessons and I have the taped messages from four of these different series. The transcription work from taped lessons, is one, unless you have done such, that you cannot comprehend. A great many hours and a number of days go into such an undertaking, but it is a work that is needful in order to be absolutely correct in what is being said. The first tape that was transcribed was twenty-seven pages typewritten. In these four series there are, if I have been accurately given the same, a total of eighteen messages.

I now am going to list *where* these were given, *when*

they were given, *the theme* of each series and *the specific titles* (full information was not available on each series). I am doing this for various reasons, and at the very outset, as the material is all basically the same. What I am saying is that if one has heard one full set, four to six lessons, he has, in essence, heard the four series. Indeed, the presentations do vary in some thoughts, examples, wordings, etc., but essentially they are the same. Therefore, I need not, with but few exceptions perhaps, give statements from all of these. These four presentations, the four series that I have, were given as follows.

a. **Place:** Richland Hills Church of Christ
6300 N. E. Loop 820
Fort Worth, Texas 76180

Date: February 3-4, 1990

Theme: "The Church In The 90's: The Challenge Of Change."

Topics: "A New Look At The church."
"How Will The Church Hear God?"
"How Will The Church Worship God?"
"How Will The Church Share God?"
"Christians Only... Questions Of Fellowship."

b. **Place:** Missouri Street Church of Christ
1600 N. Missouri Street
West Memphis, Arkansas 72301

Date: April 20-21, 1990

Theme: "The Church Of The 90's: The Challenge Of Change."

c. **Place:** Pepperdine University
24255 Pacific Coast Highway
Malibu, California 90265

Date: April 25-27, 1990

Topic: "If Jesus Were A Church."

d. **Place:** Church of Christ at White Station
1106 Colonial Road
Memphis, Tennessee 38117

Date: October 7-9, 1990

Theme: "The Second Incarnation: A Theology For The 21st Century Church."

Topics: "The Second Incarnation: Introduction."
"Scripture And The Church."
"The Identity Of The Church."
"The Nature Of The Church."
"Worship: Encounter With God."
"Evangelism: The Church's Reason To Be."

For the most part, I will be giving quotes, transcribed statements, from the series that were given at the Richland Hills Church of Christ on February 3-4, 1990 (when a change is made, it will be so indicated, as per the series listed above), which series they termed as a "Church Renewal Weekend" (*Rejoice*, Vol. 14, numbers 2, 3, 4, 5 and dated January 10, 17, 23, 31, 1990). Let me also state, that even if the three lessons already were given, which are going to be given at Northeastern Christian Jr. College in Villanova, Pennsylvania, March 24-27, 1991, under the theme, "Christian Service: The Fellowship Of The Towel," the material basically would be the same. I say this, as three times brother Shelly is speaking on "The Second Incarnation" (*Atlantic Christian*, Winter 1991, pp. 6,11; Quarterly Published by the College).

As the following statements are made by brother Shelly, we need to keep in mind a statement he made at various times. He says that he is "field testing," "trying it out on you," as he speaks, and that "the material is in the process of being written." The book, he says, will be entitled "The Second Incarnation," and "basically, it is an attempt to get at a theology for the church, an ecclesiology, that is both biblical and holds the prospect of being able to allow our fellowship of people to have something meaningful to do in the twenty-first century landscape of religious thought and activity" (Pepperdine Tape #1). He stated that he and Randy Harris, "a young scholar, a New Testament theologian" at David Lipscomb had been working on this material for about nine months, and the subtitle will be "A Theology For the 21st Century Church." He said he was "field testing a lot of it on you," and at Pepperdine he said, "I delivered a Reader's Digest condensed version of the material at Richland Hills in Fort Worth about two months ago" (*Ibid.*). He said, "Randy and I are receiving a number of requests right now that we could abandon our other jobs and make at least a short-term career of delivering this material" (*Ibid.*). He speaks of new realities being upon us and "changes that I know was initiated by the Spirit of God... that revitalization, that moving of the Spirit of God, the blowing of fresh winds... not happening just in our fellowship, but thank God it is happening in our fellowship of people... some people... have a theology of fear. But the mainstream of our people realize that some things needed to change and that God has set about to change them" (*Ibid.*).

Brother Shelly had said, at various times, he had not changed except in attitude and disposition. As you read the following, that I have personally and painstakingly, carefully, conscientiously and concentratingly transcribed, you can ascertain for yourself about this idea of "no change" or "change" (*quotes are in order of the lessons given*).

"We've not faced up to the calling of God to be on the cutting edge of relevance with a message that is still biblical. And we have separated those two and we have held them, and, and in contraposition to one another and we're not ready by in large as a fellowship of people...we're not ready for it. We don't even know the issues, much less are we doing much to provide answers...

"...or are we going to curse the change? Are we going to hold on to the 20's...40's...50's, or God help us the 80's or 90's, or are we going to be God's people at the moment for the time in the situation of change and crisis that God lays before us as a great opportunity to lift up Jesus Christ?

"I intend to try with all of my heart and with whatever I can do to influence any body else, to look at the present moment and to be a prophetic presence for Jesus Christ in that moment and to be a part of the second incarnation, as God does his work...Of all people, Christians probably hate change the most. We've adopted metaphors that pretty well imply that we don't intend to change. We make a fetish of nostalgia... The issue for me is not any more should we have it (a meeting) in July, but whether we ought to even have gospel meetings in the traditional sense that we've talked about...where I am, I think its a waste of time, energy and good money. We don't do it any more. That's not the way to reach people with the message of Jesus Christ.

"We've constructed a theology that's, well, one

of the buzz words 'the old paths,' and very often that's nothing more than stubborn traditionalism dressed up in religious... If by 'the old paths' we mean what I'm going to talk about in a moment in terms of faithfulness to biblical theology, You betcha, I'm for 'the old paths,' but frankly that's not what we mean... Most often we mean...

"...metaphor...its unfortunate I think that we chose to accentuate the ones that smack of rigidity, unbendingness and...maybe some times even pig headedness...I'm just speaking confessionally folks...if it indicts any body else, maybe it just means some body else has been just like me...There are, indeed, some core things that are unalterable...the fact remains though that the God of the Bible is a God of change. He is a God of freshness every morning...always stirring the waters...a new name...new covenant...new spirit...God's into stuff...

"New wine is poured into new wine skins... tired forms won't work with an exuberant message...He wasn't just talking about Pentecost...the gospel is always bubbling. The wine skins are the forms, and the institutions, and the models and programs that work at a given time for the sake of allowing that gospel to ferment and do its work, but those touch points between the gospel and the culture... whatever those wine skins are, those models and programs, there always going to have to change because...the abiding challenge to the people of God is to distinguish the wine from

the wine skins...the gospel from the traditions. Tired forms just won't work any more and the deep ruts of customary practice are not adequate to call the highway to holiness.

"The alternative to rigidity and destruction is to experience renewal that's constant. Individual believers need ongoing invigoration from the Spirit of God, and we've got to quit being afraid to talk about the Spirit of God and we've got to be open to the Spirit of God and we have to seek the fulness of the Spirit of God... Whole churches have to be open to the Spirit of God, to move among, to transform and to give life...as an alternative to the static institutional model most of us have of the church.

"The tired, uninspiring event we call worship in traditional churches has to give way to the exhilarating experience of God that exhibits and nurtures life in the worshippers.

"The life of the church must be less a series of promotions and programs and a loving atmosphere for sin-confessing, faith-sharing, support-giving believers. And the church must realize... A.A., N.A., whatever, they are the church of the modern time is because they are doing what the church has not been willing to do. They're closer to the church many times than we are in a non-judgmental, non-stifle way in relation to sinners. Every body is allowed in whose just tired of being a sinner...And if we'd been the church, society would not have invented the secular alternative to it that's helping the people we've run off...we've got

to understand...rather than retreating from it into the insulated forces of smug religiosity... We've got to have a concern about social justice...

"The church has got to change. If it doesn't change my kids are not going to stay with it. I'm probably going to stay with it - not sure - if it doesn't actually let God's presence breathe in it. But I intend to stay. I'll probably be here til I die, in this fellowship of people. I don't intend to be run out - fellow tried - I don't intend to be run out. I'm not about to quit on it. But my children won't stay with it, if it doesn't address the issues that are real in their world. Mine was the last generation that would tolerate indoctrination...Mine was the last generation that would tolerate indoctrination and sit through things we knew were mockeries of the reality we were giving lip service to and tolerate it. My kids won't...One of these days there will be grandchildren. They won't stay with a tired institution that calls itself the church, if that institution doesn't begin trying to be the church...I am not threatened. I am not depressed. I feel better about...than I have been able to feel in my adult life because I am convinced that the Spirit of God is stirring us up to do good things.

"I love this church (meaning, Richland Hills, GM). You're one of the places...you said... business as usual isn't God's way.

"Our own perfectionistic theology was depressing all of us and gouging us under heel and crushing us. We are not able to give God

perfection...Let's not be perfectionists. Let's be Christians who live on the cutting edge of God's grace...The church has got to change... Jesus knew that most people would prefer the taste of the old wine to the new, and so this text that I read (meaning Luke 5:36ff, GM) ends at verse 39. 'No one after drinking old wine wants the new, he says, 'The old is better.' The old is familiar and comfortable. It makes no demands. It produces no tensions. It causes no discomfort...The kind of perfectionistic theology, the sorta list theology and checking it off...The Christian faith isn't manageable folks. The Christian faith is bubbling new wine...it is not something capped that you let out, you know, just a little spurt at a time on your whim.

"Moving beyond the sphere of the gospel's new wine...let's determine to be instruments of God's purpose to renew His church for the 21st century, because without renewal we'll become increasingly irrelevant to God's purpose in the world and we'll be broken, spilling and wasting the precious wine of the gospel. Without renewal we'll have no value to the purposes of a holy God or the needs of a lost world.

"It absolutely astonishes me that I once thought that the depository of truth on God's earth was the fellowship of people called the church of Christ, and that the only place God was working was in our narrow little .0012% of the world's people.

"It astonishes me that I could ever believe that

my God was so narrow... small... self-contained that He couldn't work except in situations that I found comfortable, in ruts I'd been traveling that were so deep.

"A church that is inseparable from Jesus Christ must discover and affirm its identity in Him. So we begin at the beginning. We start in the gospels to find what the church is supposed to be rather than in the epistles or Acts. Restoration groups almost all live in Acts, because their mistaken assumption is that what they're trying to restore is the church of Acts, the church of the 1st century. I don't mind being part of a restoration movement, but I want you to know what I'm trying to restore. I'm not trying to restore the first century church. I'm trying to restore the thing the first century church was trying to do.

"Most restoration groups are at this third level (he spoke of 'copying the copy,' GM). The model is Jesus. The sculptors, and painters and... trying to reproduce His image, that is the first century church. Here we are, 21st century setting as our goal, 'copying the copy?'... In His own person and work, Jesus of Nazareth is the standard for the church... I do not want to compare or measure up to a norm of a first century attempt to paint a picture which was never right! They never had it right! Perfectly right! They didn't get Him down on canvass just exactly the way He should have been. Not in the life of the Jerusalem church, not... Antioch... Corinth.

"We must focus on the person to be His

church, rather than focusing on the history of churches which have given us only imperfect glimpses of His flawlessness... They never get it right. I'm copying a flawed copy... reproduce the flaws... introduce more flaws.

"The first century church tried to take what Jesus was about in His incarnation, God in the flesh and put it into a second incarnation which was the church as spiritual body of Christ. 21st century I want to do what they were doing. I don't want to do it just like they did it. My culture is not like theirs...

"The hermeneutic we use says our grid has to be the first century church, and its commands, examples and inferences... and if they did it, we do it. And our big concern is, when are examples binding? The answer is never, Never. What is binding is whatever theological principle caused them to do what they did in their culture and that theological principle is binding, brother. It is absolute because it expresses the nature of God in relation to man and his needs... The old hermeneutic will not make that distinction. What we've done is by intuition, by intuition, intuition. We've made some distinctions that our hermeneutic really doesn't allow us to make. And we've done better than our system should ever have generated. Common sense saved us (I don't always mention it, but a lot of laughs came from his statements, such as at this particular point, GM)... I'm as serious as a heart attack. Common sense and intuition saved us...

"Is there a hermeneutic that allows you with

consistency and with spiritual insight to make that kind of distinction without getting caught up and tripping over your feet as we have (he had previously spoken of kissing, foot washing, one cup and taking care of orphans, GM)? I believe there is. I cannot spin it out for you in full detail, but I can give you the outline of it and I'll leave some of you to work with me on it and with Randy. And we'll do better.

"The point of all this is to pry our thinking away from the institutional focus to a personal focus. The church is not an institution...its an organism. The church's identity is not the sum total of its doctrinal behavior components as witnessed in Acts and the epistles. Its identity is found in duplicating the life of Jesus as originally seen in the gospels. For the purposes of formulating a theology of the church that can have hope of surviving the century ahead and meeting needs allegiances are going to have to shift. Denominational loyalty has to give way to loyalty to Christ. Commit to a local church must be a means to an end of commitment to Christ, and not an alternative to it and Christ must be all in all with our imperfect approximations...seen for exactly what they are, imperfect approximations.

"Two different models of church history. One of them Randy and I call the golden age great pit theory of church history. This is the one you know...this is that ideal church which never existed...apostasy...about 150 years ago there came a restoration movement and you and I got right back to where it was over here

(using the board and drawing a diagram, GM) so we're exactly what they were back there and for all this intervening centuries folks were in the great pit. From the golden age past the great pit, there we stand. That is an awful self-serving of mockery of truth and reality... Which church do you want to restore? Jerusalem, with its lack of evangelistic zeal? Or restore Corinth with its open fornication and, and drunkenness in church services around communion time? What about Colossae with its heresy? What about Ephesus? What about Laodicea, that church that says, 'We've got it'? And He said you're dead as a hammer and don't know it (laugh). They said, 'We don't need anything' and He said, 'You need everything.'

"There's another model for the church that's much more biblical that starts at the same place as the other one... This is the ideal. This is Jesus instantiated in the corporate life of a body of people. That's why it is a church. And here is the history of the church, this church, Woodmond Hills church, American restoration movement church, all church history, from Pentecost forward. Some days we do better than others and some churches some times with certain challenges and prophetic voices are closer and farther. None has ever been there (pointing, pecking on the board, GM). Its a radically different model, isn't it? I won't ask for a show of hands...just ask you to be honest in your own heart, which one represents reality? I know which one looks better on a chart for self-serving purposes. It is sorta like that sermon all of us use to preach. 'The

marks of a true church.' And by the time we got through, whatever church we were preaching for, of course, we described. The name, not 'a' name, the name of the church was church of Christ. And the organization was, not necessarily the one at Jerusalem or Philippi, but the one we had with this man, and the worship, and da da da (?) and whether or not you gave to orphan homes and by the time you got through, add it up, whats you got? What we are. Most self-serving, I don't preach that sermon any more. Because it is just really an exercise in arrogant hypocrisy. It was designed to defend us, not discover truth and move toward it.

"Here's the text. This is the text that I've been exegeting for you for 35 minutes. Ephesians chapter one and we'll begin the reading at 18... I believe its the greatest complement ever paid the church in the Bible... or more naturally it seems to me to say... that the church somehow brings Christ to fulness. Now, you have to be very careful here. In His first incarnation, Christ didn't exist apart from his physical body. In his second incarnation Christ does not depend in any sense for his existence on us... The passage in question presents the church as Christ's spiritual body, and in this context the passage can be seen to make perfectly good sense... ***pleroma****... if that's Paul's meaning he's saying that the church carries on in its corporate spiritual life what Christ began in His physical presence... Our present challenge is to understand the church after a new, more biblical model, as a second incarnation.*

God lives in this world via His spiritual body. The church takes up and continues the life of God in the flesh that was begun with the historic person of Jesus. Many things about the nature, mission and function of the church can be understood only against this background understanding of the church's identity.

"The misunderstandings of the church...the commoner mistake among believers is to say 'the church is what we are.' And circle the wagons and be defensive. Therefore the church is a group of folks in religious assemblies like this...or its narrow-minded bigots, or its cold-hearted insensitive people, or its just people who are fundamentally no different in their moral spiritual lives than the non-Christians with whom they live and the flattering or unflattering images of what the church is, depending on what they see in us. Those images define the church for most people.

"We have to realize that there is no finality for the church in any of its corporate manifestations, Jerusalem, Corinth, Antioch, Richland Hills...If there were a perfect church, of course, it would be the one where I am (said facetiously, GM)...our proper task even then would not be to reproduce its form, but to capture for ourselves this vision of modeling Christ that made it a church. See the distinction?...but to model in a corporate body what Jesus was in His first incarnation as God among us...

"Our goal of being the church must derive from a personal love relationship, discipleship

relationship with Christ rather than a reproduction of form, ritual and methodology. I am no longer looking for a list of items to reproduce in corporate life. I'm trying to see Jesus, so I can live Him. We need to acknowledge the Jesus of the gospels as the standard for the church rather than the projects in Acts or the organization of the epistles...the rallying cry that we've lost, no creed but Christ, is fundamentally sound and needs to be reembraced.

"God help us to be a pilgrim church with a personal rather than institutional focus that will allow us to change so as to be God's people." (***All quotes from tape #1.***)

"I am going to talk about hermeneutics...taking a text, making sense of it, understanding the author's intentions and meaning and then doing whatever is appropriate with that meaning...imaginary dialogue...What should the modern church be like? If you ask this question of members of churches of Christ someone will always reply, 'The church today should be like the first century church we read about in the New Testament.' Sounds so simple...all we have to do...any body with one eye and half sense can, go back and read what they were and did, set it down where you are...go back to our person to whom the question has been placed...you mean we should have open fornication and abuses of the Lord's Supper like in Corinth?...then we...have charismatic worship services including tongue speaking... (he says, 'Oh, I see,' or 'Oh, I guess you'll want us...' or ..., between each answer,

GM). Then I guess you'll want us to tear the New Testaments out of our Bibles since the early...only Old Testament scriptures?...(the imaginary one now says, 'I've stated it correctly,' after another try at answering what has been thrown back at him, and now we hear) Ah, I say, so we must practice foot washing, women must wear veils,...? 'What I mean is,' this fellow now says, 'I really don't know what I mean' (laughter). I think...the answer is not as simple as...

"Our task in this segment of the study is to try to understand the role of scripture in developing a vision for the modern church...in building a theology for the modern church...three questions ...nature of scripture...meaning of scripture...how do we do the applications... apply the text to my contemporary situations...

"Luke did his research. He said, Look, I've followed this out real closely and read the accounts that are circulating, whatever they were, Mark, Q, what, I don't know, scraps, listened to preaching, but when he sat down the Spirit of God so guided him that when he pulled all his notes together and his recollections, what he put down was a proper account, an accurate account, a theologically appropriate account for his purpose. Obviously the purpose was different than Matthew's purpose. One of the worse things we've ever done with the gospels was to study them in a harmony of the gospels fashion.

"Well, sometimes we try to understand the Bible and we use the Bible, scissors and paste,

proof text preaching, string of pearls theology, grab a verse here, grab a verse here...string of pearls but it gets to the conclusion I want and that is all that counts. Some of us have formed our hermeneutic that way.

"How do you derive the pattern? Pattern theology has been our undoing. Pattern theology we have learned to generate by a hermeneutic of command, example and inference...it assumes that the Bible is all of a kind in terms of literature, that all of it is case study legislation, so you take this system and you put the grid over it and what you come up with is your pattern. None of the Bible is written as English case law...You see, we juggled all sorts to make it fit that hermeneutic, and we have done better than our hermeneutic should have allowed. Sanctified common sense has kept us from doing the things that hermeneutic would really have required of us...the extreme right...have been more consistent with that hermeneutic than we've been. But we regard them as eccentrics.

"How do I apply the text to my contemporary situation, if not by string of pearls, command, example, inference, pattern theology? If there were an exact correspondence between my situation, my culture, my crisis, as between those in scripture in those cultures, in those crisis situations, there would be no problem. I'd simply address the situation in the exact manner mandated by scripture, but that's almost never the case. Maybe never...So what principle or principles allow us to move

responsibly from the biblical world...to our world? We would argue that the only thing that would allow it is not this, not the search for, derivation, artificial creation of a pattern theology. But the scripture can be applied to our situation only through theological principles. In a moment I'll add one other term to that.

"What do you mean by theological principles? A theological principle is some statement of truth that has to do directly with the nature of God and His salvific work on our behalf. Since God is unchanging, principles drawn from His nature are always going to apply...The fullest and clearest revelation of God, person and work is Jesus Christ...So these theological principles generate a Christocentric, Christ-centered, a Christocentric theology...not the commands...all the commands are binding. Really? Go sell everything you have and give to the poor. Greet one another with a holy kiss...When is an example binding? Never. An example is never binding. An historical precedent simply shows that at one time in one place...Its the theological principles, those that deal with the nature of God as seen in Christ, ultimately as seen in the salvation work of the cross...We believe that these particular forms or expressions are binding if and only if they are inextricable from the theological principle from which they are an expression. That's the hardest statement I'll make all morning and the one you need to hear most clearly (statement repeated, GM). Now let me explain. This means I reject a rigid pattern

theology.

"A woman ought to be able to testify along with a man in any setting, public or private... discussions in class rooms, devotionals, prayers, men and women praying together in homes, in devotionals, in small groups...I want to conclude by saying directly to the topic of ecclesiology, the church, a theology for the church...and we want to be led by scripture to embody God's truth and ways that speak to our time and our place. Scripture demands no more and we must settle for no less. And by this we can even settle the issue that has plagued us so long, so, with so much difficulty. If in fact we followed a Christocentric hermeneutic realizing that Christ and His salvific work on the cross, Christ and Him crucified, that that's central...some things are more important than others. Some things are going to be a test of fellowship for me, some ain't. I'm going to argue for acapella music because I think its consistent with the theological principle with regard to worship, let it edify. Let it communicate. But now is that the front end issue, is that the one I want to settle first, is that going to be for me the ultimate acid test to whether the person is a child of God or not, no, because that's not as near the cross, as baptism is, let's say.

"We affirm scripture as the word of God, word of man to be handled responsibly and to be lived under in consecrated discipleship. Not around the notion of rigid pattern, and scissors and paste and string of pearls. But a theology

of Christocentric interpretation so that the value, the worth, the centrality of any issue, the bindingness of whether or not this is sign or a symbol, whether it's cultural or whether it relates to something eternal, is grounded in the theological principle that underlies it and whether or not that particular expression embodies in some way that theological truth or is incidental to it.

"Father,...and to the end that you would change us and renew us, that you would liberate us from deep ruts and an inadequate methodology with scripture. A poor hermeneutic that has no way of distinguishing except by a sort of list mentality, and my list can never match any body else's. God, let us, let us have a person focused theology. Let it have to do with the principles that are eternal, transcultural, and let us have the freedom and liberty under grace to apply in our own culture those principles in meaningful ways that, that liberate souls from bondage and lift up Jesus Christ to be glorified. For its in His name that we pray. Amen." ***(All quotes from tape #2.)***

"This is the first time I've presented some of this material... This is the first time in coming to Dallas, Fort Worth, the metroplex area, to Richland Hills for me to present the material. I'm not yet as articulate with it as I intend to be, as I want to be. There's some things I'm sure that I haven't thought of yet that needs to be done. I, I call this field testing the material on you... These issues are the ones people who are going to be leaders in the church of this

21st century are wanting to address. Randy and I are under no illusions of arrogance that we have the final word on any of these things. You see, that's one of the beauties we think we've discovered in understanding God. He doesn't expect us to have the last word on it. And it's all right if we only make some contributions to it, hit some things and miss others and leave other folks to work it out. That's okay. I've gotten beyond perfectionism as the spiritual base for life and the notion that works righteousness is the way that I have to get to heaven. So we are doing the best we can to help...to address the issues where we know they have concern, but we have no illusions that what we're offering is final or definitive. We do want it to be helpful. I appreciate the affirming things that I have seen, heard from you. Some of you are here probably because you came determined to disagree but to get some good notes, so you could be among the first people to expose and write articles...you may be right in everything you're going to say...And I will be in dialogue with you if you will ever allow that. And I will not reject you, and I am sorry that you have felt compelled to reject me...for the people who maybe are not here but who'll get the tapes...be so open...we just create a new church where the atmosphere is not one of eager typewriter and yellow journalism and expose lectureships, but where we really create the body of Christ.

"We've got to stop this silly business of suicide. This business of bleeding ourselves to death when there's a Christless world facing a Christ-

less eternity...be able to live within a diversity that is still the body of Christ. And we must not preserve the illusions that we're the only honest truth-seekers in the world. We just need to be honest truth-seekers. We need to stop being sectarian in mindset and attitude. We need a hermeneutic, we need an attitude toward God and toward one another that will allow us to get beyond a check list mentality. So that I can only love the people who are just like me and who think the way I think or who let me think for them...I want to be part of a process that challenges people to let God stretch us, and cause us to think, and to find a way to give Him glory...I happen to be in a particular religious heritage that I believe has some right-headed notions, at least some rhetoric that's good and I've always taken the rhetoric seriously...not claiming to be the only Christians, but just concerned to be Christians only...be the church, not yellow pages, sectarian identity, but the church of a sort that was created in the New Testament, because it had a vision and a goal to reproduce Christ in its life. If we can do that in our local churches, God has a place for us. God has something for us to do. And if we get our hermeneutic right, so that what is central to the heart of God, and what's critical to the saving work of Christ, those are the mountain peak issues. The really, really important issues...we realize...landscape can have some variation, and that there can be some diversity within our fellowship and in other fellowships that still can be affirmed as biblical. That can still be acknowledged to be Christ-honoring, truth-seeking, Bible-believing...then our image will change...I pray for that day. I preach for it. I write for it. I beg for it. I want to be part of it where I am, and I want today to make some positive contribution to that in you.

"You begin to realize that the Bible is a radical continuity, not a radical discontinuity. All of a sudden the Old Testament has a place in your theology as well as the New Testament. And you realize that the same God wrote both. We almost have an idea that God was converted at Pentecost (laughter)...There was not a non-gracious, non-loving, hard-nosed God in the Old Testament who grew up and matured and became a Father in the New Testament...Every theological truth that is evident, instantiated, codified in the Old Testament in a particular historical cultural situation is still just as true today as it was in Eden, or...Noah...Moses... Jesus preached from the mountain...there is radical continuity, not radical discontinuity...A lot of what we're going to have to learn... about worship...will come from finding theological principles that are in the Old Testament and realizing that those principles are New Testament principles...eternal theological truths...This was the Bible of the early church and it's still our Bible... And what's there about worship in the Old Testament that we've discounted, that we've said, 'that's the Old Testament, it doesn't count...instruments... clergy...none of that counts,' that's wrong. There is no more majestic insight into worship, that we need to bring into our

worship, than what comes in Isaiah chapter six.

"Worship is suppose to be an existential moment. There are different models of worship, ours is principally an educational model... that's what is supposed to happen when we worship, we are supposed to meet God... Worship is a mysticism... Worship is an existential experience...but the principle that worship involves the head has sometimes, for rationalists like us, and boy we have that heritage...we've forgotten that the heart is there too... Our people have been content to believe, that given whatever hermeneutic, that if they get the item right, sequence them in some reasonable flow, worship will have occurred... Worship has to be an existential event of seeing the Lord high and lifted up...existential, encounter moment. If there's anything the church needs to change, the church as I know in my heritage and tradition, is worship. Worship needs to become an encounter experience...an encounter with God, that you have had a holy ***WOW****. You saw the Lord. You heard a word from God that addressed your life, and I know I've worshipped.*

"Worship is not getting there and going through a boring routine, predictable, you know what's coming next...the sermon is about as remote from life as can be. It addresses the 1940's, HEAD ON (laughter)...leaves me to face a 21st century without a word from God. And I leave...so empty. Or, depending on the nature of the preaching, I came needing

to be bathed in the love of God and to know that He has purged me and that I'm clean by His grace, and I am leaving beaten, and bloodied, and depressed...and what I got was a dose of guilt that is just the last kick in the gut I could stand. There is no reason to go on... When people meet God they leave with a sense, everything's just about like it ought to be... If you understand who God is, worship is spontaneous and unavoidable...it's the holy ***WOW****.*

"...and a lot of the stuff we do in our music is not worth doing. Its theologically abhorrent and obscene... A criterion for the music we use needs to be a theological criterion... A lot of those old songs I grew up singing, I don't sing any more... There is a lot of contemporary Christian music being written and performed in this world that we need to get into our worship...a lot of it is WONDERFUL... And why when a church introduces one or two of those are they written up for three months?... (much laughter here is caused by the way he speaks about the songs, and I have no desire to give it, GM)... Somewhere we got the idea that is (speaking of a capella) the only kind of singing that we can do, and that it's unscriptural to have a solo, sung by male or female or a quartet, male, female mixed or a chorus or a choir. CAN'T DO THAT!... (laughter and clapping)...a deep rut we've worn called tradition.

"...enjoy hearing...we could be instructed by...exhorted by special music. We've got to

admit what all of us usually do privately. 'Well, I don't think there is a thing in the world wrong with it, but I'm just not comfortable with it because we have never done that.' If it is appropriate to the principles of worship and gives God glory and edifies, let's be open to doing it.

"Let's highlight communion...we do something special...we do something special. Sometimes I do it, sometimes others do it to focus in on the communion, and we commune! And that is our fellowship...affirmation...declaration..." (it seems to me that he is light-hearted in speaking about, that is, his tone, etc. when he says, 'and now repent and be baptized, shall we stand and sing. You know when it's ending, he starts tacking this three minute thing on about the invitation...Is the public standing singing the invitation mandated in every assembly? Of course, it isn't. Try not having one Sunday morning,' GM).

"Let there be a period of confession...God there's people here...right now there is some of us who need to do business with you...God right now, listen to the hearts...God right now some are going to confess to you things going on in their families, listen, God, there's some people carrying secret vices here who want to be set free from them, alcohol, homosexuality, greed. God listen to them pour out their hearts to you right now...God hear them...and then why can't we do a priestly absolution? In the name of Jesus I can affirm to people every promise that's in the word. I

can say at the end of that prayer, to every one of you, children of God in this room in covenant relationship with Jesus Christ, with whatever sin you brought, with whatever hurt, whatever pain, whatever...if you have just offered it to God, now on the authority of that same God, I tell you, HE TOOK IT. And in the name of Jesus. I absolve you. It's His absolution. I am the one speaking at this moment to affirm His promise to you. Believe it and claim it and let a choral group, or let a solo, or let a song be led (quotes the second verse of "It Is Well With My Soul," GM)... You think people could not go through an hour and fifteen to twenty minutes of worship like that and leaving feeling other than whipped, beaten down, depressed, and wishing they hadn't come to this boring thing? I can tell you the tales of worship experiences in the church that I'm with that I live and get to share in...it's just by the turning loose of our people by the elders. Use your mind, your hearts, your creativity that are gifts from God in the context of helping us learn to worship. You don't have to do anything unscriptural, but you need to break some calcified molds...

"When Jesus met with the Samaritan woman, what he told her then was still true. God is a Spirit...those are not the...issues...the issue is, God is a Spirit, can you worship Him in spirit and truth...Spirit there means spirit to Spirit. God is a Spirit, can you lift your spirit to His. Will you let your worship be spiritual, not just form, of place...will you come in spirit and truth, and if you will, you can

worship...May God help us rise above the familiar, and comfortable and routine to worship Him, in spirit and truth (lots of loud clapping, GM). ***(All quotes from tape #3.)***

"I bring you greetings from the Woodmont Hills Church in Nashville, a sister church to you in many, many ways...the kind of church each of us is trying to be and the many common things we share...It is important that we be part of the change that is happening in the world and not be left behind by it. The gospel is new wine and we can't keep it in old wine skins...The church must change. The church must change in terms of its form and its methodologies because the world changes... The church is a living organism and it must change to live and thrive. But what the church says, stays the same.

"We provide the encountered experience with God. The church is a place where we meet God. The preaching of the word of God is an encounter with the living Christ...please open with me to my favorite text in all the Bible, it's in Philippians chapter two. And from this text I want to preach the gospel. I want to answer the question, 'Who is Jesus Christ?' (prayer).

"In...Paul is talking to the church as a community of the cross. Talking about how we live and why we live that way...Why would God become a man? No, there's not a great deal of logic to it. After all, we're not saved by amazing logic, we're saved by amazing grace (Shelly himself kinda laughs)...Salvation is by grace

through faith, it's not by what you have done, will promise never to do again, or will someday do to give God glory, no sir. Salvation is by grace, free gift,...you don't add any thing to it, you don't dot an 'i,' you don't cross a 't,' you don't finish it off, you don't add point 001% to what God has done in the main, you accept it, if you accept it all as a free gift, by faith... That's why we're the community of the cross and that's the message we proclaim...the hope we embrace...his body the community of the cross." ***(All quotes from tape # 4, side 1.)***

"You know you're a model church in a lots of ways. YOU DON'T KNOW the degree to which you are looked at as a model church. I know that sometimes you have the idea that you are a target church...some people who don't understand, who will not hear, or who out of a set of fears that they can't deal with feel compelled, really believe it's the will of God, that they should chastise, critique, and, don't get angry, don't fight back and don't answer them...Stay about your task. You're a role model church in a way that you can't understand being a part of it...You can't see it as an insider...role model church...a marvelous model...a role model church in many ways and I love you and respect you, and to know that I have a link with you.

"This week I've had one of the most exciting experiences in my life...best weekend I can remember, I feel more exhilarated than I have in ages...my spirit is so refreshed and lifted up...I've taken some material that I have been

working on for some time, 44 years now (laughter)...to field test on you and to try out on you...God is the one leading the direction, charting the course and that they're people like you and a church like this open to that and determined to follow that leading without fear. The theme this weekend has been renewal, change, getting ready for something that's already on us, the 21st century. How do we handle it?...We need to change. The church is not fixed and static. The church is a pilgrim church. Our model of the church that we've sometimes developed that something's finished and back in place that once was in place and people lost, that's just a false model. The perfect church has always been an abstract ideal, unrealized in any particular place and time...the church has always...been a pilgrim church...we've missed the ideal, it is not to re-establish the first century church...grab the same vision the first century church had, which is to instantiate Christ in a corporate life. Our goal is not to take an institutional model and reset it in another setting, but to take the model of the living organism. The church is the body of Christ.

"The church is supposed to be the second incarnation. Jesus of Nazareth was the first incarnation of God...The church is supposed to be taken up in its corporate life, the church is the spiritual body of Christ where he left off...

"Pray as we begin...renew us, change us, create in us a yearning for you that will not be

appeased by the empty things we've persued and been content with in the past...we're tired of playing church and mocking the cross, tired of sermons that stroke our egos but fail to challenge our spirits. And God, we're tired of programs that perpetuate an institution, but do nothing to put people in touch with Jesus' power to save. God we don't want any more of that. We want to be changed...we're sick of squabbling over...renew us and change us. Don't let us be content with things as they have been...Let us be your spiritual body in this world extending in our corporate life as a church, a fellowship of people...Amen.

"A concept of church history that I call the pilgrim Church and set that over against the idea that once that there was a church ideal as God meant it to be...apostasy...we've set it back right like it is supposed to be. 150 years ago we discovered it and fixed it right and we are, and none others are. We haven't done well with the issue of fellowship...I'm talking about the larger doctrine of fellowship of embracing one another in the body, affirming one another all of those who are our brothers and sisters in the Lord...a true oneness...as opposed to living with a fractured, fractious, sectarian spirit, chip on the shoulder mentality, self-serving concept...let's be where God wants us and every other person and group to be set at nought...

"We have our priorities inverted. We've majored in the minor things and we're letting the world go to hell in the process...the

joke...St. Peter showing around in heaven and...a little group huddled by themselves... Sh, that's the church of Christ over there, they think they're the only ones in the place...My goal is to be a Christian only and I do not see entailed in that the claim that I, and the folks just like me are the only Christians in this world. I don't believe that. And if you ask me how I know that there are Christians outside the fellowship with which I identify and work most often. My answer...some outside our fellowship by the same means I know there's some inside. I've had conversations with them where I've heard them express their faith... told their reception of Jesus Christ...and I see in their lives the fruit of the Spirit. I don't keep the roll for the church of Christ in the sense that that term is used in the Bible. In the Bible, the church of Christ is never used as a title, as a church name. The church is described as Christ's church, church of Christ... It's never used in the way we use it, in a sectarian sense. I call it yellow pages church of Christ...I don't keep the roll of the church of Christ that God defines that term...We've invented the doctrine of the invisible church... I'm equally sure there are some names on God's roll that are not any where on the ones we keep.

"In 1st John chapter one...important theological principle to deal with...fellowship...walking in the light again has not to do with perfect theology and perfect performance, but walking in grace. It has to do with an orientation of a light, not perfect performance within

that light. What we haven't read, always, what we've not always taken as a base of fellowship is what's in that opening paragraph...John says I'm concerned about fellowship at this level...this depends on that...our fellowship with one another is sometimes confused and garbled, and not quiet clear...that really grows out of a prior fellowship that each of us has with God and that's the critical, base line for fellowship. That's why I said a moment ago, God knows those who are his own. Since I don't know hearts, since I can't read minds, since I don't know everyone's background, I may make some presumptive judgments that because someone is in a fellowship other than mine, that maybe he doesn't believe, has not responded to, has not embraced the Savior through the gospel of Jesus, but you see, that may be a false, sectarian, totally unwarranted judgment. There are just as many bright people out there and just as many honest hearts out there as there are in here. I've met so many of them...God alone knows the heart...What does the church of Christ believe about so and so, and I say, well, just about everything (laughter). You name it, I can spot you somebody who'll believe that one.

"I don't want to be any body's mind. I don't want to do any body's thinking for them. I want to challenge folks to think. I'm basically a school teacher, and my role as a school teacher is not to spit out facts and get them regurgitated. It's to try to make people think...Folks can think in lots of places other than our fellowship...God knows those who are his.

"A young lady signed a visitor's card a while back... been coming about six to eight months... she wrote on her attendance card, 'I'd like to have an appointment with...' (She explained about her reading Romans 6, talking with her father, a deacon, and then asking her pastor to immerse her into Christ, and... 'now what do I need to do to be a member of the church of Christ?') I looked her right in the eye and said, My dear, since the day that happened you've been a member of the only church of Christ I care to be a member of or to be affiliated with. If you want to identify with this fellowship and be a part of our corporate life as a church, all you have to do is just say so and I'll tell the church... And so the next Sunday... Would you have a problem extending full fellowship to that lady? Oh, I hope not. If so, you don't understand how great God works. You don't understand how we're saved by grace through faith. You don't understand what Romans six is about... And the Lord almighty saved her... And I believe God will bless every truth in all kinds of settings... You see, salvation is not the possession of the church of Christ... our extending our fellowship to people is not the same as God extending his open heart to people through Christ on the cross.

"I want us to be a fellowship of truth seekers. I want us to be a body of people so in love with Jesus Christ... Fellowship exists at, at least two levels (purchase level and practice level; this is his 'F' and 'f' levels of fellowship, GM). Purchase level has to do with what I describe with regard to the gospel. At a

purchase level fellowship is extended from God to all of us who through our faith in Christ have been incorporated into His body by virtue of the new birth of water and the Spirit. At that purchase level fellowship is not mine to dispense or withhold, God creates it. When God births somebody into His family, it is not up to me to decide whether he's my brother, whether she is my sister...All those who are born of the water and Spirit, they're spiritually our brothers and sisters...second level...call practice level...individual beliefs, pecularities, and convictions...sometimes separate us from others...isolate ourselves off from others. The views about the millennium, church support of institutional bodies to help and assist in various works...widows...or Herald of Truth or, or instrumental music, or dispensational theology, or capital punishment, I mean the list just goes on and on. At that level we don't have to extend fellowship to one another on every issue...We've let too many of those things divide us needlessly. Because we've not kept the focus of the purchase level...we've let our issues be central...

"I don't know how to answer all the questions...want to oppose in our body. I know we can't extend fellowship to folks who are not born anew into the family. Our fellowship can't go where God's grace through Christ has not gone by the application of His blood...I can respect that (referring to one of those four elements of Christian faith that relates to the person and work of Christ in salvation, 2 John 7-9...John says anybody who denies that...

docetics, these gnostics... can't be in the body... in fellowship, GM), any body who denies one of those core truths of the Christian faith... I know... 1 Corinthians chapter five... How many churches do you know that have split over the atonement?... Ours trace to those inconsequential issues, the mole hills we've made into mountains, about the millennium, and hats, and grape juice, the war question. Those issues should have never divided us... instrumental music... still affirm at the purchase level their brotherhood, their fellowship in Christ...

"I don't know how to answer all the questions about fellowship that I'm sure you'd want to ask if we had the time. I just want to call us to pitch the issues differently than we have historically. I want us to pitch it not at the basis of our ego, and our pride and our tradition. And the hammering home of the issues that, that we've made much more important than they ever have been to the heart of God. What position do you think folks had on grape juice versus wine in communion on Pentecost? What view of the millennium do you think those three thousand had? What do you think their position was on instrumental music? or, or on institutions and orphan homes? What, you say, 'Well I suspect they didn't have a position.' I suspect they didn't either. What they had was the knowledge of a crucified Savior, and over a period of time they created things to quarrel about and to divide over.

"I don't think we'll ever get rid of all of those things. I don't think we'll ever come back to any sort of institutional oneness. I don't think that will happen. Some of the wall, unlike the Berlin wall will never come down... Maybe some day we'll at least quit throwing rotten tomatoes over the wall or hand grenades, and we'll ask for God to do some healing in our hearts so that we'll not continue to make the cross a spectacle to an unbelieving world.

"Father, we don't have answers to the questions that plague us most urgently, about our fractured, divided state, just as a fellowship of people. A tiny, little, fractured fellowship of people, much less our relationship to other fellowships of believing, Christ speaking people. But God, we know it's your will that we should not be so fragmented and so divided. We know that you want your people to be one so that the world can believe. And God we confess that the scandal of unbelief in our world is largely due to the division that we have created and perpetrated in the name of Jesus. God we know that's not your will. And we know that the body is not supposed to be biting and devouring itself as it has.

"So God, in all the change that you're going to bring about in your larger church, in that invisible body of people whose roll we don't call but where everyone is known to you. God, with all the change you're bringing about in the world, change we never thought we'd see in Berlin, or the Soviet Union, lots of other places. God act among your people to take

some walls down or at least put some patches in those walls. Where with integrity and without compromise we can move back and forth, praise, and study, and search, and seek truth, and teach, and, yes, God, learn. So that as you are changing things you will change them for the better to bring about a unity that right now doesn't exist. And even if it's never an organizational unity, never an institutional unity, can still be a rallying around the cross and a lifting up of Jesus Christ without turning the New Testament upside down to make so important the trivial things and to make sole trivia, the issue, the issue.

"We plead for it, Father, and some of us can pledge in good faith to be a part of it under your grace, and to seek it, to encourage it, to foster it, and to live it. In the name of Jesus Christ. Amen.

*"If at a purchase level you don't know Jesus Christ by virtue of the confessed faith that has led you to be buried with him in, in water to be born anew of water and of Spirit, before we close this service we want to give you that opportunity, while we stand right now and sing." (**All quotes from tape # 4, side 2.**)*

Before I go any further, I want to again assure my love for brother Shelly. I have always loved him, love him now and never expect to stop, however, this does not mean, even though I have not a single item against him as a person, that I endorse what he has taught. Yes, he has both verbalized and written many good things in the past, but in the last few years he has taught, and this is my judgment and my own studied conviction, and is teaching error publicly. I need not, at this point, to specify that error, as all the quotes I have given in the preceding several pages prove it. Brother Shelly is not preaching today what he has always taught. How well do I remember, for example, when brother Tom Warren first wrote (December 20, 1977) about the Institute for the Advancement of Christian Theism (I-ACT), and we both participated in this and were both listed in the "A Partial Directory Of Workers Of I—ACT." But those are days past, and I stand today opposed to the error he is teaching.

I also want to make it extremely clear that I have been as careful as I possibly could be in my transcriptions of his tapes. Also, I've gone the second, third and fourth mile in trying to make sure that each item is fully documented. I want to list this as one example of what I mean. When I received the tapes from Pepperdine, they were labeled RUBEL SHELLY, PEPPERDINE UNIVERSITY, 1990. Besides the number of the tape and the side one and side two, A and B marking, not one other item was on the tape. This was a rather professional label in red color. There was no date, no theme, no topic, etc. I called several men who had the tapes and found confusing results. One had two tapes in his series, one had three and one had four. The only topic designation among any of these was on the tapes of the man who had two (he thought he had the complete series), and they were labeled, "If Jesus Were A Church." When I heard my first tape, I knew the subject was "Scripture in the Church" (p. 7 of my transcription) and when I heard the second tape (p. 3 of my transcription), Rubel said: "...yesterday, as I talked about scripture in the church,..." This is twice he stated his subject, so I thought the labeling on the tapes in Ohio was wrong. Rubel had read, in his second lesson, the table of contents in the book that he and Randy Harris were working on and said: "I will read you the table of contents: Scripture in the Church, (the material from yesterday), The Identity of the Church, The Nature of the Church (I'll be combining those two today)..." (p. 1 of my transcription). I thought for sure something was wrong about those labels with the topics listed. Therefore, on February 18, 1991, at 2:00 p.m., a call was made to Michael Hinton at Pepperdine and he was sure that there were three lessons, three tapes and the topic of each was, "If Jesus Were A Church." Also, there was no particular or specific theme. If, on the page where I listed the four series of Rubel's lectures, Pepperdine is incorrectly listed (he also informed that they were conducted in the auditorium), I feel it is not my mistake. The same is true with all four series, as I have checked them the very best, that is, as thorough as I possibly could. However, I found out, that at times, even those "at the church" did not know of the dates, subjects, themes, etc. (I did not list, for example, that Rubel spoke to the ladies while at White Station, but he did and it was the sixth of the seven lessons he gave there).

Now I have taken this time and this space at this time, to make these things clear, as I would not misquote or misrepresent any one of our brothers or anyone else (this is just pure Christian living, behavior, cf. Matt. 7:12). Then, too, I am constantly hearing this same thing time, time and time again: "He misquoted me," or "He misrepresented me," or "He took me out of context," etc. This is one of the reasons I give such long quotations, as I do my best to keep the thought of "misrepresentation" or "misquotation" from even coming up. If you do not think that our brethren play up and avoid issues if a location is wrong, if a month is wrong, if a year is wrong, if a subject is wrong, then you absolutely do not know what you are talking about. Even in a debate, if you win the audience, even though perhaps you lost the argument, you have "won the debate" as far as people are concerned. Yea, how we need to be "wise as serpents, and harmless as doves" (cf. Matt. 10:16).

In the fall of 1990, brother Shelly wrote: "So many still believe the monstrous lie that...ARBEIT MACHT FREI!" This was the title of his article. In this article he says, "In English, they mean (speaking of those German words) 'work liberates' or 'work sets you free.'" He made a "take off" from Auschwitz, "an end-of-the-line death camp," where these words were over the gate as you passed through it. This is where, during the time of Hitler, 1940-1945, some 4,000,000 had died. He said: "There was no mercy in the death camp...work without reward...False hope of freedom for those who believed a lie."

It is at this point he makes his transition, "Yet how many people do I know who live by the same lie in their spiritual lives! They have put their hope in obeying enough of the 'essential' commandments, attending enough of the 'required' assemblies, and developing enough of the 'necessary' Christian virtues to go to heaven." Now, please watch the following:

> *"It is a scandalous and outrageous lie to teach that salvation arises from human activity. We do not contribute one whit to our salvation. **Arbeit macht frei!** is the falsehood against which both Romans and Galatians protest. Then there is his theological thunderbolt against it in Ephesians: 'For it is by grace you have been saved, through faith - and this not from yourselves, it is the gift of God - not by works, so that no one can boast' (2:8-9)" (**Loveliness**, Vol. 16, Num. 45, October 31, 1990, inside right page, "The weekly bulletin*

of the Family of God at Woodmont Hills").

I had planned, at this point, to give many quotations from the "earlier" writings of brother Shelly. However, the quotations of the previous pages do not need to be contrasted with what he has previously written to show he has changed in more than just in attitude or disposition. In fact, they show drastic changes. If you do not believe what I am saying, and many will not, I give the following so you can check it out for yourself. That is as honest as I can be, yea, as open as I can be. Truth has nothing to fear, and nothing to hide. Note the following articles and books; BE HONEST!

1. In *The Spiritual Sword* (Getwell Church of Christ, 1511 Getwell Road, Memphis, Tennessee 38111) there are various articles:

a. *Some Basic Errors Of Liberalism* (Vol. 1, Num. 1, October, 1969, pp. 41-43).

b. *Biblical Prophecy As An Evidence Of Inspiration* (Vol. 1, Num. 2, January, 1970, pp. 29-32).

c. *If You Love Me...* (Associate Editorial, Vol. 1, Num. 3, April, 1970, pp. 45-49).

d. *You Can Be A Member Of The Church* (pp. 35-38) and *Restoring The New Testament Church* (pp. 42-47) both in Vol. 1, Num. 4, July, 1970.

e. *God Is No Respector Of Persons'...* (pp. 20-27) and *No One Has The Gift Of 'Tongues' Today!* (pp. 42-49) both in Vol. 2, Num. 1, October, 1970.

f. *The Example Of Paul In Evangelism* (Vol. 2, Num. 1, December, 1970, pp. 39-43).

g. *The Biblical Account Of The Origin Of Things* (Vol. 2, Num. 3, April, 1971, pp. 43-49).

h. *The Works Of The Flesh* (pp. 39-43) and *Is There An Absolute Standard Of Morality?* (pp. 43-48) both in Vol. 2, Num. 4, July, 1971 (the last article was "Feature Article For The Quarter").

i. *Can The Bible Be Trusted Completely?* (Vol. 3, Num. 1, October, 1971, pp. 40-44).

j. *The Bible Solves All Problem Areas* (pp. 39-41) and *Some Marks Of Modernism* (pp. 42-44) both in Vol. 3, Num. 3, April, 1972. The one on "Some Marks Of Modernism" was "Feature Article For The Quarter" and it is great and needs to be read by all as it is right on target for what is now going on. (In fact, brother Wayne Coats printed this article in full in his book, *Rubel's Rubbish*, pp. 7-11, 184 Hillview [now 705 Hillview], Mt. Juliet, TN 37122).

h. *What About The Ecumenical Movement?* (pp. 30-34) and *How Should Men Regard The Bible?* (pp. 46-50) both in Vol. 3, Num. 4, July, 1972. The article about the "Ecumenical Movement" is the one that brother Roy C. Deaver published in its entirety in *Biblical Notes* (Vol. 17, October, 1983, pp. 65-74 and the current address of *Biblical Notes* is 7401 Glenhaven Path, Austin, Texas 78737) and it is an excellent, very splendid article. (DO READ BROTHER DEAVER'S "CONCLUDING RE-MARKS," pp. 26-29).

Surely these sixteen articles are enough to produce to be read.

2. In the *Gospel Advocate* (current address: 1006 Elm Hill Pike, P. O. Box 150, Nashville, Tennessee 37202. I said current as it use to be at 711 Spence Lane years ago), there are various articles:

a. *Liberalism: Threat To The Body Of Christ* (1972, pp. 434).

b. *A New Book On Liberalism by Rubel Shelly* (article by Pat McGee, 1973, p. 180).

c. *Oh, For An Honest False Teacher* (1971, p. 283).

3. Two of Rubel's lectures (of course, there are others, but these hit home):

a. *Young Preachers Face Today's Issues* (Harding College Lectures, November 22-25, 1971, theme: "Faith In Conflict," pp. 264-277, published by Firm Foundation Publishing Company, P. O. Box 610, Austin, TX, but the new address is P. O. Box 690192, Houston, Texas, 77269-0192).

b. *Liberalism* (Harding College Lectures, 1973, pp. 208-219, the theme was: "Age Of Crisis," publisher was the same). I suppose, if you wanted to really "be on target" with Rubel, then to note the contrast in this man, you need to read these two excellent lectures. They deal with such thoughts as: "The Character of the Bible," "Bible Authority," "Fellowship Within The Restoration Movement," "What Is Liberalism?", "What Is It Doing To Us?", "What Can We Do About It?" Yes, you need to read what he "use to say."

4. Two of Rubels books ought to be noticed:

a. *Liberalism's Threat To The Faith* (Simple Studies Publishing Company, 625 Poplar Avenue, Memphis, Tennessee 38104 and also Bible & School Supply, Montgomery, AL, 1972). This book has thirteen chapters and ninety-one pages. It, too, is a must to read to see how he has changed. Some chapters are as follows: Liberalism Among Churches of Christ,

The Ecumenical Movement, How Important Is Truth?, We Must Have Bible Authority, The Question Of Fellowship, A Valid Test Of Christian Fellowship? Instrumental Music (note that one very, very carefully), The Future Of The Church, etc.

b. *What Shall We Do With The Bible?* (National Christian Press, Inc., P. O. Box 1001, Jonesboro, AR 72401, 1975). This is an excellent book of twelve chapters and brother Thomas B. Warren wrote the introduction for it. It deals with prophecy, unity, scientific accuracy, inspiration, etc., etc., of the Bible. It, too, is a very fine book.

Again, let me say that I have not been as thorough as I could have been, but I have given sources to show the major contrasts in the quotations that I have given from brother Shelly. Again, if you think that he has not changed, just ask him if he would affirm again all of the following propositions, as he once did.

1. "Resolved: The Use Of Mechanical Instruments Of Music in Worship To God Is Unauthorized In The New Testament And Must Be Regarded As Sin" (*Shelly and Dunning Debate*, March 15-18, 1976 in Mason City at the 5th Street Church of Christ building and published by William C. Johnson, Inc., West Monroe, LA 71291, 1977).

2. "Resolved: Baptism In The New Testament Was By Immersion Only And Must Be So Practiced Today" (*Shelly and Moore Debate*, March 24-28, 1975 at the Harding Academy, 1000 Cherry Road, Memphis, Tennessee 38117 and published by Lambert Book House, Box 4007, Shreveport, Louisiana 71104, 1975).

3. "Resolved: New Testament Baptism Is To Be Administered Only To Believing And Penitent Adults

Unto The Remission Of Past Sins" (*Ibid.*).

4. "Resolved: Supernatural Creation As A Theory Of Origins Should Be Taught In Public Schools As A Serious Alternative To The General Theory Of Evolution" (*Shelly and Powell Debate*, April 12, 1984, at Clark College in Atlanta, Georgia and published by 20th Century Christian, 2809 Granny White Pike, Nashville, TN 37204, 1984).

In almost every section of the specific heading of this chapter, I have listed various things that were "strange" and "uncertain," but this time I am letting them stand as they are. To quote Rubel, "If a person has one eye and half sense..." then he can note wherein those changes are. However, I am not so much concerned merely about "the fact" of his changing as I am about the fact that he is now teaching error. Therein lies my greatest and number one concern. It was in 1984 when Rubel first wrote "I Just Want To Be A Christian" (250 pp.). In 1986, he produced a "Revised and Expanded" edition of the same book (276 pp.). On page xvi he said, "In rethinking my own beliefs, I am not aware of having moved away from any fundamental doctrine I have held since late adolescence." He continued this thought on page xvii by saying:

> *"In my own case, there has been no 'repudiation' of the basic beliefs in my life. There has been study, reordering of priorities, and alterations of understanding within a relatively stable web of belief. If one thinks he sees more change than consistency in the positions of then and now, I can only say that I prefer to change than to persist in a belief or attitude I now believe to be wrong" (20th Century Christian).*

Although I mentioned some thoughts on Mark 9:38ff

in Part II of this chapter's headline, just let me add another thought or two as this was Rubel's beginning point back in 1982/1983. This, I truly believe, has fueled several of our younger men. If they could just be made to see and understand some of the things that others have seen and understood (Franklin Camp, Hugo McCord and J. Noel Meredith), such as:

> *"I raise the question, Where does Jesus suggest that John needs to find this man and get him to come out of some denomination? Where is there any indication that Jesus suggested that John was not to leave this man entirely alone? Where is the thought implied that John was to do anything to change this man in any way? The answer is, there was none.*
>
> *"Now, if this is an argument to justify there being people in the denominations that are Christians, then it also justifies those same people staying right where they are. If not, why not? This deserves an answer. I do not believe that one can read this event and have a knowledge of the Scriptures and ever make it harmonize with the fact that it would justify one's staying in some denomination. But, if this is an example of one's being in a denomination, then it is an example of one's staying there. That which proves too much proves nothing.*
>
> *"One of the problems that the Jews had was their attitude toward other people. This was surely a problem at the time that Jesus rebuked John concerning his forbidding someone. May it not have been that it was simply one who was not one of the apostolic band? To fit the*

modern application, it should have been one who belonged to one of the sects of that day - the Sadducees, the Pharisees, or the Herodians. Yet in the context Jesus had already warned about the danger of the leaven of the Pharisees and the Herodians. There is no indication that the one that John forbade and the one that Jesus defended was associated with something that was contrary to the will of God. Can this be said about those who are in denominations today?

"Is the one who is in a denomination in a place contrary to God's will, and is one engaging in things that are not in harmony with scriptural truth? If so, are we going to say that one is all right while one is in this situation? If not, then what is the point in the illustration used in Mark?" (Franklin Camp, ***The Word Of Life****, August, 1983, pp. 2-4).*

"Just because the exorcist of Mark 9 was not personally known by John does not mean he was a false teacher. On the contrary, Jesus approved of the man, and we know that Jesus would not approve of a false teacher (Cf.: Matthew 7:15-27). The man actually cast out devils in Jesus' name, a thing no imposter could do (Cf.: Acts 19:13-16)" (Hugo McCord, ***Gospel Advocate****, September 15, 1983, p. 560).*

"...brethren have pointed out that the saved person is added by the Lord to the Lord's church, that all the saved are added to the Lord's church, and therefore there is no such thing as a saved person outside the Lord's church (Acts 2:1-47). Also, it has been pointed

> *out that no person who is not born of water and of Spirit is in the kingdom of God, that all persons who are born of water and of Spirit are in the kingdom of God, that one is in the kingdom of God if and only if he is born of water and the Spirit, and therefore born again (John 3:1-5). Mark 9:38-42 simply tells of a person John saw who was casting out demons. The man was doing it in the name of the Lord; he was doing a mighty work. The man was on the Lord's side, even though he was not traveling with the apostles. This does not teach that one can be in a denomination and still be pleasing to the Lord" (J. Noel Meredith,* ***Christian Light****, October/November, 1983, pp. 3, 9; Thompson,* ***op. cit.****, p. 23).*

I can only pray, since Mark 9:38ff has been the BEGINNING point of some of our younger men, that these remarks will help it to be the ENDING point of such usage of this passage to find denominationalism with "sincere, knowledgeable, devout Christians scattered among all" of them. God forbid that Jesus taught all those things that He did about the church, his body, his being the saviour of IT and then for some of us to teach such about the denominations!

One thing for sure, Rubel seems to be practicing what he taught (or preached) at the Richland Hills Church of Christ: "some people who don't understand, who will not hear, or who out of fears that they can't deal with feel... they should chastise,... *and don't answer them*... stay about your task" (tape #4, side 2, emp. GM). I say this, as on December 17, 1990 brother Wayne Coats wrote, and among other things, said: "Would you consent to meet me in a public debate relative to the ideas expressed in your speeches (Wayne told Rubel he had heard the speeches given at West Memphis, AR, Pepperdine, and at the premillennial church in Gallatin), which of course I deem to be false? Propositions, time, place and other pertinent matters can be resolved in due time" (705 Hillview, Mt. Juliet, Tennessee 37122). To this letter, Rubel responded on January 23, 1991, saying: "Dear Mr. Coats: Thank you for letting me know that you have heard the tapes of the speeches..." The closing three sentences, of this six sentence letter, said: "I have neither desire nor time to discuss the possibilities of a 'debate' with you. I certainly have better use of my time than to argue with you. I hope you find fruitful use for your time in this new year" (Woodmont Hills Church of Christ, 2206 21st Avenue, South, Nashville, TN 37212). Brother Coats then, on February 17, 1991 wrote his second letter to Rubel and in the letter, among other thoughts, reminded Rubel of what he had said on one of the tapes: "Randy and I want to argue that this is..." and added, "I thought that you might rather 'debate' as to 'argue' and you well know there is a difference." At this writing, no response has been given by Rubel (this does not mean that one will not be given by him). It is also of interest to note that on January 2, 1991, brother Coats also wrote Randy Harris and said: "Would it be assuming too much to ask you to meet me in either a written or oral debate relative to, 'The Second Incarnation'"? At this writing, almost two months later, brother Coats has received not a single word from brother Harris. Maybe he, as well as Rick Atchley (remember he was the one who failed to respond to a brother's first letter, and then when the certified, signature requested letter came, it was returned marked "refused"), has also taken Rubel's advice: "don't answer them." However, these things will be answered as brother Coats has already written "A Review of the Second Incarnation" ideas as per Rubel's speeches and it is at this time "on the press."

Faithful brethren have always defended the truth against any and all error (cf. Jude 3; note the chapter on "...Preaching..." for the scriptural proof of the same) and will continue to do the same. For the love of truth, abiding by its principles, and for the love of the souls of men, the elders of the Knight Arnold Church of Christ (4400 Knight Arnold Road, Memphis, Tennessee 38118) wrote to the elders of the Woodmont Hills Church of Christ on February 3, 1991 about their deep concern over what brother Shelly "is teaching." The letter stated: "We are convinced that he has publicly, and in many parts of the nation, taught serious error, and we are unalterably opposed to the error that he teaches." After making sure of their motive, etc., they said: "Therefore, as elders of the Knight Arnold Church of Christ, we have requested brother Garland Elkins, one of the instructors in the Memphis School of Preaching, to represent the Knight Arnold Church of Christ and the Memphis School of Preaching in a public debate with brother Shelly,..." Not only did these godly elders ask brother Elkins to do the debating, but they also asked brother Cates to sign the letter along with the elders, which he "readily agreed to do so."

This letter, three pages in length, and signed by elders James A. Bobbitt, Bert Embry, Floyd M. Hayes, D. H. Kirby and Harold Mangrum, along with Curtis A. Cates, contained the following "Propositions For Debate."

I.

The Bible teaches that salvation from sin results from the grace of God alone, totally and completely apart from any human activity.

Affirm: ________________________________

Rubel Shelly

Deny: ________________________________

Garland Elkins

II.

The Bible teaches that salvation depends upon both (1) the grace of God and (2) the faithful, loving obedience of the individual human being.

Affirm: ________________________________

Garland Elkins

Deny: ________________________________

Rubel Shelly

This letter covered about every aspect for such a debate, and it closed by the elders once again emphasizing their motivation: "the love of God and love for the souls of men," along with "Brethren, if you think us to be wrong you will recognize the responsibility to correct us." It even included a separate sheet with the propositions "which we request that brother Shelly sign and return" (be it noted that a carbon copy was sent to Rubel Shelly).

Under the date of February 12, 1991, the following letter was received by the elders of the Knight Arnold Church of Christ.

"Dear Brothers:

We have received your letter of February 3.

Our views, and those of all the people on our ministry staff, are best stated in the following words: 'For it is by grace you have been saved, through faith - and this not from yourselves, it is the gift of God - not by works, so that no one can boast. For we are God's workmanship, created in Christ Jesus to do good works, which God prepared in advance for us to do' (Ephesians 2:8-10).

We hope this clarifies the matter in your minds.

Yours truly,

Roy Newsom
Chairman of the Elders."

I did not feel that I had the space to give all of the three page letter from the elders of the Knight Arnold Church of Christ, but I thought I did have the space for this few-sentenced letter.

On February 25, 1991, the elders of Knight Arnold Church of Christ once again wrote the elders of Woodmont Hills Church of Christ. This was a two-page letter and it specified the particular teaching which brother Shelly had given publicly in their bulletin dated October 31, 1990: "It is a scandalous and outrageous lie to teach that salvation arises from human activity. We do not contribute one whit to our salvation."

Naturally, they began their letter by emphasizing once more that they wrote in "Christian love for you, and for the cause of Christ around the world," as well as ending it "in sincere Christian love" as they spoke about the debate. They also said: "If brother Shelly prefers to use his own words then let him affirm what he averred when he wrote, "It is a scandalous and outrageous lie to teach that salvation arises from human activity."

I am sure, at this writing, it is too early to have heard again from the elders of the Woodmont Hills congregation. We only hope, as well as pray, that they not only respond, but that they also accept to defend on the polemic platform what Rubel has publicly and very extensively taught.

10. **Strange And Uncertain Sounds From Denny Boultinghouse.** Denny Boultinghouse was managing editor of *Image* when brother Reuel Lemmons was the editor (at the first the paper was published at 151 Warren Drive, Suite D, West Monroe, LA 71291-7256). Brother Lemmons died on January 25, 1989 (*The Christian Chronicle*, Vol. 46, Num. 2, February 1989, p. 1, Oklahoma Christian College, Box 11000, Okla. City, Oklahoma, 73136-1100), and the paper had only been published since June, 1985, which was volume one. Brother Boultinghouse became the editor after brother Lemmons' death (presently the magazine is being published at 3117 N. 7th Street, West Monroe, LA 71191-2227 and volume 7 is now being published, that is, beginning with 1991).

A person only has to read his articles, both what he is saying, what is implied by his statements, and what he is not saying, as last year he wrote some articles that are perhaps just a little bit, at least to me, rather "strange" and "uncertain" in some "sounds." If you will observe the following:

> *"It is imperative that we muster up every ounce of tolerance.*
>
> *"Remember, one of the greatest strengths of the Restoration Movement of the 1800's was the renewed emphasis upon personal, individual study of the Word of God. People were encouraged to arrive at their own conclusions.*
>
> *"Another observation is that many who are against the 'new hermeneutic' are not even*

able to define exactly what it is.

"And besides, I am not so sure that anyone has ever fully explained the 'old hermeneutic.'

"Another observation: No one is saying that examples have no purpose. People are just suggesting that if you accent the premise that examples are binding in nature, it must be clear why certain examples are binding and others are dismissed.

"Nor is anyone suggesting that certain inferences serve no role at all. We just shouldn't make human inferences as binding as Scripture.

"Yes, we may discover that some of our sacred doctrines are closer to sacred cows than Scripture. And yes, we may learn that some of the ways we have been content to look at Scripture just don't work in our current world. The weakness...lies in our faulty assumptions.

*"...our people...want God real...They want arguments that make sense from Scripture,... if our purpose is to protect some of our practices" (**Image**, The 'New' Hermeneutic, Vol. 6, Num. 2, March/April, 1990, pp. 4, 29).*

"Brethren should not be forced to leave our fellowship in order to express honest convictions.

"We should be glad that so many are no longer willing to merely parrot a party line, but instead want to be honest with the text. We should be thankful for those who do not propagate tradition, but instead want to be loyal to the text. Don't you want your speakers

to have a greater loyalty to the text than to our tradition?

"Scripture gives no one the title of 'Brotherhood Protector of the Faith.'

*"Free speech is essential in examining the cultural baggage that has accompanied us on our spiritual pilgrimage" (**op. cit.**, Freedom of Speech, Vol. 6, Num. 5, September/October, 1990, pp. 4, 21).*

"If the church is to impact the world, it must change. There is no option about this. If your church is not willing to change, the death warrant of your church has been signed.

*"When you hear folks wanting the church to be like the 'good ole days,' know that you are listening to someone who will not impact the future. Love them, hug them, care for them. But do not listen to them" (**op. cit.**, Tomorrow Will Not Be Yesterday, Vol. 6, Num. 6, November/December, 1990, p. 27).*

Observe with me, if you will, some things that are said, that are implied and/or not said.

a. *It is strange* to me how that an editor will write the above editorials, three complete ones, about fifteen columns and never use a single scripture. I might understand this, if he were giving some kind of a political article in a newspaper, but not in one of the religious journals, magazines or papers.

b. *It is strange* to talk of tolerance, but does he intend it to apply to doctrine also? He surely did not say.

c. *It is strange* to hear him speak of "our own conclusions," as if whatever we decide a verse means, that is, if we arrive at such, that is as great strength. He is extremely non-specific.

d. *It is strange* that an editor will state that "many who are against the 'new hermeneutic' are not even able to define exactly what it is," as I would like to know "who they are"? Really, now, are they "many" who are so unlearned? Why not prove what you say?

e. *It is strange* to hear him say, "I am not so sure that anyone has ever fully explained the old hermeneutic." By stating an item or two about examples and inferences, you'd surely think he understood such, at least in "the wrong way."

f. *It is not strange* to hear him speak of "some of our sacred doctrines are closer to sacred cows than Scripture," as you'd expect that from those who are so loving, kind and who use the word "tradition" as they do. *It is strange* that he did not mention any of those "sacred doctrines" that are so close to what he calls "sacred cows."

g. *It is not strange* when he spoke of "faulty assumptions," as this is what he may even believe, but brother Denny, next time tell us wherein they are "faulty" and wherein they are "assumptions."

h. *It is strange* to hear him say, "our people want arguments that make sense," as that implies "our arguments do not make sense." Please explain wherein no sense is made by...and name the argument and who uses it and how.

i. *It is not strange* that he never explained the

meaning of the word "tradition." Never once did he use it as the scriptures do or give the idea that we might be using it that way. We need to let all know that "tradition" is a scriptural word if used as Paul used it. Can "tradition," if used correctly, be what you say as being "loyal to the text"?

j. *It is strange* that he would mention "Brotherhood Protector of the Faith" and yet not explain that one does have the sacred right to warn against false teachers. Brother Denny, is a person all right in your own mind if he does do what 1 John 4:1 says?

k. *It is not strange* that I read of his usage of "cultural baggage," but please explain what that is and what all it does contain. I'm sure you must know or you would not have mentioned it.

l. *It is not strange* that you can be dogmatic about the church and the fact that it must change and say, "There is no option about this"? As well as to state so emphatically, in the same context, "...the death warrant of your church has been signed." I would just like to know "who signed it"? Brother Denny, do you think you could afford some of us to have the same dogmatism?

I have just written these few items, as sometimes we fail to observe "what is strange and uncertain" about the way some of our brethren do write. One has to note what is said, what is implied by what is said, as well as being keenly aware of what he is not saying, etc. Indeed, some "strange" and "uncertain" sounds are being issued forth, yea, even by the editor of *Image*. However, that seems to be par for course, for it, eh? Prove it you say? I have already by noting the articles by brethren Randy Fenter, Randy Mayeux, Jim Hackney. If you want more proof, read some by Jim McGuiggan, Gary D. Collier, Bill R. Swetmon, Calvin Warpula, Cecil Hook, etc.

On January 22, 1991, brother Boultinghouse spoke to a preachers' luncheon on the subject, "To Preserve Unity" (Wyatts Cafeteria, South Post Oak, Houston, Texas). Indeed, let me remind you again that if I cannot document it, I will not say it (for those exceptions, if any, it is purely an oversight on my part). Yes, indeed, I have the tape of his presentation and it included the questions that were asked. If I have transcribed it accurately, he covered the following points.

a. Continue to reemphasize Christ.

b. Continue to reemphasize the grace of God.

c. Continue to emphasize the principle of individual study.

d. We must have the freedom to differ with one another.

e. We've got to develop a healthy attitude toward questions.

f. Some folks have gotten serious about the restoration movement...No creed but Christ...Part of our problem...fellowship (I am not for sure of this particular wording for the sixth point).

Brother Boultinghouse began by explaining his assigned topic, and after saying a word about "unity," he said: "I don't believe we can do anything at all to preserve that which we do not create," and he said God is the one who does create unity. But he did say, however, that we could, "in a practical way, contribute to unity."

On his second point, as listed above, he said: "We have got to get back to really studying what the Bible teaches about the grace of God. Some people focus on what man must do...To balance Christ's work to man's work and to put them on a scale is heresy. That's heresy. If you're trying to compare them out that's unbiblical, that's blasphemy, that's heresy." He said that this would be saying that the work of God at the cross was "inadequate." He then said, "Well Denny, are you saying that we're saved 100% by grace (pause). Brother, I believe to ask a question like that indicates a problem in understanding. I believe that God did all the work for my salvation at the cross...What God did was adequate...that completed work of Christ on the cross saves 100%."

After discussing the thought about "differences," he then discussed "attitudes toward questions (questioning)." He said, "Until you talk to me, you don't know my motive. How dare you say...without talking to me...talk to me." It even makes me wonder if I can understand Paul without talking to him. I believe, if a man reads my written material on some subject, he can understand me, talk, write or...about it without "talking to me." Paul even said, "Whereby, when you read, ye can perceive my understanding in the mystery of Christ" (Eph. 3:4; cf. 5:17; 2 Tim. 2:7; etc.). Then he brought up, what is a favorite term with some today (yes, and I can prove the "some," in fact, have done so in this book), "pattern." And, of course, you must use "theological," "theological principle(s)," "theological doctrine," "theological plan," "theological tenets," etc., etc.

After the lesson, there was a question period. Brother Dobbs (H. A., "Buster") asked the first question, and it was in relation to some of the thoughts that brother Boultinghouse had mentioned about "diversity and differences." Brother Dobbs specifically asked: "Are there any areas where differences of...for instance, the use of mechanical instruments of music in the worship of God?... is that in the area of diversity? And what about the essentiality of baptism?" It is rather hard to transcribe some lessons as the tapes are not always clear, especially in a "question and answer session." However, here are some of the things brother Boultinghouse said (again, as I have tried to say about each person, there is nothing personally against brother Boultinghouse, but I do believe he writes/speaks with some strange sounding, uncertain sounds/ideas). Baptism was handled first.

> *"First of all, I do believe there is room for differences and not just in the matters of preferences... (1 Corinthians and Romans). So, I do believe we can have differences in serious theological areas.*
>
> *"That question... discussed by men much greater biblical scholars than I would claim to be with a lots of differences of opinion on that. I would just say what I just said. I would teach a person that they've got to be immersed into Christ... That's what I would teach them.*
>
> *"I do believe this to be true. I am not going to sit in God's seat... If God wants to save some... God's problem not mine... I refuse to be God. I'm going to let God have the judgment on that... But I would rather lean in not taking God's position than lean the other way and take God's position. Okay? (Lots of differences of opinion on that also stated in this thought earlier, GM).*
>
> *"I would hope noboby among us would say they've got all the answers to every question. I don't... questions I still have to study... still*

studying.

"I can just tell you what I personally believe... Some... of our arguments about the instrument don't hold the water any more. And I think if we're honest about that subject, some of our arguments just don't hold the water.

"I feel, and I must say, some of our argumentation in a lot of areas is weak.

"I will tell you what I personally understand, personally about the instrument. Okay? I personally do not believe I can worship where the instrument is being played. I personally do not uh, sing, you know, I don't listen to instrumental, contemporary Christian music. I don't listen to that, personally, I, uh, and I think I'm consistent in that. I don't even believe you do that at home... You know, some of you think it's okay to sit around your house and do it, but you just don't do it in the assembly. And I, I, I'm more, I think I'm consistent. I don't do it in the house, I don't do it at... that's where I am personally. And in my mind, I've got some biblical reasons for that. But, uh, I know we, that my reasons don't persuade everybody. That's okay... I keep studying...

"I tried to answer your question, Buster.

"I believe Scripture is absolutely true. I believe in the inspired word of God. That every word is inspired. And I believe that's the authority that we have.

"And I do, I, but I'm going to go ahead and

get myself in trouble. I don't believe that, that, the, the instrument is in a salvation context of scripture. I don't believe that when I baptize someone into Christ, Now I don't say, 'Now what do you think about the instrument?' before I put them under the water.

"And I believe you can be dead wrong...and you're still my brother, Buster...

"I became a Christian by the grace of God and I'm still a Christian by the grace of God. And it's only by the grace of God I'm going to be saved. It is not by my religiosity...I'm saved by the grace of God...

At this point there were other questions asked about various items, and here we just notice one or two thoughts.

"We have a certain direction I want the magazine to go. I believe there is some diversity in our magazine. Some freedom of opinions expressed...more than some, less than others.

"Comment by one present: 'Somebody said in the magazine that there is no such thing as a law of Christ...' ***Comment:*** *I believe...no passage says obedience earns salvation. Again the man says, 'I am discussing law...'* ***Comment:*** *Uh, you know, I, I believe the New Testament obviously uses the term law. Again the man speaks. 'Is there a law of Christ? It is a very simple question, sir.'* ***Comment:*** *Is there a will of Christ, Yes. Again the man says, 'No, law...'* ***Comment:*** *I do believe it depends on what you mean by that. The man: 'Okay, This is my problem exactly with the* ***Image*** *magazine. Paul said...Perfect law of James...I wish you could*

clarify that up for me.' ***Comment:*** *Well, I'm not for sure. I believe that the will of God and the will of Jesus Christ. The man speaks up: 'No, I understand about...the law of Jesus Christ...I'm talking about.'* ***Comment:*** *Uh, I believe, I believe, all of the passages in the New Testament where the term law is used. Yes, I believe in every one of those passages, okay?*

"Now, I do not believe obeying a law in a sense of obedience that earns us salvation...I, I, I, I do believe there is some real...I don't think it is a simple question. I think there is some discussion as to what law means.

You can read for yourself and see if you find anything "strange" and "uncertain" about the answers that brother Boultinghouse gave to the questions asked of him. There is no need for me to point those out. I do want to remind everyone that the one answering those questions is the man who is the editor of *Image*, holds a rather key position in this area of a religious paper, and you can decide for yourself as to the ability he has in the handling of Bible questions (cf. 1 Pet. 3:15; Col. 4:6; etc.).

I do want, however, to include the thoughts that brother Dobbs presented at the very next preachers' gathering. Under the title of SUBJECTIVISM, he gave the following.

"The dictionary definition of 'subjective' is, 'affected by or produced by the mind or a particular state of mind...resulting from the feelings of temperament of the person...determined by and emphasizing the ideas, thoughts, feelings...having to do with the perception or conception of a thing by the mind as opposed

to its reality independent of the mind...existing or originating within the observer's mind or sense organs, and hence, incapable of being checked externally or verified by other persons.'

"A person speaks subjectively when he talks about what he personally believes, thinks, feels, supposes. Subjectivism is appealing to one's attitude and feeling as the determinant of moral and aesthetic values.

"The opposite of subjectivism is objectivism. When we accept the Bible as absolute, attainable truth, and the only acceptable basis for determining right or wrong in religion, we are accepting an objective standard. To appeal only to the Bible as authority in religion is undenominational. If a person follows the directions of the Bible absolutely he cannot properly be charged with a sectarian spirit. Example: a person hears the word of God, and believes it to be true. He repents, confesses, and is baptized in order to obtain the remission of sins. God adds him to the church. He is not denominational, or sectarian, but is simply a saved person, because he is following the standard of divine revelation, and not his personal opinions. He is not a member of a denomination because he has not done those things necessary to become a member of a denomination. He is a part of the one body - the one church - described in the New Testament as purchased by the blood of Jesus.

"On Tuesday, January 22, 1991, Denny Boultinghouse, editor of ***Image Magazine****, made the following statement at the Houston Preachers'*

lunch: (here brother Dobbs gave the quote that I earlier listed. Read it again. It begins with, "I will tell you what I personally understand, personally about the instrument. Okay?" GM).

"No appeal was made to the teaching of the objective standard of God's word, but the entire matter was put into the context of what Denny Boultinghouse personally believed, thought, and felt. Under the definition of subjectivism, brother Boultinghouse gave a subjective answer and thereby made himself a subjectivist. Such an attitude is sectarian, and denominational, because it follows human thoughts and prejudice rather than the rigid rule of revelation. Brother Boultinghouse thinks it is okay if his reasons do not persuade others." (Permission granted to use the above on 3-1-1991, 9:00 a.m., from H. A. "Buster" Dobbs.)

Brother Dobbs' thoughts about subjectivism are right on target, as can be witnessed by anyone who was there and who listened well or who has heard the tape. From the very beginning, he began by saying, "I don't believe," and kept this up throughout the lesson. He said: "I believe," "I believe it," "I believe to," "I believe that," "I believe we've," "I think," "I understand," "I teach," "I would," "I have trouble," "I am," "I refuse," "I don't," "I would teach," "I personally believe," "I feel," etc. Although he mentioned a few references, like the ones in Romans and 1 Corinthians, that was about it.

Before I bring to a close these chapters on "strange" and "uncertain" sounds, there is a book that would help everyone if we could just get people to read it. In 1986, brother Thomas B. Warren wrote: *The BIBLE ONLY makes CHRISTIANS ONLY and the ONLY CHRISTIANS* (National Christian Press, Inc., P. O. Box 1001, Jonesboro, AR 72401). This book of eleven parts (chapters) and two hundred and seventeen pages needs to be read and studied. Indeed, it would greatly help our troubled times!

Chapter Nine

THE PATTERN - AND IS THERE AUTHORITY IN BIBLICAL "SILENCE"?

THE PATTERN - AND IS THERE AUTHORITY IN BIBLICAL "SILENCE"?

I earnestly, seriously and sincerely, pray to God that we will all forever cherish and defend "the faith" (Jude 3). After all, it has been, as my English text says, "once for all delivered unto the saints" (*ASV*). I must be, to be pleasing unto the Master, one approved of God, "a workman unashamed" and the only way to do that is to diligently study and "show myself" approved by being able to handle aright or rightly divide the word (2 Tim. 3:16-17).

Evidently, few there are who know "how to study" and realize the absolute value of "correct reasoning," or, if you prefer, "valid reasoning." To come to grips "with the fact" that we "can know," that "the evidence" is sufficient, that we are "authorized" by the Almighty and have "the written" as our instruction manual, our pattern, guide, model and blueprint, is, indeed, "blessed assurance!" Without a norm, a rule, pure subjectivism is the canon.

In this chapter, for the very best possible results for every reader, I request that you diligently pay attention to the various "major topics." This chapter centers around these ten particular thoughts.

THE AUTHORIZATION IS: "IN THE NAME OF THE LORD JESUS"

In being as practical as I possibly can be through this chapter, for the profit and benefit of the widest possible range of readers, many examples employed and scriptures used will be those of concrete clearness. Therefore, no more unmistakable and unquestionable, authoritative and absolute passage could be used as a text for this section than Colossians 3:17. It explicitly avers: "And whatsoever ye do, *in word or deed, do all in the name of the Lord Jesus*, giving thanks to God the Father through him" (emp. GM, *ASV*). "In word" concerns our preaching and teaching, and "in deed" refers to our practicing. Therefore, irrespective of our preaching or practicing, it absolutely has to come under the canopy of "doing all in the name of the Lord Jesus." Inspiration has spoken!

"In the name of" means "by the authority of," and this is easily proven by Acts 4:7-10.

> *"And when they had set them in the midst, they inquired by what power, or in what name, have ye done this? Then Peter, filled with the Holy Spirit, said unto them, Ye rulers of the people, and elders, if we this day are examined concerning a good deed done to an impotent man, by what means this man is made whole; be it known unto you all, and to all the people of Israel, that in the name of Jesus Christ of Nazareth, whom ye crucified, whom God raised from the dead, even in him doth this man stand here before you whole."*

Here the apostles were asked, "By what power, or *in what name*, have ye done this?" Peter answered, "Be it known unto you, and to all the people of Israel, that *in the name of Jesus Christ* of Nazareth, whom ye crucified, whom God raised from the dead, even in him *doth this man stand here before you whole*." It must be, to almost (ought to be for "all") everyone, crystal clear that "in the name of the law" refers to that authority vested in a person as an instrument of the law. Just so, it is bright as the sun to see that "in the name of Jesus" (Jesus Christ, Christ Jesus, Lord Jesus, etc.) refers to that "authority of Jesus." After all, he said he had "all authority" in both heaven and earth (Matt. 28:18).

In our government today we have various kinds of authority, executive (President), legislative (Congress) and judicial (Supreme Court). The authority of the Supreme Court is not to invade that of Congress nor is that of Congress to intrude the executive branch. But in the matter of the Bible, Christ has "*all authority*." He has the power to legislate, the power to execute and the power to judge. May it ever be observed that all authority abides and resides in Jesus. This means that "everything" in our preaching (teaching) or practicing must be done by his authority.

His authoritative Word, the New Testament, is that means by which his authority is executed today. This can be seen from a galaxy of verses, such as Jude 3; 2 Timothy 3:16-17; John 14:26; 1 Peter 4:11; Galatians 1:6-9; John 16:13; 12:48; Revelation 22:18-19; James 1:25; etc. Now in a study of the New Testament, we come to realize how the Word authorizes. Therefore, I now list the following:

1. **BY AN EXPLICIT STATEMENT.** "And Peter said unto them, Repent ye, and be baptized every one of you in the name of Jesus Christ unto the remission of your sins; and ye shall receive the gift of the Holy Spirit" (Acts 2:38). This is an example of an explicit, direct statement. If we respect the authority of Christ, as exercised through his word, we will teach that New Testament baptism was "*for*" or "*unto*" the remission of sins, for the passage so states it clearly and simply. We will become baptized penitents.

2. **BY AN IMPLICIT STATEMENT.** "He that believeth and is baptized shall be saved; but he that disbelieveth shall be condemned" (Mark 16:16). You see,

you and I have been baptized by the authority of "an implicit statement." Nowhere did God ever say, "*Goebel Music*, you believe and be baptized..." The Bible does say, "He that believeth and is baptized..." It is "implied" that Goebel Music is part of the "he" in that verse! Yes, I know that it is true, as God implied it in this statement. It is authorized because *God has implied it*, not because *I* have accurately reasoned it. Everything the Bible teaches it does so either explicitly or implicitly, and one is just as binding as is the other. We teach the truth when we say that Lot went down into Egypt, although the Bible never states this specifically (i.e., in so many words). This truth is implied from (1) the fact that Lot was first in Canaan (Gen. 12:5) and then (2) is said to have gone up out of Egypt (Gen. 13:1).

3. **BY AN "APPROVED" EXAMPLE.** (I deliberately placed quotes around the word "approved"). "And upon the first day of the week, when we were gathered together to break bread, Paul discoursed with them, intending to depart on the morrow;..." (Acts 20:7). It is not mine here to discuss the requirements of an action that make it binding, but I can say that if it is an *example*, it is binding. When the rules of hermeneutics (reading the verse per se, reading the immediate context, reading the remote context, and applying my common sense) are applied, then I will understand this is an example, an account, happening or event by which the Word of God authorizes. (It would be a wonderfully wise thing if you have not read Thomas B. Warren's book, *WHEN IS AN "EXAMPLE" BINDING?* to do so. Especially, chapters 10 and 11 just for this point).

4. **BY EXPEDIENCY.** In the great commission the Lord said, "...Go ye therefore, and make disciples of all the nations, baptizing them into the name of the Father

and of the Son and of the Holy Spirit: teaching them..." (Matt. 28:18-20). I am obligated to "*go*," and "implied" (implication) in this word is a "method" of "means" I must employ. This means that I am left free to choose the method of going that would expedite the command. It could be "flying," but at other times it might be "driving." We can employ that which is expedient (as long as it is *lawful* - growing out of that for which there is a direct statement, an implication, or approved example) to help us carry out His teachings upon us (directives, commands). Indeed, it is authorized.

The Bible authorizes by the above-mentioned ways, and if we do that in religion for which we do not have at least one of these ways establishing Bible authority, then we do that thing "without divine sanction, without Bible authorization." No one can be pleasing unto God unless he has Bible authority for what he does. Doing a thing without Bible authorization is displeasing to God.

THE AUTHORITY IS: "AT TIMES SPECIFIC AND AT TIMES GENERIC"

This can be seen from both the Old Testament and the New Testament. When, for example, God told Noah to build the ark (that was an explicit statement), he made it clear that it was to be out of "gopher" wood. It would take the very opposite of a "wise" man to fail to see that this was a "specific" type of wood (Gen. 6:14). The same is true when God specified a lamb and a dove, as a lamb is a "specific" kind of animal and a dove is a "specific" kind of bird. Even though it is not mine to discuss it at this particular point, we need to see that when God specifies the obligation but not the "various details," then those details are left up to human discretion. In the case of the ark the size of the tree, tools, etc., were left up to Noah's discernment. Let it also be noted that when a thing is proven to expedite the obligation, it is proven to be authorized. Indeed, there is "generic authority." It falls within the matter of faith if it is truly an expedient (Rom. 10:17).

In the New Testament the directives of "go," "teach," and "baptize" are all part of the great commission - two are "generic" and one is "specific," that of "baptism" (Matt. 28:18-20). Again, we are "authorized" by what method or means we choose that will best expedite the commands of "go" and "teach." In the method employed that we deem in human wisdom to be the most expeditious in carrying out these obligations, we find it "authorized" by scripture. It is a matter of faith for us. Baptism, on the other hand, is "specific," therefore, since it can only be an immersion, a burial (cf. Rom. 6:3-4; Col. 2:12), we dare not sprinkle or pour as this would be a violation, acting against what is authorized or doing that which is unauthorized. Yet, here again we need to make known that there is an area of expedience involved. When God gives a law but not the "how" of that law, then it (the how) is involved in the law; part of the law, yes, but a part which employs human judgment. Again, when the law gives the manner of doing a thing, then every other manner is unauthorized and the manner of procedure is as binding as the thing to be done, as *it is part of the law*. God did not "specify" a river, a pool, a pond, a baptistry, etc., but that which is most expeditious is authorized. The same is true with cold or warm water or whether a person is sitting down, squatting, or is baptized (as I have done) on a stretcher, in a chair, in a bathtub, in a physical therapy tank in a hospital, etc. These items are authorized as the details of such are left to human prudence and what expedites the directive of "baptize" is authorized else the obligation could not be fulfilled by us.

Recently, a man wrote me about my tract, "Music - Instrumental or Vocal." He was concerned about "the generic," and Thayer's statement relative to a word being "generic." I answered the few lines he had written to me with a four page letter (Nov. 27, 1990). I did not know at the time that he had written others about my tract. Later, I received a letter from one of the men he had written, T. Pierce Brown. Brother Brown also wrote the man and both of us received a second letter. Brother Brown, out of this man's failing to understand the full meaning of the term "generic," wrote an article on "The Generic Question." He said it would be published in *Beacon Of Truth* in January, 1991. I mention this for two reasons: (1) people today just absolutely fail to understand the full significance of "generic," and (2) also to help anyone desirious of reading an article just on the generic and various thoughts about it. My thoughts on this particular subject are certainly not exhaustive, therefore, it is good for "the reader" to know about other material that is available on the subject.

THE LEGISLATION IS: "DO NOT GO BEYOND THE WRITTEN"

It is in 1 Corinthians 4:6 (*ASV*) that we read: "Now these things, brethren, I have in a figure transferred to myself and Apollos for your sakes; that in us ye might *learn not to go beyond the things which are written*;..." John 12:48 says, "He that rejecteth me, and receiveth not my sayings, hath one that judgeth him: *the word that I spake*, the same shall judge him in the last day." We read "...books were opened...another book was opened, which is the book of life: and *the dead were judged out of the things which were written in the books*,..." (Rev. 20:12; all emp., GM).

It is explicitly stated: (1) do not go beyond what is written, (2) it is the word that Christ spake that will judge us, and (3) the dead are going to be judged by what is written. If this is the case, and inspiration says it is, then I should never concern myself about that which "is not written" as that is not going to judge me! It is the Word that "*is written*" that is to be my judge. Biblical silence is not my judge!

If I were to go back to the Old Testament, I could show this time and time again. Space does not allow a listing of all of these to be given in typed-out form, but I can give some locations (Num. 22:18, 35; 23:20, 26; 1 Kings. 22:14; Acts 15:7-9, 24; 2 John 9-11; Heb. 1:5, 13; 7:13-14). Indeed, 2 Timothy 3:16-17; 2 Peter 1:3; 1 Peter 4:11; James 1:25; etc., should declare unto us it is "the things written" that we need to know, observe and carefully follow. We need to realize that "the written covers every area" of our life in one manner (principle) or by another (specifics). (Bro. Warren's book already mentioned, speaks to this point on pages 41-43. Compare also *The Book Of Romans*, ed. by bre. Elkins and Warren, pp. 60, 66-70, 293-297).

Jesus said, "If ye love me, ye will keep my commandments" (John 14:15, 21, 23), and John said, "For this is the love of God, that we keep his commandments" (1 John 5:3) and "And hereby we know that we know him, if we keep his commandments. He that saith, I know him, and keepeth not his commandments, is a liar,..." (1 John 2:3-4; remember that liars are going to be lost, as per Rev. 21:8; 22:15). Paul said that we are to "...rightly divide the word..." (2 Tim. 2:15). I just wonder how one can keep "that which is *not* written" (how would he know what it was?) and how can one "rightly divide" what is *not* written (that would be an amazing feat indeed!)? I say all of this in view of the fact that we today have "it written" down for us.

THE WALK IS: "BY FAITH FROM THE WORD"

In 2 Corinthians 5:7, Paul says, "for *we walk by faith*, not by sight" (emp., GM). In the book of Hebrews we have this statement, "and *without faith it is impossible to be well-pleasing unto him;...*" (11:6; emp., GM). On top of this, we have a climaxing statement about "this faith" when Paul writes, "So *faith (belief, ASV) cometh of hearing, and hearing by the word of Christ*" (Rom. 10:17; emp. GM). In gleaning thoughts from these three passages, we note: (1) the only way to walk is by faith, (2) the reason is that without faith you cannot please God, (3) this faith, without which I cannot please God, comes "from the Word," that is, that which is "written," (4) and I remember that it "is the written" that I am not "to go beyond," as "it is the word that Christ spake that will judge me," and the Judgment Scene does have men "judged by that which is written."

Faith, then, is "taking God at his *word*!" If this is the case (and it is), then it means to please God I cannot refuse to follow his instructions. This faith, since it comes by hearing the word of Christ, is that which is well-pleasing unto God. It also means that "where there is no word of God" there can be no faith and without such we cannot please God. How on earth does a man, any man, think he can please God by that "which is *not written*"? Why do I ask this? For the simple reason that today many both "in the church" and "out of the church" have and hold to the mistaken idea that "silence constitutes" authority. This idea has been around a long time, yea, even before the time of the "restoration movement." Many think "where the Bible is silent" I am free to act, but that is contrary to everything we have noted in our last few thoughts. And which thoughts, I might add, are in harmony with "in the name of the Lord Jesus" (Col. 3:17).

God has never asked any man to believe without adequate *"evidence."* Our evidence is clearly "written down" for us (cf. John 20:30-31; Heb. 11:1ff). This is why I do not appreciate people referring to Thomas (the man called by the name of Didymus, cf. John 20:24-29) as a "doubter." He simply asked for the "evidence" and when it was given he expressed his faith. Do you want to understand why, at the first, when Saul first came to Jerusalem that they were fearful (afraid) of him? It "is written" in Acts 9:26, "not believing that he was a disciple." Why did they not believe? Simply because they did not have the "evidence!" Without this evidence, upon which our faith is based, no man, not a single one, can be well-pleasing unto God. At times we have abused the passage of 2 Corinthians 5:7 by stating that "faith rules out sight." This is totally false! Faith may be contrasted with sight (empiricism). But in the case of what Jesus told Thomas (John 20:29), we know "his seeing was believing." Yet, the Master quickly said, "Blessed are they that have not seen, and yet have believed." (We might also add that faith does *not* rule out knowledge, cf. John 4:42; 6:69. In these two verses twice it is said "we believe" and "we know." In fact, one needs to study the two words for "know" in these verses. The perfect tense of these verbs is tremendously important).

THE TRUTH IS: "MAN OFTEN VIOLATES THE INSTRUCTIONS"

If I can see the "authorization," the "authority," the "legislation," and the "walk," all which deal with that which is authorized, that which is written, then I also need to be aware of THE TRUTH that God does not accept nor have respect to that which is not authorized, that which is not written (it produces no faith). This was true as far back as Genesis chapter 4, in the case of Cain (vss.

2-5, and we certainly note Abel's worship, in deep contrast, as it was "by faith," Hebrews 11:4, and we know "how faith comes"). Just because something is offered to God "as worship/in worship" does *not* mean that God is obligated to accept it. In fact, he won't accept anything, unless it is in harmony *with his instructions*.

What I have stated with reference to the worship of Cain is also true in relation to Nadab and Abihu (Lev. 10:1-2). They, too, did what they did not have the authority to do in that they offered "strange fire" before the Lord. These things (cf. Rom. 15:4) ought to serve us well as divine reminders that God will not just accept anything we offer, even if we offer him the best. The "best" with God comes from my heart and soul doing *what* he has instructed and *because* he instructed it to be done. This is the faith that is pleasing unto God - taking God at his word!

Man has and man can violate God's written word, therefore, God has been diligent in his warnings to man. Note the following scriptures very carefully.

1. *2 Peter 3:16*, "...*wrest*...the other scriptures,..."

2. *2 Corinthians 4:2*, "...handling the word of God *deceitfully*..."

3. *2 Corinthians 2:17*, "...*corrupting* the word of God..."

4. *Mark 7:13*, "*making void* the word of God by our own..."

5. *Galatians 1:6-9*, "...and would *pervert* the gospel of Christ..."

6. *Deuteronomy 4:2*, "*Ye shall not add* unto the word..."

7. *Deuteronomy 12:32*, "...thou shalt not add...*nor*

diminish..."

8. *Deuteronomy 18:20,* "...speak a word *presumptuously*...die..."

9. *Proverbs 30:5-6,* "...*add thou not*...reprove thee,... liar..."

10. *Jeremiah 23:16, 31,* "...speak *a vision out of their own heart*, not out of the mouth of Jehovah...*use their tongues, and say, He saith.*"

11. *Numbers 22:18,* "...I cannot *go beyond* the word of Jehovah my God, *to do less or more.*"

12. *2 John 9-11,* "...*goeth onward* and *abideth not* in the teaching...*bringeth not* this teaching...partaketh in his *evil works.*"

13. *Revelation 22:18-19,* "*...If any man add...if any man shall take away...*"

14. *Matthew 22:29,* "...*Ye do err*, not knowing the scriptures, nor the power of God."

15. *John 12:48,* "He that rejecteth me, and *receiveth not my sayings,...the word* that I spake, the same *shall judge him*...last day."

16. *Numbers 24:13; 1 Corinthians 4:6,* "...I cannot *go beyond* the word..." and "...*learn not to go beyond* the things which are written..."

17. *Romans 3:4,* "God forbid: yea, let God be found true, but every man a liar; *as it is written,*...mightest prevail when thou comest into judgment."

A rule for man to follow is that which is laid down in Deuteronomy 29:29, as it binds the "written" and "forbids" that which is not written. "*The things that are revealed belong unto us* and to our children forever, *that we may do all the words of this law*" (emp., GM). Would any person like to take a few minutes with these (and let me assure you that *these are only a few* of the ones that could be given) scriptures and apply them to "the silence of the Scriptures"?

THE FACT IS: "RELIGIOUS DIVISION IS OVER BIBLICAL SILENCE"

Some hold to the idea that we cannot "understand" the truth, but that is not what the Bible declares. The Bible can be understood. How *just* would God be to place my salvation upon "that which is written" and then give me "that which is written" (the Bible) knowing all the time that I could *not* understand it? The word "understand" occurs about 300 times in the Bible, and Paul wrote, "Wherefore be ye not foolish, but understand what the will of the Lord is" (Eph. 5:17). He also said, "whereby, when ye read, ye can perceive my understanding in the mystery of Christ" (Eph. 3:4; cf. 2 Tim. 2:7). I think it must be "kinda difficult" to "read" silence, that which is not written, don't you?

If the Bible cannot be understood, only one of two reasons would explain why. Either *God does not want us to understand it* (verses just given prove otherwise, cf. 2 Peter 3:9; 1 Timothy 2:3-4), or *He is not able to make the word understandable* (and who would accuse God of this?). The word is truth (cf. John 17:17; 8:31-32; 7:17) and we can "know" it (cf. Psm. 119:60; 117:1-2; Prov. 23:23; John 1:17; 2 Thess. 2:10-12; etc.). If there is no truth, there is no error; there is no sin and Jesus died for nought!

There can be only one correct understanding of the word of God and this comes to us by faith, which is by the "hearing of the word of God" (Rom. 10:17). I am quick to say that anything other than an understanding is a "misunderstanding." "To understand" means to comprehend the meaning of, to receive the correct meaning of words and signs. There is a rule of logic that says two things cannot differ on the same subject and both be right. If you "understand" and I differ, then I necessarily "misunderstand." If I tell you my phone number is 283-3634 and two weeks later you try to call me by calling 283-3436 and then tell me that "I understood you to say..." No, you did not, you *mis*understood me to say 283-3436.

We can agree "on what is written," but we "disagree" when talking of the "silence" and "what the Bible does not say." Note these very great examples.

1. **Exodus 3:1-3.** God spoke to Moses out of a "bush that burned with fire." We can know it was a "burning bush," but when we speculate on "what kind" of a bush it was that burned, then we disagree. The answer is simple as to the disagreement - the Bible is "silent" on the "kind" of bush it was.

2. **John 3:1-2.** We can all agree that Nicodemus came to Christ "by night." However, disagreement comes when we force an "opinion" on "the why" he came by night. Unity comes on the clear statement "by night," and *dis*unity comes when we try to make opinion a basis for unity.

3. **John 8:1-8.** This scripture explicitly states that Jesus "wrote on the ground." What did he write? We do not know. The reason that we do not know is because the Bible does not say. On this we can all be united. Unity comes from "that which is written." Why? There is that on which we can agree. We will all disagree on "that which is *not* written." Why? There is no authorization for my opinion. Faith and opinion are not the same thing. It

is that which is written that produces faith and is the standard, the norm, for unity. The Bible does not demand unity on our opinions, and they come from the "silence," that is, that which is not written.

4. **2 Corinthians 12:7-10.** I guess, at times, much discussion is centered on Paul's "thorn" in the flesh. Usually people have their minds made up as to what it is. Indeed, much has been said about this "thorn," and many "ideas/opinions" have been expressed as to "what" it is. We can agree Paul had a "thorn" in the flesh. We may never be, no, we will never be, united on what it was, as the Bible is "silent" on that!

There is no authority in this "silence" upon which men can agree. God does not require unity where there is no authority. What God teaches he expects, and what God has omitted, he rejects. Again, God does not demand unity in matters of human opinion, speculation, judgment or wisdom.

THE PRINCIPLE IS: "ACCORDING TO GOD'S DIRECTIONS"

Although I have already referred to this, I wanted just to say a word about this in a specific way. In Genesis 6:22, in reference to Noah's building the ark, the record says, Thus did Noah; *according to all that God commanded him*, so did he" (emp., GM). In Exodus 25:1-40, we have God instructing Moses as how he was to build the tabernacle. In fact, God said, "According to all that I show thee, the pattern of the tabernacle,..." (vs. 9; cf. Heb. 8:5). Later, and I emphasize, "Thus did Moses: *according to all that Jehovah commanded him*, so did he" (Ex. 40:16). In 1 Chronicles 28:11-12, David gave to Solomon his son "the pattern" of the temple, which he said, in verse 19, "*All this have I been made to understand in writing from the hand of Jehovah*, even all the works of this pattern" (emp., GM). It is interesting to note what David said to his son Solomon, "...*and do it*:..." (vs. 20).

Today we have problems with "doing what is written!" Faith demands of us that "we just do it." No questions are to be asked and the silence is to be just that, silent! When we have a "thus saith the Lord," or an "it is written," we are not dealing with God's *suggestions*, we are dealing with God's pattern and conformity to it must be made.

THE ILLUSTRATION IS: "WHEN YOU SAY WHAT A THING IS YOU DO NOT HAVE TO SAY WHAT IT ISN'T"

I have often thought that if we applied what we use in every day language to the scriptures, we would have much less trouble. I now list only a few things to show the simplicity of "saying what a thing is, eliminates saying what it is not." We are to observe that "the authority" is in the statement of "what is said," not in "the silence of what is *not* said."

1. **In Cooking.** When a recipe calls for, as an example, 4 eggs, does it or must it state, "now this does *not* mean 1,000 eggs"?

2. **In A Wedding Invitation**. When the date and time are listed, such as Thursday, September 21, 7:30 p.m., must it also state, "now this does *not* mean to come at 2:00 or at 9:00 p.m. or on Saturday, or on the 23rd"?

3. **In Advertising Our Worship Privileges.** When we list the time of Bible study at 9:00 and the assembly at 10:00, must we explain to people we do *not* meet at 7:30 for Bible study and 11:15 for the assembly?

4. **In Giving My Telephone Number.** When I give

my telephone number to someone, do you think that it is necessary that I tell them how to dial it? That is, must I say, "Now you must dial it in the order that I give it, and be sure you do *not* invert the order"?

5. **In Ordering Shoes.** Many times I have ordered shoes through the mail. If you were doing such, would you feel constrained to inform them of every size that you did *not* wear? That is, when you state, for example, my size is twelve, would you also feel coerced to inform them to be sure and *not* send a ten and a half?

6. **In Naming A Child.** In the case of Zacharias and Elisabeth, when (the reference is Luke 1:13, 60, 63) Zacharias wrote, "His name is John," did he have to write that his name is *not* George or Henry?

7. **In Buying A Car.** If you were to go to a GMC dealer and tell the owner you would like to purchase a Buick, would it be necessary to tell him that you do *not* want a Cadillac, a Chevrolet, etc.?

As I said, I listed only a few of the many examples, and in various fields they could be given, but perhaps these are sufficient to see wherein we live, work, worship and buy by "the thing stated, not by what isn't stated." The answer to all of the above items, is, of course, "*no*." The reason is so simple. It is what I have been trying to stress from the very opening of the chapter. Authority is in "the stated," "the written." If you doubt this, order a hamburger and tell the waitress you want lettuce, tomatoes, and mustard on it. If she puts "sauerkraut" on it, regardless of "the instructions" you gave her, what will be your reaction? Did she violate your order? Or, must you eat it regardless of "whatever" she were to put on it?

THE ANSWER IS: "THE BIBLE AUTHORIZES BY WHAT IT SAYS"

I have already stated that everything the Bible teaches, it does so explicity or implicitly. I also discussed various ways by which a thing is authorized (here I want us to keep in mind the caption of our topic), and I've briefly mentioned "specific" and "generic" authority. I now want us to understand that an item is either "*authorized*" or it is "*not authorized*." If an item is "not authorized," then we cannot do it and be well-pleasing unto God (cf. Heb. 11:1-6; Rom. 10:17). Man can only do that which is authorized if his desire and aim is to please his Maker. If the examples of Cain and Abel (Gen. 4:1ff) and Nadab and Abihu (Lev. 10:1-2) teach anything to us, it is that God does not permit, admit, sanction or approve that which is not authorized.

Evidently today some people are confused about what is "silence" and what is "generic" authority. This should be clear from what I have started already, but when someone says "We have no authority for a church building, no authority for classes, for pews, for song books, for baptistries, for communion cups (individual ones), etc., etc.," *they are mistaken*! These items are all covered under "generic" authority. Generic authority involves implication and human judgment. The command to "assemble" necessarily involves a place (it is quite difficult to assemble and not be in a place!), and this involves that which is most expeditious, be it a building (buying, renting) or meeting under a tree or in a house. The command to "study" involves human wisdom and therefore we have Bible classes. It is expedient to have such and it is related to the command to "study." This is true about a number of items.

Not only is the positive true, but the negative is

likewise true. What I am saying is that there are items that are *"implicitly forbidden."* This is the negative aspect of that realm of the generic. The Bible does not say "thou shalt not" wear short-shorts (and a lot of other things), but we need to ask, "is it condemned by a Biblical principle?" Would the principle of "modest apparel" (1 Tim. 2:9) condemn such? How can one read passages such as Deuteronomy 4:2; 12:32; Proverbs 30:5-6; Jeremiah 26:2; Leviticus 10:1-2; Matthew 4:1-11; Hebrews 7:14; Acts 15:24; 2 John 9-11 without a realization that there are some things "implicitly forbidden"? Would the divine thoughts about our worship (right object, in truth and in spirit, John 4:21-24) inform us that it is absolutely wrong to "count beads in worship"? Would the divine thought about "singing" in worship (Eph. 5:19; Col. 3:16) implicitly tell us that the usage of mechanical instruments in worship is wrong? Indeed, must we not realize that there are things "explicitly" forbidden (cf. Gal. 5:19-21) and also things that are "implicitly" forbidden (2 John 9-11; Col. 3:17)?? If we can see that there are things that are *"obligatory"* (cf. Heb. 11:6; Acts 17:30-31; John 3:5-7), why then cannot we see there are things that are also *"optional,"* such as already mentioned? We cannot allow what is forbidden nor can we forbid what is allowed and be well-pleasing unto God. Indeed, the Bible authorizes *by what it says*, yea, either explicitly or implicitly, specifically or generically.

THE PATTERN IS: "THE SCRIPTURAL LAW IS THAT OF INCLUSION"

If I am to speak "as the oracles of God" (1 Pet. 4:11), realizing how our God authorizes and that he does not accept what is not authorized, then I believe we need to emphasize that which is "included" (the stated, the written, the voiced, the word, the commandments, the statutes, etc.). Perhaps it might be wise for me to say that we had best be careful about using the term "the law of silence." I personally see no reason for using it, but a big one for it not to be used. This is not to say that we do not respect the silence of the Word. I now list, for our contemplation, the following secular examples, as I believe they can speak to us and make us more receptive to our thrust in this chapter.

1. For the invitation song, number 482 was announced. While exhorting for people to see the message, I asked 9 year old Stacey Edge why she did not turn to song number 716. She replied, "Because he said 482." She knew what was given was authorized, nothing else was (think of all the chaos if each person present said, "Well, he did *not* say...so I'm going to sing number 641, etc.!).

2. Also at this meeting in Clarkson, Kentucky, there were two men who were brothers, Ben and Victor Duvall. Ben was a pharmacist and Victor was a doctor. Publicly that night I asked Victor if he would use his brother (if he would not repent) if Ben operated by filling prescriptions on the basis of "what was *not* written" ("Well, he did not say not to use...") instead of "the written prescription." You can imagine what Dr. Duvall said! Of course, not only the doctor but also the patient would not use him as his pharmacist.

3. While conducting my first meeting in Redwater, Texas, I asked Dale G. Stinson "how" to drive (the road to take) from the Kings Row Inn to the church building in Redwater. He informed me about Stateline, where to turn, when to get on the interstate, when to get off and the highway I was to take, it was number 59, etc. After leaving the interstate, driving on highway 59 toward my next "landmark," I noticed a sign that said "Redwater Road." I slowed down and almost turned on it. After all, I

am going to Redwater and this is Redwater Road! Then I thought, "He told me the road to take off highway 59." I then put into practice what I had taught (*the law of inclusion*). (Later I told Dale of this - he informed me what would have happened had I taken that road! Another preacher heard us talking... said he took it... said it showed him his...).

4. While visiting a patient in a hospital in Fort Worth, there was no place to park. The driver of the car pulled into a parking space that had a wheelchair emblem on it, after all, it did not explicitly say that no one else could park there. We came out of the hospital after our visit, only to find "a ticket" on his car windshield. He learned "from one experience" that the emblem only authorized *just such patients*.

Now let us note some thoughts about some sacred examples.

1. Is it not clear that Genesis 6:14 "only authorized gopher wood"? Let us see what was "included," not what was "excluded."

2. Is it true that we do not take the Lord's Supper on Thursday night because of the example of Acts 20:7, or is it true that "we have no authority to take it on Thursday night"? (Note: Does an example "exclude"?)

3. Why would it have been wrong for Noah to have built the ark 700 cubits? (Simply because the instructions of 300 cubits were inclusive as to its length, Gen. 6:15).

4. Upon what basis is humming, whistling, yea, even the piano wrong in our worship to God? (The answer is the same. None are authorized and God does not accept that which is not authorized, Eph. 5:19; Col. 3:16. The command authorizes vocal music and it is inclusive.

Perhaps I need to add that we are not authorized to make "instrumental sounds with our voices either." God only authorized one thing - singing!).

5. Is it because God did not tell "Naaman "not" to dip twelve times the reason he dipped 7, or is it because God told him "7 times"? (2 Kings 5:14 says, "Then went he down, and dipped himself seven times in the Jordan, *according to the saying of the man of God*;..." (emp., GM). The reason twelve times would have been wrong is that twelve times was not authorized).

Such examples could be multiplied many times, but we need to learn that the "excluding" factor is "no authority." We, therefore, highly respect the silence of the scriptures. Yea, the Bible authorizes *by what it says, not* by what it does *not* say.

CONCLUSION

THE TEACHING IS: "Reject God's word and he will reject us." I suppose that I would not have belabored these points, but at 11:20 a.m. there came a long distance call to me (8-11-1989), and among other things the person said this: "There is no place it says you cannot have one elder is there?" If this is in any way "characteristic" of our people today, then we *need* all the repetition in our teaching that we can get! Yea, it shows the dire need of "rightly dividing the Word," as a diligent, studious workman unashamed.

We have long tried to emphasize in our preaching (especially in our gospel meeting work, etc.) that whenever a man rejects the word of God, *he rejects God* (cf. 1 Sam. 13-15). Also, if a man acts outside the realm of that which is "authorized," *he is rejected by God* (this is equally true, of course, in the first thought). Only when men trust, obey (in full acceptance) and do *as God says* does God bless them. Man must realize that he cannot direct his own steps (cf. Jer. 10:23; Prov. 14:12; 16:25; 19:21; 21:2). When he tries, he fails and that failure brings rejection by God.

THE QUESTION IS: "Is There Authority In Biblical 'Silence'"? The Old Testament answers "No." The New Testament answers "No." Therefore, from the totality of the Book, I conclude "the answer is 'NO.'"

Chapter Ten

THE PATTERN - AND THE NEW TESTAMENT CHURCH

THE PATTERN - AND THE NEW TESTAMENT CHURCH

It is, indeed, a remarkable thing to study both the Old and the New Testaments. To be able to sit in the quietness and peacefulness of one's study, and to have the exalted and blessed honor of having a Bible, the freedom to study it, and the glorious birthright, privilege and prerogative of having it in my own tongue, with the thrill of being able to worship God as He has prescribed, is almost beyond description. When it comes time for us "to count our many blessings," surely this fact ought to be uppermost in our thoughts. May we cherish it. May we never take it for granted.

I fully realize that many do not like to study the Old Testament, but perhaps they fail to realize that without such it is very difficult to understand the New Testament. While growing up, I heard a statement that I have long remembered. In fact, I just repeated it to my namesake, G.G.Jr., this past Saturday morning: "The Old Testament is the New Testament concealed, and the New Testament is the Old Testament revealed" (I do not know when or from whom I first heard this). I think, from my own perspective and experience, that one reason people fail to enjoy the Old Testament is that they have really never studied it, think it to be just "for the past," do not know how to study it, have not understood the principles in it and fail to understand how it relates to the New Testament. For this reason, I gave a few thoughts in this book on that grand and glorious statement by Paul: "For whatsoever things were written aforetime were written for our learning, that through patience and comfort of the scriptures we might have hope" (Rom. 15:4).

In this chapter, on "The Pattern - And The New Testament Church," we will observe the value of the Old Testament as it "looks forward" and "points to," not just to the Christ, but to that unshakeable kingdom (cf. Gen. 3:15; Dan. 2:31-45; 7:25-26) as well. It is in Jeremiah that we find this statement to Judah: "Thus saith Jehovah, Stand ye in the ways and see, and ask for the old paths, where is the good way; and walk therein, and ye shall find rest for your souls: but they said, We will not walk therein" (6:16). Many years after the death of Isaiah, this grand prophet spoke of "the old paths," a way that was "right," and wherein God wanted his people "to walk," as it was here they would find "rest for their souls."

THE OLD TESTAMENT AND THE CHURCH

I need not reiterate, repeat and rehash, the idea of "the pattern" by the wording found in the Old Testament. But rest assured, know without a doubt and understand with all the heart, that in the Old Testament there is much to be learned from it about the dwelling place of God, the New Testament Church. Indeed, these things constitute the plan of God for the New Testament Church.

1. **God Purposed The New Testament Church.** When we think of this word "purpose," our minds go immediately to a statement by Paul in the Ephesian letter.

> *"Unto me, who am less than the least of all saints, was this grace given, to preach unto the Gentiles* ***the unsearchable riches of Christ;*** *and* ***to make all men see what is the dispensation of the mystery which for ages hath been hid in God*** *who created all things; to the intent that now unto the principalities and the powers in the heavenly places* ***might be made known through the church the manifold wisdom of***

> ***God,*** *ACCORDING TO* ***the eternal purpose*** *which he purposed in Christ Jesus our Lord" (3:8-11, emp. GM).*

Again, we observe what he said to Timothy: "Be not ashamed...but suffer hardship with the gospel ACCORDING TO the power of God; who saved us, and called us with a holy calling,...ACCORDING TO *his own purpose and grace, which was given us in Christ Jesus before times eternal"* (2 Tim. 1:8-9, emp. GM). These declarations clearly set before us let us see that the Church of the New Testament was included in that purpose.

I recall a sermon that many of us have preached through the many years of our preaching. It would cover (1) the purpose, (2) the promise, (3) the prophecy, (4) the plan and (5) the perfection of the New Testament Church. This still needs to be preached today, yea, and perhaps more diligently than ever before. We, seemingly, have forgotten the promise of Genesis 3:15 about "the seed," and the fulfillment of that promise in Galatians 3:15-18, esp. vs. 16. We fail to see, any more, the relation of Genesis 12:1-3 and the covenant that God made with Abraham to the New Testament Church, as well as observing such thoughts found in Genesis 26:4; 28:14 and 49:10. What a soul-chilling thrill it is to read of and to know the meaning of "until Shiloh come." Indeed, the Messiah would be, as foretold by Genesis 49:10, a descendant of Judah (cf. Heb. 7:11-28, esp. vs. 14). God was preparing (planning) for the Christ, and all vital things, such as the gospel, which would convert a people and these would be His Church.

Some of the prophets pinpointed both "the time" and "the place" when this New Testament Church would begin. It was Isaiah who so exactly specified this:

> *"**The word** that Isaiah the son of Amos saw **concerning Judah and Jerusalem.** And it shall come to pass **in the latter days,** that the mountain of Jehovah's house shall be established on the top of the mountains, and shall be exalted above the hills; and **all nations shall flow unto it. And many peoples** shall go and say, Come ye, and **let us go up to the mountain of Jehovah, to the house of the God of Jacob;** and he will teach us of his ways, and **we will walk in his paths** (wonder if these were like 'the old paths' of Jer. 6:16, GM): for **out of Zion shall go forth the law, and the word of Jehovah from Jerusalem"** (2:1-3, emp. GM).*

It was also Isaiah who spoke these words: "Thus saith the Lord Jehovah, Behold, I lay in Zion for a foundation a stone, a tried stone, a precious corner-stone of sure foundation: he that believeth shall not be in haste" (28:16). And, it is well just here we note this reference being made known in the New Testament (cf. Acts 4:11; Psm. 118:22; 1 Cor. 3:11; Rom. 9:33; 1 Pet. 2:1-10, eps. vss. 4-8).

Yea, we can see "the unfolding" of God's actions, as we have seen something of the purpose, the promise, the prophecy and now we can read more as to its beginning and duration: "And in the days of those kings shall the God of heaven set up a kingdom which shall never be destroyed, nor shall the sovereignty thereof be left to another people; but it shall break in pieces and consume all these kingdoms, and it shall stand for ever" (Dan. 2:31-45; we saw only verse 44; cf. 7:13-14).

2. **God's Plan Was Perfected In The New Testament Church.** It was after the resurrection, on the way to Emmaus, that two discussed the happenings concerning Jesus, "a prophet mighty in deed and word before God and

all the people" (Luke 24:13, 19). Cleopas, one of them, said they had hoped that it was this man who was to "redeem" Israel (vs. 21). It is just here that Jesus, unknown to them at the time, said: "O foolish men, and slow of heart to believe in all that the prophets have spoken! Behooved it not the Christ to suffer...And beginning from Moses and from all the prophets, he interpreted to them in all the scriptures the things concerning himself" (vss. 25-27). Before this piercing chapter closes, Jesus again speaks, this time he says, "These are my words which I spoke unto you, while I was yet with you, that all things must needs be fulfilled, which are written in the law of Moses, and the prophets, and the psalms, concerning me" (24:44).

Surely it is evident by now that God, way back in the Old Testament times, yea, even before, purposed the Church of the New Testament. If we had nothing else to go by, the statement from Christ about "all the things in the scriptures, from Moses and from all the prophets, were wrapped up in him," fulfilled in him, would be sufficient. However, Peter adds yet another thought:

> *"Concerning* ***which salvation the prophets*** *sought and searched diligently,* ***who prophesied*** *of the grace that should come unto you:* ***searching what time or what manner of time*** *the Spirit of Christ which was in them did point unto, when it* ***testified beforehand the sufferings of Christ****, and the glories that should follow them.* ***To whom it was revealed****, that not unto themselves, but unto you, did they minister these things, which now have been* ***announced unto you through them that preached the gospel unto you*** *by the Holy Spirit sent forth from heaven; which things angels desire to look into" (1 Pet. 1:10-12, emp. GM).*

Indeed, God purposed the New Testament Church, and finally, the plan was perfected by the gospel being preached.

THE NEW TESTAMENT AND THE CHURCH

With all things "written aforetime" (the law of Moses, and the prophets and the Psalms) now fulfilled in Christ (cf. Matt. 5:17; John 17:4; 19:28-30), which, of course, included his death, his resurrection, ascension and the sending of the promised Holy Spirit of God (cf. 1 Cor. 15:1-3; Luke 24:46-47; Heb. 9:15-17, 23ff; Rom. 4:25; Acts 1:9-11; 2:1-4; 1:8; etc.), we now turn our minds back and commence, in the New Testament, reading of the promise of the church to be built by Christ. This included its coming into existence and being the "unshakeable kingdom" which has now been, for ages, received, preached and taught as the body of Christ (cf. Col. 1:18; Eph. 1:22-23; 5:23; Col. 1:24; Eph. 4:4), and as "THE WAY" and "THE ONLY WAY" (cf. John 14:6; 6:44-45) wherein man could be saved. It is here he reaches the blood of Christ, the only power in the entire world to remit sin (cf. Eph. 1:7; Rev. 1:5; Rom. 6:3-4).

1. **Jesus Promised To Build "My" Church**. It was in Caesarea Philippi where Jesus asked his disciples two questions: (1) "Who do men say that the Son of man is?" and (2) "But who say ye that I am?" In answer to the first question (Matt. 16:13), it seems that there was as much confusion then as there is today. However, in his answer to the second question, Peter exclaimed, "Thou art the Christ, the Son of the living God" (vs. 16). It is at this point we find the Master's statement:

> *"And Jesus answered and said unto him, Blessed art thou, Simon Barjonah: for flesh and blood hath not revealed it unto thee, but my Father*

> *who is in heaven. And I also say unto thee, that thou art Peter, and* ***upon this rock I will build my church;*** *and the gates of Hades shall not prevail against it. I will give unto thee the keys of the kingdom of heaven: and whatsoever thou shalt bind on earth shall be bound in heaven; and whatsoever thou shalt loose on earth shall be loosed in heaven" (16:17-19, emp. GM).*

In the Old Testament, we read "that *not one thing hath failed* of all the good things which Jehovah your God spake concerning you," and "Blessed be Jehovah, that hath given rest unto his people Israel, ACCORDING TO all that he promised: *there hath not failed one word* of all his good promise, which he promised by Moses his servant" (Josh. 23:14; 1 Kings 8:56). We can now make the same statement about the promise of Christ to build his church, as the rest of the New Testament makes that abundantly clear.

2. **The Church Was Brought Into Being On Pentecost**. That which God had purposed, that which God had promised, that which was purposed and promised was prophesied by the prophets. Further, it was prepared by the work of John the Baptizer and was also taught by the Master Himself during His personal ministry (those principles set forth so clearly by the Christ, the Messiah, the Anointed and Holy one of God would be found in His Church), made possible by the shedding of the blood of Jesus for the remission of man's sins, and now, on Pentecost, the plan of God had so unfolded step by step that it was now being perfected. Indeed, it was on Pentecost that it, the New Testament Church, came into existence! (cf. Matt. 5:17-20; Heb. 9:23-28, esp. vs. 26; Rom. 4:25; Acts 1:9-11; etc.).

Jesus had taught that the "church" and the "kingdom" were one and the same divine building. During his earthly ministry, he also made the statement: "Verily I say unto you, There are some here of them that stand by, who shall in no wise taste of death, till they see the kingdom of God come with power" (Mark 9:1). It was not long, after the ascension (Acts 1:9-11; Luke 24:44-49; esp. vss. 47-49), only a matter of a few days, that Jesus sent forth the Holy Spirit upon the apostles just as He had promised (cf. Acts 1:4-5). This day on which the Holy Spirit came was Pentecost (cf. Lev. 23:15-16, as it informs us about the day "when" Pentecost occurred, etc.), yea, it was the day of "power" (Acts 1:8).

If a man can add two plus two and get four, then I believe a man can add one, plus one, plus one and get three. Yes, three! You see, *the kingdom was to come with power*, that is one. *Power was to come with the Holy Spirit*, that is two. And *the Holy Spirit came on the day of Pentecost*, and that is three! If a man takes God at His Word, and that is faith, then he, too, will believe that *the church, which is the kingdom*, came into existence on the fiftieth day after the resurrection of Christ from the grave (cf. Acts 1:3-4; Luke 24:46-49; Acts 1:6-8, 9-11, special attention to verse 12; 2:1-4, 14-16; cf. Joel 2:28-31), the day of Pentecost! And that is no flapdoodle! The "wise" man can comprehend this, the "otherwise" man will perhaps wiggle, squirm, twist and turn, but the fact remains the same. The New Testament Church Was Brought Into Being On Pentecost, as on that day people were "added" to it (cf. Acts 2:41-47, esp. 47).

3. **The Gospel Was Powerfully Proclaimed And People Performed Its Requirements.** People today want to be saved "at the point of faith," which means "without manifesting anything else." This has never been taught in

the New Testament, in fact, there have always been conditions for man to meet, yes, even in and throughout the Old Testament (cf. Num. 21:4-9; Josh. 6:1-21; 2 Kings 5:1-14). Therefore, such a teaching is nowhere found in the Bible, and when such is put into practice today it is so done without faith. There can be no faith where there is no word of God! To say that a man is saved at "the point of faith" without manifesting any further act of obedience is to show either (1) a total disregard for the pattern, those instructions contained there, or (2) an ignorance of the Word that must be corrected (nothing wrong with being ignorant, as those on Pentecost were ignorant and had to ask what to do, but they did not stay in ignorance - that is the thing that is wrong).

For thirty-one years I have written and produced a *Daily Bible Reading Tract Calendar*. Very often, on the inside of the back cover, I will put an outline of various items relative to the New Testament Church. One of those items mentioned "the seed of the kingdom" (Matt. 13:3-23; Luke 8:11-15). Seed must be sown and thus it was on Pentecost with Peter and the other apostles being the sowers of the seed. What commenced here is traceable throughout the New Testament, therefore, we list those things which culminated in people being added to the body of believers.

a. The death, burial and resurrection of Christ were always present as "the core" of *gospel preaching* (cf. Acts 2:14-36; 1 Cor. 15:1-4; Acts 3:11-26; etc.).

b. *Faith* was produced in the hearts of those who heeded the message (cf. Acts 2:36; Rom. 10:13-17; Acts 15:7; note it is "the faith" in verse 9, as per the Greek).

c. Being pricked in their hearts, they were always

told to *repent* (Acts 2:37-38; 3:19), which was a command of God (Acts 17:30). (Note the difference in being "pricked" in the heart and in being "cut" to the heart, cf. Acts 5:33; 7:54).

d. *Confession* had been taught by Jesus, therefore, those who repented of their sins confessed Christ (cf. Luke 12:8-9). The only other alternative for these believers was that of denial, the price of which no man would want to pay (cf. Matt. 10:32-33). If confession is not necessary, then a person must deal with such passages as Romans 10:9-10; Acts 8:37; 1 Timothy 6:12-13.

e. The last step they took, which design, pattern, structure, put them "into" Christ was *baptism* (Acts 2:38; this is not *rantidzo*, sprinkling, and neither is it *cheo*, pouring), and it was "in order to receive" the remission of sins (cf. Acts 2:38 with the same Greek construction, *eis aphesin harmartion*, as found in Matt. 26:28, as whatever it means in Matt. 26:28, it means here in Acts 2:38. No man will give it as "because of" in Matthew!).

f. Being immersed *"into" Christ*, they *"put on Christ,"* and, having come in contact with the blood of Christ, they were now in the Church of Christ, the Kingdom of God, the Body of Christ, etc. (Gal. 3:26-27; Rom. 6:3-4; John 19:33-34; Col. 1:13, 18, 24; Eph. 1:22-23; 1 Cor. 12:13; Eph. 5:23). Indeed, they had obeyed the commission of the Master (cf. Matt. 28:18-20; Mark 16:15-16; Luke 24:43-47; Acts 22:16; Rev. 1:5; 1 Pet. 3:21; Eph. 5:25-27; 1 Cor. 12:27; Rom. 12:3-5, esp. vs. 5).

Many times I have been referred to, styled as and singled out as one of the "five finger" boys, fellows. This causes laughter, but it is done in derision, mockery, sarcasm, disdain, disrespect and also in pure scorn. However, I look at my hand, and theirs, ask them about the "pattern" for a hand as made by God and ask them to count those items on mine or theirs, etc. Then I let it be known that I am glad I have "five fingers," as it "fits the pattern." I also let it be known that I would never belittle one with a hand that did not have "five fingers," as that would be "less than the pattern," and is not a beautiful sight. Then I make the transition, as a sinner, who does "less than the pattern," is a pitiful sight, and he might as well cry out, "Wretched man that I am!" You see, faith is taking God at His word. No man dare tamper with the pattern, the last testament of our Lord! Yes, the grace of God in vain! (cf. 2 Cor. 5:17-6:1, esp. 6:1). Or, to use another phrase from Paul (and just the phrase, not the context, "Do not make void the grace of God" (cf. Gal. 2:21).

4. **The New Testament Church "IS" Designated.** If it is not termed, identified, depicted, described, defined and characterized, then a lot of scriptures are most confusing about this part of the pattern.

First, let us just notice some of the appellations as found in our New Testaments (cf. Eph. 3:15):

a. *Church of God*, singular and plural (1 Cor. 1:2; 10:32; 15:9; 1 Tim. 3:5; Acts 20:28; read the footnote in the *ASV* on this verse; 1 Cor. 11:16; 1 Thess. 2:14).

b. *The body of Christ* (Col. 1:18, 24; Eph. 4:12; 5:23).

c. *Churches of Christ* (Rom. 16:16).

d. *The kingdom of God* (Mark 9:1; 14:25; Acts 1:3;

8:12; 19:8; John 3:1-7, esp. 3, 5).

e. *The kingdom* (Acts 1:6; 1 Cor. 15:24; Heb. 12:28).

f. *The kingdom of heaven* (Matt. 16:19).

g. *The kingdom of the Son of His love* (Col. 1:13).

h. *The church*, singular and plural (Matt. 18:17; Gal. 1:2; 2 Cor. 8:1; Rev. 1:4; 2:1, 8, 12, 18; 3:1, 7, 14).

i. *The church of the Lord* (Acts 20:28).

j. *The temple of God* (1 Cor. 3:16-17).

It might be of worth at this time to note why the church is so signified. The word from which we get the word "church" is a beautiful Greek word. It is *ekklesia. It is that body of people* who have been "called out of the world" (cf. Col. 1:13). However, let me hasten to add that every time the word *ekklesia*, basically an assembly, is found in the New Testament it does not always refer to the church (cf. Acts 19:32, 39, 41). The church is a people (1 Pet. 2:9-10). It is a people who were all sinners before they were saved (Col. 1:21-23; 2:13-15; Eph. 2:1-3, 11-12), a people who still do sin (cf. 1 John 1:8-10; Rom. 3:9-23), and a people in constant danger of apostasy (Acts 8:18-24; Phile. 23-24; Col. 4:14; 2 Tim. 4:9-10). But, indeed, a people who have separated themselves from the world.

It is a reborn people, i.e., a believing, confessing, penitent, and baptized people, therefore, it is called a "house" (1 Tim. 1:3-4; 3:14-15; Acts 20:17, 28; Rev. 2:1).

It is a purified people, and so it is called a "bride" (cf. Rom. 7:4; Rev. 21:9; Titus 2:11-14; Eph. 5:25-27; "bride to be" in 2 Cor. 11:2-3).

It is a ruled people, and that is why it is called a "kingdom" (Gal. 6:11-16; Phil. 3:16; Gal. 6:2; James 1:22-25; 2:8, 12; Rom. 8:1-2; 2:27; etc.).

It is a Spirit-filled people, therefore, it is called a "temple" (1 Cor. 3:16-17; 6:19-20; Eph. 2:19-22).

It is a united people, and we have it designated as a "body" (1 Cor. 12:27; Col. 1:18, 24; Eph. 1:22-23; 4:4).

Indeed, the church of Christ is the people of God. If you are one of God's people, then you are a member of the New Testament Church. Note 1 Peter 2:9-10; Titus 2:11-14; Ephesians 1:3-12, as they speak to this "people concept" of the church and prove that the church is a people. Let me hasten to point out two thoughts: (1) it is never claimed that the church is sinless, but rather that the Christ has forgiven its sins (Eph. 2:1-3, 11-22; 1 Cor. 6:9-11; Col. 1:21-23; 1 John 1:7-10), and (2) the Bible never says the church saves you, but rather that the church is the composite number of the saved (Acts 2:47; cf. Colosse, Col. 1:1-2, 12-14).

It might be well, in the third place, to observe some negative aspects, that is, what the church is not.

a. *It is not a sect or a denomination,* because it is not a part of anything. It has no religious divisions (Eph. 1:22-23; 4:4; Col. 1:18, 24). Note Paul's statement in Acts 24:14, 5-6; 28:22.

b. *It is not a social club*, that is, it is not designed to sponsor dances, pie suppers, cake walks, etc. (1 Pet. 2:9-10).

c. *It is not a building*, as the church can meet in a private home (Phile. 1-3; Rom. 16:5; 1 Cor. 16:19; Col. 4:15), or in...

d. *It is not a recreational club*, as it is designed for the spiritual exercise of man, not the physical (cf. 1 Tim. 4:6-8; 1 Cor. 9:24-27; Heb. 5:12-14).

e. *It is not the family of Abraham*. Its membership is the seed of Abraham, but in a spiritual realm (cf. Matt. 3:9; Gal. 3:7, 26-29).

f. *It is not the old Jewish order*. Nicodemus was of that order (a good one, a ruler), but he was told to be "born again" as per John 3:1-7. The church is distinctively of the New Testament. It is not a continuation of the Sinaitic covenant.

Over in the state of Tennessee I was amazed, in driving between Manchester and McMinnville (some on the side roads), to see for my first time signs with the caption: The Baptist Church of Christ. It reminded me of something I heard years ago. A certain religious group was raising funds to build a church building. As they knocked on one door and told the gentleman their purpose and also their plan, he finally said, "All right, I will make a donation to the building program, if you will erect a sign that says, 'This is the Church of Christ.'" They immediately said, "We cannot do that." To which the man replied, "Well, I'll tell you what. I'll still make a donation if you will erect a sign that says, 'This is not the Church of Christ.'" They said, "No, we cannot do that either." Guess what? They left without a donation.

In Acts 16:13-15, we have the conversion of Lydia, and her household. After her baptism, she said, "If ye have judged me to be faithful to the Lord, come into my house, and abide there. And she constrained us" (vs. 15). Notice she said, "...*my house*." Now I am sure made to wonder about this house. That is, just whose house was it? Could I say, "This is Lydia's house"? Would it be correct for me to say, "This is the house of Lydia"? Would both be right? Now then, if I were to say, "This is Music's house," would that be all right? If I said, "This is the house of Music," how about that? Or perhaps you might want me to say, "This is the Music house of Lydia." How would that strike you? What does "my" show? That is, what kind of a pronoun is it? If you introduce your wife to me, and if your name is already known to me (let's say, it is Picklesimmer), but I had never in my life met your wife, you might say, "This is *my wife*." Would I be within my jurisdiction to say, "I'm glad to meet you, Mrs. Picklesimmer"? Keep in mind, you did not give me her name, you just said, "This is my wife." How would I possibly know to say, "Mrs. Picklesimmer"? Could I employ, utilize and apply the same amount of just good ole common horse sense to the statement made by Christ, when he said, "I will build my church," and know whose it is, whose name it is to wear? Remember, the church is "the bride" of Christ. If it does not make any difference, we might as well let the sign read: "This Is The Baptist Church of Christ." However, I am accelerated to say that such thinking is just pure absurdity and senselessness, plain ole tomfoolery! And any reasonable, rational, common sense and logical thinking person knows it to be so. Let's keep the name "ACCORDING TO" those divine designations that we find in the Scripture and never go beyond them.

5. **The New Testament Church Worshipped ACCORDING TO The New Testament.** It would be strange, wouldn't it, if we had a New Testament, and with the blood of Christ it was sealed, authorized, sanctioned, endorsed and stamped, and we went along and worshipped *according to* an (the) Old Testament? Even though the mediator today is Christ Jesus, of this "new and better covenant" (cf. Heb. 9:15-17; 8:6; Matt. 26:28; Heb. 7:11-

28, esp. vss. 22, 27-28), wouldn't it be rather odd if we still tried to go through Moses? These things make about as much sense as those who go to the Old Testament to prove an item or two of (in) their worship.

We need to be reminded, "And whatsoever ye do, in word or in deed, do all in the name of the Lord Jesus, giving thanks to God the Father through him" (Col. 3:17). Christ has "all authority," and it was Christ who said, "God is a Spirit: and they that worship him must worship in spirit and truth" (John 4:24, check the Greek *dei*, "must" by Greek authorities and see if we have an option here; "all authority," Matt. 28:18). This means that God is to be worshipped, that God is to be worshipped by the worshipper having the right motive or attitude, and that God is to be worshipped by the truth, that which is authorized by Christ to be the truth. If this is not a pattern, and one for acceptable worship, pray tell me what it is. God is not obligated to just accept anything for worship, nor has He ever been!

Now with this pattern in mind, either the New Testament Church did or did not worship ACCORDING TO the standard, ACCORDING TO that which is written. If we are not to go beyond "that which is written" (1 Cor. 4:6), not to "add nor to take away from the written" (Rev. 22:18-19; Gal. 1:6-9), then all we must do is to see just how they worshipped, that is, what they did in their worship.

Within the pages of the New Testament, the standard, the norm and the rule that governs man today, we find the following:

a. The disciples came together *"to break bread"* (Acts 20:7, Greek is *klasai*, 1 aorist act. infin., "purpose clause;" 1 Cor. 11:23-29).

b. The disciples *prayed* (cf. Acts 2:42; 1 Thess. 5:17).

c. The disciples *were taught* when they assembled (Acts 2:42), as they continued in the apostles' teaching (cf. Matt. 28:20; Acts 20:7).

d. The disciples *sang* psalms, hymns and spiritual songs (cf. Eph. 5:19; Col. 3:16; yea, they "sang" the "*ode*," Greek for the general word for "song," cf. Rev. 15:3, and rest assured the word for the word "sing" is the Greek *adousin*. So, according to Ephesians 5:19, Colossians 3:16, they "sing" [*adontes,* from root *ado*] the spiritual "songs" [the Greek is *odais*, from the root *ode*], so do not be led astray when someone tries to hang the instrument on this general word, *ode*).

e. The disciples *gave* according as they had prospered (cf. 1 Cor. 16:1-2; 2 Cor. 8:1ff; 9:6-7, as well as other verses in these two great chapters on giving).

If they (the disciples) "walked by faith" (2 Cor. 5:7), which is from "the word of hearing" (Rom. 10:7), then they "pleased God" (Heb. 11:6), and this they must have done. Why? I do not read that they were ever condemned, only praised, therefore, what they did must have been authorized and it must have been acceptable, being offered to God and in and with the proper motive. Therefore, if we do what they did in following "the pattern," "the rule book," that which had "divine authorization," then, we, too, can please God ("never condemned" is in reference to these avenues of worship only). But to please God, be it known that it must be **according to that which is written**. If not, then just do whatever pleases you as God will just have to be obligated to accept "whatever" we do (cf. Judg.

17:6; 21:25).

6. **The New Testament Church Was Organized By The Divine Standard.** When a church had so grown and matured spiritually, it was to be organized by having a plurality of men called "elders" (Acts 14:23, if someone tries to deter your thoughts by it not being "every" because the Greek is *kata* and not *pas*, inform them that *kata* is used distributively with numerals and places).

Since putting the above note in parentheses, I thought perhaps it might be of benefit (people today are looking for any loophole) and help to explain that "every church" is correct in Acts 14:23, and also compare it, prove it, by the same usage in other places. **Note:**

a. *In Acts 5:42*, we have "every" day, but again it is the word *kata*, not the word *pas*.

b. *In Acts 22:19*, it is rendered "every" synagogue, but it is *kata* also here.

c. *In Titus 1:5*, it is "every" city, and the word again is the Greek *kata*.

d. *In Revelation 22:2*, it is "every" month, and, yes, the word is *kata*.

e. In each of these five places, the word *kata* is used and is translated as "every," although the word *pas*, "every" is not employed. This is why it is correct to translate 1 Corinthians 16:2, "Upon the first day of 'every' week." (Bro. Andrew Connally gave me a new Greek Testament, not one like I have, and I have just tonight checked it along with my other Greek Testaments. This new one is the one edited by men like Aland, Metzger, Wikgren, Martini and Black. All that I checked agree on the word *kata*).

I have given the above for the simple reason that many today say that "each" and "every" church does not have to have elders. This is false to the core, that is, if they have so grown, matured, and have qualified men (cf. 1 Tim. 3:1-7; Tit. 1:5-9; 1 Pet. 5:1-3). It is not ACCORDING TO the written for a church to decide to use majority rule, a pure democracy, a government by the people, popular government, as some have done! The church is to be overseen by men called elders, presbyters, pastors, shepherds, bishops and overseers (cf. Acts 20:17, 28). There are three basic words in the Greek New Testament, *presbuterous* (elder or presbyter), *poimen* (pastor or shepherd) and *episkopos* (bishop or overseer), and all three of the Greek words (the six in English) are used in Acts 20:17, 28! Two of the three are used in Titus 1:5-7 and two of them are used in 1 Peter 5:1-2, *presbuterous* and *episkopos* respectively. Also, one can note the verb *poimanate* (1 aor. active imperative from *poimanio*) is used in 1 Peter 5:2. (For a full discussion of these words and the various usages check my book, *The Faith Demands Efficient Leadership In The Church*).

In the New Testament, we also find a group of men called "deacons." These men were servants to the elders, serving in whatever capacity they could to assist the eldership (yes, it is correct to use the word "eldership," cf. Gen. 40:21, the word "butlership" and how it is therein used). Their qualifications are observed in the same book and chapter with those of the elders (1 Tim. 3:8-10, 12-13). When Paul wrote "to all the saints in Christ Jesus that are at Philippi," he said, "with the bishops and deacons" (Phil. 1:1). In regard to the passage in Philippians 1:1, do we not realize that the "bishops" and the "deacons" are distinct from "the saints." Is not every church to have deacons? It is interesting in a study of the Greek *diakonos*, to read what Thayer says: "one who executes the commands of another" (p. 138). Indeed, these are the men who serve as special servants to and for the elders in their work. The passage in Acts 6:1-6 needs to be thoroughly studied. I say this, as in verse one we have *diakonia*, ministration, and in verse two the word *diakonein*, serve, is used. Both of these are akin to the word for deacon, *diakonos*.

Another brief word here needs to be said, especially since today we have an "abuse" of the word "deacon." For those who would jump to the conclusion that the church, officially, needs to have an office wherein we have "deaconesses," and try to support the same by the use of the term *diakonon* as used by Paul of Phoebe (Rom. 16:1), let me suggest that these need to study the word *diakonos*. I say this as there is a "general" use of the word, as well as a "technical" use. Surely we ought to know that every single time we find the word "elder" in the New Testament, the word "assembly" in the New Testament, the word "apostle" in the New Testament, that they are not always used in their "technical" sense. And so it is with this word (cf. Matt. 20:26; John 2:5,9; 12:26; Rom. 15:8; 1 Cor. 3:5; 2 Cor. 3:6; Eph. 6:21; Col. 1:7,23; 1 Thess. 3:2, perhaps these few times it is used will be a "good beginning" in case one is so inclined to argue with the above). It is no wonder to me that, in his book on hermeneutics, Dungan spoke of "common sense" as a rule to be used in Bible study.

In the local church we also note they had an "evangelist" who labored with them. He, too, worked under the oversight of the elders (cf. Eph. 4:11; 1 Cor. 9:1-16; 1 Tim. 4:1-16; 5:19-21; Titus 2:15; etc.).

7. **The New Testament Church Is Ruled And Regulated By The Rule, The New Testament.** The pattern for the New Testament Church does not stop with the six things that I have previously discussed, and those

just briefly. Be it emphatically stated, punctuated and pronounced, that the New Testament is the rule for every aspect of the Church of the New Testament. This, in itself, would take a book, but let me be rather laconic, concise and to the point, as I list other thoughts by which the New Testament pattern is to govern the church, yes, as it is, and I repeat, in every aspect. The New Testament pattern is not to be a "hit" and "miss" type of guideline, that is, I cannot just pick and choose "this" item and then "omit" that item. We do not have the prerogative to be selective and just obey one or two pieces of the pattern (let any woman try to make a dress by only cutting out for the dress her favorite sections and throwing the rest of the pieces, the designs, away!). God never gave any man, any local church, that option! It is a must, a mandate, a divine legislation that we obey (teach, preach and practice) "the whole counsel of God" (cf. Acts 20:27). What I am saying needs to be said! No local church can live in harmony with the divine blueprint and throw out "church discipline," for example, regardless of how "tasteless" it is (cf. 1 Pet. 2:1-3, esp. vs. 3).

I feel almost "out of place," and some may think that I am almost "out of mind," by stressing, reasserting and reaffirming, that the New Testament Church is dictated, supervised and superintended, disciplined and directed by the New Testament and it alone, and by all of it. Christ is the testator (cf. Heb. 9:15-17) of the New Testament (cf. Matt. 26:28), that which is "perfect" (cf. James 1:25) has been made known, fully revealed and written down (cf. 1 Cor. 13:8-11) and it is (present tense) to make the man of God complete (cf. 2 Tim. 3:1-17). It is not to be "added to," and *oh how we know about that, but* the text also says **"No man is to subtract" from it** (cf. Rev. 22:18-19). Those who do not let it govern the "entirety" of the life and of the actions of the New Testament Church are guilty of "taking from or subtracting from" what is written! Take away "church discipline" and you are "subtracting from" it, for example (cf. 2 Thess. 3:6ff). We know about "false teachings or perversions" (cf. 1 Cor. 4:6; Gal. 1:6-9; 2 John 9-11), but when are we going to realize that we ourselves may be our very own worst enemy (cf. Acts 20:29-30, "from among your own selves...").

a. *The church and its members.* I recall also, in the *Daily Bible Reading Tract Calendar*, in the outline of the New Testament I previously mentioned, referring to a listing of designations for the individual members (cf. Eph. 3:15). I listed such as: (1) Saints (Rom. 1:7; 1 Cor. 1:2; Phil. 1:1), (2) Brethren (Col. 1:2; Gal. 6:1; Luke 8:21), (3) Disciples (John 15:8; Acts 11:26), (4) Children (Gal. 3:26; 1 John 2:1; 3:1-3; Eph. 5:1), (5) Christians (Acts 11:26; 26:28; 1 Pet. 4:16), (6) Members (Rom. 12:4; 1 Cor. 12:27; Eph. 5:30), etc. These all show a relationship to one of the ways that the New Testament Church is designated, such as "brethren in the family of God," "members of the body of Christ," etc.

b. *The church and the world.* Such verses as 1 John 2:15-17; James 1:27; 4:4; 1 Thessalonians 5:21-22; John 17:13-19; 18:36, as well as many others, tell us of this pattern for us and the world and how we are to live in the world. Yes, "in," but not "of!"

c. *The church and righteous living.* It should be sufficient to read Titus 2:11-14, but there are also admonitions in 1 Peter 2:11-12; Philippians 2:5-9; Romans 8:6-13; 1 Peter 2:21; etc., and we are definitely to let "our light shine" (cf. Matt. 5:14-16; Phil. 2:12-16).

d. *The church and its mission.* We need to be reminded of the "marching orders" of the church (Matt. 28:18-20; Mark 16:15-16; 1 Cor. 1:18-21; Rom. 1:13-16; 1 Tim. 3:14-15; 4:6-16; John 6:44-45) and realize why it is here on the earth. I certainly believe the secondary meaning of Ephesians 3:10 teaches this, the gospel made known by/through the church. The value of the soul demands "full speed ahead" (cf. Matt. 16:24-26; Col. 1:23), as the saving of souls is the number one mission of the church and we accomplish this by preaching, benevolence and edification.

e. *The church and the poor* (destitute, needy, indigent). A passage in 1 John ought to "shake us up" when it comes to the pattern we are to follow: "But whoso hath this world's goods, and beholdeth his brother in need, and shutteth up his compassion from him, how doth the love of God abide in him?" (3:17). We must be concerned and demonstrate it to others who are in need (cf. Acts 2:44-45; 4:32-37; James 1:27; 2:14-18; Acts 6:1-6; Gal. 6:10; etc.).

f. *The church and the erring.* Let it be sufficient here just to list those scriptures dealing with this subject (Matt. 18:15-17; Rom. 16:17-18; 1 Cor. 5:1-13; Eph. 5:11; 2 Thess. 3:6-15; Titus 3:10-11), as surely they are self-explanatory. (My book, *A Crucial Study Of A Critical Subject - Fellowship*, deals with this problem, as well as with false teachers.)

g. *The church and false teachers.* Some of the same scriptures I listed above also apply here, such as Romans 16:17-18; Ephesians 5:11; Titus 3:10-11. Some of the erring, you see, may be so because of false teachings, others may be immoral, etc. One scripture that needs to be captivated in practice is 2 John 9-11. Yes, we in the church do have this divine mandate (cf. 1 John 4:1; 1 Thess. 5:21, Greek is *dokimadzo*, "prove," note Luke 14:19, it is also used in 1 Cor. 16:3; etc.).

h. *The church and God's dwelling place.* This surely should be taught more often, as it might help us in our holiness and our attitude toward the church, each other, etc. (cf. Eph. 2:19-22; 1 Cor. 3:16-17; Heb. 3:1-6). God's dwelling place is not in any denomination! A church (?) not erected ACCORDING TO THE DIVINE PATTERN does not have God dwelling in it, no more than if Moses had not built the tabernacle according to the pattern (cf. Heb. 8:5; Exod. 25:9,40; 40:16). A human institution is not a divine one nor can it serve in the place of one. God will be with "His" people (Rev. 21:1-3).

i. *The church and its warning.* Again, there is perhaps some overlapping in thoughts/scriptures (cf. Matt. 15:7-9, 13-14; 1 Tim. 4:1-3; 2 Cor. 11:2-3; Gal. 1:6-9; Rom. 16:17-18; Acts 20:29-30; 2 Tim. 4:1-5; etc.), but brethren, beloved of God, we must heed the warning about being warned! Hebrews 2:1-3; 12:25; Acts 3:22-23; Romans 2:4-11 have a message for the church today and only a fool will fail to be moved by it. In this, as in all things, the Father is saying unto us, "This is my beloved Son, in whom I am well pleased," and "hear ye him" (cf. Matt. 3:17; 17:5). What hope do we have if we "hear not" the Christ of God, His chosen? (cf. John 5:28-29; Matt. 25:46).

There are other items, of course, that need to be studied, and with diligence, but perhaps enough has been covered to handle some of the "oft-asked" and "misunderstood" pieces of the pattern in the New Testament Church. Not only that, but also areas in which our study has been lacking. I just believe "if we will put the brethren in mind of these things," "be diligent" in them, "give ourselves wholly to them," "take heed to ourselves," and "to our teaching," progress will be made and we shall "save both ourselves and them that hear us" (cf. 1 Tim. 4:6-16).

Chapter Eleven

THE PATTERN - AND CRUCIAL QUESTIONS ABOUT THE NEW TESTAMENT CHURCH

THE PATTERN - AND CRUCIAL QUESTIONS ABOUT THE NEW TESTAMENT CHURCH

I have learned, from trying to preach and teach for about the last forty years, that just because someone says, "You did not answer my question," does not mean that the question was not answered. It simply means that the person did not grasp or that he failed to see the answer given. It could mean that he saw the answer, but would not accept it and "this statement was his 'out.'" There is something I perhaps need to add to this thought about questions. I have learned this especially in trying to handle questions on the subject of "mechanical instrumental music" in worship to God. It seems to me, when every positive statement in the Bible has been given, there are still some who will try to justify it by offering objections, "in the form of questions," to the very explicit command of God "to sing." For an example, after almost exhausting the subject ACCORDING TO that which is written, someone is always asking, "What about David and the book of Psalms, especially Psalm 150"? or, "The Bible does not say, 'Thou shalt not use the instrument, does it?'" Therefore, it seems that it is just not sufficient, for some, to give "what is written." And this, even though one has labored to make it known that we will not be judged by that "which is not written." Then, even if you have shown this particular thought, they will ask, "Just how far can you go with the thought about not going beyond that which is not written?" For some, it seems, the plain statements of the Bible are just not adequate.

The matter of questions is most imperative. It is,

indeed, a marvelous and wonderful way to teach the Bible. In the last two years, and for the second time, I have gone through and listed all of the questions that I found asked in the Bible. I found over 1700 questions asked in the Old Testament. I found over 800 questions asked in the New Testament. Believe me, I have typed out every single question that I have found, and to have over 2,500 questions typed out is "a very large stack of questions." I take it then, since so many have been asked in the Bible, that they are extremely useful and important. Jesus was the Master teacher, and it was a great technique of His to ask questions (cf. Matt. 21:23-27).

Even though some of the material that I have tried to present in the various chapters thus given has been rather extensive, exhaustive, and encyclopedic, it is still gnawing at me to think someone is going to say, "Yes, but..." and then "ask a question." Therefore, I want now to take a little time and space and answer a few questions that have been and are being asked about the New Testament Church. I do this, as there is a precious soul involved in every question that is asked. Also, every Bible question deserves a Bible answer. It is not just sufficient to receive "an answer" to a Bible question, one must receive the right answer, the Bible answer. Then, too, we are charged by God "to give an answer" (cf. 1 Pet. 3:15).

The following few questions are not going to be given in any particular, specific and special, sequence. I do not want anyone to think I have given them by a certain classification or categorization. These are given at random, indiscriminately, but each question has merit and will stand, I trust, "as a unit" of special thought. There is a certain "background" to each one of these questions, but that parentage, conditions and circumstances, is not mine to give. The procedure will be simply to set forth the question, and then seek to give a logical, sound and sensible, answer.

IS CHURCH MEMBERSHIP ESSENTIAL?

The vast majority of religious groups in our world today do not even include the name of him who died to save them. Yet, in Matthew 16:18, we have it said by Jesus: "And I also say unto thee, that thou art Peter (the reader should be aware of the difference in two Greek words, *petros* and *petra*, Peter and rock, as used in this passage), and upon this rock I will build my church; and the gates of Hades (Hades is the correct term, as this is not the word for hell, as found in the *KJV*) shall not prevail against it." The remainder of the New Testament bears witness to the fact that this promise was fulfilled, as it tells of His Church.

In the world of today, the world of denominationalism, and I perhaps need to add that this "thinking" (?) has crept into the minds of some of the members of the Family of God, we find two ideas very often expressed. "No, church membership is not essential," and, "Yes, a man can be saved and never be a member of the church." This error is widespread. Ask the person on the street and he will immediately tell you that the church is not essential. Ask him if he wants to go to heaven, and he will say that he does. There is something we need to learn "just here." Human aspiration does not equal divine inspiration.

There is a reason for such a false doctrine (teaching). In fact, every false doctrine rests upon some misunderstanding of the Bible. People today misunderstand the Church. Most of them think of it as a building. At the very best, it seems, they think of it as one denomination among others, to which particular one you do not have to belong to be saved. They also misunderstand the plan of salvation, as the vast majority teach it is by faith only (they never do see the connection between the two). Also, there is the conception that it is something "to join" after you are saved, that is, if you want to do so. It is no wonder then that people think that the church is non-essential.

The Bible teaches, Yes, church membership is essential. No, one cannot be saved and not be a member of the church (that is, if accountable). Please understand that I am discussing The New Testament Church, the one that Christ built. I am not referring to any denomination, for you can be saved and never be a member of a single denomination. Indeed, to be saved, you cannot be saved in a body of which Christ is not the head (cf. Eph. 5:23). I am explicitly saying that you cannot be saved without being a member of the Lord's church, and that the church exists in a visible sense. Of that visible body, you must be a part, if you expect to be saved.

1. **The Church Is The Called Out.** I refer here to the Greek word, *ekklesia*, which we have translated as "church." This word has a very special relationship to the world, as it means "to be called out" and, of course, "called out of the world and called into the service of Christ" (cf. Col. 1:13).

In the New Testament we have "called through our gospel" (2 Thess. 2:14), "called into God's kingdom" (1 Thess. 2:12), "called out of darkness" (1 Pet. 2:9), "called by the suffering of Christ" (1 Pet. 2:21), "called into the fellowship of his Son" (1 Cor. 1:9), "called into one body" (Col. 3:15), "called with a holy (divine) calling," (2 Tim. 1:7-9; cf. Heb. 3:1), and "called to be saints" (Rom. 1:7), etc.

Is it necessary to be: called by God? called by the gospel? called out of darkness? called unto salvation?

called into God's kingdom? called into the fellowship of God's Son? called by the suffering of the Christ?, etc. IF SO, CHURCH MEMBERSHIP IS ESSENTIAL.

2. **The Church Is The Realm Of The Saved.** The church is composed of the saved and all of the saved. This is not saying that all who profess to be members of the church are saved people. It is saying that God adds "the saved" to the ones being saved, the church (Acts 2:47; 5:14; 11:21). The **King James** says, "Praising God, and having favour with all the people. And the Lord added to the church daily such as should be saved" (Acts 2:47).

Whom did the Lord add? Was it not those being saved? This is not something they "joined," as the Lord "added" them. From this, if we are very astute, we know three things: (1) The church is made up of saved people, (2) only saved people, and (3) all saved people.

Since the Lord adds the saved to the church, how can a person be saved and remain outside the church? It simply cannot be done. Is it necessary to be in the realm of the saved? IF SO, then CHURCH MEMBERSHIP IS ESSENTIAL.

3. **The Church Is The Reconciled Body.** The following from Paul's pen sets this forth without a question or a doubt.

> *"Wherefore remember, that once ye, the Gentiles in the flesh, who are called Uncircumcision by that which is called Circumcision, in the flesh, made by hands; that ye were at that time* ***separate from Christ, alienated from the commonwealth of Israel,*** *and* ***strangers from the covenants of the promise, having no hope*** *and* ***without God*** *in the world.* **But now in Christ Jesus** *ye that once were far off* ***are***

> ***made nigh in the blood of Christ.*** *For* ***he is our peace,*** *who* ***made both one,*** *and brake down the middle wall of partition, having abolished in his flesh the enmity, even the law of commandments contained in ordinances; that he might* ***create in himself of the two one new man,*** *so* ***making peace; and might reconcile*** *them both* ***in one body*** *unto God through the cross, having slain the enmity thereby" (Eph. 2:11-14, emp. GM).*

That "one" body is the church, as proven by Ephesians 1:22-23; Colossians 1:18, 24. "Ye are the body of Christ," said Paul to the Corinthians (1 Cor. 12:27). To the Romans, he said, "For even as we have many members in one body,... so we, who are many, are one body in Christ" (Rom. 12:4-5). Paul frequently spoke about the members, the body, and talked of them as being united. He would mention "...all the body..." (cf. Col. 2:19; Eph. 4:15-16). He said: (1) the body, the church, (2) his body's sake, which is the church, (3) to the church which is his body, (4) members of one body, (5) reconciled in one body, and then climaxed it all by stating (6) there is one body (Eph. 4:4). If the church is the body, the body is the church, there is but one body, then how many churches are there? How many bodies does your head have? It is the same way with Christ. He is the head of only one body, and we have Paul's word for it: "...as Christ also is the head of the church, being himself the saviour of the body" (Eph. 5:23). That is so clear that even I can understand it.

The word "reconciliation" really means "to make friends again," as "re" means "again," and "to conciliate" means "to make peace between" or "make friends." This was done by bringing both Jew and Gentile into one body, the church, through the Cross.

Is it necessary to be restored to God's friendship? Is it necessary to be reconciled to God (cf. 2 Cor. 5:17-21; Rom. 5:8-11)? Is it necessary to know where reconciliation takes place? IF SO, then CHURCH MEMBERSHIP IS ESSENTIAL.

4. **The Church Is The House Of God** (family). "But if I tarry long, that thou mayest know how men ought to behave themselves in the house of God, which is the church of the living God, the pillar and ground of the truth" (1 Tim. 3:15).

The word "house" means "family." This can easily be seen from the following verses: Hebrews 11:7; Acts 16:31-34; Hebrews 3:6; Ephesians 2:19; 3:15; Acts 10:2; etc. God is the Father (cf. Eph. 3:14; 4:6; Matt. 23:9) and all the saved are his children. Christ is a son over the House of God (Heb. 3:6), and Christians are his brethren (Heb. 2:12; Matt. 25:40; 1 Thess. 1:1; Rom. 8:16f; Gal. 3:26-27; 4:7). Does God have any children outside his own family? Note the following, as it does us good to set it forth by way of a syllogism.

Major Premise: All God's children are in God's Family.
Minor Premise: God's family is the Church.
Conclusion: All God's children are in the Church.

Is it necessary to be in God's family? Is it necessary to be a child of God? IF IT IS, CHURCH MEMBERSHIP IS ESSENTIAL.

5. **The Church Is The Kingdom Of Christ.** It was, as we have already noticed, in Matthew 16:18-19 where Jesus promised to "build my church." We have also seen that the word church means "the called out," indeed, "called out of the world of darkness" and "translated into the kingdom of the Son of his love" (Col. 1:13). No

wonder it was said by Jesus, after promising to build the church, that he said to Peter, "I will give unto thee the keys of the kingdom" (cf. Matt. 16:19). He called us "unto his own kingdom" (1 Thess. 2:12).

The book of Revelation was written to the seven churches of Asia (cf. Rev. 1:4; 2:1,8,12,18; 3:1,7,14). In this book, we very often read of the kingdom (cf. 1:6,9). Also, it is stated in this book that "the kingdom" was purchased by the blood of Christ (Rev. 5:9-10; cf. 1:5). The amazing thing is that the same blood, the blood of Christ, purchased the church (Acts 20:28). Now if Christ built the church and called it his kingdom, and did so when he died and shed his blood, and that blood purchased both the church and the kingdom, then the church is the kingdom and the kingdom is the church (and I am certainly not saying that this is the only way the word "kingdom" is used in the New Testament).

Is it necessary to have Christ as your King? Is it necessary to be in the Kingdom? Is it necessary to observe the supper that is in the Kingdom (cf. Luke 22:29-30)? Is it necessary to render service in the Kingdom? IF SO, CHURCH MEMBERSHIP IS ESSENTIAL.

6. **The Church Was Purchased With The Blood Of Christ.** No clearer statement could be made than that by Paul to the elders, bishops, at Ephesus: "Take heed unto yourselves, and to all the flock, in which the Holy Spirit hath made you bishops, to feed the church of the Lord which he purchased with his own blood" (Acts 20:28). If you know who the Lord is, then you know it would be all right to say "to feed the church of Christ which he purchased with his own blood." It was in the book of Ephesians where Paul stated: "Husbands, love your wives, even as Christ also loved the church, and gave himself up for it; that he might sanctify it, having cleansed it by the

washing of water with the word" (5:25-26).

We are "redeemed" by the blood of Christ, the lamb of God (1 Pet. 1:18-19); his was the blood of the New Covenant (cf. Matt. 26:28). It is said by the Hebrew writer, "And according to the law, I may almost say, all things are cleansed with blood, and apart from shedding of blood there is no remission" (9:12). Indeed, his blood "cleanses us" (1 John 1:7).

Can a man be saved without the cleansing power of Christ's blood? When Christ lived, every drop of blood was in his body. When He died every drop went for the church, His body. There is no blood outside his body, when he lived or when he died. If a man can be saved apart from the shedding, coming into contact with that blood, of the blood of Jesus, then it will not be any harm to count it unholy (cf. Heb. 10:29). But that is not the case. He did not die in vain. He did not die for nought. IF CHURCH MEMBERSHIP IS NOT ESSENTIAL, HE DIED IN VAIN AND HIS BLOOD WAS UNNECESSARY.

7. **The Church, Their Names Are Written In Heaven.** In Hebrews 12:23 we read: "to the general assembly and church of the firstborn who are enrolled in heaven, and to God the Judge of all,..." (be it known that the word "firstborn" in this passage is plural, being in Greek *prototokon*). In Philippians 4:3, Paul spoke about his fellow-workers "whose names are in the book of life" (cf. Luke 10:20). Indeed, there are names "written in heaven."

Is it necessary to have your name written in heaven? Note: "And if any was not found written in the book of life, he was cast into the lake of fire" (Rev. 20:15). Again, "And there shall in no wise enter into it anything unclean, or he that maketh an abomination and a lie: but only they that are written in the Lamb's book of life" (Rev. 21:27). Yes, indeed, you must admit it is. When you do, you are admitting something about church membership. The fact that you are embracing is: CHURCH MEMBPERSHIP, MEMBERSHIP IN THE LORD'S BODY, IS ESSENTIAL.

I could write on, but perhaps enough has been said. You see the Church is called "the bride of Christ," therefore, is it necessary, a must, to be married to Christ (cf. Rom. 7:4)? The Church is the temple of God, God's temple, and is it necessary to dwell in God's temple? If so, then church membership is essential. It is also a fact that the Church is the Vineyard of Christ. Is it necessary to be a branch in the vine (cf. John 15:1-8)? If so, then church membership is essential.

To say that CHURCH MEMBERSHIP IS NOT ESSENTIAL TO ONE'S SALVATION, is to say that one can go to Heaven without:

a. Being called by the gospel.

b. Being saved.

c. Being reconciled.

d. Being a child of God.

e. Being a citizen in the kingdom.

f. Being purchased by the blood of Christ.

g. Being enrolled in heaven.

h. Being married to Christ.

i. Being in a spiritual house.

j. Being a branch in the vine.

Do not let anyone speak evil of the beautiful bride of Christ. I trust, in the matter of MEMBERSHIP IN THE

CHURCH, you will make your "calling and election sure" (cf. 2 Pet. 1:10).

IS THERE MORE THAN ONE WAY TO ENTER THE CHURCH?

Several years ago, when I was much younger, I recall conducting a gospel meeting with the Smith Grove church (September, 1965) just out of Woodbury, Tennessee. During the course of that meeting, I had drawn a chart on the blackboard, using a circle, some arrows, etc., and had the word "Christ" and the word "Church," preceded by the word "in," inside that circle. On the line with the arrows that pierced the circle, going into it, I had written the word "into." Under that word, I had listed two scriptures, Romans 6:3-4 and Galatians 3:27. These verses read as follows:

> *"Or are ye ignorant that all we who were* ***baptized into Christ Jesus*** *were* ***baptized into his death****? We were buried therefore with him through* ***baptism into death****: that like as Christ was raised from the dead through the glory of the Father, so we also might walk in newness of life" (Rom. 6:3-4, emp. GM).*

> *"For as many of you as were* ***baptized into Christ*** *did put on Christ" (Gal. 3:27, emp. GM).*

I mentioned that these were the only two verses that I knew of that stated "...into Christ." I did not know at the time (of course, it would have made no difference) that there was a Baptist preacher, and a man many years my senior, in the meeting. Later, after we had dismissed, the man, laughingly said: "Why you've just got two verses...." The next night I redrew the circle, etc., and then, on the other side, drew an arrow piercing the circle, etc., and under the line drew just one line. The Baptist preacher was again present. I made a statement about what the man had said after the last worship (last evening). I challenged him to list, not two, but just one verse that used the word "into" to show me anywhere in the New Testament where a person came "into Christ" any other way than the ones I had listed. In fact, I said, "I'll just leave this little diagram on the board and he can just write it on the line I have prepared for it." The diagram stayed on the board all that week, and the night the meeting closed, I remarked about there being no verse of scripture on that line. Then, laughingly I said, "Only two verses... that is exactly two more than you have." The point made **the point** about the only way there is to "get into" Christ.

Some eleven years ago, I met another man, one more schooled, and in the course of our debate, he wanted to prove that one could get "into" Christ by faith. Among other things, he commenced using the verses, like John 1:12; John 3:16; etc., and wanted to prove, since the Greek word here is *eis*, and not *en*, and, therefore, it should be translated "into." However, what this Dr. failed to know was that the grammar will not allow it to be so translated. Sure it is the word *eis*, but did all of the translators of the *King James* and the *American Standard* not know that? If they knew that, then what caused them to translate *eis* as "in" and not "into"? It is the rule of grammar that is stated: "The verb *pisteuo* followed by *eis* with the accusative is to be translated by 'I believe in or on.' Thus *pisteuo eis ton kurion* means 'I believe in the Lord or I believe on the Lord.'" (J. Gresham Machen, *New Testament Greek For Beginners*, p. 84, # 184). This "believe in" or "believe on" the Lord is often found in the New Testament, such as in John 2:23; 3:16, 18; 5:24; 6:40 (cf. vs. 47); 8:30; etc., but it is "in" and not "into." Not a single soul on earth can show where any man ever came into Christ by faith without any further act of obedience!

Whether it is "into" Christ, or "into" the body, the thought is the same. "For as the body is one, and hath many members, and all the members of the body, being many, are one body; so also is Christ. For in one Spirit were we all *baptized into one body*, whether Jews or Greeks, whether bond or free; and were all made to drink of one Spirit" (1 Cor. 12:12-13, emp. GM). We need to observe that there is a difference between "in" and "into." I have, for many years, used the examples of these two words in relation to "coming into or in *being in* a room," "getting into or *being in* one's clothes," "coming into or *being in* a building," etc. One I used on this Dr. was about his car. I said, "Dr. ...I saw you drive up *in* your car. Will you also go home *in* your car?" He replied that he would. I then asked him a very simple question: "Can you go home 'in' your car without first of all getting 'into' your car?" This made him change his mind about his statement that there was "no difference" between "into" and "in." If it isn't clear, let me state it emphatically. **There Is Only One Way To Get Into Christ And Into The New Testament Church**, ACCORDING TO THE PATTERN. Man's word does not matter, and it sure will not "hold water" (a good country expression) in the day of judgment.

There is yet perhaps to be given the most powerful, explicit, unambiguous and unequivocal, unconditional and unmistakable statement, and it is one from the lips of the Master to a man by the name of Nicodemus. It is as follows:

> *"Now there was a man of the Pharisees, named Nicodemus, a ruler of the Jews: the same came unto him by night, and said to him, Rabbi, we know that thou art a teacher come from God; for no one can do these signs that thou doest, except God be with him. Jesus*

> *answered and said unto him, Verily, verily, I say unto thee, Except one be born anew, he cannot see the kingdom of God. Nicodemus saith unto him, How can a man be born when he is old? can he enter a second time into his mother's womb, and be born? Jesus answered, Verily, verily, I say unto thee,* ***Except one be born of water and the Spirit, he cannot enter into the kingdom of God*** *" (John 3:1-5, emp. GM).*

To Nicodemus, Jesus said in verse three, "Except one be born anew (footnote, "from above"), he cannot see the kingdom of God." Nicodemus, it is evident, did not understand about "this birth," but he knew that Jesus had mentioned "a birth." This is made clear as a crystal by his statement, as he said, "How can a man be born...old... second time into his mother's womb, and be born?" I know this is the case, as then in verse five, Jesus clarified what was so puzzling to Nicodemus. It is in verse five where Jesus told Nicodemus explicitly "how to" get "into" the kingdom of God. Jesus said, "Except one be born of water and of the Spirit, he cannot enter into the kingdom of God." From this conversation, we can learn various things. *Note:*

a. The subject was not physical birth (if so, one would have a hard time with a "dry" birth, it being *anudros* "without water").

b. The subject of being "born again" related to an entrance into another realm.

c. The subject of being "born again" had two ingredients, water and of the Spirit.

d. The subject of being "born again of water and the Spirit" was directly related to the kingdom of God.

e. The subject of being in the kingdom of God was described by "being born from above" (Greek, *gennethe anothen*), as well as by "being born of water and the Spirit (Greek, *gennethe hudatos penumatos*) before one could "enter into" (Greek, *eiselthein eis*) it.

f. The subject of this birth would allow one to draw the conclusion that this was an important subject.

g. The subject of this birth would also allow a person to draw the conclusion that how to "get into" the kingdom was an essential without which no man could get "into" the kingdom.

h. The subject of this birth, being preceded by the word EXCEPT, informs us that *this is the only way possible* to gain entrance "into" the kingdom of God (Greek, *ean me*, is "except," and this is a negative conjunction and means "unless," "if not," "except," or "without," Thayer, p. 162; Arndt and Gingrich, p. 210).

i. The subject of this birth is given twice, verses three and five, but both mean the same as the kingdom of God is mentioned in both verses, therefore, "to see" is the same as "to enter," and "born anew" is the same as "born of water and of the Spirit."

j. The subject is explained again in verse six, with the thought of "being born again" intensified by "Ye *must* (Greek, *dei*, means, for us, "no alternative, no option, no choice, etc.") be born anew" (vs. 7).

k. The subject of Christ to Nicodemus undoubtedly

must be that of how does one enter the kingdom of God.

1. The subject, if it relates to one's salvation, and it does, has two important components, being in the kingdom of God, and how one gets into the kingdom of God. Both factors are of great significance.

There are now a few items that must be recognized from our study thus far about the most important subject relative to the entrance into the New Testament Church. We find that one is baptized "into" Christ, baptized "into" his death, baptized "into" one body, "born anew" and "born again of water and of the Spirit" and thus "enters into" the kingdom of God, and that there are no exceptions to this pattern as given by Jesus. It is an essential, as the same Master said, "Ye must be born anew." This is the one and the only one way to get "into" Christ, "into" the one body, and "into" the kingdom. Earlier in our study we found out that the "kingdom" and the "church" were the same institution, just different designations. Therefore, if one must be "born anew," "born of the water and the Spirit" and baptized into Christ to get into the body, which is the church, and the church is the kingdom, then *there is one and only one way to get into the New Testament Church. If this is not the case, then* we can draw this conclusion, THE WORD "EXCEPT" DOES NOT MEAN "EXCEPT."

IS THERE ONLY ONE NEW TESTAMENT CHURCH?

Anyone who is deadly serious in the asking of the above question needs to try and grasp various Biblical examples and thoughts. Once again we bring into focus some Old Testament items for our consideration, and then we will progress to the New Testament for a more complete or fuller answer.

1. God gave Noah only one pattern for the ark, as revealed in Genesis 6:14-22.

2. God gave Moses only one pattern for the tabernacle, as revealed in Exodus 25:9,40; 40:16; Hebrews 8:5 (cf. Acts 7:44).

3. God gave David, who delivered it to his son Solomon, only one pattern for the temple, as revealed in 1 Chronicles 28:11-12, 18-19.

4. God gave Joshua only one pattern for the destruction of the walls of Jericho, as revealed in Joshua 6:1-21; Hebrews 11:30.

5. God gave only one pattern to Naaman, by his prophet Elisha, for the cleansing of his leprosy, as revealed in 2 Kings 5:1-14.

6. God gave only one Son (the only begotten Son, cf. John 1:14,18; 3:16,18; 1 John 4:9) to shed his blood on the Cross and seal only one New Testament as the only pattern for man today (Matt. 26:28; Heb. 9:15-17,26).

7. In the New Testament, the pattern of sound words (cf. 2 Tim. 1:13; 1 Tim. 6:3), we have:

a. Christ promising to build one church (Matt. 16:13-19).

b. Christ stating that his blood was that of the New Testament, as seen in Matthew 26:26-28.

c. Peter quoting Moses as the prophet, Christ Jesus, that people in the New Testament were to obey or be destroyed (Acts 3:22).

d. Paul speaking about the gospel as the power of God to save mankind (Rom. 1:16; 2:16; 1 Cor.

1:18, 21).

e. Paul saying that the revelation of the mystery hid in God so long has been revealed (Rom. 16:25).

f. Paul stating that all nations is given the commandment unto obedience of faith (Rom. 16:26; footnote saying "the faith").

g. Paul declaring the gospel contained the death, burial, and the resurrection of Christ (1 Cor. 15:1-4) and that the authority is from the Lord (2 Cor. 13:10).

h. Paul made it known that we are Abraham's seed, heirs of the promise, only if we are Christ's (Gal. 3:29).

i. Paul revealed that God had purposed the church in his eternal purpose (Eph. 3:10-11).

j. Paul publicly stated that he was made a minister to fulfill the word of God (Col. 1:25; 1 Tim. 1:11; 2 Tim. 1:8; Titus 1:1-3).

Step by step the Bible, from the Old Testament, into and through the New Testament, the plan, the guideline, the pattern, and blueprint of God unfolded as it progressed. Finally, the virgin gives birth to the Christ child, he grows, matures, is immersed to fulfill all righteousness, has a three to three and a half years public ministry, promises to build His church, and lays down the principles by which it is to be governed. He chose twelve men and sent them out to preach the message. Later, Paul, by the divine authority of heaven (cf. 1 Cor. 14:37; 4:17) proclaimed the gospel, God's power to save. It is in the gospel, the norm, the standard, the pattern of sound words, the rule, that we find the answer to our question.

Thus we find, in the New Testament, the pattern, many things divinely stated (these men were inspired of God and so they spoke, cf. 2 Pet. 1:19-21; 1 Cor. 2:9-13; 2 Tim. 3:16-17).

a. The Church (termed by Christ "My" church) was to be built by Christ (Matt. 16:18).

b. Paul said, as well as did others, it was purchased by the blood of Christ (Acts 20:28; Eph. 5:25-27).

c. Paul also stated, as well as did others, that Christ was the foundation of the church (1 Cor. 3:10-11; Rom. 9:30-33; Isa. 28:16; Acts 4:11; Psm. 118:22; 1 Pet. 2:4-8).

d. The Church, also called the kingdom, was to come while some who heard Christ speak were still living, was to come with power and was to come with the coming of the Holy Spirit and all of this came about on Pentecost when the New Testament Church came into existence (Mark 9:1; Acts 1:8; 2:1ff).

e. People were added to the church (Acts 2:47; 5:14; 11:24) as it was in existence and local churches were being established in various cities (Acts 14:23; Titus 1:5; Rev. 1:4).

f. Inspiration, through these men, especially in the writings of Paul, spoke of "the body," "the church," "the body which is the church," "the church which is his body," "one body," "baptized into one body," "many members but one body," "one body in Christ" (Eph. 1:22-23; Col. 1:18, 24; Eph. 4:4; 1 Cor. 12:13, 27; Rom. 12:3-5; esp. vs. 5).

g. In the pages of the New Testament, the pattern, we find that the church was termed:

(1) The Church of God (1 Cor. 1:2).

(2) The Body of Christ (Col. 1:18, 24; Eph. 4:12; 5:23).

(3) The Churches of Christ (Rom. 16:16).

(4) The Kingdom of God (Acts 1:3; 8:12; 19:8).

(5) The Kingdom of Heaven (Matt. 16:19).

(6) The Kingdom of the Son of His Love (Col. 1:13).

(7) The Church (Rev. 2:1, 8, 12, 18; 3:1, 7, 14).

(*) **Note**: Never do we read about Christ promising to build His churches. Nor do you read about Christ building some denominations, sects, social clubs, recreational centers, etc. You only read about one New Testament Church, that which was purposed in the mind of God, promised by God, prophesied by the prophets, prepared for by John and others and then brought into perfection.

h. The New Testament, the pattern for man today, speaks about the SINGULARITY of THE CHURCH.

(1) Being called "The Bride Of Christ," one just has to ask about how many brides did Christ have? (Rom. 7:4; Rev. 21:9).

(2) The church is called God's habitation, God's temple, and how many did God have? (Eph. 2:19-22; 1 Cor. 3:16-17).

(3) The New Testament has Christ saying, "I am the way, the truth and the life" (John 14:6). How many ways?

(4) The New Testament has Christ as the saviour of the body, which is the church, therefore, as Christ is the way, the saviour and of the church, the New Testament Church is the way to heaven! (Eph. 5:23; John 14:6; 6:44-45; Acts 2:47).

(5) The New Testament Church is called the Family of God, so the question is, "How many families does God have?" Does God have any children outside His family? Is there a familial inheritance anywhere else except in God's family? (Eph. 3:15; 1 Tim. 3:14-15; 1:3-4, "house" is "family").

(6) Ephesians 5:23 reads as follows:

(a) "For *the* husband
(b) Is *the* head
(c) Of *the* wife,
(d) As Christ also is *the* head
(e) Of *the* church,
(f) Being himself *the* saviour
(g) Of *the* body."
(*) If these seven "the's" do not convince you of one and only one, then one of the two of us needs to go back to school to find out what a definite article is! Just as a husband has one wife, is the head of only one wife, so Christ is the head of only one body, the church. Yes, just one!

(7) Furthermore, in the reading of Ephesians 5:22-23, I find the following "definites":

(a) The Lord.
(b) The Church.
(c) The wives (of their husbands).

(d) The church...gave himself up for "it."

(e) That he might sanctify "it."

(f) Having cleansed "it."

(g) The Word.

(h) The Church.

(i) That "it" should be holy and without blemish.

(j) The Church.

(k) We are members of his body.

(l) The two shall become one flesh.

(m) Christ and the church.

(n) The wife is to reverence her husband.

While growing up, I led singing for brother Joe W. Laird in many gospel meetings (such as Taylor, Oklahoma). He was a very dear friend of the family, and there are many, many things I could say about Joe Laird. He and Hoyt Huffines published a book entitled: *Oft-Asked Questions* (which I have had since it was published in 1960). It was the beginning of a "seed thought" for a marvelous sermon. The sermon that I preached was given the title: "Is The Church 'The Only One'?" It speaks about various religious groups (I did not say "churches" as there is but "one" and it is the only one that is "the called out"), and the fact that most of them have at least one or more "bits and pieces" of the truth of God's pattern. But I often have made this challenge, it is only in the New Testament Church, the Church of Christ, that a person can believe and practice all of these things at the same time. I know of no other group where you can believe in the plenary verbal inspiration of the Scriptures, understand the complete difference in the Old and New Testaments (law, rules and regulations), worship in song without mechanical instruments of music, commune upon the first day of every week, practice baptism in the name of the Father, and the Son and the Holy Spirit, an immersion into Christ for the remission of sins, be organized by the scriptural government as the New Testament has outlined, have the scriptural name for both the church and the members, having Christ as the only head (no earthly hierarchy or headquarters except in heaven), teaching the relation of the church to the world, being benevolent and evangelistic, etc., etc. As I said before, some may practice one, two or more, but only in The Church of The New Testament, The Church of Christ, can you believe and practice all of the pattern at the same time!

Indeed, there is only one New Testament Church, as this is all that Christ promised to build, and neither Christ nor God lies. The pattern does not give different signals (cf. 1 Cor. 14:8), that is, the idea that "different bits and pieces from various, all, denominations and sects, make up the pattern" is completely foreign to the New Testament. Only the New Testament Church was eternally purposed in the mind of God, lovingly purchased by the blood of Christ and beautifully perfected by the Holy Spirit of God.

DO I HAVE TO BE RIGHT ABOUT THE NEW TESTAMENT CHURCH?

One of the most explicit, clear and distinct statements that ever fell from the lips of the Master may be the following recorded for us by John: "Jesus therefore said to those Jews that had believed him, If ye abide in my word, then are ye truly my disciples; and ye shall know the truth, and the truth shall make you free" (8:31-32). Since I know that Jesus said this, then I know (Greek, *ginosko*, "I know") it is possible for me to know the truth. If a man can come to a knowledge of the truth, is he under obligation to do so, or does the truth really matter? We are not talking about a man being benevolent, dedicated to what he personally believes, earnest in his endeavors, or fervent in his life's actions, we are talking about the truth, and does a man have the responsibility before God "to know the truth"? I ask this, as Jesus said it was "the truth" that makes a man free. I also bring to our remembrance that Jesus said, "I am the truth." He stated, "If any man willeth to do his will, he shall know of the teaching, whether it is of God, or whether I speak from myself" (John 7:17). If a man does not have to know the truth, then what differences does it make anyway? That is, why have the Bible, the New Testament, the pattern and why should we not just "do whatever we are big enough to do"? Just let the "law of the land" be the norm, the standard and the rule for all of my conduct, after all, what difference, if any, does it make? If this is the case, I can shave off any part of the truth, some of the truth or all of the truth.

In our world today, there are agnostics (Greek, *aginosko*, "I do not know") who claim that we cannot know that the Bible is truly the inspired word of God. But I think, as far as I am personally concerned, I am hurt much more by those "in the church," our brothers and our sisters, who are governed by existentialism, humanism, situation ethics, etc., and other false philosophies. We are, today, living in a "ME-DEEP" society where the major concern is self, what pleases me, the "I-owe-it-to-myself" feeling, or the "I deserve to be happy syndrome," etc., etc. Why do you think today that our own members question the indispensability of the church, Bible authority or even as some do now, water baptism, in the name of the Father, and the Son and of the Holy Spirit for the remission of sins? We need once again to comprehend what the Bible teaches by such declarations as found in John 8:31-32; 14:6; 6:44-45; Hebrews 5:8-9; 1 Peter 1:22-25; 1 Timothy 4:6-16; 2 Timothy 4:1-5; 3:16-17; 2 Peter 1:19-21; 1:3; etc. If you read these verses, then you will "know" that a man is not just to seek the truth, but he is to "hear" and to "learn" the truth. Can a man not, by valid reasoning, that is, reasoning from the evidence that God has given to man, know certain things? Is not there any internal evidence in the Bible, the self-authenticating kind of evidence, that would let me know that I know certain things? **EITHER:**

1. There is a God or there is not a God, but both cannot be true.

2. The Bible is the word of God or the Bible is not the word of God, but both cannot be true.

3. Jesus the Christ is the Son of God or He is not the Son of God, but both cannot be true.

4. The Church is the New Testament Church or it is not the New Testament Church, but both cannot be true.

5. A man can know the truth or a man cannot know the truth, but both statements cannot be true.

6. A man must know the truth or a man must not know the truth, but both cannot be true.

7. Jesus told the truth in John 8:32 or He did not tell us the truth in John 8:32, both cannot be true.

8. God lies or God does not lie, but both cannot be true.

If it does not matter about the truth and about whether or not a man can know the truth, must know the truth, etc., then none of the things above really matters. That is, it does not matter if there is a God or not, if the Bible is God's word or not, if the Church is the New Testament Church or not and it does not matter if a person is even in the Church or not. But you and I both know that IT DOES MATTER! We have the Word of Jesus Himself on this subject: "Ye shall know the truth, and the truth shall make you free" (John 8:32). If I, as Jesus said, "Shall know (again, I want to emphasize that this is the Greek *ginosko,* "I know") the truth," must I know it to be made free? Is there anything else that can make a man free? Does a man have to be free? What does it mean to be free? Will error make a man free? If error will do what the truth will do, why be concerned about the truth? If error will not make a man free, and a man must be free, then does a man have to be right about the truth? If a man does not have to be free, then it does not matter about that, the truth, which makes a man free! If a man is not to draw any conclusions, conclusions that are authorized, justified and guaranteed by the evidence, then why is a man commanded to study and why were people commended for searching the scriptures (2 Tim. 2:15; Acts 17:10-11)? Why is a man told to be "ready to give an answer" (1 Pet. 3:15), if the answer does not matter? In fact, why did the Holy Spirit through Peter tell us to be ready to give an answer when a person cannot even know the truth? If, on the other hand, we are told "...that ye may know how ye ought to answer each one" (Col. 4:6), then is there not placed on us a God-given responsibility to "know how to answer each one"? I challenge everyone to study the words "believe" and "know" in such verses as John 4:41-42; 8:55.

I know that there is among us today both agnosticism and subjectivism. All one has to do to prove this is just use his eyes and ears! But that is not all that is among us, as today we face both *logophobia* (Lionel Ruby, *Logic: An Introduction*, p. viii) and *misology. Logophobia* is the fear of logic, the fear of using the principles of sound reasoning, actually, a distrust of reason. *Misology* is really the rejection of logic, or perhaps the hatred of logic. For some reason, people like "sound reasoning" in almost every field but that of religion. Yet, the Bible specifically charges us to "prove all things; hold fast that which is good" (1 Thess. 5:21, it would be well to study the Greek *dokimadzo*, "prove" in this and other places where it is used). If this is the case, and it is, then there are some things about which a man MUST be right. How I remember a Ph.D. taking hold of my arm and saying to me, "Goebel, you can't know anything." Then he said, "You don't know anything," and I thought he was just joking. In fact, I said, "Please do not tell my brethren this, as they think I know something." However, I very quickly learned he was serious, therefore, I said, "Do you know that?" Those four words blew his mind. You see, if he "knew" that I did not know, then why couldn't I "know" that I know? What he really did was to affirm and deny the same thing, which is, of course, self-contradictory. How could he claim "to know" that "I did not know," when "no one" can "know" anything? But, God says for us to "prove" all things, therefore, I am certain that there are some things about which we must be right. *Note the following:*

1. Must one be right about God (cf. Psm. 14:1; 53:1)?

2. Must one be right about faith in God (Heb. 11:6)?

3. Must one be right about the gospel (Rom. 1:16; 1 Cor. 1:18-21)?

4. Must one be right about obeying the gospel (2 Thess. 1:7-9)?

5. Must one be right about repentance (Luke 13:3, 5; Acts 17:20)?

6. Must one be right about baptism (Acts 2:38; Matt. 28:19; Rom. 6:3-4; Col. 2:12)?

7. Must one be right about worshipping God (John 4:24)?

*. Then if the answer to these seven questions is "YES," what is the answer to: "Must One Be Right About The New Testament Church?" (Matt. 16:18; Eph. 5:23; 4:4; 1:22-23; Col. 1:18, 24). Of course, we should not just stop with the seven questions I asked, as there is the concern of Christian living, sound doctrine, the judgment, heaven, hell, and eternity (James 1:27; 4:4; Titus 2:11-14; 2 John 9-11; 2 Cor. 5:10; Rom. 14:12; Heb. 9:27; Matt. 25:46; John 14:1f; Rev. 20:10-15; 21:8).

On one occasion, brother Marshall Keeble was speaking about error and "the plants which God did not plant" (cf. Matt. 15:13-14). He made reference to those who thought that such did not really matter, not if we were sincere and really believed what we were doing was right. Then he said, in relation to the plants that God did not plant and that are going to be "uprooted," "If you do not believe it, then just stay around til 'rooting time'." And I say to those asking this question, "Do I have to be right about the New Testament Church?" If you do not think so, "just stay around until 'rooting time'!"

Chapter Twelve

THE PATTERN - AND THE PREACHING THAT PLEASES GOD

THE PATTERN - AND THE PREACHING THAT PLEASES GOD

If you believe that God is your creator, and the Bible says that he is (Gen. 1:26-27), if you believe that in him we live and move and have our being, and the Bible says we do (Acts 17:22-31), then you must believe that God has created you and is sustaining you (cf. Psm. 3:5) for a specific purpose. Is not this purpose to be pleasing unto God (cf. Prov. 16:7, a general rule is herein stated)? Some people purpose to please themselves, but this is not a worthy or a New Testament purpose (cf. Rom. 15:1-4). Some purpose to please others, and this is a strong incentive for there are those on every hand crying to be pleased, but this, too, the New Testament says is not a worthy purpose (cf. Gal. 1:6-10; esp. vs. 10; 1 Thess. 2:3-6). Few there are, evidently, who realize that man was placed on earth for one purpose, and one purpose only, that of pleasing God (cf. Prov. 16:7). Pleasing God is imperative (cf. John 8:29)! If I had the time and space, a galaxy of verses could be listed on this thought. I am speaking about verses with the word "please," "delight," "pleasure," "well pleased," "displeased," etc. (cf. Gal. 1:10; 1 John 3:22; Hag. 1:8; Heb. 13:16; 3:17; 10:38; 11:6; etc.).

Preaching is indispensable in the salvation of mankind. It was Paul who penned, "For seeing that in the wisdom of God the world through its wisdom knew not God, it was God's good pleasure (note the word "pleasure") through the foolishness of the preaching to save them that believe" (1 Cor. 1:21). Indeed, when we preach, we please God, but only if we preach it exactly as it is (1 Cor. 1:18-25; 2 Tim. 4:1-5). It is hard to preach the truth if you are trying to be a man-pleaser, to become prominent, to take the lead in some movement, to become recognized, etc. However, if we are trying to please God, then one of the easiest things to do is to preach the truth. I say this, and have no fear of the statement, regardless if the subject is unity, worship, the church of the New Testament, the plan of salvation, marriage, divorce and remarriage, eternity, etc.

Preaching that pleases God is obligatory. After that marvelous and magnificent statement of 1 Corinthians 1:18-25, Paul continued through verse five of chapter two about who is to get the glory, and just where "the power of God lies." He then proceeded to let all men know that God's word is verbally inspired (1 Cor. 2:6-13; cf. 2 Pet. 1:19-21; 2 Tim. 3:16-17). The men of the New Testament knew it was of God and that they were compelled to preach it (cf. Acts 4:18-20; 5:29; Rom. 1:13-16). We today can do no less!

PREACHING HAS ALWAYS BEEN GOD'S METHOD TO MAKE KNOWN HIS MESSAGE

Through all ages God has chosen to make known his message of salvation through the process of preaching (1 Cor. 1:18-21; esp. vs. 21). Noah was a preacher (2 Pet. 2:5), and it is so stated, but so was Abraham, Moses, and the prophets. In the New Testament we read that John the Baptist preached (Matt. 3:1ff), Jesus also preached (Matt. 4:17), and when he sent out the twelve (Matt. 10:7) and also the seventy (Luke 10:1ff), he sent them out to preach.

Paul told Titus that "God hath in due time manifested his word through preaching" (Titus 1:3, *K.J.*, *ASV* has "message" with a footnote "proclamation"). It matters not what century it is, be it the 20th or the 1st, God's good pleasure is to save the world by the process of preaching. In fact, this was the worldwide and revolutionary statement made by Jesus in what we term "the great commission" (cf. Mark 16:15-16; Matt. 28:18-20; Luke 24:46-47). In the program of preaching, that is, the extent of it, we read in the New Testament of preaching to "every creature," "to all creation," "to every nation," and "unto the uttermost part of the earth" (cf. Acts 2:14ff; 1:8 to the verses listed above). Yes, preaching has always been, is now, and will always be His method to save the lost, the world. That is one reason that this subject is so very crucial and critical for us today.

PREACHING THAT PLEASES GOD HAS ONLY ONE SOURCE BOOK

To be able to please God, preachers must understand that there is no other source book, instruction manual, blueprint, guide, rule or canon, than the New Testament from which we can learn the (only) type of preaching it is that pleases God. To learn this, one must come to grips with various words, their meanings and know how they fit together. We must remember that verbal inspiration is "word by word" inspiration, that is, it is "the words" that are inspired. God put "the words" in the mouth, not just the "hunch" in the head, or the "thought" in the heart (cf. Exod. 4:12, 15; Isa. 1:10; Jer. 1:9; Ezek. 2:7; 3:4, 10; 2 Sam. 23:2; Matt. 10:19-20; Luke 12:11-12; 21:14-15; 1 Cor. 2:9-13; etc.).

There are several words which are translated "preach," and I list only a few in reference to the many that could be given. Note carefully how the following words are used in connection with preaching.

> ***Kerusso.*** *This word appears about sixty times and is translated as "to be a herald, to proclaim*

as a herald, to proclaim, to declare, to publish, to preach" (Luke 12:3; Mark 1:45; Matt. 3:1; 4:17). This word suggests formality and an authority that must be heeded. The word itself says nothing about the message, but from it we learn the preacher is to publicly proclaim, and with authority, the New Testament message (cf. Titus 2:15).

Kerugma. *This word has about eight occurrences as "preaching" and it refers to "a proclamation by a herald" and is related to our first word. However, this word refers to "the substance" of the preaching, and does not necessarily refer to "the act of preaching" (**kerusso** is a verb and **kerugma** is a noun). One of the great verses here is 1 Corinthians 1:11. It is also used in 1 Corinthians 2:4; 15:14; 2 Timothy 4:17; Titus 1:3.*

Euangelizo. *Once again, in contrast to **kerusso**, we find a word referring to the message, the good news message, and is translated in a number of ways, but with little actual difference. It is "to preach the gospel" (Rom. 1:15; Luke 4:18; 1 Cor. 1:17; etc.), "declare or bring glad tidings" (Acts 13:32), "bring good tidings of" (Luke 2:10), etc. This word is employed over fifty times.*

Dialegomai. *The very basic meaning of this word is to "set forth argumentation," "to argue," "to debate," "to contend," "to discourse," to be a "contender for the faith." It is "reason with" (Acts 17:2; 18:19), "dispute" (Acts 17:17; 19:8-9; 14:12; Jude 9), etc. In about ten of its thirteen occurrences it has the* *meaning of "dispute, reasoning with."*

Apologia. *This word is used of giving an "answer" (Acts 25:16; 1 Cor. 9:3; 2 Tim. 4:16; 1 Pet. 3:15), "the clearing of one's self" (2 Cor. 7:11) and "defense" (Acts 22:1; Phil. 1:7, 16). It occurs about eight times in the New Testament and teaches us that it is right for the preacher to defend the gospel. The very root idea is to set forth evidence which defends one's position, an answer to the charges, a defense of one's case.*

Suzeteo. *This word, especially in the* ***King James****, is given as "dispute" (Acts 6:9; 9:29), "reason together" (Mark 12:28), "reason" (Luke 24:15) and "question with" (Mark 8:11; 9:14). In four out of ten occurrences, it has the meaning of "disputation." This word instructs, yea, informs us that it is right and proper to discuss, dispute, and debate about the sacred gospel of the New Testament.*

Elencho. *We have this word given as "reprove" (Eph. 5:11, 13; 2 Tim. 4:2), "rebuke" (1 Tim. 5:20; Tit. 1:13; Rev. 3:19), "convict" (John 8:9), "tell one's fault" (Matt. 18:15), "convince" (Tit. 1:9), etc. In fact, in twelve of seventeen times it has the very meaning of "reproof" (akin to it is* ***elenchos****, which is the evidence, Heb. 11:1) as in 2 Timothy 3:16. Herein we find the preacher is to expose, bring to light, to rebuke, admonish, call to account, refute the teachers of false doctrines and demand an explanation. This is a gospel preacher's obligation.*

Parrhesiazomai. *This is the word that puts the "starch in the wardrobe" of the gospel preacher! It, indeed, gives the forcefulness with which the preacher is to make known the message of good news. It is given as "speak boldly" (Acts 14:3; 18:26; 19:8; Eph. 6:20), "to preach boldly" (Acts 9:27), etc., and in the nine occurrences so used it deals with "preaching with boldness." It instructs the preacher of the gospel to preach boldly, plainly, and most confidently.*

Epitimao. *In twenty-four of the twenty-nine times this word is employed, it is translated as "rebuke" (**K.J.**, cf. 2 Tim. 4:2), but it is also given as "charge" (Matt. 12:16), and "straightly charge" (Luke 9:21). It is certainly within the bounds, when needed, for the preacher to reprove, rebuke, censure and to tax with fault. It is interesting to note that outside of 1 Timothy 4:2 and Jude 9, it is used only in the four accounts of the gospel. It is most frequently used of the Lord's rebukes.*

Parakaleo. *The basic meaning of this word is "to call to one's side," "to summon," "to admonish," "to exhort," "to entreat," etc. I suppose that it is justified to say that the number one meaning, at least as far as usage goes, is "to beseech." Here we find a word employed about one hundred and eight times and forty-three of those times it is given as "beseech." It refers to about every kind of a calling to a person which is meant to produce the desired reaction. Indeed, there is a place for pleading and exhorting, yea, with all of the* *compassion that one can muster in the preaching of the gospel. Yes, it is right "to beg" with compassion for the soul of man, that is, to argue in another's behalf as an advocate.*

Let it be known that I have not "touched the hem of the garment" in reference to the Greek words of our New Testament when it comes to the preacher and preaching. But if one were just to study these and no more, he would have a studious task. These alone are used, if I have noticed accurately, two hundred and eighty-seven times! However, these ten words from our study of the Greek New Testament ought to be enough to convince and convict anyone of the following thoughts:

1. *The preacher is* never to exalt himself or any man, only the Christ (2 Cor. 4:5; cf. 1 Cor. 2:1-5; Rom. 1:16f).

2. *The power to save is* not in "the messenger," but in the message (1 Cor. 1:18-21; Rom. 1:16).

3. *The basis of* the charge to preach is revealed in 2 Timothy 4:1-5.

4. *The urgency must be* viewed if one is to have the proper attitude of preaching (cf. 2 Tim. 4:1ff).

5. *The plain and positive truth of* the gospel must be set forth, yea, in clear and forthright language (cf. Eph. 6:20). A man must be convicted that he is lost.

6. *The spirit of compromise*, the "maybe so's," the "perhaps," or the "I think so's" are not to be in his vocabulary (cf. 1 Cor. 2:1-5).

7. *The faith will be* valiantly defended against every man-pleaser, religious politician, professional crier, proclamators of human doctrines, socializing counselors, lukewarm elders and the preachers who have defected into the

world, along with charismatic orators and human philosophical speculations of super-softness (cf. Acts 17:17; 19:8-9; 1 Pet. 3:15; Acts 6:9; 9:29; 1 Tim. 6:12; 2 Tim. 4:7; Acts 14:3; 9:27). The preacher knows he has a responsibility to error.

8. *The Bible teaches* the preacher to "contend earnestly" (Jude 3, Greek *epagonizomai*), "to make a defense" (1 Pet. 3:15), "fight the good fight of the faith" (1 Tim. 6:2, Greek *agonizomai*), "to put on the whole armor of God" (Eph. 6:11), "to suffer hardship" (2 Tim. 2:3, *kakopatheo*, is the Greek word here) and "to war" (2 Cor. 10:3, Greek *strateuo*). At times the preacher knows the polemic platform, for oral debate must be his. He knows this because he is a student of the Book and follows the examples of Christ, the early disciples, Paul, the apostles and elders, Apollos, etc. (Mark 9:14; 12:18-28, 34-40; 22:22-33, 41-46; Phil. 1:7, 16; Acts 9:29; 18:19; 17:17; 17:1-2, 4; 15:6-7; 18:28, respectively).

9. *The spirit of Christ will* always be manifested (cf. Matt. 19:16-22; John 8:1ff; cf. Rom. 9:1-3; 10:1-4; Gal. 4:19; Eph. 4:32).

10. *The decision that must be* made by "the hearer" will be called forth, yea, the preacher will exhort, implore, entreat, beseech, and beg (for those who think *parakelo* does not include this last word, I suggest they read Thayer on page 482) for his soul as it hesitates, yea, between heaven and hell (cf. 2 Cor. 5:11; Acts 2:40; Josh. 24:14-15; etc.). The warning, if not given, makes the preacher to be disobedient to his charge (cf. Heb. 10:31; Ezek. 33:1-16; 2 Cor. 5:11; 2 Pet. 2:1ff; etc.).

It is my observed, viewed, studied and truth-convicting belief relative to what I personally hear about "how" preaching should and should not be done, that it stems from ignorance of our source book, the Bible, the pressure of the powers that be, financial or otherwise, elders who "fear the flock," and the comfortable, lukewarm and indifferent attitude possessed by so many today. After all, what difference does it make in our very modern, affluent America where man is trying to be deified and God is being humanized! We are educated, we are popular, we have goodly houses and costly clothes, we have well-paying jobs, influential friends and business acquaintances, we own the property and for the most part (for the most of us) we have forgotten that our citizenship is in heaven and this earth is nothing more than an overnight motel! Indeed, "the voice of the people has become the voice of God." Yes, what we are striving for is "meeting human needs," "socializing the gospel," having "dollars and numbers" and that tells our own precious story for today! But, believe me, man is not the judge, no, not even on preaching!

PREACHING OF JUST ANY KIND DOES NOT PLEASE GOD

Even though I have tried diligently to set forth the above in the best way I know how, I feel it imperative to cover this point under a separate heading. How true it is in this day and age that we dare not assume anything. With a dislike for logic (from the Greek, *logikos*, which pertains to the reasoning faculty, reasonable, rational), as well as anything that deals with a syllogism (from the Greek, *sullogizomai*, to compute, to reason), it is just best to "touch all the bases." I do this now just briefly with a few scriptures as follows.

1. **1 Corinthians 1:18, 21.** We should note the difference in two items, the "foolishness of the thing preached," and the "preaching of foolishness."

2. **Titus 1:11.** Some, yea and even today, still teach things which they ought not.

3. **Philippians 1:15.** The preaching of Jesus Christ out of envy and out of strife.

4. **Matthew 15:9.** In vain do some worship the Master, teaching as their doctrines the precepts (*K.J.*, commandments) of men.

5. **Galatians 1:6-9.** A different gospel, which is not another gospel, but the gospel perverted and twisted is preached and people are troubled and under anathema.

6. **Romans 16:18.** Occasions of stumbling today are being created by those of fair and smooth speech, as they beguile the hearts of the innocent.

7. **Acts 20:28-30.** Heed is to be taken as there are those who do speak perverse things to draw away the disciples after them.

With just these seven scriptures facing us, how can anyone even dare to think that one can be saved (be pleasing unto God) by just any kind of preaching? Read these verses, meditate upon them, and then ask yourself this question: "Is this the kind of preaching by which God is pleased and the world is to be saved?" It is no wonder then that we have such admonitions as 2 John 9-11; 1 John 4:1; 1 Timothy 4:1ff; 2 Timothy 4:1-5; Matthew 15:13-14; etc. I must conclude if the preaching of a perverted gospel will make the preacher accursed, it will also make its believers accursed. His worship is vain and if that be the case then his belief is vain. Water, indeed, is able to quench thirst, but with salt it will create thirst. It can save life, but mixed with arsenic it destroys life. It certainly does matter what is believed and obeyed.

PREACHING BY PREACHERS WHO REALIZE THEIR CHARGE

There are three very important words that I want to list as covering the basis for this particular thought.

1. **Charge**. One of the most famous passages is 2 Timothy 4:1-5, as we view the work of preaching. The word for charge here is the Greek *diamaturomai* and means "to charge earnestly," "bear a solemn witness" and is so used in 1 Timothy 5:21; 2 Timothy 2:14. Another important Greek word used is *parangelia* (noun), *parangello* (verb), and refers to a command received from a superior and transmitted to others (1 Tim. 1:3; 6:13, 17). There is no way to get around the idea of "command" in this word.

2. **Stir**. Paul used this word in 2 Timothy 1:6 in relation to the young Timothy (Greek, *anazopureo*), and it is used metaphorically referring to a fire that may die out. There are other words so used, as in 2 Peter 1:13; 3:1; Acts 19:23; Luke 23:5.

3. **Provoke**. This word is found in Hebrews 10:24 and comes from the Greek *paroxusmos* (from *para* and *okuno*). It means a real stimulation, a provoking. In Acts 17:16, we find it used, and this passage brings into play the meaning of the word *okuno*, to sharpen, to incite, and to stir up. Paul's spirit was stirred within him! It is of interest to note that this is the word used in Acts 15:39 of the "contention" between Paul and John Mark.

When a preacher realizes he is under a charge, a true charge, one from a superior, a commander, his preaching will stir those who hear and will also provoke, stimulate, and arouse a man to take action. It is this kind of preaching by a preacher who realizes his job that is pleasing to the Almighty. The solemnity of our charge is seen in that it is in the presence of God, the presence of

Christ Jesus, with the realization of the coming judgment, recognition of the second coming of Christ and the very nature of the kingdom.

Talk about a stir! *Preach one God* and you will stir the idolater and the atheists. *Preach divine creation* and you will stir the evolutionists. *Preach immortality* and you will stir up the materialists. *The authority of the scriptures being preached* will stir the modernists. *Preaching one church* will stir the denominational world. *Preach the headship of Christ* and you will stir the Catholic. *Preach being "on fire"* (against our laziness, littleness and lukewarmness) and you are going to stir the majority of the church. *Preach on modest apparel* if you want to stir the bathing beauties of the long, hot summer. *Preach*, if you will, *on dancing*, if you want to stir many a daddy and a momma. *Preach of the Master's holiness* if you want to stir a hornet's nest of the drinking, smoking, chewing, revelling, lascivious and uncleanness found among us today. *Preach on foreign mission work* and you just might get the Americanization of Christianity board members to "put you across the pond." *Preach on the New Testament plan* of purposeful giving, and you may hear the cry, "Don't let your left hand know what your right hand is doing!" *Preach* boldly, *preach* negatively, *preach* as if you were expecting a response, *preach* to move the people, *preach* to rebuke and reprove, *preach* to the elders, yea, *preach* on specific sins, *preach* on the New Testament charge of discipline, etc., etc., and when you do, *preach* with your bags packed as you will have stirred the people and those under whom you serve!

The gospel of Jesus Christ cuts through old habits, exposes sin and presents a new standard at variance with the world. It is light for our darkness and salt for our corruption. The old man is not (does not die) going to die without a struggle. However, we must dispel darkness with light, spread purity in a world of immorality, convict sin in a world that loves sin and project truth in a world of error. This type of man who owes his allegiance to God and to no other, who is tender and kind, motivated by love, weeps for the lost and hates every false way will always please God by his preaching.

PREACHING TO IMPART THE GOSPEL, NOT TO IMPRESS THE PEOPLE

With all of my heart and soul, I know that we ought to be (and I do think, for the most part, we are) more concerned about winning people than in winning points. Yea, more concerned about imparting the gospel rather than impressing the people. Paul at one time instructed his hearers to "...be ye imitators of me" (1 Cor. 4:16) and then seven chapters later said, "be ye imitators of me, even as I also am of Christ" (11:1). With these two thoughts about "imitation" (Greek is *mimetes*) in our minds, let's note:

> *"For our exhortation is not of error, nor of uncleanness, nor in guile: but even* ***as we have been intrusted with the gospel, so we speak; not as pleasing men, but God*** *who proveth our hearts. For neither at any time were we found using words of flattery, as ye know, nor a cloak of covetousness, God is witness; nor seeking glory of men, neither from you nor from others, when we might have claimed authority as apostles of Christ...* ***we were well pleased to impart unto you,*** *not* ***the gospel*** *of God only, but* ***also our own souls,*** *because ye were become very dear to us" (1 Thess. 2:3-8, emp. GM).*

> *"And I will most gladly* ***spend and be spent*** *for*

your souls" (2 Cor. 12:15, emp. GM).

"For am I now seeking the favor of men, or of God? or ***am I striving to please men****? if I were still pleasing men, I should not be a servant of Christ" (Gal. 1:10, emp. GM).*

Preachers, perhaps above most of the church, need to realize they are not in some popularity contest. What we need in the pulpit today is what Paul spoke about in the preceding verses just quoted. Deception exists on every hand, but the greatest of all is that of "self-deception" (cf. 1 Cor. 3:18). I am in the pulpit of God, not to show how much I know, to tell where all I have been, to elaborate on my education, speak of my credentials, my degrees, to speak of the many jobs I have held, the programs that I have been on, to be a comedian, a news reporter, a religious politician, a public relations man, as a counselor, but as an evangelist fulfilling the high and noble task of making known the message of the Master. There is to be no competition among those of us who preach, but I feel there is as we so much want to be "the one who..." I recall the story of a famous orator, great gospel preacher, coming to town and there were two local men who so much wanted to go and hear him. One was able and one was not. The next time they met, the one who could not make it asked, "Is he as good as you?" To which the young preacher who had heard the famous man replied, "No, he is about like you."

PREACHING THE WHOLE COUNSEL, AND WITH BALANCE

Without going into all the particulars, let me hasten to say that I personally believe a man can preach the truth every Sunday and be lost, yea, the congregation also. For an example, supposing a man preached on "grace" every

Sunday, and that he preached God's grace, the favor unmerited, unearned, etc., but that is all he ever preached. If he preached on "the love of God" each Sunday, and that was it, would that be sufficient? Supposing a man preached the truth on faith and on baptism, but never preached "repentance," would that be all right and pleasing to God? Would that suffice the plan of God for man?

It was the apostle Paul, to the Ephesian elders, who said, "For I shrank not from declaring unto you the whole counsel of God" (Acts 20:27). Oh, how much I love the man who prayed for my preaching and said, "...that brother Music may always have balance in his preaching." When I think that we are "to preach the gospel," then that is exactly what we are to preach, not just "one facet" of it.

A gospel preacher, to be pleasing to God with his preaching, absolutely must include the following:

1. *The negative as well as the positive* (cf. 2 Tim. 4:1-5; Rom. 13:9-10; cf. Jer. 1:10). When one preaches on the qualifications of elders, he must preach on all twenty-six, and eighteen of them are positive and eight are negative.

2. *The law of God as well as the love of God* (cf. James 1:25; 2:8; Rom. 8:1; 1 Cor. 9:21; etc.).

3. *The two natures of God*, that is, *his severity and his goodness* (Rom. 11:22).

4. *The Lion of the tribe of Judah as well as the Lamb of God* (Rev. 5:5).

5. *The sins of man as well as the salvation of God* (1 John 3:4; 1 John 5:17).

6. *The heart of man* (included is the intellect, the will and the emotions) *and the mind of man, with the proper*

appeal to all (cf. Matt. 22:34-40, the whole man is to love God).

7. *The fear we need as well as the faith we must have* (2 Cor. 5:11; Heb. 10:31).

8. *The hell of the devil as well as the heaven of God* (Matt. 25:46; Rev. 20:10ff; 21:8; 22:15).

9. *The duty of man as well as the devotion to his master* (Eccl. 12:13; cf. Luke 17:10).

10. *The compulsion in our pleading as well as the compassion in our preaching* (cf. 2 Cor. 5:11, 14; Matt. 23:37).

There is not a Bible subject upon which a gospel preacher is not to preach. If anyone, including the elders, tries to hinder him from preaching any such subject, then he must remember to whom his allegiance belongs. Whether with his pen or his voice, he belongs to God, to him and to no other! Many fear the subjects of church discipline, marriage, divorce and remarriage, pure Christian living, sinful habits, etc., but these are not to be feared by any "mouthpiece" of God, as he has a job to accomplish, and like the Son of God, when he bends his head in prayer or bows to death, his one thought is "not my will, but thine be done," along with "it is finished" and I have "fought the good fight and kept the faith."

PREACHING PAINFULLY PLAIN THESE POWERFUL POINTS

The longer I preach (it is almost four decades that I have been trying), the more preaching that I hear, the more people with whom I talk, both in and out of the body of Christ, the more I read and become aware of our religious world and its teachings, the greater I keenly feel the need of always making known the following prominent and paramount, singular and salient points. Note these, and note them carefully, please.

1. *Jesus did not come to make people religious, but to make them religiously right* (cf. John 8:31-32; 7:17; 17:17).

2. *Christianity is religion, but not all religion is Christianity* (cf. Acts 17:22ff; Matt. 6:24; 15:7-9).

3. *It is not enough to give a question an answer, it must be the only answer, the right answer, the Bible answer* (cf. 1 Pet. 3:15; Col. 4:6).

4. *There is a body of truth that is absolute, objective, attainable, and unchangeable, fully explained* (cf. John 8:32; 17:17; 14:6; 6:44-45; 7:17; Jude 3; Eph. 4:4-6; Acts 6:7; 15:9; 2 Tim. 4:7).

5. *We must have Bible authority for everything we preach/teach and or practice* (Col. 3:17; 1 Pet. 4:11).

6. *It is not sufficient to love what God loves, as I must also hate what God hates* (cf. Prov. 8:13; Amos 5:15; Psm. 97:10; Heb. 1:9; Jude 23; Psm. 119:104).

7. *It is not adequate to preach and or live the truth, one must defend the truth* (cf. 1 Pet. 3:15; Jude 3; 1 John 4:1; 1 Thess. 5:21; 1 Tim. 6:12; Acts 6:9; 9:29; 18:28; Greek *miseo*, hate, 42 times).

8. *Any time a man rejects the Word of God, he rejects God* (1 Sam. 15:3, 21-30; 8:3-7).

9. *The world is not divided over what the Bible says, but over what it does not say* (cf. Exod. 3:1-3; John 8:1-11; John 3:1-3; 2 Cor. 12:7-10).

10. *Fighting soldiers, servants of God, are loving saints trying to be pleasing unto God* (cf. Gal. 1:10; John 8:29; Gal. 2:20; 6:14; 1 Thess. 2:3-4; 2 Cor. 4:2; 2:17).

Unless our preaching is true to the "old paths" (cf. Jer. 6:16), and has a distinctive and clarion sound (1 Cor. 14:8), are we true to the blood that purchased us? If we just preach what any person would preach, without making known the body of absolute truth, which is objective and unchangeable, are we truly His preachers? If we fail to make known "the faith" and let people know they are lost without the gospel of Christ, where do we stand? (Jer. 9:3). Does it not behoove each preacher to love the truth more than life itself?

PREACHING TO TURN THE WORLD UPSIDE DOWN

In Acts chapter seventeen, after Paul and Silas had gone through Amphipolis and Appollonia, they came to Thessalonica and for three sabbath days "reasoned" (Greek, *dialegomai*) and "alleged" (Greek, *paratithemi*) that Jesus was the Christ. Soon the city was in an uproar, the house of Jason was assaulted, some of the brethren, along with Jason, were taken before the rulers of the city and the charge was "These that have turned the world upside down are come hither also" (Acts 17:1-6; esp. vs. 6).

Have you ever wondered why we in this century have not turned the world "upside down"? Have you ever pondered why we are not stirring the world like the first century did? Could it be because we are not "reasoning" (to dispute with others; cf. 17:17; 18:4,19; 19:8-9; 24:25; etc.) and "alleging" (the setting of subjects before one's hearers by way of argument and proof) as these men did? How long will it be before we get on television, on radio, in the newspapers and magazines, and declare with all boldness and challenge the world to refute the claims that:

1. Jesus is the Christ, the Son of God, and there is no other name by which/in which man can (must) be saved

(Acts 4:12).

2. The church is the one body of Christ and one must come into contact wth the blood of Christ to be "in that one body" (Eph. 1:22-23; 4:4-6; 1:7; Col. 1:18,24; Rev. 1:5).

3. Man cannot be saved out of the church, and one religious group is not as good as another (Eph. 5:23; Matt. 16:13-18).

4. The gospel of Christ is the only message in the world that has the power to save the soul of man, there is no other (Matt. 7:21-23; 7:13-14; John 8:32; 17:17; 7:17; 2 John 9-11; Gal. 1:6-9; 2 Thess. 1:7-9; 2:10-12).

5. Faithfulness to Christ must, absolutely must, be put above all other things and people (Acts 21:13-14; 1 Cor. 4:11-13; 2 Cor. 6:1-10; 12:7-10; 2 Tim. 4:6-8; Rev. 2:10).

The world needs to be turned, and we have the spiritual dynamite, the gospel (1 Cor. 1:18; Rom. 1:16), with which to turn the world "right side" up (2 Cor. 2:14). Let's give it our very best. Let's preach like we believe it, for, indeed, we must believe it.

PREACHING THAT IS ADDRESSED TO THE RATIONALITY OF MAN

The Word of God, as expressed in the New Testament, is rational communication, language, and thus an appeal for man to receive and to understand God's communication by means of his rationality. That we have adequate evidence in the New Testament of such, can be easily proven. We have hundreds of words that convey the idea of rational activity. These imply that man must both receive and understand the communication from God, the New Testament.

This thought alone would take a book, not just a chapter in one or a small tract, much less one segment of one chapter. However, I can make some comments that will show/prove this point.

1. **Some words convey the rational faculties of man**, such as *nous*, the mind, intellect, or *dianoia*, the thinking of the mind (these two words occur about 37 times) and there are others so translated.

2. **Some words give the reasoning process**, and we have a host of such (Greek, *logizomai, suzeteo, logos, dialegomai*, etc.) and so we find in English words like reasoning, thinking, examine, judge, thought, consider, prove, answer, persuade, exhort, etc., and these are used from (translated from) some 37-46 Greek words and found from 1 to 330 different times.

3. **Some words refer to the impartation of knowledge**, such as the word teaching (Greek, *didasko*, used about 93 times), disciple (Greek, *mathetetho*, 4 times), teaching, instruction (Greek, *didache*, about 30 times) and we have various words for preaching, learning, edification and expounding, etc.

4. **Some words deal with verbal communication**, such as the Greek word *logos*, perhaps used as much as any word we might discuss in these areas (over 330 times). There is the word gospel (Greek, *euangelion*, 154 times), and it, the gospel is usually proclaimed by a herald, an evangelist, and it is to be obeyed. Then we have also words in Greek which give us our English words like epistle or writing, book, scripture, message, revelation, etc.

5. **Some words relate to intellectual inquiry.** In fact, we have the word "inquire" (among the various words for this one word in English is the Greek *diaginoseo* and *zeteo,* used over 100 times) as well as "question" and

"search" or "examine," from other Greek words.

6. **Some words inform us of disputation, refutation, controversy or confutation**, such as "dispute" (Greek, *dialegomai*), and there are many others (defense, correction, to call in question, find fault, and each one from other Greek words). I've always enjoyed the word in Greek, *diakatelegchomai*, as found in Acts 18:28 (argue or debate right down to the finish line).

7. **Some words tell us of the conclusion of the mind,** and so we have such words as "conclude" (Greek, *krino*, for example), "understand" (Greek, *noieo*, for example), and we have other words for our words "establish," "approve," "determine," etc.

8. **Some words describe the certainty of the mind,** which is just a great thought for those who say that "one cannot know..." This calls for such words as "know" (*ginosko* in the Greek is found over 200 times), and then there are other words from which we get our English words "assurance," "sure," "certainty," "confirm," "prove," "evident," etc.

9. **Some words detail certainty of fact.** So, we "know" there is "truth" (Greek, *aletheia*) and we know there is something that is "genuine" (Greek, *alethinos* or *alethes*), and these three words alone are used some 150 plus times.

10. **Some words even describe, tells us of, ignorance and unreasonableness** (the negative side of learning, believing, knowing, understanding, etc.). We have the Greek words *alogos, agnoia,* and *amathes* as examples of "unreasonableness," "ignorant" and "unlearned," respectively. (For those who know the language, they will immediately observe the "negating alpha" on each word).

May each reader realize, as I said before, I only

touched, yea, if I even did that, "the hem of the garment" in the language of the New Testament. It truly can be said that "no man turns on logic, until logic turns on him." The revelation of God is attainable. I know that we can "know," as the Master himself said, "...know the truth..." (John 8:32; check the thought of Romans 1:18-23; 1:28 and you can prove that their desire kept them from "knowing" God).

PREACHING AS A DYING MAN TO DYING MEN

When Paul penned his famous "charge" to the young preacher, Timothy, he said, among other things, "...preach the word; *be urgent* in season, out of season;..." (2 Tim. 4:2, emp. GM). The Greek word for "urgent" is *ephistemi* (*K.J.*, instant) and means "to stand by," "be at hand," "come on," "to be ready," and so is translated as "urgent," or "be instant." We must have a ready spirit (Tit. 3:1; Rom. 1:15; 2 Cor. 12:15), be able to seize opportunities (Col. 4:5; Eph. 5:15-16) and "imitate" the great apostle who wrote these words (cf. Rom. 1:14-16).

In the negative, this does not mean "in the summer" or "in the winter," "when I feel like it" or "when I want to do it." This means "at all times," including the covenient and inconvenient, easy and difficult, opportune and inopportune, at home and abroad, near and far, as there is no "off season" for the Christian. I am speaking of a twenty-four hour a day, seven days a week most urgent matter. We are like those described in 2 Chronicles 24:5, as we, too, "hasten it not."

We must learn that Christianity is not seasonal. God demands constancy of us, that is, we can never quit (Luke 9:62). Indifference and slothfulness are everywhere condemned, and no place shows this as does Revelation

3:14ff. I belong to a God whose religion is one of "always" (cf. 1 Cor. 15:58; Col. 4:6; Phil. 2:12; 4:4; 1 Pet. 3:15; etc.). Paul was faithful "in prison and out," "in the presence of kings and governors, or a jailor," "in perils or in palaces," "with friends and without friends," "when supported and when not supported," etc.

I personally feel, to a great degree, our sense of urgency is lacking! Do I really preach "as a dying man to dying men"? Are we truly convinced that men are lost without the gospel? Are we sure that the gospel is the only means that can save man? How true it is that we are standing between a "go" (Mark 16:15) and a "woe" (1 Cor. 9:16).

While in another state, up north of us, about three years ago, an elder asked me, "Do you always preach this way?" He was talking about the message, the contents, and the urgency felt in its deliverance. I just kinda believe there is a difference "in a sermon to preach" and "a heart-burning message to deliver." Indeed, I preach that urgency everywhere.

Recently, while listening to a man close his lesson, he made the statement that he would not "beg" anyone to respond. Within the scope of the promises and the warnings, I personally would implore, beseech, plead, appeal to, seek, request, ask, call upon, yea, from the Greek word *parakaleo*, I would "beg for a man's eternal spirit." The people of Jonah's day may have had 40 days, but you and I are not promised 40 seconds!

May God help us to realize there is a preaching that is pleasing unto God, but there is also one that is displeasing unto God. May this study help us to strive to please God in our preaching, by the preaching of the Christ, of the Cross, of the Gospel, of the Word of God,

Remission of Sins and of the Kingdom of God. I trust that it can be said of us, as Jesus said about himself, "And he that sent me is with me; he hath not left me alone; for I do always the things that are *pleasing* to him" (John 8:29, emp. GM). *Preacher*, even before you preach that next sermon, ask yourself, "Will this sermon please God?" *To every reader*, when you hear your next sermon(s), ask yourself the question, "Is that the type of sermon (preaching, and I here make reference to 'the content of it,' not the manner of delivery) that is pleasing to God and one that would save the world?" Preacher and reader, remember this, there is that which is displeasing unto God. *Elder*, remember when you hear the next sermon that your preacher(?) delivers, to ask, "Is that the preaching that will be pleasing unto God and that which it takes to save the world?" It might be, if you (elder) have read this, that you need to ask, "Have we, as elders, encouraged or hindered 'our preacher' in being true to the real work of an evangelist?" That is, "Have we been honest and true to THE BOOK AND ITS CONTENTS that 'our preacher' is to preach?" I repeat, there is a preaching that is "pleasing" unto God, and there is a preaching that is "displeasing" unto God.

Chapter Thirteen

THE PATTERN - AND THE COMMAND OF REPENTANCE

THE PATTERN - AND THE COMMAND OF REPENTANCE

A study of the vital subject of repentance may come from various New Testament books, but I seriously doubt that any of the verses we could mention could excel in depth, meaning, and comprehension what we find listed in the New Testament book of 2 Corinthians. Indeed, we are delving into a subject that roots itself throughout God's Word. In the New Testament, we find it mentioned in one-third of those twenty-seven books!

The study of repentance is not too difficult, but the application of what is learned is perhaps one of the most Herculean elements the non-Christian or the Christian will ever face. Years ago there was a book written on "the forgotten commandment," discipline. In fact, that was the title of the book. Repentance might well be called "the most misunderstood commandment," as, indeed, it is the commandment, and perhaps the only commandment, that is so unpracticed and unheeded when the completeness of its requirements are fathomed. This can further be seen when one observes that it bears directly on the subject of discipline, the so-called "forgotten commandment."

I have forgotten just exactly where I read it, but it was brother J. W. McGarvey who said: "If God should give spiritual gifts as he did in the first century, I would not ask for the gift of healing, prophecy, or tongues, but the gift that would enable me to help men repent of their sins." It has rightly been termed "the hardest command" for man to obey. As this subject is developed, I believe we all will come to understand why.

This is a subject on which we have been negligent. Yes, I know that it has been preached on time and again, even as I have in every local work I've done. Yes, I, too, know that it is a subject about which some have written. In fact, I wrote a tract, *"The Bible Doctrine of Repentance"* and published the same in 1986. I did this, as I could not find a single tract (at the time) that was in any way thorough as to the subject of repentance. In this tract, which was centered around certain questions, I covered these:

1. Is Repentance A Divine Requirement?

2. Is Repentance Divinely Defined?

3. Is Repentance Divinely Mirrored?

4. Is Repentance A Divine Teacher?

5. Is Repentance Produced By Divine Motives?

6. Is Repentance Necessary For Forgiveness?

7. Is Repentance Truly A Divine Act?

I also had a chapter in my book, *"Divorce,"* entitled "Divorce and Repentance" (pp. 227-243), both of which I felt were fairly complete. Still I am fully aware that this God-given mandate, both in our teaching and practicing of it, has not occupied eminence in the mind and heart of the individual or in the classroom or assembly room of the local church. Far too few of our men, I personally feel, as they begin to preach, say, "The elders have asked me to preach on the subject of repentance today." If we think the "except" of John 3:3, 5 is important, let me remind us that the same word is used, and by our Master, in Luke 13:3, 5, and it is used regarding "repentance."

THE CALL TO REPENTANCE

In traveling from church to church across our country in the work of Gospel evangelistic meetings, in the reading of all the church bulletins that come across my desk, in noting what is written in many of our Gospel papers, and in listening to sermons, lectures, and various conversations, I am convinced that there is far too little said about that which is so emphasized in the New Testament, the need for people to repent. Evidently we have the idea that the thrust of the local church is to gain new members. This certainly is a most vital and necessary part. However, if that is all we think about, it could very well leave the impression that the local church, the members, are all in good standing with God and thus cause the assumption that there is no need for repentance on their part. I am convinced, and have been for a good many years, that one of the greatest needs of the people of God is more repentance. This implies that we understand what all is involved in repentance. Brethren are sometimes shocked when you preach to them. While in Vanderbilt University and preaching in Coffee Country, Tennessee, one good brother said to another: "Say, he is preaching to us!"

Just here let me remind all of us it was to "the church of God which is in Corinth" (1 Cor. 1:2; 2 Cor. 1:1), that Paul penned these words:

> *"For though I made you sorry with my epistle, I do not regret it: though I did regret it (for I see that that epistle made you sorry, though but for a season), I now rejoice, not that ye were made sorry, but that ye were made sorry unto repentance; for ye were made sorry after a godly sort, that ye might suffer the loss by us in nothing. For godly sorrow worketh repen-*

tance unto salvation, a repentance which bringeth no regret: but the sorrow of the world worketh death" (2 Cor. 7:8-10).

"Lest again when I come my God should humble me before you, and I should mourn for many of them that have sinned heretofore, and repented not of the uncleanness and fornication and lasciviousness which they committed" (2 Cor. 12:21).

1. **A Call To The World.** There are many examples in the Word of God relative to the call to repentance, and some of these are to people in the world, people who have no relationship to our Father: the alien, the non-Christian. This can be seen from the preaching of John (Matt. 3:1-2), of Jesus Himself (Matt. 4:17) in His personal ministry, and also in the preaching that Jesus told the twelve to do (Mark 6:2). Yes, it is true, as we all know, that John did preach to the Jews who were God's people, but people who had wandered away from God and who needed to repent and come back to God. On the day of Pentecost, when believing sinners cried out, "Brethren, what shall we do?" Peter said unto them, "Repent ye, and be baptized everyone of you in the name of Jesus Christ unto the remission of your sins;..." (Acts 2:38). Paul declared that God commands "all men everywhere to repent" (Acts 17:30, *K.J.*).

2. **A Call To The Church.** In addition to the call to the world, God also calls every unfaithful child of His to repent (cf. Acts 8:20-24). This call that God has for His own people is not just to isolated individuals, but is sometimes given to entire churches. If a church is guilty of the sin of lukewarmness, as was the church at Laodicea (Rev. 3:14-22), if a church is guilty of leaving its first love, as was the church at Ephesus (Rev. 2:1-7), if a church is

guilty of being dead, as was the church at Sardis (Rev. 3:1-6), if a church is guilty of condoning religious error, false doctrine, as was the church at Pergamum (Rev. 2:12-17), and if a church is guilty of permitting sin, as was the church at Thyatira (Rev. 2:18-29), then God's call is "repent or perish."

How true it is then that God desires all men everywhere to repent of their sins (cf. 2 Pet. 3:9; 1 Tim. 2:3-4). Yes, those in the world and those in the church! All men have sinned (Rom. 3:23) and sin violates the law of God (1 John 3:4). Since no sin can enter into Heaven, then sin must be forgiven and this demands repentance (cf. Rev. 21:27; Isa. 1:10-20, esp. vs. 18; Luke 13:3, 5; Acts 17:30).

THE CIRCUMSCRIPTION OF REPENTANCE

When it comes to the definition, the delineation, and delimitation of repentance, we find, perhaps, our greatest difficulty. I say this both from what I have observed and also studied. Therefore, it is deemed necessary to list both the negative and the positive.

1. **Considering The Negative.**

a. *It is not just regret*, as clearly seen in the case of Judas in Matthew 27:3. Here we find remorse or regret, but not genuine, full, repentance.

b. *It is not just fear*, although the Bible emphasizes the need of godly fear (cf. Eccl. 12:13; Prov. 1:7; Acts 10:34-35; Rom. 3:18; Psm. 36:1). It could be that some are just scared, as is the man in the foxhole, but that is not godly fear. Note also Felix in Acts 24:25.

c. *It is not just conviction*, for one might be convicted and yet not truly repent. Men must be convicted of sin to be saved (cf. John 16:8; Eph. 6:17), and many today state that they have sinned, but there is no real change in their lives (no real conviction). King Saul said he had sinned, but it did not change his life.

d. *It is not just being sorry*, as there is a sorrow of the world and also a godly sorrow (2 Cor. 7:8-10). I am sure the Pentecostians of Acts 2 were in sorrow about their sins (2:36ff), but they were not then forgiven.

e. *It is not just a reformation of life*, as one may quit some sin and then reform his life for some selfish reason and still not obey God (cf. Matt. 3:1ff; Luke 3:7-8). It is connected with repentance, but it is not repentance.

f. *It is not just prayer*, as clearly seen from Proverbs 28:9. We might pray ever so fervently, but that is not repentance.

g. *It is not just confession*, as sins must not only be confessed, they must also be forsaken (cf. Prov. 28:13).

h. *It is not just ceasing to do wrong.* One might stop stealing and feel that he can keep the money and be all right, but this is not repentance (cf. Acts 8:20-24; 2:36ff).

i. It is not just assembling with the saints for worship, as this is not what covers sin (cf. Psm. 32:1; Prov. 28:13; 1 Pet. 3:8-12). Some negligent members "slip" or "slide" back in, occupy a pew once more, and think this is repentance. It is a far cry, yea, a very far cry from it!

j. *It is not an "if" statement.* This is not confessing

sins, but bespeaks of an attitude that is not right. This is a long way from what David did in Psalm 51:1-3. Note that he said: "My sin," "my iniquity," and "my transgression."

2. **Considering The Language.** A brief study of two Greek terms is necessary at this point, both to establish the previous section and to introduce the section to follow.

One is the word *metamelomai*, used six times in the New Testament as a verb (the adjectival form is used twice). I suppose the classic use of it is in Matthew 27:3 in reference to Judas. It is also used in the first of our two references in 2 Corinthians 7:8, twice, and then again in verse 10. Simply stated, this word means regret, remorse. It could lead one to true repentance, but, as in the case of Judas, it could leave one with only remorse. Judas did regret his sin, but he did not turn back to God and change his directions. He was a lost man (cf. Acts 1:25).

The other word is *metanoeo*, and is used some 34 times in the verb form and 24 in the noun form. This is the word used in the New Testament to note genuine repentance, indicating that the sinner must make "a spiritual change." It is almost always (only one exception, I believe) used in reference to repentance from sin. In this word there is a "change of mind" and it results in a "change of conduct." W. E. Vine wrote: "...this change of mind involves both a turning from sin and a turning to God" (p. 281). Joseph H. Thayer stated: "...the change of mind of those who have begun to abhor their errors and misdeeds, and have determined to enter upon a better course of life, so that it embraces both a recognition of sin and sorrow for it and hearty amendment, the tokens and effects of which are good deeds..." (p. 406).

3. **Considering The Positive.** If I were to give one

basic sentence, a single thought, in my explanation of what repentance is, it would be this: "Repentance is a change of mind, brought about or produced by godly sorrow, that results in a change of life." As far as I am able to detect from all the Word of God on this subject, nothing else is true repentance. I want to make it ever so clear that repentance is not godly sorrow, which, evidently, many believe. Note just here some thoughts about this change of mind.

a. *Regret.* The sinner must feel regret, as he now understands his sins have transgressed God's law and he has incurred God's wrath (cf. 2 Cor. 7:10).

b. *Resolve.* We know, from such verses as Matthew 21:29 and Luke 15:18, that the sinner must change his will.

c. *Reform.* This change of conduct is seen in the life that he now lives, that is, the fruit thereof is ever so clear (cf. Matt. 3:8; 1 Thess. 1:9; Acts 19:19).

d. *Restore.* This is a thought that is most difficult, perhaps at times even impossible (the one I have sinned against may be dead), but the desire and effort are absolutes. If I have stolen something, I must return it, as this is the idea herein expressed.

Thus far, we can clearly see that genuine repentance is more than regret or remorse (cf. Jer. 4:28; 2 Cor. 7:10), more than simply saying, "I'm sorry," more than a reformation of life, more than conviction, yea, more than all those things already discussed in the "negative" section.

THE COMMAND OF REPENTANCE

Earlier in our study we noted there was a "call" to repentance, both for the world and the church (Acts

17:30). Now I use the same passage to show that repentance is a command, one coming from God Himself: "The times of ignorance therefore God overlooked; but now he commandeth men that they should all everywhere repent." The word "commandeth" is correctly translated (Greek is *parangellei*, and is from *para*, beside, *angello*, to announce), as it means to give order, give a charge, a command, and such like.

The Lord, our Master, during His personal ministry uttered these words: "I tell you, Nay: but, except ye repent, ye shall all in like manner perish" (Luke 13:3, 5). It would take an "unwise" man to miss the exceptive clause in the Master's statement.

As the beloved physician, Luke, closed the book that bears his name, he included his account of the great commission in Luke 24:46-47. "Thus it is written, that the Christ should suffer, and rise again from the dead the third day; and that repentance and remission of sins should be preached in his name unto all the nations, beginning from Jerusalem."

When the day of Pentecost dawned and the fulness of time came for the proclamation of the Gospel, Peter delivered the sermon recorded in Acts 2. When inquiring sinners asked what to do to be saved, he said, "Repent ye, and be baptized every one of you in the name of Jesus Christ unto the remission of your sins; and ye shall receive the gift of the Holy Spirit" (v. 38). In the very next chapter we have recorded yet another sermon by this man, wherein he said, "Repent ye therefore, and turn again, that your sins may be blotted out, that so there may come seasons of refreshing from the presence of the Lord" (v. 19).

The book of Revelation reveals the letters to the seven churches of Asia in which we find the Lord telling five out of the seven to "repent or perish" (Ephesus, Pergamum, Thyatira, Sardis, and Laodicea). Thus we have, in a rather short survey, seen that this is a command of God from the synoptics through the Apocalypse of John. When a person views even these few Scriptures, it will be clearly seen that repentance is, indeed, a mandate from Heaven itself.

THE CHALLENGE IN REPENTANCE

I believe there are at least two reasons why this has been termed "the hardest command" for man to obey, as indicated below:

1. **A Challenge To Self.** The command of repentance is aimed directly at the will of man, and herein lies the difficulty. It is hard to get man to give up sin, as "self" is the hardest man in the world to crucify (cf. Matt. 19:16-22; Acts 8:13-24; 17:32-34). Very few can say with Paul, "I have been crucified with Christ; and it is no longer I that live, but Christ liveth in me: and that life which I now live in the flesh I live in faith, the faith which is in the Son of God, who loved me, and gave himself up for me" (Gal. 2:20).

Our Lord Himself taught that we must "deny" self. "If any man would come after me, let him deny himself, and take up his cross,..." (Matt. 16:24). Luke made it even clearer, if possible, when he wrote Luke 9:23 and Luke 14:25-35. Three times in this latter passage he made a statement, a condition, and stated if this is not the case with a man, "he cannot be my disciple" (vss. 26, 27, 33). The Lord knew man (cf. John 2:24-25) and knew that he was quick to justify self and avoid guilt. He also knew that man was an egotistical and self-serving individual. Man must get rid of self. He must crucify self, as "no man can serve two masters" (cf. Matt. 6:24). If self is enthroned, then Christ is dethroned! Indeed, the command to repent, when fully obeyed, dethrones self and enthrones Christ as his ruler. This is a real challenge to self.

2. **A Challenge In Restitution.** The thought of "restitution" is perhaps one of the most frightening, and this may be the reason that we are constantly asked if repentance involves restitution (so many today teach that it does, but only in certain realms). Unless I have missed someone, only eleven people in the Bible said, "I have sinned." As we have already seen, however, conviction is not full and genuine repentance.

Let us here note some Biblical examples to prove the definition of repentance given earlier: "a change of mind brought about or produced by godly sorrow that results in a change of life."

a. *Matthew 21:28-29.* In this passage of Scripture let us observe what was the mind of the boy who said, "I will not," in reference to his father's command to go work in the vineyard. But he repented, that is, he changed his mind. He then went and worked in his father's vineyard. The change of mind was repentance, and the going and working in the vineyard was reformation of his life. The knowing, the going, and the working are all important.

b. *Luke 15:11-24.* The prodigal son asked for all that was his and his father gave it to him. We see him in his preparation to leave home, his leaving home and his departure into a foreign, a strange, land. It was in this land that he went as low as a Jew could go. Then the Bible says he came to himself (vs. 17). This proves that one in sin is not really at himself. Now note what he said: "I am going back to my father and I am going to say that I have sinned." Here again is godly sorrow. He said, "I will arise and go," and this is his change of mind. He had been going away from his father and now he has resolved to go back to his father. In verse twenty we have this statement, "He arose and came to his father." This is his reformation of life. Here again we have a change of mind brought about by godly sorrow that resulted in a change of life.

c. *2 Corinthians 7:7-11.* Paul wrote a letter to the church at Corinth because they were not behaving themselves as Christians. He stated a thought we want to note. He said that though he made them sorry with a letter he did not repent, that is, he did not regret it. He then pointed out why: It had worked godly sorrow in their lives. This godly sorrow worked repentance, but the sorrow of the world works death. Then, in verse 11, he spoke of "the earnest care it wrought in you, what clearing of yourselves, yea what indignation, yea what fear,..." Paul's letter produced godly sorrow in their hearts. It caused them to change their minds and verse 11 says it caused them to change their lives. The correct meaning of repentance is herein found. It is a change of mind, which change of mind is brought about or produced by godly sorrow and results in a change of life. Anything other than this is not Bible repentance.

However, we should be careful to observe that repentance involves restitution, that is, as far as possible. This is the element that perhaps is overlooked, not heeded, in this subject. It is so easy to get up, come to the front, say, "I have sinned," and then do nothing about the sin committed. Restitution means restoring that which belongs to another, giving back, replacing, and repaying. This has always been a part of God's law to man.

a. *Leviticus 6:1-6* (cf. Num. 5). Under the law of Moses, if a man wronged another (perhaps taking something from him) he was to restore it, adding a fifth part. If the man were dead, he was to give it to the next of kin. If the next of kin were dead, he was to give it to the priest to be used in God's work. *This is restitution.*

b. *1 Samuel 12:1-5.* After the people of God had rejected Samuel, since he was old and his sons no longer walked in the way of the Lord, he stood before Israel and said, "Whose ox have I taken? or whose ass have I taken? or whom have I defrauded? whom have I oppressed? or of whose hand have I taken a ransom to blind mine eyes therewith? And I will restore it." *That is restitution.*

c. *Luke 19:1-8.* Here is a man by the name of Zacchaeus, a chief publican, a rich man, a man who desired to see Jesus. When Jesus saw him in the sycomore tree and told him to come down because he was going to abide with him, Zacchaeus said, "Behold, Lord, the half of my goods I give to the poor; and if I have wrongfully exacted aught of any man, I restore fourfold" (v. 8). Jesus did not tell the man this was a matter with which he did not have to be concerned, but He rather approved his actions. Zacchaeus recognized a principle that many today seemingly do not understand. *The principle is that of restitution.*

Restitution must, as far as is humanly possible, be made. I repeat, some things cannot be "undone" (e.g., if I have killed a man). However, I can do for the family what I can and try to overcome the wrong I've committed. The same is true if I have stolen something; I will try, as far as possible, to replace it. If I have lied, slandered, or gossiped and harmed, hindered, or destroyed someone's character, I will make it right as far as I possibly can. Anything less than this will not give me the joy of heart that I should have. In fact, *in Matthew 5:21-24 restitution is essential if one intends to worship God in an acceptable manner.* Jesus explicitly said, "...if therefore thou art offering thy gift at the altar, and there rememberest that thy brother hath aught against thee, leave there thy gift before the altar, and go thy way, first be reconciled to thy brother, and then come and offer thy gift" (vv. 23-24).

It does not take long to repent, but it may take a lifetime to carry out and to accomplish what I have resolved in repentance if restitution is involved. Luke 17:3-4 proves it does not take long to repent, as does Acts 2 (vv. 38ff). But let us all keep in mind the teachings of the Master found in Matthew 22:39; 7:12. This particular thought is the difference in our two Greek words. The first word mentioned refers primarily to "after-care," but the second, the one that brings about a change of mind, means "after-knowledge." In Matthew 12:41 we read, "The men of Nineveh shall stand up in the judgment with this generation, and shall condemn it: for they repented at the preaching of Jonah; and behold a greater than Jonah is here." Jonah preached, just as God directed, the people believed the message, and then they demonstrated it. Jonah 3:10 declares, "And God saw their works, that they turned from their evil way; and God repented of the evil which he said he would do unto them; and he did it not." Please note that God called this repentance. Therefore, so do I, and so does any faithful preacher of the Gospel!

THE CLASSIC CASES AND CHARACTERISTICS OF REPENTANCE

Although we perhaps have already mentioned enough proof of the meaning of repentance, let us now notice some examples in the Word of God that demonstrate that repentance, and I am referring to GENUINE REPENTANCE, bears fruit that no one can question or doubt. Note the following New Testament cases:

1. **Matthew 12:41.** This passage refers to Jonah, his preaching, and the turning by the people of Nineveh. God saw their works, their turn from evil, and called it repentance (cf. Luke 11:32).

2. **Matthew 21:28-29.** This text describes a son who had declared he would not work, changed his mind, and then went and worked. Verse 29 says he "repented himself," and it clearly shows that he did the will of his father.

3. **Luke 15:11-24.** The prodigal came to himself, talked to himself, arose and did that which he said he would do. He declared that he had sinned both against Heaven and his father and was unworthy to be called the son of his father. The compassion of the father did not hinder his resolution and the boy confessed (no "if" statement here) to the right person at the right place!

4. **Acts 8:20-24.** When told to repent of his wickedness, Simon proved beyond dispute his genuine repentance when he said, "Pray for me that none of the things which ye have spoken come upon me" (v. 24).

5. **Acts 16:27-34.** The jailor, when his question was answered about his soul's salvation, "took them the same hour of the night, and washed their stripes; and was baptized..." (v. 33).

6. **Acts 19:19.** "And not a few of them that practised magical arts brought their books together and burned them in the sight of all; and they counted the price of them, and found it fifty thousand pieces of silver." The cost of repentance, the price to be paid for it, is, at times, very expensive, eh? I wonder if they "counted the cost" of true repentance?

7. **1 Corinthians 6:9-11; 2 Corinthians 7:7-11.** In the first passage we find the Corinthians had turned from their devilish practices, evidenced by "...and such were some of you...," and in the second we find their change of mind caused by godly sorrow that worked repentance unto salvation, which brought no regret. They cleared themselves, proving their reformation of life.

8. **1 Thessalonians 1:9.** Paul wrote of their repentance when he declared, "For they themselves report concerning us what manner of entering in we had unto you; and how ye turned unto God from idols, to serve a living and true God." Once again, here is repentance demonstrated.

I have given the majority of the "classic cases" of repentance as found in the New Testament. From these we have learned that genuine repentance carries evidence that no one can question (cf. Lev. 6:1-7; Luke 19:3-9). We know that it involves a sense of sin, sorrow for sin, and severance from sin (cf. Matt. 21:28-29; Luke 15:11-24). Indeed, this is where the word *metanoeo*, after-knowledge, comes to light with a determined honesty, fervency, a deliberate turning from sin, and a turning to God in harmony with the will of God. It restores, as far as possible, that which can be restored.

THE CLOSE CONSTANCY WITH REPENTANCE

Having discussed the acid test, the real crucible, of repentance, it seems only natural now to show the careful application of this subject as we find it revealed in the New Testament.

1. **Repentance Is For The Alien.** On the day of Pentecost, the initial response to Peter's sermon was revealed by Luke: "Now when they heard this, they were pricked in their heart" (Acts 2:37). It was then that they asked, "Brethren, what shall we do?" Just here Peter said, "Repent ye, and be baptized every one of you in the name of Jesus Christ unto the remission of your sins;..." (v. 38). Peter had preached the Gospel and they had been pricked in their hearts, having believed what he preached. Therefore, Peter told them to repent. It is obvious that repentance is for the alien, and it is also obvious that it comes between belief and baptism.

In Acts 8:26-38, we can read of the conversion of the eunuch. The evangelist, Philip, preached unto him (v. 35) and the eunuch believed the message. The Scripture says, "And as they went on the way they came unto a certain water; and the eunuch saith, Behold, here is water; what doth hinder me to be baptized" (vs. 36)? It was not long until the eunuch said, "I believe that Jesus Christ is the Son of God," and having made that confession, was immersed into Christ (v. 38). He made his confession just prior to his immersion. Therefore, in just these two cases we have observed that the Gospel was preached, people heard it, believed it, they repented, they confessed, and they were immersed. So, repentance precedes confession, and it follows belief. This is the plan that God has for the alien sinner.

2. **Repentance Is For The Christian.** Also in Acts 8 we have the conversion of Simon. He, too, believed and was immersed (v. 13). He "continued" with Philip, beholding the miracles and was amazed. Later, when Peter and John came to Samaria, laid hands on the Samaritans,

and imparted the Holy Spirit, Simon wanted to purchase that power (vss. 18-19). To him Peter said, "Repent therefore of this thy wickedness..." (v. 22). The word "sin" is not herein used, but rather the word "wickedness" (Greek, *kakia*). In 1 John 1:9 we read, "If we confess our sins, he is faithful and righteous to forgive us our sins, and to cleanse us from all unrighteousness." Therefore, we now have the "order" for the child of God: it is repentance, confession, and prayer. Whereas the alien sinner repents of his sins and confesses Christ, the child of God repents of and confesses his sins before our God.

3. **Motives Bringing Repentance.** When I wrote and published the tract previously mentioned, one question centered around "divine motives" producing repentance. After listing two thoughts about God, I then delineated eight motives that might be used to bring men to repentance. However, here I merely want to list the motives of fear (Acts 17:30-31; Rom. 14:10-12; 2 Cor. 5:10), the goodness of God (Rom. 2:4), and the hope of reward (cf. Acts 2:38; Titus 1:2). Such motives can cause men to make a change in their lives.

THE CHARLATANS OF REPENTANCE

A charlatan is a deceiver, a beguiler, an imposter, an allurer, a fraud, a cheat, a swindler, a confidence man, trickster, a chiseler, along with other terms that I could give. Believe me, when it comes to the subject of "repentance," I fear that their number is legion. If time and space permitted, I would like to show how repentance relates to idolatry (Acts 17:23-24), murder (Acts 2:23), impurity (Rom. 1:18-28), immorality (1 Cor. 6:9-11), serving God with zeal, but not with knowledge (Rom. 10:1-3), and such like. The fact is that all men everywhere are commanded by God to repent (Acts 17:30). This includes any sin, each sin, every sin, and all sin. However, some have the idea (and by their smooth and fair speech they have beguiled and won converts), that when it comes to marriage, divorce, and remarriage, divorce, and remarriage repentance does not apply. How can repentance, involving restitution, refer to the liar, the fornicator, the drunkard, the thief, the murderer, and others, but not to marriage and divorce?

In the book entitled "*Divorce*" that I wrote in 1987, chapter 13 is entitled "Divorce and Repentance," and I would encourage it to be read (certainly not because I wrote it). Also, chapters 6 and 7 deal with what brethren "did teach" and what some "now teach." Let me go on record in saying that it is a "damnable heresy" (note, if you will, the use of these words in 2 Peter 2:1) to teach that repentance is simply saying, "I'm sorry" and "I won't do it again," and then continuing to live in sin. If you believe this is not taught, then I challenge you to read *The Connally-Hicks Debate* of 1979. You will not have to read the entire 368 pages; just read pages 16-18 of Olan Hicks' first affirmative (Connally's reply on pages 38-41) and the questions asked of brother Hicks on pages 366-368 (this is just one of many of our men who could be quoted on this).

I want to emphasize that some are teaching that if one does sin repeatedly, all he has to do is to say repeatedly, "I am sorry, and I won't do it again." Who can believe it, except those in their desire to "cover the sin" of someone? When you become a member of Christ's body, you stop lying, stealing, fornicating, drinking, and so forth, but when it comes to marriage, divorce, and remarriage you do not have to cease your sin. No indeed! All you have to do is just say, "I'm sorry and I won't do it again." However, if you do it again, say it again, then you're free to do it again. Again I ask, "Who can believe it?"

This is not all that is taught on this subject. How about a preacher, a marriage counselor, who will look you right in the eye and tell you that "I do not know what 1 Corinthians 7 teaches," but he advises, "Once you leave your companion, never go back." Someone like this needs to understand what "reconciliation" means in 1 Corinthians 7:11, know the Greek word *katallageto* (from *katallasso*), the tense of the verb, the voice, etc., and see if it does not mean that "the door must ever be open to reconciliation" and that "the very one who deserts is the one who is to make the move for the reconciliation." If this verb is middle, then that is exactly what it means (it may be passive). One thing for sure this is a first aorist, 3rd person singular, imperative word! The very **least** that this passage teaches is **that there is a choice**! To say **never return**, is an outright denial of the Word of God. The very tense of the verb tells that reconciliation is possible. If the situation is seemingly impossible, one will keep himself to where it can become possible. No one has the freedom, that is, the instruction from the Almighty God to so conceal himself and to make reconciliation an impossibility. How can any one teach anything but that the deserter is guilty? How can any one teach less than complete reconciliation and be in harmony with the meaning of this word? How can any person teach, "If you are not happy, leave, as the Bible says that would be an 'unreasonable service,' and we know that with God it would be and is a 'reasonable service'"(this is based on Rom. 12:1). Yes, how can any person teach, "If you leave, never return"? Talk about batting 1000% in counseling, losing every session, THIS IS IT!

Brethren, do not ask a man if he "believes in repentance," but ask him, "what do you mean by repentance?" We need to understand that THERE CAN BE NO FORGIVENESS WHERE THERE IS NO

REPENTANCE (Luke 17:3-4), and we need to know what repentance involves! For a man to be saved, he must repent, since there can be no forgiveness without it (Acts 17:30; Luke 13:3,5; 1 John 2:3-5; Rev. 21:27; 1 John 3:4; etc.). Cannot we understand that God is not going to forgive a person, any person, who will not repent? Regardless of what is said by some, we know that one can "live in sin" (cf. Col. 3:5-9). Yes, there is not only the "act" of sin, but the "state" of sin.

I have said many times that God promises forgiveness to those who repent, but God does not promise a tomorrow to those who procrastinate (cf. Prov. 27:1; 2 Cor. 6:2; Heb. 3:7; 4:7; James 4:13ff). If there is no repentance, there can be no pardon.

Repentance is *the key* to the broken homes of today, as well as the solution to so many of the problems connected with theories on marriage, divorce and remarriage. However, above all that I might say, it is *the key* to being able to hear the "well done..." and the "enter in...."

Remember, the church in Ephesus did not need a larger missionary program, the churches in Pergamum and Thyatira an extended benevolence work, the church in Sardis a bigger budget, or the church in Laodicea to become more socially involved and "meet the needs of the members." What they each needed to do, said the Lord, was to repent. REPENT OR PERISH was the message for FIVE OUT OF THE SEVEN churches of Asia, and it very well could be the message that the churches of Christ need to hear today.

Chapter Fourteen

THE PATTERN - AND THE BAPTISM OF JESUS

THE PATTERN - AND THE BAPTISM OF JESUS

In the chapter in this book, while discussing the Greek word *tupos*, the regular word for "example" (given also as "pattern," "ensample," etc.), I referred to this passage from the pen of Peter: "For hereunto were ye called: because Christ also suffered for you, leaving you an example, that ye should follow his steps" (1 Pet. 2:21). I made mention that this was not "the regular word *tupos*," example, but the Greek word *hupogrammos*.

Since I am now devoting a short, but a complete chapter, to the baptism of Jesus, it is imperative, to me, that we restate and rehearse the meaning of this Greek term. However, we do not intend to do it as thoroughly as we did before, but enough to help us to see that Jesus did leave for us an "example," a "pattern," and that we are to "follow his steps."

1. **Thayer** spoke of this word as "an example set before one" and he listed 1 Peter 2:21 (p. 642).

2. **Arndt and Gingrich** gave it as a "model, a pattern... Mostly of Christ, 1 Pe. 2:21" (p. 851).

3. **Bullinger** listed it as "a writing-copy, hence, a pattern, etc., for imitation" (p. 265).

4. **Vine** gave the word as coming "from *hupo*, under, *grapho*, to write under, to trace letters for copying... a writing-copy, an example, I Pet. 2:21,... what Christ left for believers..." (pp. 240, 54).

5. **Kittel and Friedrich** stated: "... There is little doubt that what is in the mind is a model or example..."

(Vol. 1, p. 772).

6. **Roy C. Deaver,** "the Lord is our underwriting" (Vol. XV, 1981, pp. 1-2).

The baptism of Jesus is mentioned by Matthew (3:13-17), by Mark (1:9-11), and by Luke (3:21-22). As our perfect example, Jesus left for us "steps to follow," to imitate, to pattern after, and, I personally believe that Jesus did this in his character, in his teaching, yea, in his entire life. He is our model, as we are all aware of and recognize, in resisting temptation, speaking and manifesting the truth, his display of love for all mankind, his submission to the will of our heavenly Father, his suffering and in teaching us about "how" to die, etc. Therefore, I take it that he is also our model, our pattern, our example in his baptism.

Although we have three accounts of his baptism, for this particular material we now give Matthew's account.

> *"Then cometh Jesus from Galilee to the Jordan unto John, to be baptized of him. But John would have hindered him, saying, I have need to be baptized of thee, and comest thou to me? But Jesus answering said unto him, Suffer it (or "me") now: for thus it becometh us to fulfil all righteousness. Then he suffered him. And Jesus, when he was baptized, went up straightway from the water: and lo, the heavens were opened unto him, and he saw the Spirit of God descending as a dove, and coming upon him; and lo, a voice out of the heavens, saying, This is my beloved Son, in whom I am well pleased" (3:13-17).*

Before an actual study of these verses, I want to inaugurate, set in motion and take the first step toward our lesson by interjecting some background material that I feel is imperative and which subject matter will cover for us the first verse listed, verse thirteen. So, we now observe the following thoughts.

1. **Before Satan tempted Christ** (the temptation is found in chapter four, verses one through eleven), He was baptized. The onslaught of the devil on the Son of God did not commence until after God had said, "This is my beloved Son, in whom I am well pleased." There is, even in this, a lesson, as when one sets such a high and lofty goal before him, that of being baptized and becoming a son of God, it is then the devil truly begins his arsenal of darts flying.

2. **In the matter of Jesus' coming to John**, we need to be keenly aware that he came for the express purpose of being baptized. The text reads: "Then cometh Jesus from Galilee to the Jordan unto John, *to be baptized* of him" (vs. 13, emp. GM). There is a powerful thought in the Greek word from which comes "to be baptized." I say this as *baptisthenai*, from *baptizo*, is a 1st aorist passive infinitive. This most distinctly and definitely shows "the purpose" for the coming of Jesus to John.

3. **The place from whence Jesus came** is also important for a very special reason. Our text reads: "Then cometh Jesus *from Galilee to the Jordan*..." The text in Mark says, "And it came to pass in those days, that Jesus came from Nazareth of Galilee, and was baptized of John in the Jordan" (1:9). In the gospel according to John, we read: "These things were done in Bethany beyond the Jordan, where John was baptizing. On the morrow he seeth Jesus coming to him, and saith, Behold the Lamb of God, that taketh away the sin of the world!...And John...I have beheld the Spirit descending as a dove out of heaven;...and I have seen, and have borne witness that

this is the Son of God" (1:28-29, 32, 34). Jesus came from Nazareth and this is almost surely Bethany. If so, then we have Jesus covering a vast distance. In fact, tradition has the distance as some 70-80 miles. J. W. McGarvey seems to think it was a distance of some 15-20 miles (*The Fourfold Gospel*, pp. 82, 105).

The point I desire us to meditate on is "that distance" that the Son of God traveled "to be baptized." If tradition is right, then he spent some 14-16 hours in getting to John "to be baptized." If what McGarvey said is accurate, then he journeyed some 4-5 hours to come to John "to be baptized." Yea, today many people, who say that Jesus is their "example," will not even walk the aisle of a church building, where there is nice warm water in a good prepared baptistry, in order "to be baptized."

4. **Why did Jesus come to John**, that is, what was the motivating force, the power that was behind him and enabling him to do such. We are not told, but one thing is certain and that is he did not come because John besought him to come. Remember, the text states that John would have "hindered" him. All things indicate that Jesus came because God told him to come. This shows that the baptism of John was:

a. *From heaven* (Matt. 21:23-27).

b. *According to God's Word* (Luke 3:1-4).

c. *Designed to manifest Jesus to Israel* (John 1:29-34), as it was at His baptism that He was first made known to Israel as God's Son.

d. *A part of preparing Christ's way* (Luke 3:1-6).

JOHN WOULD HAVE HINDERED CHRIST FROM BEING BAPTIZED

There was a hindrance, a stumbling block, an obstacle placed in Christ's way to keep him from being baptized. It is found in the words, "John would have hindered him" (vs. 14). The word here is *diekoluen*, from the root *koluo*, which means "to hinder, forbid, to restrain." However, the word in our text is a strengthened form. It means "to hinder thoroughly,... of John the Baptist's endeavour to hinder Christ from being baptized" (Vine, p. 221). Had Christ been proud, had he been haughty, had he wished to have asserted Himself over John, He would not have been baptized.

1. **Jesus was sinless**, yet He had to be baptized to fulfill all righteousness. No matter how good a person is, he has to be baptized to please God. Few there are who have the seven qualities I find recorded about this man Cornelius (Acts 10:1-2, 22), however, he, too, had "to be baptized." In fact, the text says, speaking of Peter, "And he commanded them to be baptized in the name of Jesus Christ" (Acts 10:48). How strange "a command" for a non-essential!

Another man who also was told "to be baptized" was the man Saul of Tarsus. Again, few men could equal such a man: "...as touching the law, a Pharisee; as touching zeal, persecuting the church: as touching the righteousness which is in the law, found blameless" (Phil. 3:1-7, esp. vss. 5-6; cf. Gal. 1:13-14). But once again, we find a man who had "to be baptized." In answer to his question to the Lord, "What shall I do, Lord?" he was told, "Arise, and go into Damascus; and there it shall be told thee of all things which are appointed for thee to do" (Acts 22:10; 9:6 says, "...what thou must do"). The answer was plain: "And now why tarriest thou? arise, and be baptized, and wash away thy sins, calling on his name" (Acts 22:16; cf. 9:18).

2. **No man**, and it does not matter from where he gets his message, as even the message of John the Baptist was from God (Luke 3:1-4; John 1:32-34), has the right, the authority or the power to forbid a person from being baptized (provided, of course, that one has repented). Note, if you will, the word "hindered" in Matthew 3:14, the word "forbid" in Acts 10:47, and the word "hinder" in the case of the Ethiopian eunuch in Acts 8:36. I often wonder what it is and why it is that so many people today are "hindered" from being baptized "into" Christ (cf. Rom. 6:3-4; Gal. 3:27).

JESUS ANSWERED JOHN, "SUFFER ME NOW"

The New Testament has always emphasized, accented and accentuated, the importance, the gravity and graveness of this matter of baptism, by its always having been done immediately. Just a few examples will prove this beyond any shadow of a doubt for anyone to examine.

1. **The Pentecostian Jews** were told by Peter to "Repent ye, and be baptized every one of you in the name of Jesus Christ unto the remission of your sins;..." and the text says, "They then that received his word were baptized: and there were added unto them *in that day* about three thousand souls" (Acts 2:38, 41).

2. **The Ethiopian Eunuch** said, "Behold, here is water; what doth hinder me to be baptized?...*And he commanded the chariot to stand still: and* they both went down into the water,...and he baptized him" (Acts 8:36, 38).

3. **Saul of Tarsus**, was asked by Ananias, "And *now why tarriest thou?* arise, and be baptized, and wash away thy sins, calling on his name" (Acts 22:16).

4. **The Philippian Jailor**, of Acts 16:29-34, was taken "*the same hour of the night*,...and was baptized, he and all his, *immediately*."

It is not amazing to me that Jesus told John, "Suffer me '*now*.'" No man is ever to put off such an important step, yea, the final one that puts a man into Christ (cf. Gal. 3:27; Rom. 6:3-4). This is why, in the Bible, it is so emphasized. In the above examples, only listing four, we are told of people being baptized in "that day," "commanding a chariot to stand still...," "asking *now* why do you tarry," and the jailor being baptized "the same hour... immediately" and this was an hour "about midnight!" (Acts 16:25-34). May I remind each reader that the little three letter word "now" is an adverb and means, "at the present time, in and under the present circumstances, at the present moment, at this time, right now, just now, at once, straightway, without delay, etc." As far as I know, every example we know about in the Bible, followed the example of the Christ, having been baptized "now." What is it today that makes the preachers of our time "put off" until next week, until warmer weather, until all the family can come home, until the close of our evangelistic series, etc., for one "to be baptized"? If this is not a direct violation of 2 Corinthians 6:2, "...behold, *now is the* acceptable *time*; behold, *now is the day* of salvation," then I am not aware of what a transgression is (Greek, *arti*, now, is in verse 15!).

AT HIS BAPTISM, JESUS FULFILLED ALL RIGHTEOUSNESS

Once again, in our text (vs. 15), Jesus said, "for thus it becometh us to fulfil all righteousness." Have you ever spent any time deliberating, considering and concentrating, what all it was that Jesus came to fulfill? Note these:

1. *The scriptures* as seen from Luke 24:44-47.

2. *The law and the prophets* as viewed from Matthew 5:17-20.

3. *His decease* as determined from Luke 9:28-31.

4. *All righteousness* as seen here in Matthew 3:15.

I need also to point us to the reason why Jesus here "fulfilled" all righteousness. Here it is outlined in a nutshell, a capsule.

1. *John the Baptist was sent by God* (John 1:6, 32-34).

2. *John's preaching was from God* (Luke 3:1-4).

3. *John's baptism was from God* (Matt. 21:23-27).

4. *Jesus came to do God's will* (John 4:34; 5:30; 6:38).

When I connect the above thoughts about John being sent by God, about his preaching being God-inspired, and that he preached a baptism from heaven, with the idea that Jesus came to do "the will of God," it is no wonder he was baptized. Jesus was *sinless*, yet he had to be baptized to "fulfill all righteousness." The commandments of the Lord are righteousness (cf. Psm. 119:170; are "truth," vs. 151), and Jesus came, as it was written, "In the roll of the book it is written of me, To do thy will, O God" (Heb. 10:7), therefore, when the Lord was baptized by John, he fulfilled all righteousness.

Jesus was *sinless*, but me, *I was a sinner and in sin*, but I, too, had to be baptized. In a sense, even though we know of the Master's sinlessness and our sin, we, too, are baptized for a similar reason, which is "doing the will of God," or "fulfilling his righteousness." Baptism is a command of God, and his commandments are righteousness (note Acts 10:33, 48; Psm. 119:172, respectively). If a man truly loves the Word, loves the Lord, he, too, will be baptized. "If ye know that he is righteous, ye know that every one also that doeth righteousness is begotten, born, of him" (1 John 2:29). We must be willing to "keep the commandments" (cf. John 14:15,21,23; 1 John 2:3-6; 5:1-3; Luke 8:17-21; 11:27-28; Matt. 7:21ff; Luke 6:46).

AT HIS BAPTISM, THE HEAVENS WERE OPENED

The heavens were opened (1) at the beginning of the ministry of Jesus (Matt. 3:16), and they were also opened at the close of His ministry (cf. Acts 1:9-11; Mark 16:9-20; Heb. 4:14-16; 9:23-24). In and after the same fashion, it may be equally said that the heavens are opened when we are baptized, for we are "united with Christ in baptism" (cf. Rom. 6:1-5; Col. 2:12; Gal. 3:26-27). It may also be said that the heavens will be opened to us again, that is, when we meet Christ at His second coming. If alive, that will certainly be when we close our ministry (cf. John 14:1-4; Acts 1:9-11; 1 Thess. 4:13-18; 2 Thess. 1:3-10). So, at the "opening" and the "closing" of our ministry, we see another thought. (Verse 16 is clear.)

AT HIS BAPTISM, THE HOLY SPIRIT DESCENDED UPON HIM

It is most interesting to observe thoughts about the Holy Spirit and of Christ, commencing with this verse, verse sixteen: "And Jesus, when he was baptized, went up straightway from the water: and lo, *the heavens were opened unto* him (the thought we just covered), and he saw *the Spirit of God descending* as a dove, and coming *upon him*." *Note:*

1. **The Spirit was on Christ fully,** as seen in John 3:34-35.

2. **The Spirit was with Christ in temptation**, as we read in Matthew 4:1-2.

3. **The Spirit was with Christ in His miracle working**, as noted in Matthew 12:22-32.

4. **The Spirit was with Christ in His preaching**, as observed in Luke 4:16-24 (cf. Isa. 61:1-3; perhaps also 11:1-5).

5. **The Spirit came on Christ at His baptism** (Matt. 3:16).

It is to be discerned that the teaching of the New Testament is that the Holy Spirit also comes when we are baptized (cf. Acts 2:38; 5:32; Gal. 4:6-7). Not only this, but the Holy Spirit is also with us through life (cf. 1 Cor. 3:16-17; 6:19-20; Eph. 1:13-14; 2 Cor. 1:21-22; 5:5).

In the case of Jesus in Matthew 3:16, we can surely note that it was "after his baptism" when the Holy Spirit descended upon him. I read, "And Jesus, when he was baptized, went up straightway from the water:...and...the Spirit of God descending as a dove, and coming upon him." A man would have to be the opposite of "wise," not to see "when" it was that the Holy Spirit came. So it is with us today. Why then do so many teach that they "receive" (get) the Spirit "before" baptism?

AT HIS BAPTISM, A VOICE CAME FROM HEAVEN

The next statement of our text is: "And lo, a voice out of the heaven,..." (vs. 17). Here again it is most enlightening to see the times when "a voice came from heaven to Jesus while He was upon earthly shores." Therefore, we note:

1. **At His birth**, as made known to us in Luke 2:10-12.

2. **At His baptism**, as already noticed in verse seventeen.

3. **At His transfiguration**, as related to us in Matthew 17:1-5.

4. **During the last days of His ministry**, as revealed in John 12:28.

One of the many things wrong with our world today is that people are not "hearing the voice of God." God speaks to us today "through his Word," as we are told "whereunto he called you through our gospel, to the obtaining of the glory of our Lord Jesus Christ" (2 Thess. 2:14). Faith comes "by hearing the Word" (Rom. 10:17; John 6:44-45). Every one who becomes a child of God does so because he has "heard" and "hearkened" unto God's calling (cf. Matt. 7:21-23; Luke 6:46; John 6:45; Rom. 10:13-17; etc.). We, today, have a choice to make, we can either "heed" the voice of God as He calls us by the Word, or we can "dismiss" such a calling (cf. Luke 8:18; Mark 4:24; Heb. 2:1-4).

This is not the only time we will "hear" the voice of God. All of us need to be reminded of the following:

1. **If we are alive**, at his second coming, we will hear his voice as the Bible says, "For the Lord himself shall descend from heaven, with a shout, with the voice of the archangel, and with the trump of God:..." (1 Thess. 4:16).

2. **If we are dead**, and in the grave, we will still hear him when the call is given. "Marvel not at this: for the hour cometh, in which all that are in the tombs shall hear his voice, and shall come forth;..." (John 5:28-29).

3. **When we stand before God in the judgment**, we will, yet once again hear his voice. "Then shall the King say...Come,...And the King shall answer and say unto

them,... Then shall he say also unto them on the left hand, Depart from me,... then shall they also answer, saying, Lord,... Then shall he answer them..." (Matt. 25:34, 40, 41, 44-45). What a conversation! This will be the last time that any of us, according to the Word, will ever hear "the voice," therefore, we had best "heed it today." We have a choice today as to what we will do "with the voice of God," but when God speaks to us at the judgment, **not a single one of us will have a choice, even though we may argue with the King** (cf. Matt. 7:22; Luke 13:25-27).

AT HIS BAPTISM, GOD FIRST CALLED JESUS HIS SON

It is also in verse seventeen that we read, "...saying, This is my beloved Son,..." It is imperative that we realize we become sons of God when we are baptized "into" Christ (cf. Rom. 6:3-4; Gal. 3:26-27). I want us to be aware of the following, although I feel that I cannot take the space to write out all of the verses. The Bible speaks about us being:

1. **Born of God**, as in John 1:11-13.

2. **Born from above**, in John 3:3.

3. **Born of water and of the Spirit**, John 3:5.

    a. Note these verses on the Spirit and the Word (Eph. 6:17; 1 Pet. 1:22-25; 1 Cor. 4:14-15; James 1:18).

    b. Study these verses on baptism, "washing of water" (Eph. 5:25-27; Titus 3:4-7; Heb. 10:22; Acts 22:16).

4. **Now the sons of God**, as witnessed by the statement of the beloved John (1 John 3:1-3).

As far as I know, this is the first time on public record that God called Jesus his Son. It is in John 1:28-34, when John was in Bethany beyond the Jordan that Jesus came to him and this is when John called him "the Lamb of God" (1:29). John witnessed to those present that this was the one of whom he had spoken (vss. 30-31). He also spoke about seeing "the Holy Spirit descending as a dove" upon Jesus (vss. 32-33), and then made the statement: "And I have seen, and have borne witness that this is the Son of God" (vs. 34).

I stand staggered that people can read this and know that it was "after his baptism" that God called Jesus, "my beloved Son." Yet, I am aware that many today are taught, and they believe it, that they can become "a son of God" before being born again, born of water and of the Spirit, born from above, yea, being baptized "into" Christ.

AT HIS BAPTISM, GOD FIRST SAID, "IN WHOM I AM WELL PLEASED"

God showed His pleasure at Christ's baptism, as the record states so beautifully: "And lo, a voice out of the heavens, saying, This is my beloved Son, in whom I am well pleased" (vs. 17). On one occasion Jesus said, "And he that sent me is with me; he hath not left me alone; for I do always the things that are pleasing to him" (John 8:29).

One of the best questions that we can ask ourselves is, "Do I do that which is pleasing unto God?" "Will this please God?" It could be that some should ask, "When is God pleased with me?" To this, we answer by noting a few of the ways that the Bible says we please the God of heaven.

1. **When we believe** (Heb. 11:5-6).

2. **When we are baptized** (Mark 1:9-11; Luke 3:21-22).

3. **When we are steadfast** (Heb. 10:36-39; 1 Cor. 10:1-5).

4. **When we live the life** (Rom. 12:1-2; 14:16-19; Gal. 5:25; Heb. 13:16; 1 John 5:11-12).

5. **When we give as we should** (Phil. 4:15-18; 1 Cor. 16:1-3; 2 Cor. 8:1ff; 9:6-8).

6. **When children obey their parents** (Col. 3:20-21).

7. **When we do His will** (Heb. 13:20-21).

The very top priority of our lives should be to seek to please the Almighty, our heavenly Father. How sad it will be someday to hear him say, "depart from me..." and all because we failed the very God of heaven by being displeasing unto Him.

AT HIS BAPTISM, JESUS WAS PRAYING

We turn now and note the record of Jesus' baptism as penned by Luke: "Now it came to pass, when all the people were baptized, that, Jesus also having been baptized, and *praying*, the heaven was opened, and the Holy Spirit...and a voice came...Thou art by beloved Son; in whom I am well pleased" (Luke 3:21-22, emp. GM).

The New Testament does record "prayer" at some of the various examples of baptism.

1. **Cornelius** (Acts 10:1-2, 22, 43-48).

2. **Saul** (Acts 9:10-12).

3. **Pentecostian Jews** (Acts 2:36-42).

4. **Lydia** (Acts 16:13-15).

It makes me wonder if we should not stop more often than we do and "take time" to pray with those who are about to be or who have just been baptized. This is, perhaps, the most important decision one will ever make and, it seems to me, we need to ask heaven for its blessings on us.

AT HIS BAPTISM, THE GODHEAD WAS MANIFESTED

As we look back, beginning with verse sixteen, we can note the Lord Jesus was "being baptized," the Holy Spirit was "descending as a dove, and coming upon him," and then there is the Father, who, in verse seventeen, "...saying, This is my beloved Son, in whom I am well pleased." And so it will be at our baptism, for the Lord Himself said: "All authority hath been given unto me in heaven and on earth. Go ye therefore, and make disciples of all the nations, baptizing them into the name of the Father and of the Son and of the Holy Spirit: teaching them to observe all things whatsoever I have commanded you: and lo, I am with you always, even unto the end of the world" (Matt. 28:19-20).

I have not tried in this study to cover all the many passages in the New Testament on the subject of baptism, as that was not my intent and purpose. In keeping with the caption of this book. BEHOLD THE PATTERN, I felt we needed to look "at the pattern" in reference to "The Baptism Of Jesus." Indeed, there is much to cover in it, and I do not want anyone to even think that I covered all of the points that I could have. *For example:*

1. The use of the plural "us" in verse fifteen is most important to us and to our baptism being handled correctly (Greek, *hemin*).

2. The word in verse sixteen is *baptistheis*, from *baptizo*, the Greek word for immersion. When someone sees the often-photoed picture of Jesus being sprinkled, this word should settle that quibble once and for all as it is "specific." The word for sprinkle is the Greek *rantizo* and

the word for pour is the Greek *cheo*. Each of the three words is specific and must be rendered by specific meanings.

*. Should any one desire to delve into the subject of baptism in the New Testament, then he will find *baptizo* (to immerse, baptize), listed 80 times, *baptisma* (baptism, immersion), listed 22 times and *baptismos* (baptisms) listed in Hebrews 6:2, with John being called "the Baptist" (Greek, *baptistes*), 14 times. It is, indeed, a subject found in many passages in the New Testament and one that needs to be seriously and most thoroughly covered.

I trust you will investigate, consider and contemplate, the four things that happened when Christ was baptized (immersed). Ask yourself if these items happened BEFORE or AFTER Christ was baptized:

1. When were the heavens opened?

2. When did the Holy Spirit descend on Jesus?

3. When did God speak and call Jesus His Son?

4. When did God say, "In whom I am well pleased"?

If there is not "a pattern" for us in the baptism of Jesus, then I very seriously doubt that one can be found within the pages of our New Testaments.

Chapter Fifteen

THE PATTERN - AND IT SPEAKS OF GRACE AND LAW

THE PATTERN - AND IT SPEAKS OF GRACE AND LAW

It should not be a surprise to anyone to hear the statement that we are saved by grace, and that by the grace of God we are what we are. Neither should it astonish anyone to hear that we have the gospel as the power of God to save the soul and that it must be obeyed from the heart, as man is not without law to which he must be obedient (cf. Eph. 2:8-10; 1 Cor. 15:1-10; Rom. 1:16; 1 Cor. 1:18,21; Heb. 5:8-9; Rom. 1:5; 16:26; 4:15; 1 Cor. 9:21). However, it is the idea that grace and law are mutually-exclusive, the gospel is not law and we are not under law today that is stunning and hits like a ton of bricks to the serious student of the Bible. Therefore, as we have the New Testament as our pattern, our guideline and rule, we turn to it for our education, our training and teaching, our indoctrination and instruction. We now study the grace of God and watch how inspiration teaches it in relation to God's law.

THE MEANING OF IT

The Greek word for "grace" is *charis*, and, according to Mr. J. B. Smith's *Greek-English Concordance,* it is used 156 times in the New Testament (*A Tabular and Statistical Greek-English Concordance Based on the King James Version With an English-to-Greek Index*, p. 372, #5385). Out of that number, it is translated as "grace" about 130 times. It is also translated as "favour" (6), "thanks" (4), "thank" (4), "thank you" (3), "pleasure" (2) and there are some seven miscellaneous uses. Paul, alone, used the word 102 times out of the 156 times it is employed and out of those 102 times it is given as "grace" 91 times. (This does not include the 8 times it is found in Hebrews, all of which are translated "grace".)

We find that "grace" has various uses. Both the first (Luke 1:30) and also the third (Luke 2:52) time it is found, it is translated as "favor." It is given as "grace" in Luke 2:40 and means "favor." In 1 Corinthians 16:3 it is "bounty" (*ASV*) and "liberality" (*K.J.*). Also, in reference to the contribution for the poor at Jerusalem, we find it listed as "grace" twice (2 Cor. 8:1, 4, the word "gift" is found in vs. 4 of the *K.J.*). In 2 Corinthians 9:15 we have it listed as "thanks." In the *ASV* we find it also listed as "joy" in Philemon 7, "acceptable" in 1 Peter 2:20, and as "words of grace" in Luke 4:22. So, it has a manifold use.

One of the most frequently used definitions is "unmerited favor." Of course, it is the "favor" that God bestows upon man, desirous of his salvation. While looking at this word in Thayer, I find another definition that is a great way also to explain this magnificent and marvelous term. While speaking of that which affords such things as joy, sweetness, charm, loveliness, delight, etc., I find this statement: "Moreover, the word *charis* contains the idea of kindness which bestows upon one what he has not deserved: Ro. 11:6;...the N.T. writers use *charis* pre-eminently of that kindness by which God bestows favors even upon the ill-deserving, and grants to sinners the pardon of their offences..." (*Greek-English Lexicon of the New Testament*, pp. 665-666).

The point that I want to emphasize here is something that is "needed," but not "deserved." This can easily be seen in the story of the prodigal son and the Samaritan woman. I see it in the direct statements of Jesus as revealed in Matthew 5:38-44, as well as in his actions in John 8:1-11, Luke 19:1-10, 7:36-50, 23:34. Indeed, the world *did not deserve* a Saviour to come out of the ivory palaces, *but it needed one*. This ought to be the dominating principle of our lives. It is to Him alone (only) that we do return what HE DESERVES, but He gives us what we need (cf. Titus 3:3-5).

THE MATRIX OF IT

God is the genesis and origin of divine grace (cf. James 1:17; 1 John 4:7; John 3:16; Rom. 5:8; 8:35-39). He is the author, that is, the Father of the second mile religion and this is easily seen in the case of Adam and Eve. Grace gave them the place and position they had, but it was the breaking of the divine prohibition, as seen in Romans 5:12, that caused sin to enter into our world. We can clearly and most explicitly state that the love of God, in spite of man's sin, then worked out a plan for man to be redeemed. This motion, scheme, was because of the magnanimity of God, as God was not obligated to do what he did.

Man has, since the time of Adam and Eve, found himself in the world of sin and of death. Accountable man who violated the great and good will of God sins (1 John 3:4), and so it is that we "all have sinned, and fall short of the glory of God" (Rom. 3:23). Man need not deny his sin, therefore, his need for God's divine grace (1 John 1:8-10). Thank God he has extended that grace to man!

THE MEANS AND MEDIUM OF IT

Perhaps the clearest statement that can be found relative to the method, the happy medium of grace, is: "For the law was given through Moses; grace and truth came through Jesus Christ" (John 1:17). This is verified in so many places, but none as pure and perfect, defined and distinct as that of 2 Corinthians 8:9 and Romans 5:15.

It is not only "through" Christ that we have God's divine grace but it is also "in" Christ where we must be to receive it (cf. 2 Tim. 2:1), as that is where God has placed it. It is very faultless to say that "redemption is in Christ" (cf. Rom. 3:21-24), yea, it is unremarkable. Paul is even more explicit when he writes:

> *"For the grace of God hath appeared, bringing salvation to all men, instructing us, to the intent that, denying ungodliness and worldly lusts, we should live soberly and righteously and godly in this present world; looking for the blessed hope and appearing of the glory of the great God and our Saviour Jesus Christ; who gave himself for us, that he might redeem us from all iniquity, and purify unto himself a people for his own possession, zealous of good works. These things speak and exhort and reprove with all authority. Let no man despise thee" (Titus 2:11-15; cf. Gal. 2:20-21; Acts 20:32; 1 Cor. 15:10).*

THE MAGNITUDE OF THE MESSAGE

1. **Salvation Is By Grace.** "For by grace have ye been saved through faith; and that not of yourselves, it is the gift of God" (Eph. 2:8). We are speaking about a gift, unearned and unmerited (cf. Luke 17:10). This is something that we do not pay for, as it is the love of God that has bestowed such. However, we need to realize the two elements found in this passage, both "grace" and "faith." God did for us that which we could not do for ourselves.

2. **Saving Grace Is Through Faith** (Eph. 2:8-10; Titus 2:11-12).

> a. *God's Side.* God owes us nothing. All that God did he did by grace, as that is the way God acted. All that God did in order for our salvation he did by grace. Grace is the divine side.

(1) Christ is the gift of God's grace (2 Cor. 8:9).

(2) His death was an act of God's grace (Heb. 2:9).

(3) The gospel is a matter of grace (Acts 20:20, 24).

(4) His teaching is a part of grace (Titus 2:11-12).

b. *Man's Side.* All should know, but evidently many do not or else do not show it, that whereas God acted by grace, man acts by faith. This certainly is not faith without action. It is not a dead faith (Eph. 2:8-10). God's grace is conditioned on man's part; both grace and faith are necessary to salvation. Whereas God purposed the scheme of redemption (Eph. 3:8-11), promised the Messiah (Gen. 3:15; 12:3; 49:10), developed the sacred plan by and through "the fathers," sent his Son (Gal. 4:4ff; Rom. 3:21-25; 4:18-25; John 3:16) and offered man every spiritual blessing in Christ (Eph. 1:3), it is man that must respond to God's grace. Man does this by an active, living, obedient faith. No man can be saved unless his faith is operative. This is the way that we appropriate God's grace, his divine blessings (Mark 16:15-16; John 8:21, 24; Rom. 4:16; 5:1-2; 10:10; Acts 2:38). Faith is not for God, it is for man. It is man that does the believing.

God provides "what" we are to hear, but man does the hearing. He gives the testimony of faith, but it is man that does the believing. God grants repentance, but it is man that must do the repenting. God sent his Son, Jesus, but man has to confess the Christ, etc. God performed what man could not do. It is grace that makes obedience valid. Man's faith must be an active working faith (cf. Gal. 5:6; Cor. 15:10). Be it clearly understood that faith is a "gift of God," but only in the sense that it was God who gave the provisions, the plan, the testimony, the Christ that produced faith. God's grace cannot flow to man unless man's faith is there to be saved.

3. **Saving Grace Is In Christ.** "Thou therefore, my child, be strengthened in the grace that is in Christ Jesus" (2 Tim. 2:1). In chapter two and verse ten Paul says that "salvation is in Christ." In Romans 3:24 we read, "being justified freely by his grace through the redemption that is in Christ Jesus." It is only "in his name" that man can be saved (Acts 4:12). God, by grace, has provided for us salvation, and that salvation is in Christ. Man, therefore, has to be immersed into Christ, he must be immersed into Christ (Gal. 3:27; Rom. 6:3-4), in order to receive the blessings promised by God. Man, by faith, is moved to take this step to get into Christ, where we are partakers of God's grace (Rom. 5:1-2). We are then "one" in Christ (Gal. 3:28; 1 Cor. 12:13). I repeat, and I know of no gospel preacher who believes we can (some talk like some do believe it), but man cannot pardon himself.

4. **Saving Grace Is Not By Grace Or Faith Alone.** I would not debate that a man is saved by faith. Neither would I debate that a man is saved by grace. But I would debate "when" is a man saved by grace and or faith. God provides, that is, he has made the provisions for man's salvation, but man is not saved by provisions alone. Man may have many things provided for him, such as food and water, but if he does not partake of such man will die. If I were to provide clothing for a man during a blizzard (or shelter), and he chose to refuse such, the end would be the same. God has provided, but man must obey (Phil. 2:12-13; Acts 10:34-35), must accept the plan.

The Bible abounds with example after example showing and proving what I have here been saying. There is always the blessing (grace), the instructions, man's faith and then his obedience. Such can be seen in the Old Testament example of Noah and the ark (Gen. 6:14-22; Heb. 11:7; cf. Num. 21:1-9; Josh. 6:1-21; 2 Kings 5:1-14). It is equally seen in the New Testament. In John chapter nine, because had that man not "gone," and "washed in the pool of Siloam" he would not have "come forth seeing" (vss. 1-7), we have the same thing. It is the case that the Bible does not contradict James 2:24, and regardless of what Martin Luther said on Romans 3:28, etc., as faith moves to do "according to all that he hath commanded." The Bible does not say "by faith without any further acts of obedience." Faith is not nullified by acts of obedience (cf. Josh. 6:1-21 and the things they were to do), and when one obeys what God has stated, commanded, required, that does not mean he has earned God's blessings. A gift may have "conditions" attached to it (cf. Josh. 6:2; and also the "after" in Heb. 11:30). The blessings accrue to man when his faith has obeyed. God did not just give "instructions" in the Old Testament, but also in the New (cf. Tit. 2:11-14 and observe both the negative and the positive instructions).

5. **Saving Grace Involves Works.** There are the "works that God has done" (already discussed), and then there are "works" for man to do. It must be evident, since the Bible does not contradict, that if the Bible says, and it does, "saved by works" (James 2:24-26) and also says "not by works" (Titus 3:3-5), that there are two kinds of works.

a. *Works Excluded.* These are those which would seemingly have ground for boasting (Eph. 2:9; Titus 3:5; Rom. 3:27-28). This involves human ideas, plans, schemes, and glory. There are also "works" of the law (Gal. 2:16; Rom. 3:20; Acts 13:39). Naturally, we find other such works in the

New Testament (cf. Gal. 5:19; 1 John 3:8).

b. *Works Included.*

(1) Let it be noted, and carefully so, that "faith is a work." "They said therefore unto him, What must we do, that we may work the works of God? Jesus answered and said unto them, This is the work of God, that ye believe on him whom he hath sent" (John 6:28-29). This is not the works that God did, but the works that God outlined for us to do. I recall the first time I heard one of our own preachers say that there is not a single work that one has to do. At that point, being the speaker and answering questions, I said, "If that is the case, then man does not have to believe, for faith is a work." I then quoted Thayer's statement about the Greek words *"ta erga tou theou"* found in John 6:28: "...the works required and approved by God" (p. 248). Of course, there are times when "whatever you say" does not matter. One thing for sure, "they were to do the believing," as no one could do it for them.

(2) There are works of the gospel, that is, works of faith (Gal. 5:6; James 2:14-26). The examples of Rahab and Jericho, as seen in James 2:25 and Hebrews 11:30-31, ought to be observed.

(3) There are works of obedience of faith (Heb. 11:6). In both Romans 1:5 and 16:26 we have the expression that the gospel was made known "unto obedience of faith among all the nations." Until faith obeys, it is dead. James likens it to "the body without the spirit being dead" (James 2:26). In the same way, "faith without works is

dead," and a "dead faith" is one that cannot save anyone! Indeed, faith must "act" (cf. Acts 2:38, 40; 10:34-35; 1 John 3:7; Phil. 2:12; 1 Cor. 15:58).

Some still cry man has nothing to do. However, even with those in Acts 11:13-14, they had "to hear" (cf. Rom. 10:17). People are not saved first and then obey the commandments (1 John 3:23; Acts 16:30-31; 17:30). If baptism is not necessary because it is a command, then neither is faith or repentance (cf. 1 Pet. 1:22; Rom. 6:17-18; Heb. 5:8-9; 2 Thess. 1:7-9). People today talk about "the eternal security of the believer," and I believe in it also, however, you must obey to get it and remain obedient to keep it! Some works are obligatory (Rom. 2:13; James 1:22). God will not do for man what man can do. God performed only that which man could not do. The commands of grace are obeyed by faith. Works perfect faith, otherwise it is dead.

6. **Saving Grace And Law Are Inseparable.**

a. According to Titus 2:11-14, which I have already given in full, "God's grace instructs us," that is, it "teaches us." It tells us "what to deny," "how to live," and "that for which we should look." It informs us what to "leave," how to "live," and that for which we should "look."

b. God's word is a law of grace. Paul spoke about the "ministry which I received from the Lord Jesus, to testify the gospel of the grace of God," and commended those Ephesians "to God, and to the word of his grace, which is able to build you up, and to give you the inheritance among all them that are sanctified" (Acts 20:24, 32; cf. James 2:12, "a law of liberty").

c. We need to emphasize that "law" is a means of appropriating God's "grace" (cf. Rom. 1:15; 16:26).

d. When we think of the church as a purified people, we have it called "a bride," when it is termed a spirit-filled people, it is called "a temple," and when it is seen as a united people, it is referred to as "a body." Equally true, when we think of the church as a "ruled" people, we have it called "a Kingdom" (cf. Gal. 6:11-16, observe the term "rule," Greek *kanon*). All should know that "a ruled people," a "kingdom," has a "king" and follows a "law" (cf. Judg. 17:6; 21:25; Acts 17:7; 1 Cor. 9:21). Now note the following:

(1) Perfect law (James 1:25).

(2) Law of liberty (James 2:12; 1:25).

(3) Law of the Spirit of life in Christ (Rom. 8:2).

(4) Law of faith (Rom. 3:27).

(5) Law of Christ (Gal. 6:2).

(6) Royal law (James 2:8).

(7) The law on my mind (Rom. 7:23; law of sin).

(8) Law of righteousness (Rom. 9:31).

We must be an *obedient* people (John 14:15, 21, 23; 15:10, 14; 1 John 2:3-6; 5:1-3; Luke 6:46; Matt. 7:21; Heb. 5:8-9; 1 Pet. 1:22; Rom. 6:17-18; Luke 8:19-21; 11:27-28), as we are citizens in the greatest kingdom this world has ever known or will know (cf. Dan. 2:31-45).

e. We also observe that the church is a "reborn"

people, and for this reason it is called a "house." *Note:*

(1) House of God (1 Tim. 1:3-4; 3:14-15).

(2) Church of the living God (1 Tim. 3:15).

(3) Church of the Lord (Acts 20:28).

(4) The Church (Rev. 2:1; cf. Acts 20:7).

It was to these Ephesians that Paul said, "For by grace have ye been saved through faith; and that not of yourselves, it is the gift of God" (Eph. 2:8). It absolutely must be observed, **that before he said this, they had**:

(1) Heard (Eph. 1:13).

(2) Believed (Eph. 1:13).

(3) Repented (Acts 20:20-21).

(4) Confessed (1 Tim. 6:20-21).

(5) Been baptized (Acts 19:1-7; Eph. 5:25-27).

(6) Remission of sins (Eph. 1:7).

(7) The Holy Spirit of promise (Eph. 1:13, cf. these last two items **imply baptism** (cf. Acts 2:38).

THE MISSTATEMENT, MISUSE AND MESS REGARDING IT

When I refer to this subject, meaning "all grace and no law," I call it a "misstatement," which word means "a garbled version." I have reason for such a term, as can be observed by the following:

1. Jesus is not a lawgiver; he is not a Moses.

2. The Gospel is not a law, does not involve law and

it excludes and dispenses with law.

3. Grace and works are mutually exclusive.

4. Grace and law are antagonistic to each other.

5. All will be saved and without any law.

6. There is not a single work to do.

7. We are under grace and not under any law.

When I employ the term "misuse," which word means "to use wrongly," I do so because of the following:

1. The wrong meaning is attached to God's grace.

2. There is much today that IS NOT being said.

3. Some preachers today are not giving "the whole counsel."

4. We have a "false hope" being created today by what is said.

5. In speaking of "all grace," it blasphemes John 12:48.

6. The teaching of many today makes the sinner "inactive."

7. Today there is the separation of "the plan" and "the man."

8. What is said today by some rules out any and all conditions to be met.

When I speak and or write of this subject and use the word "mess," meaning a "mingle-mangle," "confused mass," or pandemonium," I do so because of the following:

1. There is today much confusion on "works of obedience."

2. People are disarrayed by having "grace" versus "gospel."

3. We note disorder among us by having "love" versus "law."

4. Turmoil is caused when we pit "the positive" against "the negative."

5. Bewilderment is seen by many when we hear that it is "the Christ," and not "the Church."

6. It mystifies the mind to hear of "the man" but not "the plan."

My Conclusion Is Confusion, if what is stated by many today is true. Therefore, we observe:

1. *There is no sin* (Col. 2:14; Rom. 2:14-15; Gal. 4:21-31; Rom. 4:15; 5:13; 1 John 3:4; 1:8-10) and Jesus Christ died for nought (Eph. 1:7; Rom. 8:2).

2. *Grace is nullified,* for if there is no law, there is no sin, hence there is no need of grace (Rom. 5:20).

3. *God has to act arbitrarily* (Rom. 11:4-5). How so, if not any obedience?

4. *Universalism faces us* (Tit. 2:11-12; Matt. 7:21ff; 25:46; 2 Thess. 1:7-9), so there must be some law.

5. *If there is no norm or standard, then why cannot we do what we feel we are big enough to do* (cf. Judg. 17:6; 21:25).

6. *We have no need in the plan for remission of sins* (Acts 2:38; 8:22; James 5:16). The reason is again very simple, as if there is no law, there is no sin and there is no need for remission of sins.

7. *Faith must be* "crossed out" (John 6:28-29; Mark

16:16; Acts 16:30-31; 1 John 3:23).

8. *We are a people without a New Testament* (1 Cor. 9:21; James 2:12; 1:25; Heb. 8:13; etc.).

9. *Implied in this is the fact that we are living under no law at all.* This is the case if the gospel is not a law, for other laws have been taken away (Col. 2:14; Gal. 4:21-31; Rom. 2:14-15). This would be why no one was guilty of sin and why Christ died in vain.

10. *We are become antinomianism advocates.*

11. *Many scriptures are very hard and most difficult to understand and to explain if* grace dispenses with law, such as:

a. *James 2:12,* "law of liberty."

b. *1 Corinthians 9:21*, "under law to Christ" (just here it is wise to be sure and note the Greek on this thought).

c. *Romans 6:17-18*, "obeying a form of the doctrine;" *1:5* "obedience of faith;" and repeated in *16:26.*

d. *Galatians 5:19-21*, "who practise such things shall not inherit the kingdom of God," (and my question is "What is it that makes these items "sin"?)

e. *Isaiah 2:3*, "the law went forth from Zion, and the word of Jehovah from Jerusalem."

f. *Matthew 7:21, 24; Mark 3:35; Luke 8:19-21; 11:27-28, etc.* "What is there 'to do," seeing there is no law, no commandments, no mandates, no stipulations, etc.?" "Why isn't every one the mother and the brethren of the Lord?"

12. *If we are not under any law, then:*

a. There is no chance to apostatize.

b. There is no need for a heaven.

c. There is no need for a hell.

d. There certainly is no need for a judgment.

It seems fitting that this chapter should close with, "Beloved, believe not every spirit, but prove the spirits, whether they are of God; because many false prophets are gone out into the world" (1 John 4:1), and "And for this cause we also thank God without ceasing, that when ye received from us the word of the message, even the word of God, ye accepted it not as the word of men, but, as it is in truth, the word of God, which also worketh in you that believe" (1 Thess. 2:13).

Chapter Sixteen

THE PATTERN - AND THE PLACE OF WOMAN IN THE NEW TESTAMENT AGE

THE PATTERN - AND THE PLACE OF WOMAN IN THE NEW TESTAMENT AGE

The caption of this chapter is, indeed, worthy of every consideration that we can give it. *It admits* that woman has a purpose, a position and a profession in the very first two words. In this we understand that she has a role, rank and a responsibility, as these things are inherent in "the place of woman." *It acknowledges* the biological difference in the sexes and it takes our minds back to the statement, "It is not good that the man should be alone; I will make him a help meet for him... and Jehovah God... made he a woman, and brought her unto the man... And the man said,... she shall be called Woman..." (Gen. 2:18, 21-23). *It accepts, abides by, and addresses*, with great appreciation the New Testament, as in deep contrast to any other Testament, rule, authority, or standard that anyone has concocted, contrived, composed or conjured up. *It avows and asserts* the affirmation that so many have denied, disclaimed, and disapproved of, that being the connection of God's New Testament with "the age" in which we now live. All of this, which could easily fill numerous pages, is wrapped up in the nine words of our topic.

First and foremost in this article will be that teaching of the New Testament relative to the place of women. However, I feel it necessary to show the need of such by observing some quotes from various sources and groups, both without and within the New Testament Church. These will serve to let us see: (1) Is woman in her place? (2) Is woman out of her place, that is, out of bounds, out of order and out-of-step? (3) Is woman trying to occupy the man's place? (4) Is woman aware of what is taking place regarding many teachings relative to her place? (5) Is woman in tune today with the exalted place and honor given to her by God, our Heavenly Father? Of course, many other "insights" will be recognized, we trust, hope and pray, by those who read what we have written.

THE FEMINISTS ARE SPEAKING

These ladies (?) have not only spoken in the past several years, but they are "forever" speaking and writing about "the place" of the woman. Therefore, please be aware of some of the things they have said and are saying.

> *"We must destroy love...Love promotes vulnerability, dependence, possessiveness, susceptibility to pain, and prevents the full development of woman's human potential by directing all her energies outward in the interest of others."*

> *"No deity will save us, we must save ourselves. Promises of immortal salvation or fear of eternal damnation are both illusory and harmful."*

> *"Marriage has existed for the benefit of men and has been a legally sanctioned method of control over women...the end of the institution of marriage is a necessary condition for the liberation of women. Therefore, it is important for us to encourage women to leave their husbands and not to live individually with men...we must work to destroy it (marriage)."*

> *"As for divorce, Dr. Bane said she sees it as a 'safety valve' for families. 'It makes for better family life,' she said. 'There's no merit in*

holding families together just for the sake of it. For this reason, divorce improves the quality of marriages.'"

"What happens to children... We really don't know how to raise children. If we want to talk about equality of opportunity for children, then the fact that children are raised in families means there's no equality."

"By the year 2000 we will, I hope, raise our children to believe in human potential, not God..."

"For the sake of those who wish to live in equal partnership, we have to abolish and reform the institution of legal marriage."

"Miss Ti-Grace Atkinson... 'seeks to eliminate sex, marriage, motherhood, and love, claiming that marriage is legalized servitude. That male-female relationship is the basis for all human oppression."

Any thinking person needs to truly examine the goals that are to be found in this movement that is so anti-family and anti-God. It is humanistic to the core and is set on restructuring all existing institutions, and this includes all of them (the home, the church, the government, etc.). They have even sought to change our language by degenderizing it. Therefore, we were not surprised in 1982 when we had a "new version" (?) of the Bible by some ultra-liberals and that God is "Mother" and "Father" of mankind. I beg each reader to be awake to their cries of "lack of identity," "do your own thing," "an anonymous biological robot in a docile mass," "slow death of mind and spirit," "you owe it to yourself," "living at a lower human level," etc., etc., then he will, to some degree, be aware of what they are saying, teaching, speaking, writing and advocating.

THE NEWS AGENCIES ARE SPEAKING

I seriously doubt that anyone can measure the full outreach that is given by the forces at work in the world which are designed for the sole purpose of destroying the Biblical concept of the institutions that I named in the above paragraph. They are set at changing the standard concept of society and this has spread throughout the world. This rapid spread of their message has been caused, to a very great degree, by the support given to these ungodly and anti-Bible views by television, radio, magazines, books, seminars, lecturers in key places, newspapers, politicians, talk shows, etc., etc.

In a period of one week, I either read, heard or observed the following this past month of November.

> *"...energy and imagination...upset the stereotypes that have kept women trapped in their cultural roles."*
>
> *"America's Fifty Most Powerful Women."*
>
> *"Women Of The Year."*
>
> *"The Super Woman."*
>
> *"Women Of The Nineties."*
>
> *"The Career Woman."*
>
> *"The Working Woman."*
>
> *"Women Warriors."*
>
> *"...women of the years from Rosie the Riveter to the Suited Yuppie of the 80's, each era had its own image of womanhood."*

Our newsmen, it seems to me, very often tip the scales to a large degree in favor of the ones favoring abortion, federal funding of the child development centers (we hear so much about this), civil rights for homosexuals, ratification of certain laws to aid their cause, and many such-like items in their arsenal, their military storehouse, of items that are eating like a cancer at the very heart of those principles upon which righteousness is to be found. How they detest such thoughts as: "Righteousness exalteth a nation; but sin is a reproach to any people" (Prov. 14:34).

SOME BRETHREN ARE SPEAKING

I am not surprised that these thoughts about women have found their way into denominationalism, yea, with their women preachers and leaders. Yes, even in the Roman Catholic system they have had to fight a battle, and, in some areas they have lost it with women priests, and with the priests being able to marry, etc. (Nothing wrong with marriage, but it goes to show the strength of this influence as it knows no boundary lines). Religious leaders have upheld many such thoughts.

The Lord's Church is no exception, that is, it has not escaped the influence of the ungodly forces at work in the world. Not only do some women hold some of the positions, persuasions and precepts of the feminist movement, but some have also spoken, written and tried to enforce their views where they worship (the local church). *Let us hear from some of our own ladies.*

> *"I believe that God intended woman to be a creature of dignity and worth in full partnership with man and given equally the task of carrying on his purposes in the world - whether it be in the marriage relationship, in the family, in society or in the church." (This, she stated,*

was her thesis toward which all I have to say will be aimed.)

"...this was one of Paul's arguments. But, in all honesty, we have to admit that one can argue the very opposite with perhaps even better logic." (She can even surpass, exceed and excel inspiration, GM).

"Now, as much as I'd like to, I can no longer put off talking about Paul, our 'thorn in the flesh' for sure."

"Paul's arguments are not logical. Apparently, he is so upset that, in perfectly normal fashion for such circumstances, he used the most extreme arguments he could think of to bolster his position. Then, he turns right around and tears most of them down."

"Surely, no one would seriously deny that women have been, at best, second class citizens in the church and, at worst, completely suppressed... Our worship services might be much warmer and more spiritual if women were allowed some part in planning and participation" (Above quotes from a seminar, and I have the manuscript, GM).

"I believe the church is changing its attitude toward women...I only know of one congregation in which women are allowed to be full participants in the church, and that is the one I attend. In our church all members have equal rights. There are no 'men only' restrictions on prayer, public reading, serving (such as passing the communion trays), business meetings, or leadership positions" (Quoted by Roy Deaver -

POWER, p. 27).

Good people, it is not only our women who are speaking out relative to the role of women, but some of our men are doing the same and all of it is a shame. *Listen now to what some of our men are saying*, as well as "what is happening" in some churches (I am limited on the number of quotes because of space).

> *"1984-85 DEACONS AND DEACONESSES. The term 'deacon' means servant, and is used in the New Testament to refer to those officially appointed by the church to serve in some special capacity. It is not a decision-making post, and obviously not limited to men. Women were given special assignments by the church in New Testament days and were called deaconesses... Here at Sunset Ridge, we currently list 42 deacons and deaconesses. These people are appointed for specific tasks and are reviewed annually." (This article* ***from them*** *listed the departments by name, the deacon and/or deaconess, etc., GM).*
>
> *In 1985, one church distributed a questionnaire by "The Worship Committee" and one item to be checked as to whether one would "agree" or "disagree" was: "Ladies speaking in the assembly."*
>
> *In 1986, "The text in I Cor. 14, which is questionable as an authentic passage,... Key question in understanding of issue: Our Approach To Scripture...legal manual, blueprint,... We need the ongoing guidance and direction of God to understand truth... Women are not to domineer but also to serve humbly -*

not only in assemblies but also in all of life... ***Bible does not address:*** *women in business meetings, women serving Lord's Supper, women leading singing (or their singing at all)...* ***Expressly permits:*** *women praying in assembly, women in official roles of service... We need to prayerfully consider what God's will is for us in these and other areas as we reflect on the scriptural teachings concerning women in the church."*

"REPORT on WOMEN'S PARTICIPATION IN PUBLIC WORSHIP. On July 31, 1988, the elders presented a statement to the Bering family concerning the use of spiritual gifts by both men and women, expressing our conviction that it is scriptural and appropriate for sisters as well as brothers to serve in Sunday morning worship roles of ushering, greeting visitors, receiving the offering, reading Scripture, leading prayers, leading singing, and serving communion. We pledged that the implementation of women in these roles would be preceded by sermons and Bible classes on the pertinent passages of Scripture. We also expressed a belief that the 'when' and 'how' in this matter involved waiting on the Lord, and sensing the congregation's willingness to be led in this direction."

"Nashville Jubilee, July 6-8, 1989, Nashville Convention Center..." Out of this, which is far too much to write about, but based on what happened, these questions were asked: "Why were women's classes with women teachers open to both men and women regardless of the gender of the teacher? Why did one lady teacher have to station women at the classroom

door to ask men not to enter nor to be a part of the class? Why was a woman asked to deliver a major lecture when one of the male speakers failed to be present? Why did one speaker ask his wife to sing a solo before the entire assembly and after the first verse she led the congregation in the rest of the song?"

"The 21st Annual Youth Minister's Seminar... October 16-19, 1989...Each October, Lubbock Christian hosts...The keynote speakers are... and Randy Mayeux. You want to talk about the issue in the 90's. There are Bible majors at Abilene Christian and Lubbock Christian who are female...In one youth group...there is a woman, a teenager...that wants to be able to preach in some fashion to men and women when she gets older. You want to kick her out?...The bottom line is that in the 1990's diversity is the only game in town,...Can a woman lead prayer in a mixed group? It's a good question. And the answer, of course, is yes she can. I mean because it is happening.

Recently, the HERALD OF TRUTH *had a conference on family. Nine hundred people came to the Dallas area. One of the sessions, in which all of the participants, nine hundred men and women came, the speaker was a woman...let me tell you what she did, she preached. And she was dynamite! Do we want to drive these people away from us?...I will tell you that the churches of Christ cannot survive the resource drain if we drive people away like that in the 1990's..."*

"...Priscilla and Aquila are mentioned six

times in the Scriptures. Four times her name is mentioned first...The early church knew the power of unleashing godly women in their homes as helpers and as teachers of scripture. I would love to see, as this church looks into the 90's, a more creative approach on our part to the role of small groups of evangelism and to the role of our women in reaching the lost. I genuinely believe the churches that survive the 90's are going to be the churches that do some very creative thinking about their current worship schedule and decide instead to put a real priority on freeing up their people as teachers of scriptures in their homes..." (Oct. 21, 1990).

THE NEW TESTAMENT HATH SPOKEN - ONCE AND FOR ALL

There should be absolutely "no reason" at all to discuss that we are living in the New Testament Age, that the New Testament is our sole authority in matters pertaining to religious items, and that the women of our age are to occupy "the place" as described by inspiration. Even though this should be "the case," I am sorely afraid it is not "the case." There is just too much evidence contrary to what should be "known and observed" by godly men and women. We, therefore, must, as Peter so explicitly stated: "...be ready always to put you in remembrance...," and "...I stir up your sincere mind by putting you in remembrance," and the reason is listed as "...ye may be able after my decease to call these things to remembrance" and "that ye should remember the words which were spoken before by the holy prophets, and the commandment of the Lord and Saviour through your apostles" (cf. 2 Pet. 1:12-15; 3:1-2).

If a person is a good student of the Bible, then he will know and understand "the why" of "the memorials" that God has given. He will note how they served to bring the offerer into remembrance of God. It is used this way in the Old Testament and bears a direct relation to one's "memory," serving as "a remembrance." It also occurs in the New Testament (Matt. 26:13; Mark 14:9; etc.), and is from the Greek *mnemosunon* meaning "a memorial, that which keeps alive the memory..." I also observe that the Greek *echo* ("to have, to hold") is used in the strengthened form (*katecho*) and is translated both as "hold fast" in Luke 8:15; 1 Corinthians 15:2, and then "keep in memory" (*King James*) in 1 Corinthians 15:2. The last passage has reference to "the gospel" by which we "are saved" if we "keep in memory what I preached unto you." If New Testament Christians needed this, then so do we today.

God knew his people "would forget," therefore, he took all means, seemingly, every advance and preventative measure, safeguard and safety valve, to keep us from "going astray from that which is written." It is no wonder that I find the words "remember" and "remembrance" so often used in the New Testament, being found in almost every book - 23 out of 27. The Greek words are found 74 times and are translated as "remember," "call to mind," "be mindful," "put in mind," "call to remembrance," "put in remembrance," "bring into remembrance," "bring to remembrance," "in remembrance," "be had in remembrance," "come to remembrance," "remembrance again," etc.

God has often said, "Beware lest thou forget Jehovah thy God, in not keeping his commandments, and his ordinances, and his statutes,... lest... thy heart be lifted up, and thou forget Jehovah thy God,... lest thou say in thy heart,... and then God said, "If thou shalt forget... ye shall surely perish" (cf. Deut. 8:11-20). Christ told Peter about his denial that was to come and the cock crowing, which he denied and even said if it took him to die he would not deny his Master (Matt. 26:31-35). However, the very sad story came to pass just thirty-five verses later when Peter began to deny his Lord. After the denials and the cock crowing three times, *we have written for us*: "AND PETER REMEMBERED THE WORD WHICH JESUS HAD SAID..." (Matt. 26:75, emp. GM). How sad to "remember" too late! I pray to God, oh, how I pray to God that we do not "remember too late!" Yea, how true it is that *we absolutely must be reminded* of the things that are written.

1. **LET US REMEMBER TO RESPECT BIBLE AUTHORITY.** "And whatsoever ye do, in word or in deed, do all in the name of the Lord Jesus, giving thanks to God the Father through him" (Col. 3:17). Acts 4:7-10 should inform us that "in the name of the Lord" means "by the authority of the Lord." To please God, we must have faith (Heb. 11:6), and faith comes by "the hearing of the Word of God" (Rom. 10:17). Where there is "no word of God," there can be "no faith." However, the child of God is to "walk by faith" (2 Cor. 5:7). We can neither "walk" as God would have us to walk nor "be pleasing" to God without "the faith" that comes "from the Word of God." It is a divine charge "not to go beyond that which is written" (1 Cor. 4:6, ASV). The reason is simple, "we shall be judged by that which is written" (cf. John 12:48), the very thing that we are not "to go beyond" (1 Cor. 4:6; cf. Rev. 20:11-15). **God does not authorize by what the Bible does not say, that is, upon its silence.** There is no Bible authority in silence.

2. **LET US REMEMBER THE CHAIN OF AUTHORITY.** Paul praised the Corinthians "that ye remember me in all things, and hold fast the traditions,

even as I delivered them to you" (1 Cor. 11:2). He then gave this statement: "But I would have you know, that the head of every man is Christ; and the head of the woman is the man; and the head of Christ is God" (vs. 3). This "chain of authority" was not just for the Corinthians because of a local problem, but is a very hallowed and heavenly, sacred and spiritual principle for all times. Remember that Paul "taught the same in every church" (cf. 1 Cor. 4:17) and that what he wrote was "the commandment of the Lord" (1 Cor. 14:37). Surely all of God's children ought to know that "principles" are binding. Therefore, the head of Christ is God, the head of every man is Christ, and the head of the woman is the man.

3. **LET US REMEMBER OUR DIVINE RESTRICTIONS.** Note if you will, that the word "our" is plural and there for a reason. We hear so much today that connects woman's limitations, being checked and curbed by the Bible, that it makes her some sort of a second-class citizen in the church and a second-rate soldier in his army. Submission to God never made anyone "second-rate" or "inferior." Man has his own restrictions and that is "not shocking," as even the only begotten Son of God had some (cf. 1 Cor. 11:3; cf. John 4:34; 5:30; 6:38; Rom. 15:3; Heb. 10:7). Indeed, man is to be in submission to Christ, just as Christ was in submission to God, and just so, woman is to be in submission to man. No one who is bent on pleasing (note what Christ said of himself, John 8:29) God, and that surely ought to be our aim and ambition, feels insignificant, lower than, less than, second-fiddle, small-time, unimportant, subservient, second-class or bargain-basement. We dare not let "women of the world" delude, deceive and defraud our Christian women, women in submission to Christ, feel as though they are second-best, low-grade and of low-quality. Submission to the divine will never has made anyone low-class.

4. **LET US REMEMBER OUR GOD-REVEALED AND BIBLE-DECLARED PLACES.** God revealed these as the Bible is "God-inspired," "God-breathed," and "Every scripture is inspired of God, and profitable for teaching,... that the man of God may be complete, furnished completely unto every good work" (2 Tim. 3:16-17; cf. 2 Pet. 1:19-21; John 16:13-14; 1 Cor. 2:9-13; Gal. 1:11-12; etc.).

Once again I employ the plural "our," as both man and woman are declared by inspiration to have their own special roles to fill in the marriage relationship. However, it is "the man," not "the woman," upon whom God has placed the responsibility of being "the head" of this divine instituiton. Paul says, "For the husband is the head of the wife, as Christ also is the head of the church,..." (Eph. 5:23; all of this paragraph, verses 22-33, needs to be diligently studied). He then admonishes the women by saying, "as the church is subject to Christ, so let the wives also be to their husbands in everything." The love we find in Christ for the church is the kind the husband is to have for his wife, and the wife is to love and reverence, honor, her husband. I give this as God's order and arrangement, not man's. God places the man as "the head" and the woman "in subjection," along with the ingredients of love and respect placed on both (cf. 1 Pet. 3:1-7, as it also informs and instructs us in God's way for our homes).

5. **LET US REMEMBER GOD'S SANCTIFIED ARRANGEMENTS.** Having just mentioned "the home," let us now, just briefly, focus our attention upon God's arrangement for the church. Again, it is "the man," and not "the woman" that is to be an elder (1 Tim. 3:1), as it is "he" that is to be "the husband of one wife,"... "one that ruleth well his own house," and "having his children in subjection..." (vss. 2-7 should be noted). The same is true with one being a deacon, as "Deacons in like manner"

are to "be husbands of one wife,..." (1 Tim. 3:8-13). In like manner, no woman, that is, with God's approval, can be a preacher, an evangelist, as the same author of the above, Paul, one chapter earlier, stated: "But I permit not a woman to teach, nor to have dominion over a man..." (1 Tim. 2:12). It is an evangelist, like Timothy, that Paul told to "...speak and exhort and reprove with all authority" (Titus 2:15). A woman, restricted by 1 Timothy 2:12, cannot fulfill Titus 2:15. We have seen, therefore, in this section, that a woman, if she intends to do as God has directed, to be pleasing to God, cannot serve as an elder, or as a deacon, or as an evangelist (and, as seen from the preceding thought, cannot be the head of the home).

I must emphasize, so that there positively will be no misunderstanding, that no gospel preacher stressing these items gives the slightest hint of any inferiority for God's woman or her estimation in the sight of God as being anything less than that of man's. Man and woman are of **equal worth and value in the sight of the Almighty**, but in the realm of the home and of the church, God assigned them their respective roles, positions, places, and these must be honored, respected and revered. That is, if we intend to please God and not mankind.

6. **LET US REMEMBER THE WOMAN IS BOTH TO PRAY AND TO TEACH.** No one knowing "the truth" in God's Book, the Bible, would ever speak, write or in any way teach that a woman was not to pray and to teach. Woman is "commanded" to teach (Titus 2:3-5), and we have Acts 18:24-26 as a good example of a woman teaching the Word of God. We also know that all Christians are to pray (cf. 1 Thess. 5:17; 1 Tim. 2:1ff). But both of these items, "the praying" and "the teaching" are to be done in accordance with the sacred principles clearly understood and with the totality of what the Bible says

about a woman's praying and also her teaching.

It is just here we recognize that 1 Timothy 2:1-15, with verses 8-15 being specifically set forth, as the passage that gives both the restriction and the reason for the restriction in this matter. Paul stated, in verse one, that prayer is to be made for all "men" (Greek, *anthropos*), however, he used another word (Greek, *aner*, form here is *andras*) in verse eight: "I desire therefore that the men pray in every place,..." Further he says, "But I permit not a woman to teach, nor to have dominion over a man,..." (vs. 12). The kind of praying or teaching that would, in any way, involve the usurpation of authority over man would be wrong. This passage does forbid a woman to teach, but only in reference to having "dominion" over a man. This also is true with a woman "leading in prayer" with men present, as it does involve the very thing Paul here states that God forbids. (The Greek is clearer than the English. I remember in third year Greek having to diagram this very verse for Dr. J. W. Roberts. The Greek words and the construction of those words cannot be overlooked.) In no realm, in no way, can a woman afford to place herself in a position of being authoritative, as per our text. Then Paul gives us the reason for the restriction (verses 13-15), "For Adam was first formed, then Eve" (reason number one), and "Adam was not beguiled, but the woman being beguiled hath fallen into transgression" (reason number two). In the last verse, Paul refers to the nature of woman's work, and it is not that of "leadership," but that of being in subjection, that she serves in subordination and subjection, aiding and abetting, and one continuing "in faith and love and sanctification with sobriety."

7. **LET US REMEMBER NOT TO BE DECEIVED, DELUDED.** The word that is often translated as "deceive"

may have reference to being deceived, that is, deceiving oneself (cf. Gal. 6:7, Greek is *planao*). It means "to lead into error, to seduce, to lead astray,"... "often it has the sense of deceiving oneself" (Vine, p. 28). We also have the word "delude" and "beguile" (both from the Greek *paralogizomai*) as used in James 1:22 and Colossians 2:4. This is the word from which we get our word "logic," and it means "to circumvent, reckon wrong, reason falsely, miscount, to cheat by false reckoning, to deceive by false reasoning" (Thayer, p. 484; Vine, pp. 112, 290).

People often have a "false sense of reasoning" and are deceived thereby. Their "logic" is no good, as it misses the point. Many today fail to heed the warning: "This I say, that no one may delude you with persuasiveness of speech" (Col. 2:4). And let it be said that a man can thoroughly and completely do this to himself (1 Cor. 3:18, the Greek word is *exapatao*). I personally feel that many today, yea, and even on this subject (as well as others), are being deceived. Remember, this strengthened form, *exapatao*, is the word used both in 1 Timothy 2:14; 1 Corinthians 11:3, about "Eve being beguiled by the serpent." I find it interesting that the same form (the intensive form) is not so used of Adam, only of Eve in 1 Timothy 2:14.

Every serious student of the Bible ought to be aware that a person can thoroughly deceive himself/herself. We need to know that false teachers can deceive (2 Thess. 2:3). We need to pay attention to the ones using "smooth and fair speech," as they are listed, by God, to be among "the deceivers." Some are ensnared, enticed, allured by his or her own lust (cf. James 1:14, Greek word here is *deleazo*). When the true character of sin is belittled, it is said we are deceived by empty words (Eph. 5:6), and the list goes on and on. Nothing in the world is more deceiving than our own subjectivism, our own likes, feelings, opinions, thoughts, and convincing ourselves, as I often have been told, "I know my God, and He would not... God knows... God..." I only point out that no one, not even a single solitary soul, knows anything about God's thoughts (Isa. 55:6-11) except those revealed to us in the Bible. To live and to disregard God's instructions, what He has stated in the Bible, is to live in ignorance. The only way in the world to find out about God, about how God thinks, about how God feels about things, about breaking His laws, commandments, statutes and ordinances, about how God treats sin, etc., is to know what the Book says. Please do not let your own subjectivism (justifying your actions by thinking, "My God..." unless it is so stated in God's Book) keep you from a knowledge of "what is written," as no man dare "go beyond that" (1 Cor. 4:6; John 12:48; Rev. 20:10-15). Again, "there can be no faith where there is no word of God" (2 Cor. 5:7; Rom. 10:17; Heb. 11:6). Not a soul knows any more about God than what is revealed in the Bible. We even have a word that informs us we can "deceive our own mind" (the Greek word is *phrenapatao*, cf. Gal. 6:3).

A GODLY, KNOWLEDGEABLE, AND EXPERIENCED MAN HAS SPOKEN

Even though this is rather lengthy, it needs to be read in its entirety time and time again. I wish it were in every home, in the hands of every family and given to those young ladies who are now Christians and those who are planning on becoming such. It would help every young couple (as well as some older ones), and I mean both the man and the woman, to read, meditate on these things from the pen, the heart and soul, of Roy C. Deaver. His article was captioned, "Admonitions For Christian Women." These thoughts are his, but I will adapt the outlining and only use what is apropos.

1. **Be Mindful of the Power and Influence Of the Christian Woman.** One of the most powerful influences in all humanity is the influence of the woman, and of the mother. One of the most powerful influences *for good* is the influence of the *Christian* woman, the *Christian* mother... It is the woman who wields the greatest influence in the lives of the *children*, because she (generally) spends more time with the children; she (generally) is more concerned about the spiritual education of the children. There is more truth than poetry in the statement: "The hand that rocks the cradle is the hand that rules the world." (We had better be careful to see to it that the world is not being ruled by a group of twelve year old "baby-sitters".) Women also exert a tremendous influence in the lives of their *husbands*. They can go a long way in making the husband what he ought to be. Be grateful for your influence, and determine to use it to the glory of God.

2. **Determine That You are Going to be a Real "Help-meet."** God said, "It is not good that man should be alone; I will make an help meet for him" (Gen. 2:18). This means: one suited to him, a counter-part, a complement to him, a helper (each is incomplete without the other). The Christian woman will be a real helper. She won't "take over." She won't "brow-beat." She won't fuss, grumble, complain. She will encourage, help, inspire. She will maintain a healthful interest in her husband's work.

3. **Recognize and Respect the Divine Arrangement.** Memorize and quote often Ephesians 5:22ff. In the family unit, someone has to carry the responsibility of being the head. Someone has to make the final decision. God has placed this responsibility upon the husband. Countless problems come because of a failure to respect this basic

point. Some women absolutely refuse to allow their husbands to be the head of the family unit. Some husbands absolutely refuse to carry this responsibility.

Don't be afraid to be in subjection. This is commanded by the Lord. This doesn't mean that the wife is a slave. This doesn't mean that the wife is inferior. This doesn't mean that the wife has nothing to say about the matter. It does mean obedience, and not just obedience when there is agreement. Even when it turns out that the husband is wrong, the Christian wife does not say: "I told you so." Know, believe, respect and teach that "...as the church is subject to Christ" so the wife is to be in subjection to her own husband.

4. **Don't Ever Allow Yourself to be Placed in a Position of "Having Dominion Over" a Man.** Read carefully 1 Timothy 2:12. The "nor have dominion over" is "explicative" in construction and has the force of, "nor in any other way to have dominion over a man." A good illustration of the wrong attitude is found in Numbers 12. God made the woman for the home, and it is as a home-maker that her greatest contribution is made. And, let her write the word "home-maker" with dignity and pride.

5. **If You Are Married to a Husband Who is Not a Christian, Then Know That Your Greatest Responsibility is to be Faithful to the Lord.** A lady asked me: "What can I do to convert my husband?" My reply was: "As things are, you cannot. You have never demonstrated to him that the church comes first in your life. You must straighten up your own life before you can have the right kind of influence over your husband." Peter (1 Pet. 3) shows that the Christian wife can convert her husband by means of her good life. (Check the Greek to see if it is "without *a* word," or "without *the* word," GM.)

6. **Be Determined to Imitate the "Holy Women" Discussed in 1 Peter 3:4-6.** Read carefully 1 Peter 3:1-6. Peter shows that the "holy women": Did not place the emphasis upon the outward adorning; did adorn themselves in a "meek and quiet spirit, which is in the sight of God of great price"; were characterized by a wonderful *faith*; were characterized by wonderful *hope*; were in *subjection* to their own husbands; were *obedient* to their own husbands; were *respectful* of their own husbands; are illustrated by Sarah, and that Christian women can be her spiritual daughters by imitating her.

7. **Be Sure to Heed the Instructions of Titus 2:3-5.** Read Titus 2:1-5. Paul tells Titus to teach the aged women: to be reverent in demeanor, not to be slanderers, not to be enslaved to much wine, and to be teachers of that which is good.

Paul tells Titus to teach the aged women to train the young women: to love their husbands, to love their children, to be sober-minded, to be chaste, to be workers at home, to be kind, to be in subjection to their own husbands (note these things), "that the word of God be not blasphemed."

8. **Train Your Daughters.** Train them by being the right kind of an example (cf. Prov. 22:6). When they are little girls, let them be little girls! A doctor friend of mine, a woman doctor, and I were talking about the eleven pregnancies in Junior High school. The doctor explained: "one of the greatest problems of our day is the fact that mothers refuse to let their little girls be *little* girls."

Try to help them to understand the tremendous difference between the female nervous system and the male nervous system. *Let them know that by a moment of indiscreet conduct they can create a dangerous and highly explosive situation.*

Teach them that there is nothing inherently wrong with the natural desires of the body: that these are God-given, that these are to be exercised for divine purposes, that these are to be exercised subject to divine rules and regulations.

Teach them to prepare themselves to be the best possible Christian companion, and then to marry someone who has made the same kind of preparation. This is the *infallible rule* for successful marriage.

9. **Learn to Live Within Your Husband's Income.** Don't place the emphasis upon material things (cf. Luke 12:15). Be determined to put spiritual matters first. Know that hardships do come, and learn to make adjustments. Some women never learn to live within the husband's income.

Do you have any idea as to how it affects a man to know that his wife wants something and he is not able to provide it? And, it is just possible that he might literally work himself to death in trying to provide it. There are lots of husbands in the cemetery today who were murdered by their wives *in this fashion*. One of your responsibilities is to take care of your husband!

10. **Don't be a Thief.** I have in mind here the physical side of marriage. The physical side of marriage is important. It cannot be separated from the spiritual. It must not be neglected.

Consider Matthew 19:4-5 and Ephesians 5:31. There is the deep and abiding love because God made them male and female. Thousands of problems come, homes are broken and souls are lost, because of a failure at this very point.

In Mark 10:19, the Lord said, "Do not *defraud*" (the Greek *apostereo*). James says, "Behold, the hire of the laborers who moved your fields, which is of you kept back by *fraud*, crieth out..." (James 5:4). Study carefully 1 Corinthians 7:2-3. Verse five says: "Defraud ye not one the other..." This is the same word used in Mark 10:19 and James 5:4.

When the husband and wife are careful to follow the instructions of 1 Corinthians 7:2-5, there can be neither rhyme nor reason for unfaithfulness to each other. (Permission was granted on December 6, 1990. I took the above from *Biblical Notes*, Vol. 7, March, 1974, pp. 119-124. Roy C. Deaver himself granted this permission).

As I bring this to a close, let me hasten to say that one of the greatest things a woman can do is to so grow in "the grace and knowledge" of the Lord (2 Pet. 3:18) that she will mirror verses like the ones in Genesis 2:18; Proverbs 18:22; 19:14. If she follows the divine order of God, as found in Titus 2:1-5; 1 Peter 3:1-7; 1 Timothy 5:10, 14, etc., we will have husbands and children loved, the home kept in its proper perspective, the devil put to shame by her godly manner of life, and many good works will be accomplished. Children, both hers and others, will also be taught. We will have older women teaching young women, the woman co-laboring with her husband (Acts 18:24-26; 2 Tim. 3:14-15; Eph. 5:22-33; Phil. 4:3; Gal. 5:22-23; Rom. 16:1-2; Acts 12:12; etc.), the Bible respected, the divine restrictions observed as a blessing, women will not be found being deceived and an impact will be made on the world like unto which it has not seen since the days of "the holy women" of old.

There is no limit to the end of the work that a woman can do. She is so talented and many are the opportunities to write good, solid and sound material, to extend invitations to the lost, the conducting of Bible classes, the opening of her home for fellowship, being involved in visitation and truly radiating the dedication that one in love with the Master and His blood-purchased cause brings forth.

With this woman, self is crucified, dethroned, and Christ is enthroned and it is no longer the "I" that liveth, but "the Christ" in her (Gal. 2:20; Matt. 6:33). This woman realizes she has a role no other human being has. In her God-ordained way, she is the servant of servants, and like her there is none other! She knows her dignity and demonstrates her worth. Indeed, her entire life is one that is "more precious than rubies, yea, greater than gold" (Prov. 31:10-31), as this woman "feareth Jehovah" (vs. 30). (I do have in my own files sources from which every quote was made, GM.)

Chapter Seventeen

THE PATTERN - AND GOD'S CARPENTERS

THE PATTERN - AND GOD'S CARPENTERS

With the thought in mind relative to God's Pattern, and with the importance attached to keeping it, we now, in a very practical way, focus and magnet our attention on "God's Carpenters And The Pattern." This is a most practical, but much needed thought. It does seem to me, that at least at times, we lose the ability or the insight we need for today's people when we fail to make things sensible, realistic, down-to-earth and, as my dad use to say, "Son, don't put the fodder up so high that the cows can't get it."

Among the great number of titles ascribed to our Lord and Master in Scripture, one of the most significant in understanding his relationship to the church is "the carpenter." It was a common practice among the Jews to train the young men for a certain occupation. Joseph, a successful carpenter in Nazareth during the first century, trained his stepson Jesus, to make a livelihood at carpentry. This is why Jesus was known as "the carpenter's son" and also as "the carpenter."

> *"And coming into his own country he taught them in their synagogue, insomuch that they were astonished, and said, Whence hath this man this wisdom, and these mighty works? Is not this* ***the carpenter's son****? is not his mother called Mary? and his brethren, James, and Joseph, and Simon, and Judas? And his sisters, are they not all with us? Whence then hath this man all these things? And they were offended in him. But Jesus said unto them, A prophet is not without honor, save in his own*

> *country, and in his own house. And he did not many mighty works there because of their unbelief" (Matt. 13:54-58, **ASV**, emp., GM).*
>
> *"And he went out from thence; and he cometh into his own country; and his disciples follow him. And when the sabbath was come, he began to teach in the synagogue: and many hearing him were astonished, saying, Whence has this man these things? and, What is the wisdom that is given unto this man, and what mean such mighty works wrought by his hands? Is not this **the carpenter**, the son of Mary, and brother of James, and Joses, and Judas, and Simon? and are not his sisters here with us? And they were offended in him...And he marvelled because of their unbelief" (Mark 6:1-6, **ASV**, emp., GM).*

It could be that Joseph and Jesus were responsible for building many of the houses in Galilee, but this is not important. He began his public ministry at about the age of thirty, as stated in the book of Luke: "and Jesus himself, when he began to teach, was about thirty" (3:23). I have often wondered if his being known as "the carpenter's son" and "the carpenter" is why he was known so well when he began his ministry and thus why he was able to enter into so many houses and teach. I wonder also if this is why the following statement is so significant: "And as they went on the way, a certain man said unto him, I will follow thee whithersoever thou goest. And Jesus said unto him, The foxes have holes, and the birds of the heaven have nests; but the Son of man hath not where to lay his head" (Luke 9:57-58). Was he so busy building for others that he never took time for himself? Of course, there are many things we do not know and that we cannot know.

Again, these things are not what is important. There is something, however, that we do know.

The item of great import, of great consequence, is that Jesus built the greatest house the world has ever seen and ever will see, the church of the living God.

> *"Now when Jesus came into the parts of Caesarea Philippi, he asked his disciples, saying, Who do men say that the Son of man is? And they said, Some say... He saith unto them, But who say ye that I am? And Simon Peter answered and said, Thou art the Christ, the Son of the living God. And Jesus answered and said unto him, Blessed art thou, Simon Bar-Jonah: for flesh and blood hath not revealed it unto thee, but my Father who is in heaven. And I say also unto thee, that thou art Peter, and upon this rock* ***I will build my church****; and the gates of Hades shall not prevail against it..." (Matt. 16:13-19,* ***ASV****, emp., GM).*

> *"These things write I unto thee, hoping to come unto thee shortly; but if I tarry long, that thou mayest know how men ought to behave themselves in* ***the house of God, the church of the living God****, the pillar and ground of the truth" (1 Tim. 3:14-15,* ***ASV****, emp., GM).*

From Jesus, the greatest master builder, and from God's other carpenters of whom we read about in God's Word, we can learn great lessons which can help us be and build as God's carpenters. All of these men of God built "according to the pattern" revealed to us in the New Testament. There are many characteristics of God's carpenters that we must imitate: "According to the grace of God which was given unto me, as a wise masterbuilder I laid a foundation; and another buildeth thereon. But let each man take heed how he buildeth thereon" (1 Cor. 3:10; cf. 1 Cor. 4:14; 11:1; Phil. 3:15-19).

GOD'S CARPENTERS BUILD ON A ROCK FOUNDATION

When Jesus promised to build his church, he built it upon the confession made by Peter that he was "the Christ, the Son of the living God." It was Jesus who said, "...and upon this rock, I will build my church." Christ also, earlier in his ministry, in Matthew chapter seven, said, "Every one therefore that heareth these words of mine, and doeth them, shall be likened unto a wise man, who built his house upon the rock:...the rain...the floods...the winds...and beat upon that house; and it fell not: for it was founded upon the rock" (vss. 24-25). Let us, therefore, observe some very peculiar and prominent points.

1. **Christ is the only sure foundation.** It was Isaiah who clearly stated, "...thus saith the Lord Jehovah, Behold, I lay in Zion for a foundation a stone, a tried stone, a precious corner-stone of sure foundation:..." (28:16; unless otherwise noted, all quotations will be from the *ASV*). Peter, in speaking of Jesus Christ of Nazareth, said, "He is the stone which was set at nought of you the builders, which was made the head of the corner" (Acts 4:11; quoted from Psalm 118:22). Jesus himself applied Psalm 118:22 to himself: "Have ye not read even this scripture: The stone which the builders rejected, The same was made the head of the corner; This was from the Lord, And it is marvellous in our eyes?" (vs. 23 also; Mark 12:10-11). Later the apostle Paul, speaking as per the commandments of the Lord (cf. 1 Cor. 14:37), said: "They stumbled at the stone of stumbling; even as it is written, Behold, I lay in Zion a stone of stumbling and a rock of offence: and he

that believeth on him shall not be put to shame" (Rom. 9:32b-33). Isaiah, Jesus, Peter and Paul most explicitly state who it is upon whom we are to build and have the assurance of the rock foundation.

2. **We, too, must build on this foundation.** It is not illumination, but rather divine inspiration, when we hear Paul saying, "...as a wise masterbuilder I laid a foundation; and another buildeth thereon. But let each man take heed how he buildeth thereon. For *other foundation can no man lay* than that which is laid, which is Jesus Christ" (1 Cor. 3:10-11; emp., GM). To the church of our Lord in Ephesus, Paul wrote: "...being built upon the foundation of the apostles and prophets, Christ Jesus himself being the chief corner stone; in whom each several building, fitly framed together, groweth into a holy temple in the Lord: in whom ye also are builded together for a habitation of God in the Spirit" (2:19-22). Note, if you will, the words "build," "buildeth," and "builded."

3. **Our very lives are to be built on Christ.** Paul could state: "...and it is no longer I that live, but Christ liveth in me:..." (Gal. 2:20). Indeed, "...they that are of Christ Jesus have crucified the flesh with the passions and the lusts thereof" (Gal. 5:24). As a new creature in Christ (cf. 2 Cor. 5:17), there is but one place to glory and that is the cross of Christ (Gal. 6:14-15; 1 Cor. 1:31; Jer. 9:23-24). Indeed, there is a standard, a norm, a rule: "And as many as shall walk by this rule (cf. Phil. 3:16 on this word "rule"), peace be upon them, and mercy, and upon the Israel of God" (Gal. 6:16). Yea, even as we sing, "On Christ the solid rock I stand, all other ground is sinking sand."

4. **This means we build our homes by His standard.** Just think of this. Peter's home life let him become qualified to be an elder in the church of our Lord (cf.

1 Pet. 3:1-7; 5:1-4). Christians absolutely must have the right kind of companions (cf. 1 Cor. 9:5; 15:33; Matt. 12:25-26).

5. **This is the guideline for the church.** With what we have said in this section thus far, we notice only this beautiful passage:

> *"...a living stone, rejected indeed of men, but with God elect, precious, ye also, as living stones, are built up a spiritual house, to be a holy priesthood, to offer up spiritual sacrifices, acceptable to God through Jesus Christ. Because it is contained in scripture, Behold, I lay in Zion a chief corner stone, elect, precious: And he that believeth on him shall not be put to shame. For you therefore that believe is the preciousness: but for such as disbelieve, The stone which the builders rejected, The same was made the head of the corner; and, A stone of stumbling, and a rock of offence; for they stumble at the word, being disobedient: whereunto also they were appointed. But ye are an elect race, a royal priesthood, a holy nation, a people for God's own possession,...who in times past were no people, but now are the people of God: who had not obtained mercy, but now have obtained mercy" (1 Pet. 2:4-10).*

GOD'S CARPENTERS BUILD WITH THE BEST MATERIALS

The materials which Jesus uses are not perfect, but they are the best available. He used Peter, a man of quick decision (cf. Matt. 16:13-19; Luke 22:31-34), but he made mistakes (Matt. 26:69-75; Gal. 2:11-14). He used Paul, a man of zeal and with a pure conscience (Gal. 1:13-14; Acts

23:1; 24:16), but he, too, made mistakes (Acts 26:9; 1 Tim. 1:12-16; Phil. 3:1-7). The Corinthians obeyed the gospel (Acts 18:8; 1 Cor. 6:9-11) and there was some "good material" (1 Cor. 3:10-15). Yet, the church, we must understand, is built on the apostles and prophets with Christ as the chief corner stone (Eph. 2:19-22; 4:11-16).

We must build with the best materials we can find, though they never will be perfect. But notice, we are to build our lives with Christian graces (2 Pet. 1:5-11; Gal. 5:22-23). We are to build our homes with a Christian partner (1 Pet. 3:1-7; 1 Cor. 9:5; 7:12-16). And, we are to build the church with sincere, godly and dedicated "vessels unto honor" (2 Tim. 2:20-21; 1 Cor. 3:10-15; Rom. 16:17-18; Eph. 5:7-12; 1 Cor. 15:33; Prov. 4:14-17; Psm. 1:1-3; etc.). It was Nehemiah who had a problem with his building, as there was just too much rubbish in it.

GOD'S CARPENTERS BUILD ACCORDING TO THE PATTERN

Noah built the ark according to God's blueprint (Gen. 6:14-22), Moses built the tabernacle according to the pattern (Exod. 25:9,40; 40:16; Heb. 8:4-6) and Solomon, as per David's instruction from the "writing of God," erected it according to the pattern (1 Chron. 28:11-12, 18-20). Therefore, we should not be surprised today, surely God's carpenters won't be, that there is a pattern for us to follow in the New Testament. In writing to Timothy, a gospel preacher, the beloved Paul said, "Hold the pattern of sound words which thou hast heard from me, in faith and love which is in Christ Jesus" (2 Tim. 1:13). Keep in mind that Paul spoke by "the words of the Spirit" as seen in 1 Corinthians 2:9-13; 14:37; 2 Timothy 3:16-17; etc. Paul also said, "And the things which thou hast heard from me among many witnesses, the same commit thou to faithful men, who shall be able to teach others also"

(2 Tim. 2:2). It is not something "different or foreign" to what Paul taught, but it is *the same thing* he taught (cf. 1 Cor. 4:17) to Timothy, to others and "in every church," that we are *to commit to others*! Why? So that faithful men can do as he did, teach others. In addition, Paul told Timothy "*to guard* that which was (is) committed unto thee, *turning away from* the profane babblings and oppositions of the knowledge which is falsely so called; which *some* professing *have erred concerning the faith*" (1 Tim. 6:20-21, emp., GM; cf. James 1:22-25; Rev. 10:11-15; 22:18-19; Rom. 2:16; John 12:48; etc.).

Regardless of the "plank" on which we are building, it must be "according to the word of God!" We must never forget "*who*" we are, "*what*" we are, "*where*" we are and "*whose*" we are. In this life there are many areas of "building," but it matters not what the area is, we need to shout, BEHOLD THE PATTERN!

I now list just a few of those areas where we need to "follow the pattern."

1. **We must conform to the pattern by/in obedience.** There are a great many verses on this particular thought. Some would have us to believe that "love" would rule out "commandments," but the Bible teaches just the opposite. "And hereby we know that we know him, if we keep his commandments. He that saith, I know him, and keepeth not his commandments, is a liar (cf. Rev. 21:8; 22:15), and the truth is not in him; but whoso keepeth his word, in him verily hath the love of God been perfected" (1 John 2:3-4; cf. John 14:15,21,23; 1 John 5:1-3). The Bible plainly speaks about the "obedience of faith" as in Romans 1:5; 16:26 (footnote says, "...to the faith"). Jesus said that "his mother and his brethren" were those who "hear the word of God, and do it" (Luke 8:19-21; cf. 11:27-28, "blessed are they that hear the word of God, and keep it").

In our obedience to the truth, we "purify our souls" (cf. 1 Pet. 1:22). having been "begotten again...through the word of God, which liveth and abideth forever" (1 Pet. 1:23-25). Paul made "obedience" clear when he said, "But thanks be to God, that, whereas ye were servants of sin, ye became obedient from the heart to that form (Greek, *tupos*, footnote has "pattern") of teaching whereunto ye were delivered; and being made free from sin, ye became servants of righteousness" (Rom. 6:17-18; *K.J.* says, "...being then made free from sin..."). When were they "made free from sin"? When they became obedient, obeyed from the heart, that form of teaching (doctrine), BEING THEN! Being then what? "Made free from sin!" When? - Then! To show this necessity, we could also list other thoughts such as those in 2 Thessalonians 1:7-10; Romans 2:6-9; 1 Peter 2:1-10; etc. These show that we can refuse to follow the pattern by disobedience to the word, for to disobey the word is to disobey the Christ. The final act that puts one "into" Christ is baptism (Gal. 3:26-27; Rom. 6:1-6). One *must* "enter" through that door, else "except" does not mean "except!" (John 3:1-7; esp. 3, 5).

2. **In the matter of church organization**, we need to ring it out loud and clear, BEHOLD THE PATTERN. If, for example, there is not a model for elders, that is, if today it is "majority rule," then what about "appointing elders in every church" (Acts 14:23), "the elders and deacons" (Phil. 1:1), "desiring the office of a bishop and meeting the qualifications" (1 Tim. 3:1-7; Tit. 1:5-9; 1 Pet. 5:1-3), etc.? It is "a fact" that we do have men "over us in the Lord" (1 Thess. 5:12), men that we are "to esteem exceeding highly in love for their work's sake" (1 Thess. 5:13). We are to obey "them that have the rule over us" (Heb. 13:7, 17). Indeed, we are to see in them our "examples" (1 Pet. 5:3), that is, these men are to be a "pattern" for us. Our study could go on by

noticing Acts 20:28; 1 Pet. 5:2; Acts 29:29-30; John 10:1-15; Luke 15:3ff.

3. **In the subject of Christian unity**, we need again to sound the alarm about "beholding the pattern." The Bible never speaks about such a thing as "unity in diversity," as that is clearly contrary to the prayer of Christ (John 17:20ff), the platform given by Paul (Eph. 4:1-6), the plea made to the Corinthians (1 Cor. 1:10ff) and a whole galaxy of verses dealing with unity (cf. 2 Cor. 13:11; Phil. 2:3; 1:27; etc.). There is, in the true sense, no such thing as "unity in diversity." There is "unity" and there is "diversity," so we can speak of "unity and diversity." Real unity, not union, will never come until we have a "unity of the faith." No, not until we walk, talk, love, act, believe, obey, and follow the pattern will we ever have New Testament unity.

4. **In the topic of marriage, divorce and remarriage**, there is a must that we pull the curtain and read again the bold headline of "Behold the pattern." Based on Matthew 5:31-32; 19:3-12; Mark 10:2-12; Luke 16:18; Romans 7:1-3; 1 Corinthians 7:1ff, I summarize the thoughts contained therein by the following:

ACCORDING TO THE "ONE" BOOK
INSPIRED BY THE "ONE" GOD
REVEALED BY THE "ONE" SPIRIT
PRESENTED BY "ONE" MIND
WE OBSERVE THAT "ONE" MAN
IS JOINED TO "ONE" WOMAN
BY THE ONE AND ONLY "ONE" GOD
TO BECOME "ONE" FLESH
FOR "ONE" LIFETIME
RESTATED BY "ONE" JESUS
AS AT THE "ONE" BEGINNING
BUT NOW WITH "ONE" EXCEPTION

(Written by GM in 1987 and used on page XIII in his book entitled, DIVORCE).

5. **In the question of Christian teaching and preaching**, we take a "look into the perfect law of liberty" (cf. James 1:25). In doing this, we once again see the urgent need to "Behold the pattern." I realize this is a very broad subject, like the ones above, but my desire has been just to "touch" on these to show the work of God's carpenters. Indeed, there is a "pattern" to follow in the following imperative items if we intend to be well-pleasing to God. Who among us would dare say that there is not a "pattern" in:

1. New Testament Doctrine (cf. 2 John 9-11).

2. New Testament Worship (cf. John 4:21-24).

3. New Testament Assembling (cf. Heb. 10:25; Luke 4:16; Acts 17:1-3; last two for examples of Jesus and Paul).

4. New Testament Righteousness (cf. Tit. 2:11-14).

5. New Testament Purity (cf. 1 Pet. 2:11-12).

6. New Testament Morality (cf. James 1:27; 4:4).

7. New Testament Study and Prayer (cf. 2 Tim. 2:15; 1 Thess. 5:17).

8. New Testament Honesty (cf. Heb. 13:18).

9. New Testament Labor (cf. 1 Cor. 15:58).

10. New Testament Discipline (2 Thess. 3:6ff).

It is evident from the Bible that when we refuse to follow the pattern it is because of disobedience to the Word. When a man rejects the living word of God, he rejects God (cf. 1 Sam. 15:21ff). To reject the word of God is to reject the Christ of God, his chosen (cf. Matt. 7:21; Luke 6:46). Truly, if a man has the capability to preach, then he must preach the Word just as God gave it.

GOD'S CARPENTERS BUILD TOGETHER

You just cannot build a house all by yourself. You must have at least some help. Thus, we work together as we build (cf. Heb. 3:4; 2 Cor. 6:1). In the case of Nehemiah, he agonized (1:4), analyzed (1:5), organized (2:18) and supervised (5:14) and they built the wall (cf. 4:6).

Christ has a plan that is world-wide and revolutionary (cf. Matt. 28:18-20; Mark 16:15-16; Luke 24:46-47; Acts 1:6-8; cf. 1 Thess. 1:6-8; Col. 1:23; etc.), but it is failing because each man is not doing his part (cf. John 9:4; 14:12; Matt. 9:36-38; Luke 10:2; John 4:35). Here again we need to cry, "Behold the pattern." If we could but work together (cf. 1 Cor. 12:18-27) and observe that each member of the body is (1) in a God-given position, (2) relies and depends on one another, (3) cares for each other, and (4) complements each other, and, "with a mind to work," we, too, could "bridge the gap" (cf. Ezek. 22:33; Neh. 4:6) and "build the wall."

There are many descriptions of the beautiful bride of Christ revealed to us in the New Testament, but there is none more exciting or thrilling to read than expressed in the following:

1. Perfected Together (1 Cor. 1:10).

2. Fitly Framed Together (Eph. 2:21).

3. Tempered Together (1 Cor. 12:24).

4. Builded Together (Eph. 2:22).

5. Fitly Framed and Knit Together (Eph. 4:16).

6. Supplied and Knit Together (Col. 2:2, 19)

7. Striving Together (Phil. 1:27)

When we continue:

1. Steadfastly with one accord (Acts 2:46),

2. Being of one heart and soul (Acts 4:32),

3. Following after things that make for peace (Rom. 14:19),

4. Edifying one another (Rom. 14:19),

5. Speaking the same thing (1 Cor. 1:10),

6. Being of the same mind (1 Cor. 1:10),

7. Having the same judgment (1 Cor. 1:10),

8. Allowing no divisions (1 Cor. 1:10),

9. Living in peace (2 Cor. 13:11),

10. Giving diligence to keep the unity of the spirit in the bond of peace (Eph. 4),

11. Standing fast with one spirit and soul (Phil. 1:27),

12. Having the same mind (Phil. 2:2).

13. Showing the same love (Phil. 2:2).

14. Being of one accord (Phil. 2:2),

15. Counting others better than self (Phil. 2:3),

16. Doing all things without murmurings and questionings (Phil. 2:14),

then, and only then will we, as God's carpenters, build together, and, according to the pattern! Indeed, each man is to do his part. The Old Testament also shows us such examples in Joab and Abishai (2 Sam. 10:9-12) and Aaron and Hur (Exod. 17:11-13). We need, as God's carpenters to have the spirit of Nehemiah and his fellow-workers. Therefore, (1) let us rise up and build (Neh. 2:17-18), and (2) let us have a mind to work (Neh. 4:6), and (3) may there be no "no nobles" among us (Neh. 3:5) who put not their necks to the work of the Lord.

Many years ago, I worked for one of my uncles, an excellent carpenter, for one entire summer. I learned a great deal about carpentry. Especially did I learn "the absolute necessity" of following the pattern. My uncle David, regardless of how many boards he had to cut "of the same length," always went back to "the pattern." He never once cut a board "from the pattern," and then cut the next board from the board he cut "from the pattern." I saw this done in a house in Little Rock, Arkansas, and I also saw "the builder" tell the carpenter to "tear it all out, as it was not according to the pattern." Many times my mind has gone back to Amos and the plumbline that was in the hand of Jehovah (7:7-8). God's carpenters have no right, authority, to build, except "by the pattern."

Chapter Eighteen

THE PATTERN - AND THE UNITY THAT IS IN CHRIST

THE PATTERN - AND THE UNITY THAT IS IN CHRIST

If a person is just casually familiar with the New Testament, then he will know of the Lord's prayer before he went to Gethsemane as recorded in John chapter seventeen. Some thoughts from it are given below:

> *"...Holy Father, keep them in thy name which thou hast given me, that they may be one, even as we are...Neither for these only do I pray, but for them also that believe on me through their word; that they may all be one; even as thou, Father, art in me, and I in thee, that they also may be one in us: that the world may believe that thou didst send me" (vss. 11, 20-21).*

This prayer was constantly in the mind of Paul and he, too, spoke of it frequently and we have the written messages from him pleading for the same. Note his thoughts on "unity."

> *"Now I beseech you, brethren, through the name of our Lord Jesus Christ, that ye all speak the same thing, and that there be no divisions among you; but that ye be perfected together in the same mind and in the same judgment" (1 Cor. 1:10).*

> *"I therefore, the prisoner in the Lord, beseech you to walk worthily of the calling wherewith ye were called, with all lowliness and meekness, with longsuffering, forbearing one another in love; giving diligence to keep the unity of the*

Spirit in the bond of peace. There is one body, and one Spirit, even as also ye were called in one hope of your calling; one Lord, one faith, one baptism, one God and Father of all, who is over all, and through all, and in all" (Eph. 4:1-6).

No doubt you have often heard and read of this subject, for if you know the above passages, then you know that "unity" is the thought of them. Indeed, "unity" for the world of denominationalism, as well as for the church, is "in Christ." Christ did not pray just "for these alone," but Christ also prayed "for them also which shall believe on me through their word." He added His same thought for them that He did for the apostles, so three times we find it said; "that they may be one," "that they all may be one," and "that they also may be one in us." The world of denominationalism must, by the Word, come to Him.

This is, indeed, a most tremendous and paramount topic for us today, and I am speaking about "the religious world." I have often said "Hell's foundation trembles at the shout of grace, but all of Satan's throne would crumble at the cry of unity!" This word is found, as far as I can find out, in only two books of the Bible. One is in the Old Testament (Psm. 133:1) and one in the New Testament (Eph. 4:3, 13, it is found twice here), therefore, we read:

"Behold, how good and how pleasant it is for brethren to dwell together in unity!" (Psm. 133:1).

"Giving diligence to keep the unity of the Spirit in the bond of peace" (Eph. 4:3).

"Till we all attain unto the unity of the faith, and of the knowledge of the Son of God, unto

a fullgrown man, unto the measure of the stature of the fulness of Christ" (Eph. 4:13).

These verses are among the most beautiful and stand out as beacons to those of us who desire such unity as mentioned by the Holy Spirit of God. God's unity is not just any kind of unity, it certainly is not man's union (not unity "in" diversity, which is really unity "and" diversity), but as our caption is, "The Unity That Is In Christ." Or, if you please, "Sacred Unity," "Scriptural Unity," "Biblical Unity," and this is said because it can only come in harmony with "the seed," that is, "the Word of God" (cf. Luke 8:11; Gen. 1:11-12). As bad as we desire, work for and pray for unity, we totally reject the idea of unity at any price. Truth is never to be sacrificed! No, Never! Not Ever!

It may seem to be too much repetition, restatement, recounting and reiteration, but it is an absolute "must" that we learn the deep, yea, the very profound meaning of scriptures like 2 Corinthians 5:7; Romans 10:17; Hebrews 11:6; 1 Corinthians 4:6; Revelation 20:12; 22:18-19 and John 12:48, for if such are not followed there never will be unity, only division. When men and women are "God's Carpenters," and when, like Noah, Moses, etc., they build "according to the Word of the Lord," we can expect unity. The reason is simple. They are following God's divine blueprint, His Pattern! And just as surely as they had a pattern to follow, so do we today, and it is the one that has the power to bring unity (cf. 2 Tim. 1:13; Rom. 6:17; Acts 7:44; Heb. 8:5; etc.).

The Church is a people who have separated themselves from all of the world (cf. 1 Pet. 2:5-10). As a people the church is a united people, and this is the reason it is designated as a "body" (1 Cor. 12:27; Col. 1:18, 24; Eph. 1:22-23; 4:4). Indeed, the "body is one and hath many members, and all the members of the body, being many, are one body; so also is Christ" (1 Cor. 12:12). Surely we can all understand why the figure of the body is "unity." As the human body, with its many members functions as a unit, so does the church of our Lord. Each has only one head and it is "from the head" that we move "according to its directions for perfect harmony." It is so clear from such that the New Testament church is not a denomination. A denomination is a part, but the church of the New Testament is a whole. In fact, the word "church" is never once used in the New Testament to refer to a denominational body. We do, however, read about local churches, such as that in Corinth (1 Cor. 1:2), in Jerusalem (Acts 8:1), in Ephesus (Rev. 2:1; cf. the seven of Asia, Rev. 1:4; 2:8, 12, 18; 3:1, 7, 14), as well as the "church" in the "universal" sense (cf. Matt. 16:18). In fact, we read about the local church assembled (cf. James 2:1-2; Heb. 10:25; 1 Cor. 11:17-18, 20, 33-34; 14:23; different Greek words herein used, *sunagoge, episunagoge,* and *sunerchomai*). Oh how people, brethren, today need to guard their lips when they speak about the church, the beautiful bride of Christ. Some today refer to "the church of Christ denomination," or speak about "the church and other denominations." The New Testament Church never has been and never will be a denomination. There is not a single denomination that can compare to the New Testament Church, for it was God-planned, Blood-purchased, and Holy Spirit perfected and we have "the written Word of God" for it. Not a single drop of the precious blood of the Lamb of God, Prince Immanuel (cf. John 1:29; 1 Pet. 1:17-21), went for any man-made and human institution (cf. Acts 20:28).

SOURCES OF DISUNITY

It is my own personal belief, conviction, that one of the greatest dangers we in the New Testament Church face is the danger of facing ourselves! Note the charge that Paul gave the Ephesian elders when he sent from Miletus and called them to him. "Take heed unto yourselves, and to all the flock, in which the Holy Spirit hath made you bishops, to feed the church of the Lord which he purchased with his own blood. I know that after my departing grievous wolves shall enter in among you, not sparing the flock; and *from among your own selves shall men arise, speaking perverse things*, to draw away the disciples after them" (Acts 20:28-30).

The emphasis, of course, is mine in the preceding scripture, but the thought is the Holy Spirit's through Paul and is the thought that I want to indelibly implant upon those who read this. I want to make it a thought that is not to be obliterated, one ineffaceable and unerasable, one so deeply dyed and ingrained that it will be permanent, and also, unforgettable! I have never known of someone from the "outside" to come in and break the unity of a local church, but I have known, as many who read this have known, time and time again, "the unity of the Spirit" to be broken by men on the "inside," men "from among our own selves!"

Claiming to want unity, while clamoring to be satisfied is to wind up biting and devouring one another and the end is consumption of ourselves. Many today are not, to use the Spirit's wording, "thus-minded" and, therefore, are enemies of the cross of Christ (cf. Phil. 3:15-20). Indeed, their fair and smooth speech beguiles the hearts of the innocent (cf. Rom. 16:18).

UNITY OF BELIEVERS

Paul wrote in 1 Corinthians 1:10, "Now I beseech you, brethren, through the name of our Lord Jesus Christ, that ye all speak the same thing, and that there be no divisions among you; but that ye be perfected together in the same mind and in the same judgment." In most cases, when I hear this passage used, it is urging "unity in the world." However, I deny that this was the intent of the passage when Paul wrote it. Keep in mind he wrote "unto the church of God which is at Corinth" (1 Cor. 1:2). Brethren, it is the church that is to be *united* and the world will never be "won" to Christ until we are "one" in Christ.

Unity (Greek, *henotes*) means "oneness," a "togetherness" that can only come by, be created by, the all-powerful word of God. This is why the ecumenicity of the religious world will never be that of "endeavoring to keep the unity of the Spirit in the bond of peace." It should be noted very carefully that when the Lord gave his farewell prayer in John 17, he stated: "*I pray for them: I pray not for the world*, but for those whom thou hast given me; for *they are mine*...Holy Father, *keep them* in thy name which thou hast given me, *that they may be one*, even as we are...*I have given them thy word*...Sanctify them in the truth: *thy word is truth*...And for their sakes I sanctify myself, that they themselves also may be sanctified in truth. Neither for these only do I pray, but *for them also that believe on me through their word*; that they may all be one...*that the world may believe* that thou didst send me...*that they may be perfected into one; that the world may know*..." (vss. 9, 11, 14, 17, 19-21, 23).

This is the only kind of unity that hell, with all its forces, all its power, cannot destroy! A unity based on *The*

Word. However, its effect on the world was to be through the apostles and those who believe! *Note:* "keep *them*... that *they* may be *one*...sanctify *them*...for *their* sakes... that *they themselves*...that *they* may be perfected *into one*: that the world may know." Brethren, it puts the "burden" of unity squarely on our shoulders! This is something we cannot blame on someone else.

Any time we do any thing that would in any way distract, mar, hinder and harm this admirable, beautiful quality among the children of God we commit perhaps what might be called "a cardinal sin" (you understand, of course, I am just trying to emphasize its terribleness). Our trouble, most generally, comes from "within," not from "without." No wonder, then, our Lord prayed so very fervently for the *unity and oneness of his followers*! Disunity among members eats at the body of Christ like a cancer!

In these thoughts on "unity," I am speaking about the unity of the local church, the body of Christ, for that is the only unit known to God through which He is going to accomplish his work. (Of course, unity ought to exist among all the local churches worldwide.) Any time any one begins to rip apart, with the sawblade of dissatisfaction, the blood-bought body of Christ, he ought to find himself at the foot of the cross and feel the almost unbearable weight of the blood of the Lamb of God, Jesus the Christ! Those today, speaking such contrary, foreign, strange and uncertain sounds, need to have "their mouths," as Paul said to Titus, "stopped" (1:11), and may godly elders realize it is a charge that is directly given to them. Oh today for godly elders who know the Book, hold to the faithful word, exhort in sound doctrine, and convict the gainsayers (cf. Titus 1:9-11).

MARKS OF UNITY

The type of local church that hell, with all of its power and pressure, might and muscle, strength and stamina, force and fire, grip and grit, drive and dominion cannot shake is one that is described by the Holy Spirit of God as being "together." When God does something He does it perfectly! When the church (the analogy of the human body is so beautifully marvelous in this figure) is really "one" and "together" it maintains a unity where friction and fraction are unknown. Do note very carefully, observedly, the marks of "oneness":

1. PERFECTED TOGETHER ....1 Cor. 1:10
2. TEMPERED TOGETHER .... 1 Cor. 12:24
3. FITLY FRAMED TOGETHER ......Eph. 2:21
4. BUILDED TOGETHER ....Eph. 2:22
5. FITLY FRAMED AND KNIT TOGETHER ....Eph. 4:16
6. SUPPLIED AND KNIT TOGETHER ....Col. 2:19
7. STRIVING TOGETHER ....Phil. 1:27

Show me a church with the above characteristics, and I will exhibit one before the world that the devil and all his sinful, deceitful, crafty, cunning, powerful and tempting ways cannot tear apart, splinter, divide, shake, shatter or scatter from the love of God and the power of His Word. Our dying need is to "*attain unto the unity* of *the faith*, and of the knowledge of the Son of God, unto a fullgrown man, unto the measure of the stature of the fulness of Christ" (Eph. 4:13). Note now the "reasons why," "what it takes," and "how it is to be done," as well as "wherein" comes true church growth.

> *"That we may be no longer children,* ***tossed to and fro and carried about with every wind of doctrine****, by the sleight of men, in craftiness, after the wiles of error; but* ***speaking truth in love****, may* ***grow up in all things into him****, who is the head, even Christ; from whom* ***all the body*** *fitly framed and knit together through that which* ***every joint*** *supplieth, according to the* ***working in due measure of each several part, maketh the increase*** *of the body unto the* ***building up of itself*** *in love" (vss. 14-16, emp. GM).*

It was to this church, the Ephesian church, that the unity of the Gentile and the Jew (Christians) is so excellently set forth (cf. Eph. 2:13-33). Paul, by the Holy Spirit of God, tells us just how this was accomplished. He spoke of them as:

1. In Christ Jesus.

2. Made nigh by the blood of Christ.

3. Having Christ as their peace.

4. Being one new man.

5. Reconciled in one body.

6. Reaching God the Father through him and having that access in one Spirit.

7. Now being fellow-citizens with the saints, and of the household of God.

8. Built on the same foundation, that of the apostles and the prophets, Christ Jesus himself being the chief corner stone.

9. Groweth into a holy temple in the Lord.

10. Builded together for a habitation of God in the Spirit.

If there is anything else, any other way except through the teaching of Christ, that such scriptural unity can be achieved, and such fellowship endorsed and maintained, the pattern does not declare it. You will observe that this "one new man," who now "had peace," and being "reconciled in one body unto God through the cross," had equal access unto the Father. It reads: "for through him we both have our access in one Spirit unto the Father." Talk about fellowship which was created by the truth of God! Here it is, and on such teaching it stands! This scriptural and sacred unity, brought about by that gospel which had made both Jew and Gentile free, made them enjoy true Biblical unity and fellowship. This passage, with its tremendous teaching that has been set before us, absolutely defies the damnable doctrine which says there can never be real unity on the basis of a pattern concept! When people "walk in the light, as he is in the light," then they experience a fellowship like unto which the world knows nothing about (1 John 1:3, 5-7). What Paul and John described was brought about by people doing as the pattern instructed. Indeed, one can leave and return to darkness, in that case we follow that set forth in verses such as 2 Corinthians 6:14-7:1. However, it has been the positive note that has been the key thought here at this time.

PICTURES OF UNITY

The New Testament picture, pattern, of baptized believers, born again people, is the one that serves today as our guideline, our own pattern, for the kind of unity the world needs to see. Note very accurately, exactly, precisely and correctly, just a few of the many thoughts that the Holy Spirit of God inspired on this multipotent subject:

1. ALL THAT BELIEVED WERE TOGETHER (Acts 2:42).

2. CONTINUING STEDFASTLY WITH ONE ACCORD (Acts 2:46).

3. WERE OF ONE HEART AND SOUL (Acts 4:32).

4. NO STUMBLING BLOCK IN A BROTHER'S WAY (Rom. 14:13).

5. FOLLOW AFTER THINGS WHICH MAKE FOR PEACE, AND THINGS WHEREBY WE MAY EDIFY ONE ANOTHER (Rom. 14:19).

6. SPEAK THE SAME THING, BE OF THE SAME MIND, IN THE SAME JUDGMENT AND HAVE NO DIVISIONS (1 Cor. 1:10).

7. BE PERFECTED, BE OF THE SAME MIND, LIVE IN PEACE (2 Cor. 13:10).

8. GIVE DILIGENCE TO KEEP THE UNITY OF THE SPIRIT IN THE BOND OF PEACE (Eph. 4:3).

9. EVERY JOINT IS TO SUPPLY (Eph. 4:16).

10. STAND FAST IN ONE SPIRIT, WITH ONE SOUL (Phil. 1:27).

11. BE OF THE SAME MIND, HAVING THE SAME LOVE, BEING OF ONE ACCORD, OF ONE MIND (Phil. 2:2).

12. EACH IN LOWLINESS OF MIND COUNTING OTHER BETTER THAN SELF (Phil. 2:3).

13. LOOK EACH OF YOU TO THE THINGS OF OTHERS (Phil. 2:4).

14. DO ALL THINGS WITHOUT MURMURINGS AND QUESTIONINGS (Phil. 2:14).

15. SPEAK NOT ONE AGAINST ANOTHER, BRETHREN (James 4:11).

I have listed only fifteen of the many passages in the New Testament that describe "the kind of unity that hell cannot shake." *This is why* they "turned the world upside down" (Acts 17:6), and "preached the gospel to every creature under heaven" (Col. 1:23). *It is the reason* for their being able to go "from house to house" (Acts 20:20), "publicly and privately" (Acts 5:43) and "declare the whole counsel" (Acts 20:26-27). *It is the source* of their persecution (1 Cor. 4:10-13), yet also of their rejoicing (Acts 5:41).

BASICS OF UNITY

If the New Testament is the "pattern" for us to follow, and just as surely as Noah had one (Gen. 6:14-22) and Moses had one (Exod. 25:9,40; 40:16), we have one (2 Tim. 1:13) today and we must "imitate" it to the very best, yea the limit, of our ability. When the church started on Pentecost (and today, some among us even deny this beginning point for the New Testament Church), they *continued steadfastly* in: (1) Doctrine, (2) Fellowship, (3) Breaking of Bread, and in (4) Prayer.

Beloved, *you cannot underestimate* any one of these things and even for a minute hope to have "unity." However, with doctrinal soundness, the sweet association by joint participation, unity around the table of the Master and the right attitude in prayer, we can display and demonstrate a unity that the strongholds of hell, yea, with all the demonic angels of the devil, cannot shake! For this to be, there must be an accurate comprehension through diligent study (2 Tim. 2:15; 3:16-17) of these precious jewels of "oneness."

The "Unity of Diversity" (I have already stated that this is contradictory, should be listed as "unity and diversity") idea is an insidious, treacherous, crooked and double-tongued "doctrine." It is sectarian to the core and totally unbiblical! The Bible never talks (speaks) about "diversity of faiths!" Real unity will never be until there is a "UNITY OF THE FAITH."

The idea that every "believer in Jesus" regardless of his doctrinal beliefs, teachings and practices is a faithful child of God and is to be fellowshipped is totally absurd when such is faced with the teaching of the New Testament. Then a "twin sister" to this idea is that there can be "no disfellowship" for any cause, which, as most who read this will know, was pushed by Garrett and Ketcherside. This is also an untruth (and I should perhaps have stated that exactly for what it is, a lie). It is based on *a distinction they have made* between "gospel" and "doctrine," but which distinction is not made by the inspired writings of the New Testament. If one will just be aware of certain verses such as John 7:17; Acts 5:28; 13:12; 17:19; Romans 6:17, note the words "teaching" (*ASV*) or "doctrine" (*KJV*) as being from the Greek *didache* and observe that it can be either to the "outsider" or to the "Christian," that part of the battle will be won. The same is true with the word "gospel" (which, these men say refer only to those who are not Christians). The Greek *kerugma* is the word "preaching" in Romans 16:25 and Paul addressed his letter to the "saints in Rome" (Rom. 1:7). Paul used "my gospel," and then spoke of "preaching of Jesus Christ," and it was to Christians. The same is true in Acts 20:25, but herein the word *kerusso* (this is a verb, *kerugma* is a noun, the *cognate* of *kerusso*) is used when he (Paul) says, "...I know that ye all, among whom I went about preaching the kingdom,..." The same message by which one is called to become a Christian, called out of the world (cf. 1 Cor. 1:9; Col. 1:13) is for the Christian also (Vine, pp. 201-202).

The idea that one cannot be disfellowshipped (some say this matter of fellowship is a state, always used as a noun, never a verb, but they need to note the language in Phil. 4:14-15; Heb. 2:14; 2 John 11; 1 Pet. 4:13; Eph. 5:11; Gal. 6:6; Rom. 12:13; 15:27; 1 Tim. 5:22) shows an abiding ignorance of the Word (cf. 2 Thess. 3:6; Rom. 16:17-18; in this Roman passage the word doctrine is *didache* and if one is contrary to that doctrine he is to be marked and turned away from). The same thought is found in 2 John 9-10. Yes, once again it is the word about which we hear so much (doctrine here is once again the Greek *didache*) and no one is to give even a greeting to one who does not abide in the teaching (doctrine) of Christ. Therefore, we know that fellowship can both be "extended" (cf. 1 John 1:3,6; Gal. 2:9) and "withdrawn," and the disregard for a good dose, a large one, of 2 Timothy 2:15; 1 Peter 3:15 would go a long way in helping to cure this spiritual malady.

We must believe the same thing to speak the same thing! My Bible, as well as your Bible, emphatically states "*till we all* attain unto the UNITY OF THE FAITH" (Eph. 4:13) and also says "and of the knowledge of the Son of God, unto a fullgrown man, unto the measure of the stature of the fulness of Christ." How many? All of us! How many relative to faith? One! The Faith! What else? Knowledge! Knowledge of whom? The Son of God! Why? To be a fullgrown man! To what degree is it? Unto the measure of the fulness of Christ! Indeed, we need truly to meditate on Ephesians 4:11-13, especially verse thirteen. *There is but one:*

1. GOD (THE UNITY OF WORSHIP).

2. LORD (THE UNITY OF AUTHORITY).

3. SPIRIT (THE UNITY OF LIFE).

4. FAITH (THE UNITY OF MESSAGE).

5. BAPTISM (THE UNITY OF PRACTICE).

6. BODY (THE UNITY OF ORGANIZATION).

7. HOPE (THE UNITY OF DESIRE).

Until all of these things mean what they must, we will never have the oneness so clearly outlined by the Holy Spirit of God in the New Testament of our Lord Jesus Christ. But, if we can and do have these items, we will have **unity perfected**!

COMMITMENT TO UNITY

Unity, the kind that hell cannot shake, comes from people being "crucified with Christ" and saying with Paul, "It is no longer I that live, but Christ liveth in me" (Gal. 2:20). Show me an individual who loves the Lord's Body, with the kind of love that is pure New Testament love, and I will attest to one who, if need be, will sacrifice, freely and willing be sacrificed, for the blood-bought cause. *This man, Paul, who said:*

1. "I have been crucified with Christ."

2. "No longer I that live, but Christ liveth in me."

3. "I hold not my life of any account as dear unto myself."

4. "I glory not, save in the cross of our Lord Jesus Christ."

5. "I know nothing...save Jesus Christ, and him crucified."

6. "Be ye imitators of me, even as I also am of Christ."

7. "Our old man is crucified with him."

8. "They that are of Christ have crucified the flesh."

Also said:

1. "I will most gladly spend and be spent for your souls."

2. "I am debtor both to Greeks and to Barbarians."

3. "I have fully preached the gospel of Christ."

4. "I shrank not from declaring unto you the whole counsel of God."

5. "I am a fool for Christ's sake."

6. "I have been made as the filth of the world."

7. "I imparted my own soul unto you."

8. "I am pure from the blood of all men."

What I am trying to say is this. There must be a complete denial, a loss, of self, that is, a thorough crucifixion of self in our obedience to the gospel. Only then will this unshakable unity come to pass. The insertion of self, self's wishes, desires and personal items, likes and dislikes, to the disruption of plans, progress, attitudes and emotions is nothing but a dagger in the body of Christ and in the unity for which it stands. Each member of the body, and they are many, must be completely inundated with "NOT MY WILL BUT THINE BE DONE."

The very best example, I personally believe, to be found in the New Testament for this is 1 Corinthians 1:10ff; 2:1-5; 3:1-9. Here there were some following one man, some another, some wanting "this" and others desiring "something else." The division at Corinth was a complete mockery to the spiritual man and *so is ours today when we enthrone self and dethrone Christ!*

DECISION TO HAVE UNITY

It seems that the only time the early Christians stopped in their going everywhere with the word (cf. Acts 8:4), was to fight the sin and quench the self-seeking that began to create divisions among them. Sometimes they took their eyes off the Master, forgot who they were and why they were here, looked *at their crosses instead of through them* to the joy beyond in the "house of many mansions" (John 14:1), and when this happened they began to be as "carnal" men (cf. 1 Cor. 3:1ff). When instructed and put in remembrance with the fire rekindled, the sin was either covered or the sinner disciplined. Then, once again, the bond of love was as the bands of steel, unbreakable.

To have "the kind of unity that all the horrors of hell, all of the powers of the forces that stand against the purity of the New Testament Church in doctrine, organization and worship," we absolutely must let the Word of God have "free course" (cf. John 8:37, Greek *choreo*), and this means in the life (heart, mind, soul and spirit) of each individual member! The finest quotes from the Bible that I personally know relative to assisting us in our "March for the Master," in unity, attitude, work, instruction and determination are as follows (and only a very few are listed):

1. "Let all *the people* go, *every man* unto his own place."

2. "*The congregation* was assembled *as one man*."

3. "*The people* had *a mind to work*."

4. "And *all the people* gathered themselves together *as one man*."

5. "*We* ourselves *together will build* unto Jehovah."

6. "*Let us go*, we pray thee,...and take thence *every man a beam*,..."

7. "And *the people* stood *in their place*."

8. "And the saying *pleased the whole multitude*."

9. "And *the people* gathered themselves together *as one man* to Jerusalem."

10. "*Every man determined* to send..."

11. "*Speak every man* truth with his neighbor."

12. "*The leaders* took the lead...*the people followed them willingly*," "...great resolves of heart."

Brother Roy C. Deaver, an outstanding man in "handling aright" the Word of God, wrote an article, a brief one, entitled: "GOD'S ONE-DERFUL PLAN" and introduced it by the following statements:

> *"God's plan for man is characterized by distinctive exclusiveness. The God of the Bible is not a god among many gods. The Christ of the Bible is not a christ among many christs. The Holy Spirit of the Bible is not a spirit among many spirits. The Message of the Bible (the Gospel of the Christ) is not a soul-saving message among many soul-saving messages. The Bible is not a book among many books. The Church of our Lord (the Church of the Bible) is not a church among many churches. The Bible talks about THE GOD, THE CHRIST, THE HOLY SPIRIT, THE GOSPEL, THE WORD OF GOD, THE CHURCH."*

Then, after briefly discussing the idea of the fundamental concept that is found in the word "body" (which word is an appositive for the word "church," as seen in Col.

1:18, 24; Eph. 1:22-23), he discussed three thoughts: (1) We need to consider carefully the religious situation *as it was* (referring to the establishment of the Lord's church in Acts 2), (2) We need to consider the religious situation *as it became* (a departure from the divine plan, cf. Acts 20:28-31; 1 Tim. 4:1-5; 2 Tim. 4:1-4), and (3) May we consider the religious situation *as it is* (speaking of the tragic division in the world, yet also the plea made by some for "Unity In Christ Jesus").

He closed the above with the following personal plea:

> *"The noble plea of the Church of Christ in your community is for a complete return to the Bible. We plead with men to turn away from Romanism, and from denominationalism, and to restore the church of the New Testament. We call upon men to speak where the Bible speaks and to be silent where the Bible is silent; to do Bible things in Bible ways; to have no creed but Christ, no name but the divine name, and and no book but the Bible; to do what the Bible says do, and in the way the Bible says do it; to do nothing in matters religious excepting that for which there is a 'thus saith the Lord.'"*

He finished the article by giving the Lord's prayer in John 17:11, 20-23 and the words of the Spirit-directed Paul in 1 Corinthians 1:10, and Ephesians 4:3-6 and said, "This is God's ONE-derful plan!" (*Biblical Notes*, Vol. 15, August, 1981, pp. 61-63).

Until we walk, talk, love, act, believe, obey, do and follow this pattern that I have tried to set forth from the pages of Holy Inspiration, this type of unity that all the strongholds of hell cannot shake will never be ours. *It does not come easy!* Sometimes, as said by men of the past, as well as some of the present, some "driftwood has to be cut loose." Do you want to know why it is difficult to have such a unity, a oneness? Self does not die without a struggle, a real battle, as self does not want to be "crucified." But when conversion is truthfully viewed as a "crucifixion" and it does take place, we can all say with the Psalmist: "Behold, how good and how pleasant it is for brethren to dwell together in unity" (Hebrew word for unity is the word *yachad*, a unit, alike, altogether, at once, etc.).

Chapter Nineteen

THE PATTERN - AND THE ATTITUDE THAT SAVES

THE PATTERN - AND THE ATTITUDE THAT SAVES

It is my honest conviction that nothing in this life is more important than a thorough knowledge of the Bible. Regardless of the extent of a man's education, he is uneducated who does not have a basic understanding of the Bible. A knowledge of the Bible is more important than a college education, as it relates, not to the timely only, but also to the timeless (cf. John 17:3). This firm persuasion and fixed belief stems from the fact that there is a life after death, a judgment to face, an account to be given and an absolute, infallible book, the Bible, as the source and standard of that judgment (cf. 2 Cor. 5:1; John 15:1ff; Heb. 9:27; 2 Cor. 5:10; Rom. 14:12; John 12:48; Rev. 20:11-15).

The Greek New Testament of 2 Timothy 2:15 makes it clear that it is hard work, stating perhaps in our common jargon, there is no short cut. A person will either pay the price or pay the penalty! Men can know the truth, regardless of what the agnostic says. We certainly can "know" (Greek, *ginosko*), and for the person who has love and respect for the Bible, there is "no problem" about knowing, as the evidence is overwhelming, meaning, of course, that the Bible is most emphatic in declaring this fact (John 17:3; 7:17; 8:32; 4:42; 6:69; 8:55; Luke 1:3-4; 2 Cor. 5:1, 6-8; 2 Tim. 1:12; 1 John 2:13-14; 2:3, 29; etc.). This knowledge does not come easy, but we are still under the obligation to study (John 7:17; Acts 17:11; Psm. 1:1; 119:97, 99; Josh. 1:8; 1 John 5:13, 15, 18-20; etc.).

God expects man to use his word. This is evident in so many Bibles passages (cf. Ezra 7:10; Deut. 29:29; Neh. 8:1-8; Psm. 19:7ff; 119:34-105; Luke 16:29-31; 2 Tim.

3:14-15; 1 Tim. 4:13; etc.), informing us that we must "look into" (James 1:25, Greek root word is *parakupto*, cf. John 20:5, 11; Luke 24:12; 1 Pet. 1:12), that is, we are "to look carefully" and "inspect curiously." We are not just to "glance" into ("beholdeth" in James 1:23-24 is the Greek *katanoeo*), "go away and forget," that is "neglect" it and let it escape our attention (the difference in these two Greek words is most significant and relates to whether or not this man is "blessed"). Truth comes by the same method of study that is applied to other branches of knowledge. God has no other truth to reveal to us (2 Pet. 1:3; 2 Tim. 3:16-17). Truth is not contradictory.

Spiritually and intellectually a man must be honest. Faith in the inspiration of the scriptures (Heb. 11:6; John 20:30-31; 2 Pet. 1:19-21), investigation with the mental powers (Luke 10:38-42; Acts 17:11; 2 Tim. 2:15), a willingness to ascertain the truth (John 7:17; Luke 8:15; 2 Thess. 2:10-12), and a pure mind (Tit. 1:5; 2 Tim. 4:3-4; Matt. 5:8) are necessary for sound hermeneutics. It is most important that we know the Bible, and we have to study it to know it.

How true it is that "the type of heart" determines the reception given to the seed that is sown by the sower. I believe this is very readily proved from the Parable of the Sower (or, the Soils) as described by the Master Teacher in Matthew 13:18-23; Luke 8:9-15; Mark 4:14-21. Take note of a brief, capsuled and curtailed outline as found in this parable as we look at the above-mentioned accounts.

1. **Some seed fell by the wayside**, illustrating people who neither understand nor believe (cf. Luke 8:12).

2. **Some seed fell among thorns**, exemplifying those cumbered with the cares of the world, deceitfulness of riches and lusts of other things (cf. Mark 4:18-19).

3. **Some seed fell on rocky ground**, demonstrating to us that there are some who are unstedfast believers (cf. Matt. 13:5,21; Luke 8:13).

4. **Some seed fell on good ground**, describing people who understand the word and bring forth fruit according to ability and opportunity, some thirtyfold, and sixtyfold, and a hundredfold (cf. Mark 4:20).

From that which is called "the science of human behavior," that is, why people "act and react" as they do, we have learned (discovered) today (in the past few decades) a simple truth founded in the Bible ages before. Simply stated, *"man's life is controlled by his attitudes,"* his inner motives. The acceptance of any truth depends on the attitude of the person who is listening (cf. Luke 8:11-14).

With the previously stated thoughts before us, and as we are almost ready to launch the text from which this chapter stems, let me set before us that "the attitude" concerns both "the teacher" and "the listener, the hearer."

> *"**If thou put the brethren in mind of these things**, thou shalt be a good minister of Christ Jesus, **nourished in the words of the faith, and of the good doctrine** which thou has followed... Faithful is the saying, and worthy of all acceptation. For to this end we labor and strive, because we have our hope set on the living God, who is the Saviour of all men, especially of them that believe. These things command and teach... Till I come, **give heed to reading, to exhortation, to teaching**... Be diligent in these things; give thyself wholly to them;... **Take heed to thyself, and to thy teaching. Continue** in these things; **for in doing this***

thou shalt save both thyself and them that hear thee" (1 Tim. 4:6-16, emp. GM).

It is "with the teacher," "the preacher," "the sower of the seed" that I am primarily concerned with at this juncture. Indeed, his attitude is most important. He must possess and declare by his own proclamation "the attitude that saves." Since the Old Testament is so rich, giving to us some of our most vivid examples, we turn to it once again for the main thrust of that which we must declare for Paul explicitly stated: "Take heed to thyself, and to thy teaching." No greater place could be found, especially at this time and need, than the book of Numbers.

As the children of Israel wandered in the wilderness, God blessed them over their enemies. They overcame Sihon, king of the Amorites as revealed in Numbers 21:21-32, and Og, king of Bashan, as shown in 21:33-35. When Israel came to Moab, the king Balak feared that the people would be destroyed even as the Amorites and the people of Bashan had been (22:1-5). Therefore, knowing that he could not defeat Israel without supernatural help, he sent to Balaam, a prophet in Pethor, to hire him to come and curse Israel (22:6-7). God told Balaam not to go. Balak sends more money and promises some great honor if Balaam would come. God sees that Balaam loves money and so He allows him to go if he wishes (22:7-20).

God is angered at Balaam's actions, when he goes to curse the people of God, and the ass speaks to him and reminds him to bless the people (22:21-35). Balaam finally tells Balak he cannot curse Israel when God has blessed them (22:36-23:12). This was after he had offered seven sacrifices.

He prophesies a second time and again declares to Balak that he must bless Israel because Israel is God's people (23:13-24). This is the time when Balak stated: "...Neither curse them at all, nor bless them at all." *Just here Balaam makes the statement that* reveals, *heralds*, and trumpets *the type of attitude* that each of us must nurse and nurture, advocate, champion and vindicate, if we intend to be acceptable to God in both our service and our worship to Him. Balaam said, "ALL THAT JEHOVAH SPEAKETH, THAT I MUST DO" (23:26). This is perhaps one of the most encyclopedic, sweeping and widespread declarations that any man could make. Let us now carefully analyze, explicate and explain, investigate and interpret as to gain its fullest import.

THE ATTITUDE OF COMPLETE SELF-SURRENDER - "ALL"

Several factors were at work to prevent Balaam from saying to Balak everything God had revealed to him.

1. **Balak had hired him in all good faith.** He might have felt honor-bound to please his employer. However, when we are speaking God's Word, God is our only employer. We do not have to answer to men for the truth. It is wrong to preach to please men. Paul informs us that a man is "anathema" (accursed, *K.J.*) if he *perverts the gospel* or preaches "any gospel other than that which we preached" (Gal. 1:6-10). Then he asked the question: "For am I now seeking the favor of men, or of God? or am I striving to please men?" "If I were still pleasing men, I should not be a servant of Christ," he declared. It is to the Thessalonians he said: "For our exhortation is not of error, nor of uncleanness, nor in guile: but even as we have been instructed with the gospel, so we speak; not as pleasing men, but God who proveth our hearts" (1 Thess. 2:3-4). It was the priest of Bethel who accused Amos of conspiring against Jeroboam. Amaziah said:

> *"...the land is not able to bear all his words. For thus Amos saith,...Also Amaziah said unto Amos, O thou seer, go, flee thou away... prophesy there: but prophesy not again any more at Bethel; for it is the king's sanctuary, and it is a royal house.*
>
> *Then answered Amos, and said to Amaziah, I was no prophet, neither was I a prophet's son;...Jehovah took me...Jehovah said unto me, Go, prophesy unto my people Israel.* ***Now therefore hear thou the word of Jehovah:..."*** *(Amos 7:10-16, emp. GM).*

Indeed, may we rise up and say, "...hear the word of Jehovah," and regardless of price, as it surely will not be like the "penalty" if we fail to do it.

2. **Balak had promised him a place of great honor.** That is, if he would curse God's people (cf. Num. 22:17). We, today, must be careful to give God the honor, all the glory, and not man. I often wonder if we have forgotten the thoughts of inspiration as expressed in Acts 10:25-26 ("...Cornelius met him, and fell down...Peter said, Stand up;..."), as it seems that man's pride, as well as "his honor," gets in his way of serving our Master. We are to give God the glory "in good works" (cf. Matt. 5:14-16). Yea, the apostle Paul says, "in everything" (cf. 1 Thess. 5:18; Eph. 5:20; Phil. 4:6; 1 Cor. 1:26-31). He knew wherein to glory: "But far be it from me to glory, save in the cross of our Lord Jesus Christ, through which the world hath been crucified unto me, and I unto the world" (Gal. 6:14).

3. **Balak offered him a large sum of money.** Again, providing he would curse Israel (Num. 22:18). Money has a way of blurring the cross of Christ, dimming the eyes

once set on the Jerusalem gospel and causing a strong wind to blow us from the stedfastness we are to maintain in Christ (cf. 1 Cor. 15:1-3; Col. 1:23; Eph. 4:14). Paul had something to say about "the love of money...a root of all kinds of evil" (cf. 1 Tim. 6:10). We have lost, to a great degree, the principle of "self-denial," which includes "earthly possessions" (cf. Matt. 4:18-22; 16:24-27).

4. **Will we honor God or man?** "Therefore now flee thou to thy place: I thought to promote thee unto great honor; but, lo, Jehovah hath kept thee back from honor. And Balaam said unto Balak, Spake I not...saying, If Balak would give me his house full of silver and gold, I cannot go beyond the word of Jehovah, to do either good or bad of mine own mind" (Num. 24:11-13). How many today leave out God's will to please men, to get honor, or to gain that which is destructive to the souls of men. If we were only aware of the many preachers/teachers who have fallen, forgotten, capitulated, surrendered and succumbed, etc., and have turned away from their allegiance to the Master, it would be most disheartening and perhaps would discourage many of our younger preachers and those now training to preach. It has always been the case for denominational preachers to fail to use good common sense with the Word of God, as they would take John 3:16 but not James 2:20-24; Romans 5:6 but not Acts 20:28; 1 Corinthians 15:3-4 but not Mark 16:15-16 as well as Matthew 26:26-29, but not Acts 20:7, etc., but it is not these men with whom I am concerned. I am deeply concerned about our own gospel preaching brethren... their handling of THE WORD.

THE ATTITUDE OF CRITICAL LISTENING - "ALL THAT JEHOVAH SPEAKETH"

It seems to be self-evident that many people have (almost) been trained not to listen to God's Word. Some have been told that God does not address Himself to human thinking and demand a choice for Him. They have been told that God addresses Himself to an indescribable part of man they call "the heart," and that they are saved by faith alone. This idea of "the heart" is foreign to the scriptures. The Bible teaches, and clearly so, that God addresses Himself by "speaking to man's mind." Many are the examples that could be given, but note (1) the case of Naaman in 2 Kings 5:1-14, (2) that of Saul in Acts 22:6-10, 16, (3) the example of Elijah as seen in 1 Kings 19:9-14, and (4) that of Amos in Amos 3:7-8.

Indeed, many "hear" (?) today but do not accept (cf. Acts 24:24-25; Jer. 6:16). More today need to be like Isaiah (6:6-10). Jesus commands us to take heed "what" we hear (Mark 4:24), "how" we hear (Luke 8:18), and "to give the more earnest heed to the things that were heard, lest haply we drift away from them" (Heb. 2:1). This demands "a critical examination" of everything, the standard being, the Bible (cf. Acts 17:10-11; 1 John 4:1; 2 Cor. 13:5; Acts 20:28-32; Gal. 2:11-14; etc.).

THE ATTITUDE OF PERSONAL RESPONSIBILITY - "I"

Balaam knew that Balak, as well as all of Moab, wanted Israel cursed. But he had a personal responsibility. No matter how many people oppose us, in the world or in the church, we must recognize and accept our own individual personal responsibility to examine God's will for ourselves and do precisely, exactly, God's will, that and nothing else.

If we, indeed, learn from both the Old and New Testaments, we will personally be aware that there is placed on man, God's own creation, a tremendous blessing, but it has a Siamese twin called "responsibility." When

Isaiah "heard the voice of the Lord, saying, Whom shall I send, and who will go for us?" he replied, "Then I said, Here am I; send me" (Isa. 6:8). When Joshua had gathered all the tribes of Israel to Shechem, called for the elders of Israel, their heads, their judges, their officers...he said, "Thus saith Jehovah, the God of Israel,..." and delivered his farewell address. As he closed it, he said:

> *"Now therefore fear Jehovah, and serve him in sincerity and in truth; and put away the gods which your fathers served beyond the River, and in Egypt; and serve ye Jehovah. And if it seem evil unto you to serve Jehovah, choose you this day whom ye will serve; whether the gods which your fathers served that were beyond the River, or the gods of the Amorites, in whose land ye dwell: but as for me and my house, we will serve Jehovah" (Josh. 24:14-15, emp. GM).*

The people's response was most gratifying, and it thrills both the heart and soul of any righteous person to hear it. "...Far be it from us that we should forsake Jehovah, to serve other gods;...therefore we also will serve Jehovah; for he is our God" (vss. 16-18).

I could multiply these verses many times (cf. Acts 5:29; Rom. 1:13-16), but to list the seriousness of that about which we are now thinking, writing, concerned, note:

> *"But thou, why dost thou judge thy brother? or thou again, why dost thou set at nought thy brother?* ***for we shall all stand before the judgment-seat*** *(Greek,* ***bema****)* ***of God****. For it is written, As I live, saith the Lord, to me every knee shall bow, And every tongue shall confess*

*to God. So then **each one of us shall give account of himself to God**" (Rom. 14:10-12, emp. GM).*

*"For **we must all be made manifest** before the Judgment-seat (Greek, **bema**) of Christ; that each one may receive the things done in the body, **according to what he hath done**, whether it be good or bad" (2 Cor. 5:10, emp. GM).*

THE ATTITUDE OF A GOOD CONSCIENCE - "MUST"

God did not force Balaam to do what he said, but Balaam knew that was the only thing that he could do and be right with God. His conscience would not let him do otherwise.

There are many "musts" in the Bible. Man is not "forced," as it must be a matter of his desire, his will, his love for God, yea his conscience: (1) must work (John 9:4), (2) must obey God (Acts 5:27-29), (3) must be about our God's business (Luke 2:49), (4) must be baptized (Acts 9:6; 22:16; John 3:1-7), (5) must worship God both in spirit and truth (John 4:21-24), (6) must not strive (2 Tim. 2:23-26), (7) must believe that God is, as well as being a rewarder of those diligently serving him (Heb. 11:6), etc.

The conscience cannot be good unless we do what we know is right.

"Hereby shall we know that we are of the truth, and shall assure our heart before him: because if our heart condemn us, God is greater than our heart, and knoweth all things. Beloved, if our heart condemn us not, we have boldness toward God; and whatsoever we ask we receive of him, because we keep his com-

mandments and do the things that are pleasing in his sight" (1 John 3:19-22).

There is coming a day, Paul said, "when God shall judge the secrets of men, according to my gospel, by Jesus Christ" (Rom. 2:16; note should be made of vss. 11-16, as well as 1 Pet. 3:18-22). We are to have and maintain an "attitude of a good conscience" (cf. Rom. 14:23).

THE ATTITUDE OF ACTIVITY - "DO"

The religion of Jesus Christ is not a "dead" religion. That is what was wrong with Judaism. Jesus came to take that away and to supply a living religion. The religion of Jesus Christ is a religion of "doing." As brother Keeble once said, "You don't get religion, you 'do' it." Jesus spoke of the man entering into the kingdom of heaven as "he that doeth the will of my Father..." and also asked, "Why do ye call me Lord, Lord, and do not the things which I say?" (Matt. 7:21, vss. 22-27 as well; Luke 6:46). When asked about his mother and his brethren, he said, "My mother and my brethren are these that hear the word of God, and do it" (Luke 8:19-21, esp. vs. 21; cf. Luke 11:27-28; 10:25-37; Mark 14:3-9; John 4:34; 15:13-15; Gal. 6:7-9).

Even though Balaam had a high and noble attitude toward his own responsibility to God, he is nevertheless remembered, not for his goodness, but for his love of the hire of wrong doing (2 Pet. 2:12-16). We need to remember the admonition: "Wherefore let him that thinketh he standeth take heed lest he fall" (1 Cor. 10:12). But just here, we need to remember Balaam's answer to Balak: "O my people, remember now what Balak king of Moab devised, and what Balaam the son of Beor answered him; remember from Shittim unto Gilgal, that ye may know the righteous acts of Jehovah" (Mic. 6:5).

These verses, in view of the way Balaam was remembered by the pen of inspiration through Peter, should be inscribed deeply upon the heart and soul of every student of the Book and of every follower of Christ. I list them, as I know of no where in all of the life of one, where so many famed and famous, unmistakable and unforgettable solid-rock statements are found. They bear being firmly burned into our great desire to please and serve God, all the while remembering Balaam "who was remembered for the wrong love."

> *"And Balaam answered and said unto the servants of Balak,* ***If Balak would give me his house full of silver and gold, I cannot go beyond the word of Jehovah my God to do less or more"*** *(Num. 22:18).*

> *"And Balaam said unto Balak, Lo, I am come unto thee: have I now any power at all to speak anything?* ***the word that God putteth in my mouth, that shall I speak"*** *(Num. 22:38; cf. vs. 35).*

> *"...And he answered and said,* ***Must I not take heed to speak that which Jehovah putteth in my mouth"*** *(Num. 23:12).*

> *"Behold,* ***I have received commandment*** *to bless: And he hath blessed,* ***and I cannot reverse it"*** *(Num. 23:20).*

> *"But Balaam answered and said unto Balak, Told not I thee, saying,* ***All that Jehovah speaketh, that I must do?*** *(Num. 23:26).*

> *"And Balaam said unto Balak, Spake I not also to the messengers that thou sentest unto me, saying, If Balak would give me his house full*

> *of silver and gold,* ***I cannot go beyond the word of Jehovah, to do either good or bad of mine own mind; what Jehovah speaketh, that will I speak?*** *" (Num. 24:12-13, all emp. GM).*

The great body of knowledge, which I have referred to previously, earlier, in this chapter, the science of human behavior, is certainly a truth, not only founded among the great and noble truths of the Bible, but we also see it practiced. It was on Paul's second tour that he encountered four different attitudes in equally as many cities. Yet, here was the same man, who preached the same message and perhaps delivered it the same way.

1. **In Thessalonica**, Acts 17:1ff, a coastal city of Turkey, he had reasoned (cf. 17:2), as well as "alleged" (vs. 3) with them from the scriptures, and a great congregation of the Lord's people began (cf. 1 Thess. 1:9-10). However, for the most part, it seems, there was not the receptiveness toward the truth by all, as many (a crowd) were filled with *jealously* and set the city in an uproar (vss. 5-9). They even took with them "vile fellows of the rabble" (vs. 5) and troubled the rulers of the city (vs. 8). Evidently, a whole host of people were *prejudiced, had a closed mind*, and let their *ignorance of the truth* guide them without being willing to ask, to study and to learn.

2. **In Berea**, Acts 17:10-14, to which the brethren had sent Paul and Silas by night, they went into another synagogue (vs. 10), and they found these to be "more noble" than those in Thessalonica. The reason is simple, as they *"received the word with all readiness of mind, examining the scriptures daily, whether these things were so"* (vs. 11). In this city, many believed, yea, "of the Greek women of honorable estate, and of men, not a few" (vs. 12). The Jews in Thessalonica, when they heard of Paul

proclaiming the Word of God also in Berea, further showed their prejudice as they came "thither likewise, stirring up and troubling the multitudes" (vs. 13).

3. **In Athens**, Acts 17:15-34, while Paul waited for Timothy and Silas, "his spirit was provoked as he beheld the city full of idols" (vs. 16). Paul then "reasoned" in the synagogue with the Jews, as well as in the marketplace, every day, with the devout persons (vs. 17). This is where Paul encountered *the philosophers*, Epicurean as well as Stoic, who, because "he preached Jesus and the resurrection" (vs. 18), brought him unto the Areopagus. All because of the truth being foreign to them (*note*, "strange gods," "new teaching," and "strange things to our ears"), as they spent their time, all of their time, "in nothing else, but either to tell or to hear some new thing" (vs. 21). We, today, do not "miss the mark," when we say that it mattered not to them whether Paul preached Jesus or Jupiter, and/or Mercury or Baal (cf. Acts 13:11-12; 1 Kings 18:21). Can we not say that these were just *totally indifferent* to the Word, and that they possessed a kind of pseudo-intellectualism (yea, which is found among us today)? It makes me want to cry out, "Oh, the philosophers! Yea, the philosophing philosophers who philosophize the truth!"

4. **In Corinth**, Acts 18:1-17, to which he had come from Athens, he found Aquila and Priscilla, abode with them as they were tentmakers, and "reasoned in the synagogue every sabbath" (vss. 1-4). He turned to the Gentiles (vs. 6), was encouraged by the Lord himself (vss. 9-10) and abode here a year and six months teaching the Word of God among them (vs. 11). The Jews once again "rose up against Paul" (vs. 12ff) and he was taken before the judgment-seat (Gallio). We should all know what "a Corinthian" was and what it meant to "Corinthianize."

Paul had now come to a city where there was *almost every type of immorality* (cf. 1 Cor. 6:9-11), but nonetheless, many responded (Acts 18:8; 1 Cor. 6:11; cf. 2 Cor. 3:18; John 12:42-43) as is very often the case because the Word is so powerful (cf. Rom. 1:16; 1 Cor. 1:18-21, 25-31; 2:1-5; 2 Cor. 4:3-4; etc.).

In every city, it seems, there are "only a few" (cf. 1 Cor. 1:26-29; Matt. 22:14; 1 Tim. 6:6-10) who have "the spirit of the Bereans and search to see if these things be so" (Acts 17:10-11). But this is the type, the kind of a spirit that pleases God (cf. Prov. 23:23; Psm. 119:151; Acts 10:33). Many today will just not "pay the price that truth demands" (cf. Matt. 16:24; 10:34-39; Luke 14:25-35; Gal. 2:20; 6:14).

May we forever cherish the attitude of, BEHOLD THE PATTERN, by doing as the noble Bereans did. We need deeply to root and establish that which will serve as a WITNESS, not only to us, but to our own precious families, our children, our grandchildren, and to the very world that is all around and about us. It may just be that in time to come, they might say, "What meaneth these stones?" (Josh. 4:6, 21). By having "*the attitude that saves*" and by "*beholding the pattern*," we will prove to the world that God has one way for all men, and that one way, one plan, is, indeed, universal and eternal. Yes, it is clearly and unmistakably, undisputable and undoubtable, the fact that God has a PATTERN, therefore, may we always, in all things, BEHOLD THE PATTERN.

APPENDICES

AN UPDATE ON THE ELKINS - SHELLY DEBATE

AN UPDATE ON THE ELKINS - SHELLY DEBATE

As I was bringing to a close the section relative to some "Strange" and "Uncertain" sounds stemming from brother Rubel Shelly, I made mention of the debate invitation extended to him by the elders of the congregation meeting at 4400 Knight Arnold Road in Memphis, Tennessee. I quoted from those elders (Knight Arnold Road Church of Christ), chapter eight, part iv of this book, and also listed the propositions for such a debate. The elders had asked brother Garland Elkins to represent the Knight Arnold Road Church of Christ.

These elders, on February 3, 1991, wrote their first letter to the elders of the Woodmont Hills Church of Christ in Nashville, Tennessee, where brother Rubel Shelly is serving. On February 12, 1991, brother Roy Newson, chairman of the elders, replied in the negative. On February 25, 1991, the Knight Arnold Road elders wrote their second letter to the elders at Woodmont Hills (and each time a copy was sent to brother Shelly), and, at the time I finished the manuscript for this book, it was just "too early" to have heard again from the Woodmont Hills elders. Therefore, the closing sentence of that material stated the following: "We only hope, as well as pray, that they not only respond, but that they also accept to defend on the polemic platform what Rubel has publicly and very extensively taught."

About a month later (March 25, 1991), the elders of Woodmont Hills wrote another letter, and, as before, brother Roy Newsom signed it. I now give that letter in its entirety.

"Dear Brothers:

It is our judgment that there will be no advancement to the Lord's Kingdom by our participating in the debate you propose.

In Him,

Roy Newsom"

If space allowed, I would include two articles from brother Thomas B. Warren: "Salvation Is By Grace - But Not By Grace Only," and "Will These Propostions Be Signed And Discussed?" The best I can do is to list where they can be found to be both read and studied.

1. *Yokefellow* (A Publication of the Memphis School of Preaching, Knight Arnold Road Church of Christ, 4400 Knight Arnold Road, Memphis, Tennessee, 38118-2948, VOL. 18, NO. 4, April 15, 1991 and VOL. 18, NO. 6, June 26, 1991. Curtis A. Cates and Garland Elkins, co-editors).

2. *Firm Foundation* (Firm Foundation Publishing Company, P. O. Box 690192, Houston, Texas 77269-0192, Vol. 106, No. 5, May, 1991, editorial office of H. A. [Buster] Dobbs).

3. *Biblical Notes* (7401 Glenhaven Path, Austin, Texas, 78737, VOL. XX, No. 3, May/June, 1991, and VOL. XX, No. 4, July/August, 1991. Roy Deaver, editor).

I do, however, want to say a word about the April 15, 1991, issue (the one mentioned above) of *Yokefellow,* as its contents are "a must" if a person wants to stay abreast, and first hand, of this most important subject. I now list those contents and do so to encourage you to order this issue and/or subscribe to this outstanding publication.

1. A Brotherly Appeal For A Public Discussion On A Crucial Matter, Curtis Cates, page 1.
2. Contending For The Faith Once Delivered, Curtis Cates, page 2.
3. They Make Light Of It, Garland Elkins, page 2.
4. *Arbeit Macht Frei!,* Rubel Shelly, page 3.
5. Reaction To Rubel Shelly's Article, Curtis Cates, page 3.
6. Correspondence Between Knight Arnold And Woodmont Hills Elders, pages 3, 4, 5.
7. Salvation Is By Grace But Not By Grace Only, Thomas B. Warren, page 5.
8. Oh, For An Honest False Teacher, Rubel Shelly, page 8.

In addition to these major articles, I deem it necessary to alert you, that is, to call your attention to, two "bordered" articles:

1. Incredible Charge; Glaring Inconsistency, page 4 (note # 5 above).
2. A Late Response, page 6.

I want to also point out that the caption, in bold letters, of the June, 1991, issue of *Contending For The Faith* (Bellview Church of Christ, 4850 Saufley Field Road, Pensacola, Florida, 32526-1798, Vol. XXII, No. 6, Ira Y. Rice, Jr., editor) was as follows: WOODMONT HILLS, RUBEL SHELLY REFUSE KNIGHT ARNOLD ELDERS, GARLAND ELKINS' CHALLENGE TO DEBATE SALVATION ISSUE. Therefore, in this issue one can also be aware of the correspondence between the two churches that I have previously mentioned (Note also Vol. XXII,

No. 8, August, 1991, pp. 2-7).

Just in case someone should object to the elders at Knight Arnold making their correspondence with Woodmont Hills known, let me show you their wisdom in this by reminding you of what they wrote in their very first letter (February 3, 1991).

> *"Since brother Shelly has taught his views publicly, and from coast to coast, we are sure that you will have no hesitancy in endorsing him to debate. And, since his views have been widely circulated, we feel sure that you have no objections whatever to our publicizing this communication" (next to last paragraph, second page).*

Evidently, the response to this material, relative to this debate invitation as per the *Yokefellow* (April 15, 1991) has been terrific. I noted these words in an issue, "The positive response by the readers of the April 15, 1991, issue has been overwhelming... Many hundreds have requested to be added to the list of *Yokefellow* subscribers" (VOL. 18, NO. 5, May 29, 1991, p. 3). Again, it was stated: "The April 15, 1991, *Yokefellow* on 'A Brotherly Appeal for a Public Discussion on a Crucial Matter' has been reprinted. Thousands of extra copies have been requested" (VOL. 18, NO. 7, July 17, 1991, p. 3). Indeed, some 17 thousand or so copies of this issue were printed. This clearly indicated the interest that is manifested in this debate and material.

The Christian life demands that we be proper, principled, and precisely painstaking when it comes to writing material and quoting various brethren. My soul will not be jeopardized by being rather "loose" with my quotations, presumptuous (disrespectful) in my statements, and a failure to reassure each of my love for the truth and the person(s) involved in the material herein produced.

For several years, I was a recipient of the bulletins from where my good friend, and brother, Rubel preached. However, in 1991 I stopped receiving LOVELINES (the weekly bulletin of the Woodmont Hills Church in Nashville), therefore, on February 16, 1991, I wrote the secretary (thinking she was perhaps in charge of such), only to be answered on the 26th by Rubel (the secretary had given my note to him). I was informed that I was one of perhaps a dozen whose names had been omitted from the bulletin list. I did not realize that I had been "overtly critical...," read with a "jaundiced eye," and "made no secret of your theological and personal opposition to my ministry," therefore, my name was omitted from the mailing list.

This letter (the above statements), more than puzzled and bothered me, therefore, on March 7, 1991, I wrote Rubel. This was a three page letter, including my gratitude for him taking the time and personally writing, that now I understood why I had been dropped from the bulletin list, etc. I informed Rubel that I would like for him to prove (I would not mind having the proof of his statement...and asked him to document it for me) what he had said. I said this, as in that letter, I mentioned that for some 2½-3 years, after his Centerville speech in 1983, that I refused to believe what I heard, defended him and never once backed down from any man regarding the same. I mentioned our togetherness in various activities, gave a specific date as an example, and stated that in those earlier years we stood on the same ground. I complimented his earlier writings, debates, and the excellent job he had done. I also declared how that I sat and wept when I heard what he was now teaching (and "how" he was saying and stating such, those intonations, inflections and modulations!). Yes, he wrote again (the letter's date is 4-2-'91), however, no proof, no document, was given of what he had said about me and my...

In the above-mentioned letter, I declared that I had been wrong in my backing of him, was very, very sorry that we no longer stood as one man in the faith, defending the same, and now, for the first time in my life, I was going to quote him (and this I have adequately done in this book). I also stated that it was just not the case that the only thing changed was his attitude. If you, dear reader, believe I am wrong, let me list another one of his articles in the *Gospel Advocate:* "Has The New Testament Church Been Restored?" (December 16, 1971). In fact, to give you just a "spiritual taste" (if no taste, perhaps no appetite!) of it, note the following:

> *"But recently there has been a great outcry against the validity of the plea for restoration.* ***Brethren have said*** *that* ***the New Testament church has not been restored.***
>
> *"I categorically deny the notion that the restoration plea is invalid.* ***I also deny*** *that* ***the goal of restorationism is yet unrealized. The New Testament church,*** the body and bride of Christ, ***does exist in the twentieth century*** *and I am a member of that body!*
>
> *"The foregoing affirmation is made in view of four primary facts: (1)* ***the New Testament*** *is the authoritative truth of God which* ***forms a fixed rule of faith and practice for*** *people of* ***every generation*** *(need I give any further proof?), (2)* ***the New Testament reveals a single plan of salvation*** *to which all men are*

> *subject, (3)* ***the New Testament authorizes*** *five acts of worship which Christians may - and must - perform* ***and*** *(4) the New Testament* ***sets forth a simple pattern*** *(please note the use of the word "pattern," as it was no slip!) of congregational organization which must be faithfully followed.*
>
> ***"We have restored the New Testament church*** *and have exactly the same situation (no cultural baggage here) which the church had in the first century. We are the body of Christ and are striving toward the ideal goal for the church which is set forth in the perfect revelation of his will to men" (I need not make myself redundant in the fact that more than just Rubel's attitude has changed. All emph. GM).*

In chapter eight, just before listing some of Rubel's articles, lectures, books and also his debates (a few pages prior to the debate invitation from the elders of the Knight Arnold Road Church of Christ), I quoted the pertinent thoughts from his article (*Arbeit Macht Frei!*), which article was the basis of the debate challenge. That article is dated as October 31, 1990, as per *Lovelines* (Vol. 16, Num. 45). Yet, with all that has been written, brother Shelly still maintains that same position. I now prove my statement from his article entitled: "This Is Heresy?"

> *"SEVERAL MONTHS BACK I WROTE an article under the title* ***"Arbeit Macht Frei!"*** *It was an affirmation of the biblical doctrine of justification by grace. It asserted that human attempts at self-justification through good works are pointless. Salvation does not arise from what we do but from what God has already done at Calvary.*

The reaction of a few to that essay has been frightening. What their response says about their concept of salvation alarms me both for their own sakes and for anyone who takes them seriously.

They charge that such a view of grace negates human responsibility, makes repentance unnecessary, denies the necessity of baptism, rejects the duty of Christian holiness, and otherwise removes human obedience from the divine scheme of things.

How utterly false - and revealing - the indictment is.

Of course we are supposed to hear and heed divine commandments. Every law God ever gave is holy, righteous, and good. None is to be despised by anyone who believes in him. Faith in God involves submission to his will, and grace gives neither liberty to set aside any command of God nor approval for any instance of disobedience.

But there's a problem. Suppose we do ***everything*** *we are told to do? We are still 'unworthy servants' with no right to claim salvation (Luke 17:7-10). The fact is, however, that we* ***don't*** *do all the things divine law requires. 'We know that the law is spiritual,' wrote Paul, 'but I am unspiritual, sold as a slave to sin' (Rom. 7:14). I confess the same deficiency.*

Here is what the New Testament says about the adequacy of our obedience to law: 'Therefore no one will be declared righteous in his sight by observing the law; rather, through the law we become conscious of sin' (Rom. 3:20).

Yes, we are commanded to repent, be baptized, feed the hungry, minister to prisoners, pray, worship, abhor sin, live in love, evangelize, etc. Nobody does all these things. Nobody does even one of them perfectly. So, while no one will go to heaven as a rebel against God, neither will anyone go there because of his prowess at rule-keeping.

In the article already cited, I called it an 'outrageous lie' to teach that salvation arises from human activity. In Galatians, Paul was even more pointed and called theology which grounds salvation in human activity 'another gospel.'

How, then, will anyone be saved? Not by 'doing enough' but by accepting what God has done for him. By grace. All-sufficient grace. Amazing - and apparently intimidating - grace!

*Legalism calls this 'heresy.' Scripture calls it Good News" (**Lovelines**, Vol. 17, Num. 19, May 8, 1991, inside right page).*

Before quoting another statement or two from his pen, be sure and note the date of the above article (May 8, 1991), compare it with the date of his *Arbeit Macht Frei!* article (October 31, 1990), as well as with the dates of the correspondence between the elders of the Knight Arnold Road Church of Christ and the Woodmont Hills elders (February 3rd and 12th; February 25th and March 25, 1991). I mention these to be sure and prove the point that brother Shelly still "maintains that same position."

Prior to the article entitled "This Is Heresy?," he

wrote:

> *"The Bible sets faith and all it consequences opposite* ***merit****, not activity. Salvation arises solely and exclusively from God's grace. No human activity - nor all of them collectively - adds one particle to it. Eternal life is a free gift! Faith is simply accepting the gift. Holding out our hands. Unwrapping the package" (****How To Do Faith****, Vol. 17, Num. 17, April 23, 1991, inside right page. See if you note any contradiction in the above quote. I only wish, and most sincerely, that space allowed me to quote and point out some of his statements as per* ***Lovelines****, same volume, but found in numbers 12, 23, 28, 29, as examples. Evidently, he loves to use Romans 3:20-22, law, obedience to law, etc., in contrast to salvation as being solely and exclusively from God's grace, no human activity, etc. Indeed, brother Shelly still maintains his teaching found in Arbeit Macht Frei!, so what we are saying must be, as per his words, "an outrageous lie" (It is good to be reminded... emp. are his unless otherwise stated, GM).*

Unless brother Shelly has removed himself from all valid reasoning, then he very truthfully knows that a precisely stated proposition is either "true" or "false." (If it is true that there is a God, then it must be false that there is no God). *If it is true, Proposition Number I,* that "The Bible teaches that salvation from sin results from the grace of God alone, totally and completely apart from any human activity," *then it must be false, Proposition Number II,* that "The Bible teaches that salvation depends upon both (1) the grace of God and (2) the faithful loving obedience of the individual human being." With this in mind, it seems clear enough to state that one of these propositions is true, and the other one is false. It seems that brother Shelly, whether he will debate it on the polemic platform or not, would at least sign one of these as to what his convictions really are. If he thinks that one of these is not a precisely stated proposition, then let him declare that matter by proving the same.

The above may sound harsh, but I certainly do not mean it to be anything but a loving desire to bring such a study to fruition. I just believe this would help us all tremendously and help to settle a tremendous unrest among us in this matter. There is no doubt in my mind about brother Shelly being one of the finest and one of the most loved soldiers of the Cross, at least in days gone by (before this great change took place). And, we still love him! This ought to be manifest by the great concern we have shown. But I must very quickly add that we no longer love what he is teaching. Neither do I believe that "our fellowship," unless awakened to certain things, will come "to be more of an irrelevance to God's purposes than we are already." No, indeed! I do not believe for a moment that we are an irrelevance to God's purposes.

The Bible is very clear on "the false teacher," the one bringing "a different doctrine" (cf. 2 John 9-11; Rom. 16:17-18; Tit. 3:10-11; Eph. 5:11; etc.), yea, the apostates, and brother Shelly knows this as well as anyone. It may just be that he needs to go back to the article he wrote (published date of May 6, 1971), and which was published in the *Gospel Advocate,* and hear himself, listen well to himself, take heed to himself and to his teaching (cf. 1 Tim. 4:13-16) and admonish himself as he admonished others when he wrote: "Oh, For An Honest False Teacher." Here are just a few of his thoughts, "back then."

"Of certain false teachers, John wrote: "They went out from us, but they are not of us; for if they had been of us; they would have continued with us: but they went out,...they all are not of us" (1 John 2:19).

They had arisen from within the church itself! They had become apostates from the truth... they did not possess the spirit of obedience which was characteristic of faithful disciples,... these...had...severed their ties with faithful churches.

Can anything good be said about such apostates as these? Yes! They were honest! When these former members of the Lord's church came to repudiate the basic tenents of the faith, they were honest enough to...make a clean break with the church.... Surely we can have more respect for a man who is honest and open about his convictions (or lack of them) than for a man who no longer believes the basic doctrines of the gospel but seeks to stay within the body of believers as a subversive. Such a person is not only a heretic Christian, he is a dishonest man!

Oh, for an honest false teacher!...

While I do not question the sincerity with which they came to their present views, I do question their honesty in remaining within our brotherhood after they have come to hold such!

...If, upon such thorough investigation, they decide that they are no longer 'of us,' let them be honest enough to break with us openly and quit their unmanly treason!" (this has been

taken from page 284 of the ***Gospel Advocate,*** *which I have on my desk at this time, GM).*

Before one jumps to the wrong conclusion, please, get this article in full and read it. You need to understand "the basic tenets of the faith," "apostates from the truth," "the spirit of obedience," "the basic doctrines of the gospel," and the use of "the church," "faithful churches," "the Lord's church," "the body of believers," "or brotherhood," etc. Brethren, this kind of article is excellent, and it certainly shows clearly, yea, crystal clear, that there is more than just "a change in attitude or disposition." The way he once wrote, the choice thoughts as presented above, and all beautifully plain and solid truth, is no longer the way he thinks (writes, lectures, or preaches). Indeed, if the above quoted descriptions of the truth have not changed, then brother Shelly has changed. What he has preached, written, lectured and taught could very well be one of the reasons he does not want to debate, as he was so precise, so very definite, so very sure, positive and determined. He knew the truth, knew that we could know the truth, knew that we knew the truth, had the truth, preached, lectured and both debated and defended the truth. Maybe just here I could use his own words (found in the last paragraph I quoted form his article above), in reference to all these men who are giving and sending forth a "strange" and "uncertain" (there is nothing "uncertain" about what they are saying, but in comparison to the way Paul used it in 1 Corinthians 14:8 it is "uncertain" as compared to that which is so certain and distinct) sound, "...let them be honest enough to break with us openly and quit their unmanly treason!" (in his third paragraph he used the word "subversive," which is a synonym for treason. You see, it is all right from those so loving to use such strong words as "unmanly treason," but just let one of us use suchlike if you want to hear "the ever-so-loving and loveable" bellow and bawl, howl and yowl, yammer and clamor. But the point for us to note is "where Rubel stood" *when he used such*).

"The third-annual *Nashville Jubilee* begins Wednesday, July 3, at 6:30 p.m."... "Thursday through Friday, daytime sessions at the Nashville Convention Center begin at 8 a.m. and continue until 8:30 p.m." (*Lovelines, op. cit.*, Vol. 17/Num. 26, June 26, 1991, as per the front page). The date of this event was July 3-6, 1991, and the theme was "Room at the Cross." "The Madison and Antioch churches have set a high standard by which this year's *Jubilee* will be measured" (*ibid.*, Vol. 17/Num. 18, May 1, 1991, front page). This event that registered 11,500, coming from 40 states and four foreign countries, with evening crowds averaging more than 700 per night above last year's, was, of course, hosted by Woodmont Hills.

I give the above, as during this event brother Shelly spoke on two of those days. His subjects were: "How the Church and Kingdom Relate," and "A Christian Antinomy: Law and Grace." As I listened to the first tape, and made my transcription, I heard again what he had already (for the most part) given (the date of the first lesson was July 5, 1991).

I then listened to his lesson on "A Christian Antinomy: Law and Grace," and made my transcription of it. It is from this lesson that I want to quote a few of the statements he made.

> *"Our salvation arises entirely and only from grace; not by one thing we bring from this system over here (referring to his diagram he had mentioned in his lesson for illustrating his points), not by one act of duty, not by one deed of obedience, not by one righteous thing*

we do. It is entirely of grace through faith.

"We have to be careful because we're in a fellowship where legalism runs... easy to fall into it.

"I know a lot of people who are living by that monstrous theological lie today (referring to his article that we've earlier mentioned, ***Arbeit Macht Frei!****, etc.).*

"I understand grace... my debt... I believe that ... I trust Jesus... My salvation is on grace alone... Not by anything I've added to that... I'm not saved because I've been... there is only one 'because of' in His plan of salvation... I trust Jesus and Him alone!" (from side two of my tape, GM).

I want to mention a few of the things that Rubel stated about "law" and about "human responsibility," as I would be very unfair to have heard his tapes and not mention these. As I have written before, we are a principled people and conduct ourselves accordingly. I want us to know what he says about "law" and about "human responsibility," as he does not deny either, but affirms both. The following I have transcribed from his tapes.

"I affirm the necessity of law... Law is how God reveals Himself... I will never degrade law... Law is therefore a holy thing... The problem is not with law, but with lawkeepers ... Grace and law are inseparable... Each absolutely necessary...

"Faith is our response..." (from side one of my tape, GM).

"Baptism... is an act of faith... It is an act of

faith done to accept and affirm the grace that has been given to us through Jesus Christ... Anything else is to prostitute baptism.

"The one step to salvation is faith... saved because of the grace of God...

"In affirming that (speaking of whether salvation is by grace and grace alone), I do not deny human responsibility. Of course, we have responsibility... I am saved by what He did... not by my believing and not by anything that in obedience to Christ I've done to demonstrate that that faith is real" (this was the end of my tape, side two. This date was July 6, 1991, at his 3:45 p.m. class in #206, GM).

On the second side of the first tape (the one earlier mentioned, but not yet quoted), he did make the following, and it is in this connection, meaning of "law and grace," so I give it.

"One fellow wrote me a letter the other day. He said... 'Grace just means that God gave us the plan by which we can save ourselves.' I wouldn't say that without letting you know I was quoting somebody else's words. Because that is blasphemy people. That's not just an aberration of understanding, that is blasphemy" (side two of my tape, July 5, 1991).

Now then, I have taken the time to give quotations from my transcription of brother Shelly's two lessons at the *Nashville Jubilee,* as this is up-to-the-minute, in the swim of his thinking and speaking, it is on the debate material and shows that he has not changed. In fact, it declares unto us, in no uncertain terms (his words are indisputable, unquestionable and undeniable), his own precisely stated feelings about debating the issue at hand. *Please note what he said.*

> *"And, No, I'm not going to debate anybody on the theory of whether salvation is by grace and grace alone. Because the Bible just makes that too plain" (side two of the July 6th, 1991 lesson as already listed, GM).*

There you have it! I stand amazed at the reason for not debating the propositions (listed earlier as per chapter eight): "Because the Bible just makes that too plain." I say this, as evidently it was so graphic, distinct, visible, vivid, apparent, and self-evident that it has taken years for brother Shelly to come to this conclusion. And if such be the case, and it is, then why not debate it with brother Elkins and let us all see just how plain, clear-cut, well-defined, obvious, manifest and unmistakable it is. Surely he would want all the world, especially all of his brothers and sisters, to "see this new-found truth." After all, he did not come to "see the light (?)" until the past few years.

Again, I do not say what I cannot document. It would be well if every reader could read the sermons preached by Rubel over the radio in years gone by. Here is a statement or two on some subjects that have a bearing on and relate to that under discussion.

> *"Baptism is essential unto salvation. It is not a command to men who are already saved, but is* ***a condition to be met by sinners in order for them to receive*** *the remission of their sins" ("What Baptism Does," p. 4, radio station WHBQ on May 17, 1970, emp. GM). He says about the same thing in his sermon, "Baptism For The Remission Of Sins," same station May 10, 1970, and in his sermon "Objections To*

Baptism For The Remission Of Sins," same station, May 24, 1970. Each one is four pages, single-spaced, and I do have them in my possession).

"Most people would be terribly shocked if anyone suggested that many sincere religious people are going to be lost eternally. They would likely cry out, 'Only God knows who is going to be saved and lost! You are judging and trying to play God when you suggest that you can know who is right and who is wrong in religion!'

***"The Word of God commands us** to distinguish between truth and error. **It requires us** to support the one and oppose the other... (II John 10-11)... (I John 4:1)... If this is not a clear requirement that men must examine, test or judge the doctrines taught by religious teachers, human language is unintelligible and meaningless!" ("Will The Good People Of All Churches Be Saved?", "The Truth In Love" radio broadcast, sermon No. 301, no date given, p. 1, emp. GM).*

In this sermon, brother Shelly made statements such as: "The New Testament teaches that Christ established only one church and desires for all men to be united in it," "The New Testament apostles and prophets recognized only one church," "The New Testament teaches that the saved are all added to the one church," and "...from a Biblical perspective, we must say that there is actually only ONE church and that all the other so-called churches are nothing more than false churches and human denominations" (p. 2). He goes on to say that "the Word of God and it alone can show what is right and wrong in religion" (and this is why we would like to have the debate, to let the Word of God settle the issue!). After that statement he begins a section on "Unity Based on the Word of God" (both on p. 3).

I believe, with all my heart and soul, dear reader, that we want to be "right." In fact, Rubel said, "The difference between being right and wrong in religion is the difference between salvation and condemnation" (p. 3). And, he went on to say that "error means condemnation" (and undoubtedly he believes that we are in error, as he no longer believes what we all at one time proclaimed) (p. 4). Let the debate come about and you can hear (perhaps) further quotations from what he once said (maybe from sermons like his "Thinking That God Is Like Man," same program, sermon No. 304).

Those of us who have taught the truth on this matter under consideration have been charged by the denominational world as being "legalists" for a long time. However, unless I have totally and completely misunderstood our good brother Rubel, he is now making the same charge against us. At various times in the two lessons given at the *Jubilee* he implied such. I want to give just one statement from him. It was given by him in the same paragraphical thought of his closing words (at least that is when my tape ended) in his lesson on "A Christian Antinomy: Law and Grace," which was his last lesson to give.

> *"My salvation is based on grace alone...I'm not saved because I believe or because I repented or because I was baptized or because I...There is only one 'because of' in the plan of salvation. I'm going to heaven because Jesus paid my sin debt...And I'll never believe anything else...I won't trust the system. I*

won't trust good works. I'll trust Jesus and Him alone.

*"**Arbeit Macht Frei!**, work will set you free. Work will make you a spiritual neurotic. Trusting what you can do and how good you are, and doing enough and keeping the essential commands will drive you nuts. Understanding the gospel will produce a fruitfulness of good works in your life that fear and law and a works system never would and you'll do it out of joy and in love, not in fear that you'd fry in hell if you didn't. And the difference in the two is not a slight... words, it's the difference in the gospel and legalism. And, No, I'm not going to debate anybody..." (documentation already given).*

I close this with words by brother Thomas B. Warren, as it does seem we need to keep repeating what we have always said and a man could not say it better than brother Warren. He said, "In the April issue of *Yokefellow* (the article was 'Salvation Is By Grace, But Not By Grace Only,' and was on page 5, GM), I affirmed (at least by implication) the following statements:

1. *It is a misrepresentation for any one to state we affirm that any human act of **obedience** to God can ever be regarded correctly as **meritorious** (that is, **earning** salvation without the grace of God).*

2. *In all of my life, I have never heard even one Christian affirm that sinners **earn** their salvation by acts of obedience (For someone to affirm that such is the case is to misrepresent the facts).*

3. *No one can **earn** his salvation.*

4. *No one can be saved without the grace of God.*

5. *People are saved by the grace of God **when** - and **only** when by faith they obey the relevant instructions of Jesus Christ (who clearly taught that only those who **do** the will of the Father will enter the kingdom of heaven (Matt. 7:21). (This involves obeying the plan of salvation which is revealed in the New Testament).*

6. *While the works of men **cannot earn** the forgiveness of even one sin, it is nevertheless the case that salvation by the grace of God is **contingent** (depends upon) on both **man's faith** and **man's obedience** to the gospel of Jesus Christ (Cf. Heb. 5:8-9; et al.).*

*This whole matter can be summed up well by noting (1) that all people who live and die in faithfulness to the gospel of Christ will be saved eternally (James 2:24-26; Rev. 2:10; Heb. 5:8-9; et al.) and (2) that all people who live and die in unfaithfulness to the gospel of Christ will be **lost** eternally (II Thess. 1:7-9; Matt. 7:13-14; et al.).*

It is because of our love for our God and for our fellowmen (including our brothers and sisters in Christ) that we call attention to these matters and urge that they be discussed in a public way so that all who wish to do so may hear those discussions which are so vital to the soul of each one of us. If we know our own hearts, we have no motivation in all of this except that of sincere love for both God and man. We sincerely love brother Shelly and pray for his welfare in every righteous way.

*We also pray that this discussion may soon be arranged and be truly profitable to all who are concerned. Surely it is the case that we - as Christians who sincerely love one another from the very depths of our hearts - will be anxious to do what will be most conducive to the resolving of a point of difference which so crucial to the salvation of souls" (**Biblical Notes,** VOL. XX, No. 4, July/August, 1991, p. 3).*

A POTPOURRI OF WHAT'S HAPPENING

A POTPOURRI OF WHAT'S HAPPENING

I absolutely, categorically and conclusively, do not see how there can be a single doubt in any person's mind as to the fact that SOMETHING IS HAPPENING among us and to us as a people of God. I would be an utter fool to say I know all of WHAT'S HAPPENING. One thing, however, I do know, I do know something of WHAT'S HAPPENING. I also, because of the vast amount of the evidence available, know THE WHY of some things HAPPENING TO US. I can safely say this, as if THE PATTERN is rejected by our preachers, elders, deacons, and members, then we can do or teach anything that we feel we are "big enough" to do and or to teach. This is the case, for where there is no standard, no blueprint, no guide, no norm, no model, etc., then it is up to man to do what he desires and wants to do (cf. Judg. 17:6; 21:25). Sacred history reveals this happened "when there was no king in Israel," and so every man "did that which was right in his own eyes." But one thing we need to learn is the fact that we, today, have "a king whose name is Jesus" (cf. Acts 17:7). Indeed, there is a law (cf. 1 Cor. 9:21).

In this section, I just want to call our attention to some of WHAT'S HAPPENING among us and to us as an army of our Master, indeed, as a "people for God's own possession" (cf. 1 Pet. 2:5-10). It is as I have entitled it, just a medley, a mixture or a salmagundi, a cross section and sampling of a few items that are both revealing and shocking. These are listed in no specific order or arrangement, but each will inform us in our "enlightened" (?) movement(s) that we absolutely "must," BEHOLD THE PATTERN.

1. **When I wrote chapter seven,** part three, I said, "Brother Randy Mayeux preaches for the Preston Road Church of Christ, 6409 Preston Road, *Dallas, Texas* 75205." I need to make an "update" on this, as I cannot go back now and rewrite that statement. When I wrote it, it was true. However, since then things have changed. Although many things have been said "by way of the grapevine," and circulated, I only can say what I can document. It was not until I heard the introduction of brother Mayeux from a taped lesson of his, that I can now state what brother Mayeux himself has said.

> *"He's just told me that he has resigned at Preston Road. He is going to finish his dissertation and receive his doctorate at USC, University of Southern California. I was told to make sure that's mentioned" (from a tape of the lesson at the* ***Nashville Jubilee,*** *July 4, 1991, 10:30 a.m. class, room # 201, where he spoke on "Ministering to Baby Boomers, Part I," and transcribed by GM).*

Later, in his lesson, brother Mayeux said, "I'm taking a six months sabbatical from ministry... My last speaking engagement for a while is the first weekend of August" (side two of the above tape).

In his next lesson, he said, "... I kinda like preaching. I, I am feeling genuine deep pain that for the next six months I don't get to preach every Sunday. I, I, I mean I'm literally hurting over that" (side two of the tape of his lesson, as above, but Part II, GM).

When I wrote of some of the "strange" and "uncertain" sounds by him, I quoted him as saying, "But I will tell you that I am very weary of the circles of criticism." Maybe brother Mayeux felt the tightening of these "circles of criticism," who knows? One thing I know, he still, as of the *Nashville Jubilee,* is sending forth some "strange" sounds. Let me just quote a few of his statements.

> *"The day is over when you will expect to stay church of Christ all your life."*
>
> *"In the 1990's, (church) membership will disappear."*
>
> *"Does it really make a difference if a person is amillennial or premillennial? To this day it doesn't really matter to me if a person is amillennial or premillennial..." (side one of the lesson, Part I).*
>
> *"The worse mistake we make structurally is having all of our meetings sitting on pews... The last thing I want is the same order of worship every Sunday. I don't want that ever again. Not ever. Not two weeks the same."*
>
> *"The biggest problem in the church of Christ is our unbending demand that our religion be only a thinking religion... We don't want our people to feel."*
>
> *"...bring them in without making them members... Women need to be represented in leadership" (two thoughts of his nine in "keys to understanding baby boomers," GM).*
>
> *"The average church in America does not care for lost people" (side two of his sermon, Part I).*
>
> *"...unchurched culture...church of Christ things in church of Christ ways...I'm tired of the absolute rebellion against the will of God while we sit and argue about junk and..."*

(sermon, Part II, side one of tape).

"Baby boomers do not want a God they never encounter. I do not want a God that I never encounter. And churches of Christ are real good at building churches where you never encounter God!"

"A church that is truly contemporary... I'll tell you what the right translation is. The one that people can understand. That's the only test. That's the only test" (this thought was given under his sub-title of "What kind of a church ...?", as he talked about biblical strategies).

"A church that tells the truth. Churches of Christ were born with a strange belief that everybody has the right and the privilege to read the Bible and draw their own conclusions. We were born with the promise that there was no creed to sign. Creeds are wrong. Denominations are wrong. It is wrong for a person in church 'A' to tell a person in church 'B' what to believe. It's wrong for a person... what to believe. You don't have a creed to sign and you don't have a denomination. And I'm telling you that if we tell these things to people today we'd better be telling the truth, and I'm not sure we are..." (this was his sixth point under the above-mentioned topic, GM).

"... but I think we are losing them because our music is not today's music. I love Alton Howard. I believe in **Image** *magazine. I think we ought to get rid of song books. All of them... There are too many thees, there are too many thous, there are too many thys... And forget all that*

stuff for a minute and ask about the tune...I think we've got to become contemporary in our music."

"If you want just a little personal comment, it is this. In my fantasy world, I would take the Lord's Supper out of every Sunday morning service, and I would put it on Sunday nights. Because Sunday morning is when the seeker will come. In America, the average person who says I think I'll check out Christianity, he thinks he ought to go on Sunday morning. On Sunday night he's watching 60 Minutes...And so let's take the Lord's Supper Sunday nights, maybe at home" (sermon, Part II, side two. I was not clear on the last three words of the above quote. He might have said, "They'll be at home," but that is four words and I only heard three. I listened to it several times before I decided it was as in the quote as I gave it, GM).

I have given the above for a reason. You see, it does not matter "where" brother Mayeux is, at Preston Road or some place else, as he is (and perhaps will be) still giving some "strange" and "uncertain" sounds. He, for example, ought to know that the doctrine of premillennialism would destroy the church, it not being in the original plan of God was just set up as a substitute and that only until Christ comes again! Oh, me, so much could be said about what brother Mayeux says! The best thing to do is to read what he writes and listen to his tapes, that is, for first hand information.

2. **Is it not rather strange,** that when the ACU Bookstore held an "Autographing Party" on February 20, 1991, featuring about five of Max Lucado's books that they

omitted the one entitled: CHRIST IN EASTER; A FAMILY CELEBRATION OF HOLY WEEK (it was co-written, as I mentioned in chapter five, by Billy Graham, Charles Colson, and Joni Eareckson Tada)?

It is of interest to note that brother Terry M. Hightower, also preaching in *San Antonio* (Shenandoah Church of Christ, 11026 Wurzbach Road, 78230-2590), invited brother Lucado to publicly discuss the following propositions.

> *"The Scriptures teach that the Bible is a blueprint, or pattern for men living today, involving rules and regulations" (Affirmative: Terry M. Hightower; Negative: __________).*
>
> *"The Scriptures teach that the Bible is a 'love letter' as opposed to a blueprint or pattern, not involving rules and regulations, but rather a 'relationship' only" (Affirmative: __________; Negative: Terry M. Hightower, Aug. 1, '91).*

However, brother Lucado sent a note and stated "...no interest in engaging in a debate" (the note was undated although both the name of the church, Oak Hills, and Max's name was on it). It was, however, received on August 7, 1991. (I might say just here that you will want to read brother Hightower's article, "Denominationalized To The Max: A Critical Review Of Max Lucadoism." This will be in the September 1991 issue of *Contending For The Faith.* Be sure to read, especially so, Max's prayer at the First Presbyterian Church in downtown San Antonio). Brethren, when will we ever practice what John taught in 2 John 9-11, as well as what Paul taught in Romans 16:17-18; Ephesians 5:11? When will some of the brethren have the courage to get on the polemic platform and defend their preaching, as well as their many associations (this question is being asked: "Did our brother Max go to Switzerland and participate with Billy Graham in a world-wide seminar?" Nay, you can hear anything. However, he did help to write a book with Billy Graham as one of the authors, so it does make one think.) with false teachers.

3. **The Fort Worth Christian High School** had a very neat and attractive brochure for their Baccalaureate and Commencement Services for 1991 (May 26, 28 respectively). On the page entitled Commencement Service, the speaker was listed as Dennis Baw, Pastor Glenview Baptist Church. On the page with the caption, Commencement Speaker, I now quote the following.

> *"Dennis Baw has a vital interest in Fort Worth Christian: His daughter Marcy is graduating, having attended here for the past two years. Next to his relationship to Christ...*
>
> *"...Reverend Baw continued his education and received a Master's degree from Southwestern Baptist Theological Seminary in Fort Worth. For the first ten years of his ministry he served as a youth pastor/evangelist in...For the past eleven years he has pastored the Glenview Baptist Church of Fort Worth.*
>
> *"Soon after Dennis became a Christian as a young adult, he...After being called to the ministry, he found his talents in music and songwriting could be best used by the Lord and His people. He continues to use those talents in addition to his preaching and pastoral ministry..." (I have a copy of the brochure and no other information as printer, etc., is given on it, GM).*

If you would like to read a very excellent letter by one

who was in attendance (I am speaking of brother Guss Eoff), then secure the July/August, 1991 issue of Biblical Notes (VOL, XX, No. 4, edited by Roy Deaver), as on page 6 the heading is: GUSS EOFF, FORMER TEACHER, WRITES TO FORT WORTH CHRISTIAN. Brother Guss, on June 12, 1991, wrote his letter to brother William Tucker, President of Fort Worth Christian High School (7517 Bogart Drive, Fort Worth, Texas 76180), with copies being sent to the Board of Trustees (and let me hasten to say he was not the only one to write), as his granddaughter was a member of the graduation class. Just in case you are not able to read his letter, I now quote just a few pertinent paragraphs.

> *"Mr. Baw was listed in the commencement Service as, Speaker, Dennis Baw, Pastor, Glenview Baptist Church.*
>
> *"Under the head, commencement Speaker, it was stated: 'Soon after Dennis became a Christian as a young adult, he left a career in professional entertainment as a singer and instrumentalist.'*
>
> *"After being called to the ministry, he found his talents in music and song writing could be best used by the Lord and his people. He continues to use those talents in addition to his preaching and pastoral ministry" (quotations that I here give are from the brochure, as these are the ones that brother Guss used in his letter. Following are some of his thoughts about such, GM).*
>
> *"I could not believe that the Board of Trustees, the Faculty, and the students would have a Baptist preacher as the speaker for the Com-*

mencement Service. What has happened to Fort Worth Christian?

"Does Baptist doctrine make Christians? Is the man scripturally right in the Baptist religion? Was Fort Worth Christian established on the belief that Baptist doctrine made Christians?

"Are the people where Dennis Baw preaches the Lord's people? Does Baptist doctrine make his congregation God's people? (Now watch carefully what he says, GM).

"I heard his speech. He told the graduates to make room in their lives for Christ. He preached Baptist doctrine, the same thing he would preach in his own building. He did not preach what the Bible teaches to be a Christian.

"Does Fort Worth Christian now believe that Baptist, following Baptist Doctrine, are members of the New Testament Church? Why did they choose a Baptist preacher instead of a faithful gospel preacher?" (Many other very fine things, of course, were in the letter and it closed with the explicit statement of it being written "in a spirit of love and kindness," yet with "I am deeply concerned about what seems to be the direction of...", GM).

It would be totally unfair of me if I failed to say that his letter did receive a reply (June 25, 1991). He was assured that the commitment of the board, administration and faculty was the same as the founders of the school. It was explained that the fathers of the graduating class, for the past several years, were the ones who had been giving the baccalaureate and commencement addresses. President Tucker admitted that he was "uncomfortable with several insertions of Baptist doctrine," said he was mistaken regarding Dennis Baw as he thought he would have been "more generic and limited to those truths upon which we all agree," and went on to speak of him as a valued friend and one whose influence has caused many students to come to Fort Worth Christian (permission granted... at 8:25 a.m. on 9-7-'91, but I chose only to give a thought or two as..., GM).

On July 2, 1991, brother Guss responded (to which rejoin to this day no answer has been received) and here are a few thoughts of that resound.

> *"So far as I know, the founders of F.W.C. never had a denominational preacher to speak at a baccalaureate or commencement, and I don't believe they would.*
>
> *"Brother Tucker, I feel that your explanation is not really acceptable. My son, Larry, is a father of one in the graduation class, and he was not offered an opportunity to speak. He is an excellent speaker, and would have been honored ... He was there for the graduation,...*
>
> *"Brother Tucker, I have found long ago that we do not use false teachers on what we agree upon. That is the problem right now with the Christian church and instrumental music... I appreciate you saying, 'I was mistaken.'*
>
> *"Regardless of Mr. Baw's influencing new students to attend F.W.C., that is no reason endorsing error... I pray that F.W.C. board, administration, and faculty... make their firm stand known and meet the challenges of the future... We are faced with so many that are liberal, God give us men that will stand, and*

faithful schools, to which we can send our children.

"Thank you again for your kindness. I shall look forward to hearing from you, and hoping you will review and modify the things that need changing."

It really makes one wonder about WHAT WOULD HAVE HAPPENED had F.W.C. had a student enrolled and whose father was a - YOU NAME THE RELIGION OF YOUR CHOICE - and who had been a value to them, influencing students, etc. In fact, it makes me wonder WHAT IS GOING TO HAPPEN when such does occur. Indeed, the precedent has been set and it will be in fight with "influence, power, popularity, support, etc.," (as this barometer, measure, prototype, model, pattern and criterion is in the dye that has been cast) when graduation comes again.

The selection of the speaker is not all that needs to be corrected, as the one who writes the full page article about Dennis Baw, COMMENCEMENT SPEAKER, as well as the page, COMMENCEMENT SERVICE, needs to KNOW the difference between "a Baptist and one who is a Christian," and he also needs to know something of the use of such terms as "pastor, reverend, pastored, pastoral," etc. How on earth could such a brochure just absolutely SLIP BY without someone knowing what was in it and saying something about it? It seems simply incredible that such was published and presented and the distinction between the Lord and His people was not set forth in crystal clear terminology. This has been publicly done and I just wonder when the public retraction of such will come. Will it be corrected or covered up? Or, does it represent the thinking of "those in charge"? It just makes me wonder where our moral fiber and spiritual spunk is.

Indeed, *God Give Us Men!*

4. **Foundations,** "Strengthening Spiritual Muscles," Gospel Advocate Family Bible Studies, Adults, Fall 1990, had a lesson headlined, "Have You Made Your Reservations?" I have that lesson on my desk as I write this and here are the first two paragraphs.

> *"I was in our local religious bookstore recently looking at new books about the epistles of Peter. The salesclerk is a very nice, very religious young lady who is hoping to be a missionary to France. When she found out what I was looking for, she asked, 'Is Peter very interesting? I've studied Paul's writings and the Gospels, but I've never even read Peter.'*
>
> *"Peter tends to get left out of Bible study. After all, his books are not very long, not numerous and not generally known for their theological depth. Anyway, wasn't he the oaf who tried to walk on water, cut off Malchus' ear and denied the Lord three times?" (Lesson 7, week of October 14, 1990, pages 28-31, p. 29 quoted).*

I had read an article that brother Thomas F. Eaves, Sr. wrote (Church of Christ, 515 Church Street, Tiptonville, Tennessee 38079 and which was published in their bulletin, VOL. 2, No. 46, January 20, 1991, via *The Edifier,* Vol. 10, Dec. 6, 1990, Num. 49, as just one example of such), and knowing him like I do, I just knew that he had already written to those who work with this material. I immediately wrote brother Eaves, and sure enough he was true to the faithfulness that characterizes him. On February 27, 1991, he responded and sent me a copy of the letter that he had received both from T. B. Underwood, Jr., and

F. Furman Kearley. Brother Eaves had sent them a copy of the article that he had written (and that was published in various papers) entitled, "Was The Apostle Peter An Idiot?" (their dates of letter response were November 15, 1990, and December 17, 1990, respectively).

Brother Eaves charged the author with "two glaring mistakes," as per the second paragraph quoted from the article above: (1) "The author charges Peter with being a shallow writer, i.e., his books are 'not generally known for their theological depth,' and (2) that Peter was an oaf." I can grant you that in both cases Thomas Eaves proved his points. On the first point, just out of the first chapter of 1 Peter, he mentioned 17 great biblical subjects of depth. On the second point he asked the question (after giving the definition of the word 'oaf'), "I wonder if those on Pentecost (Acts 2) were aware that the Gospel they were hearing was being preached by a blockhead?" He also covered some other thoughts and then closed by saying: "The author of the lesson owes an apology to God, Peter, and his readers for the flippant manner in which he has handled the Word of God. I sincerely pray that it will be forthcoming" (business address of Thomas Eaves is Tennessee Bible College, P. O. Box 865, Cookeville, TN 38503-0865, in case you should desire a copy of his article).

In response to the letter from Ted B. Underwood (Gospel Advocate Company, 1006 Elm Hill Pike, P. O. Box 150, Nashville, TN 37202), as already noted, brother Eaves wrote him on January 3, 1991 and covered some thoughts from the previous two letters (Underwood and Kearley).

> *"You indicated the author was using a technique known as hyperbole. Brother Furman Kearley, in his correspondence to me (December 17, 1990), said he thought that the author*

was intending to speak in irony or sarcasm. It seems to me that the brother wrote something which is interpreted in different ways.

"Brother Kearley suggested that I communicate with the author and ask him directly what he actually meant by his statement. If you can furnish his address I will write him about this matter.

"Appreciate any assistance you might give me with this problem."

When I first contacted him about this material, he penned me a note stating, "No answer to this letter as of this date, 2/25/'91"). Just recently I called him (August 27, 1991, 7:30 a.m.) and in his reply, he wrote, "No answer as of this date, 8/29/'91").

Again, I am shocked, startled, stunned and staggered that such an article (one that belittles inspiration and the God-inspired characters) could somehow get into one of the major papers of our beloved brotherhood! It makes me wonder about the "editing" of the material and a number of other things. To even use such a term as "oaf" (regardless of what the author may have had in mind) is very, very poor judgment and should be publicly retracted (my understanding is this man is no longer writing for *Gospel Advocate,* personnel has changed, and I see no need to list the author's name at this point). I do know some churches sent back their material and... How do you personally feel about the word "oaf"? (meaning dunce, clodpate, loggerhead, simpleton, fool, nitwit, nincompoop, numskull, saphead, donkey, deformed child, freak, idiot, imbecile, half-wit, monster, moron, dult, blockhead, lout, stupid, etc., etc., and you can check out the references on this word yourself). So now you know why Thomas Eaves wrote under the caption, "Was The Apostle Peter An Idiot?" And to believe that churches pay money for such material!

5. **A Church Bulletin Board** is torn apart, not once but twice, but is, each time, repaired or redone... "Would you please examine the picture of the board and...?" This was part of a long conversation from Willia Williamson of Tompkinsville, Kentucky at 2:00 p.m. on January 16, 1990. On the very next day, January 17, 1990, her husband, Lawrence Williamson, wrote me a letter. He began by saying, "One man can make a difference. I appreciate your courage to stand for the truth in face of opposition." He then spoke of his wife's (Willia) call, the lack of respect for Bible authority that was behind the removal of the bulletin board, the sending of three bulletins for my consideration relative to the board being unscriptural "because we used an Old Testament scripture (Mal. 2:16), and the Old Testament laws are no longer binding on us today." He also said they would be sending a picture of the board just as soon as they received them.

On February 16, 1990, sister Williamson wrote me a long three page letter and enclosed a picture (they were very sorry, as it was a double exposure, however, it is better than nothing to illustrate WHAT'S HAPPENING) of the bulletin board (the one that was destroyed twice). She said the board was up for about two weeks, and then "someone" took down part of it (the first line, God Hates Divorce, and the last line, Exception - Fornication). Only the middle part was left. She then set about (and did) replacing the missing parts, and "on the same afternoon caught the lady who had taken it down in the very act of removing it again. However, this time she tore the complete board down, destroying all the letters." She asked the lady "why?" only to hear her say, "God doesn't hate."

Then the lady told her if she put it back up she would "tear it down again." It was put back up for the third time, as one of the elders had not seen it (he had to be with his wife who was seriously ill). At this time there were only two elders remaining (one had previously resigned and one had died).

It is rather a heartbreaking story. An elder's meeting was conducted (one elder supported the board) with one elder saying "Malachi 2:16 was Old Testament scripture and did not apply today." He also gave sister Williamson about an hour lecture on "rightly dividing the Word of Truth." Later I learned this elder resigned and so "we are without elders."

Brother Williamson is 47 years old and has 21 years of preaching experience (he has a college degree, is a 1973 graduate of the Memphis School of Preaching and also has 30 hours in apologetics). He sent me a letter that I received on March 7, 1990, and enclosed a letter from "The Preachers Committee and the men of the Tompkinsville Church of Christ." You do not have to wonder about his job, as the preacher (he wrote, "Enclosed letter shows where standing for the truth and preaching sound doctrine will lead to today.") whose allegiance is to God, to Him and to no other, very often hears what he heard in the words, "You are notified that you are relieved...effective March 1, 1990,..." And, of course, it was by a majority vote.

I want you to observe (I only wish you could have seen the picture in color, as it was beautifully done) the picture of the bulletin board and I give it to help drive home something of WHAT IS HAPPENING among us and to us today.

When sister Williamson first called, and we talked for about one hour, I told her that she could mark it down "as almost a fact" that the woman who had ripped down the board had a marital problem of some kind. Guess what? The elder who had objected to it was her father-in-law, and her husband, this elder's son, had been previously married! In about forty years of preaching, I have known person after person to believe the truth on marriage-divorce-remarriage, that is, until it affected their family, and then, for some odd (in contrast to the Bible) reason (?) they changed their mind. God still hates divorce, and for the person who thinks otherwise I would simply ask him/her to read the chapter in my book (DIVORCE is the title of it), chapter fourteen, captioned, "Divorce - God Hates It!" And if you are one who thinks that God does not hate, then just read page 245 and check out the references relating to the Greek word for hate, *miseo*. She first called me because she had read this chapter.

I can only say that I would to God our so-called marriage guidance counselors (I think they prefer the word, at least some of them do, marriage "therapist" or some other fashionable term) also hated what God hates. But, be it advisor, mentor, confidant, guide, tutor, teacher, coach, leader, etc., let these men and women first KNOW THE BOOK OF GOD BY WHICH WE WILL ALL BE JUDGED SOME DAY, as there is A PATTERN for marriage-divorce-remarriage.

6. A Nashville, Tennessee paper, THE TENNESSEAN, had a screamer (title) which read "CONSERVATIVE CHURCHES MAY FOSTER INCEST, PANEL SAYS" (Thursday/June 13, 1991, page 1A, and the conclusion was on page 2A under "Churches May Foster Incest - Panel," by Ray Waddle, Religion News Editor), and I know of nothing that has caused more of an outburst of protest to those involved than this. Indeed, if I ever felt that one should sue in the name of and for the church, it was caused by this most contemptible, disgusting, abhorrent, despicable, offensive, obnoxious and foul label. The editor wrote this as an item being "sent forth" from a panel of four male church professionals at the annual David Lipscomb University Lectures.

I referred to this article causing an "outburst of protest," and that was just a mild term, as it has caused much disturbance and disruption, turmoil and tumult, yes, pandemonium, if you please. I not only speak of articles, letters, phone calls, etc., but also of real deep Christian convictions and emotions that have been as stirred as I've personally witnessed. (And, even challenges to debate have been extended, of course, they were not accepted). Such an imprint as in *The Tennessean* is sickening to the core, as it is most damaging to the Church, the beautiful Body of Christ, and to the faithful soldiers of the Cross that uphold the Truth of God. I fully understand that newspapers may not always accurately report items, and I am not one to rush into such without knowing exactly what was said.

On my desk at this time is my tape recorder and inside of it is my copy of the tape of that forum. And as I listen to that tape, I am following the transcription of it to make absolutely sure I can quote such exactly, accurately, faithfully, factually, and truthfully. Again I want to say, I would not misreport, misstate, misquote, falsify, distort, twist, pervert, exaggerate or misrepresent our brethren, *but then neither will I whitewash or make such into a "watergate" affair.* This cannot be overlooked, as it has brought reproach upon the New Testament Church in the very eyes of the public! Before going any further with this, let us read some of what was said. (Let me hasten to say the tape is far too long - double spaced the transcription is almost 40 pages - to go into detail, but we can observe enough to see if what the paper declared was true. That is, we will just touch on the major thoughts, and even though Gayle Napier was the last of the four to speak on the tape, I'll start with what he said as he was the first to be directly quoted in the newspaper.).

> *"I want to pick up first with what Gary was talking about submission. I think one of the biggest problems I see in the church of Christ is that we have so distorted this idea of headship and submission that we have created a pathological marriage model.*
>
> *"We have equated, and we have preached, folks, the idea of headship means power and control. I am in charge. I am primary. I call the shots. I am the most important one in this family. And that's my heritage. As far as the family is concerned, mother was to be in submission to dad and the relationship was that he was important and she was unimportant. In her submissionship role...second class ...emotions weren't important and she was treated like one of the kids.*

"And I hear this in therapy all the time. And the relationship takes on...mood of he is the big daddy, and she is the daughter. He has all the power and control, and he is primary and she is like one of the kids. I hear women saying, Gayle he treats me like my dad. He sounds like my dad, and I don't want to have sex with my dad. I call that emotional incest.

"...infidelity, which is psychological in my judgment. Uh, I want to know why there was an affair. There are as many reasons to have affairs as not to have affairs. And if somebody has an affair in town where they live, they're dumb. Cause eventually they get sloppy; they're gonna get caught. A blind person could follow that trail. So my assumption is you wanna get caught. Do you want to get caught (1) to punish your spouse, (2) to make them angry, because if they're angry it's easier to walk away from it, (3) you want their attention, (4) power play, (5) you're tired of making love to your mom or your dad, and there are other reasons. (Perhaps it should be stated that the question asked dealt around the fact that Gayle had mentioned there were 6 different kinds of divorces, such as psychological, emotional, social, legal, etc. I wonder if he discusses "a scriptural divorce," and "an unscriptural divorce," or would that be Bible doctrine and not "therapy"?, GM).

"I'm glad this is the last day (I put this in, as evidently as many as 3-4 tapes, maybe 5, are available). I want to put it in a broader perspective, and, uh, into the church perspec-

tive. I think theologically we have taught on organization of the church, and social, spiritual organization that is power addicted. And I think we have, uh, a perfect church setting where men in pulpits and men who are elders are power addicts, and we have taught churches to be co-dependent, to use Gary's term. And we attract people who want to be co-dependent and have people tell them what to do. We don't want to change.

"I think the first thing we have to do theologically is to understand the leadership is servant leadership. It is not power and control. And being the head of my wife is not a power and control, it's a servant leadership. And I think our whole theology has to change.

"I'm going to say something that's going to get me in hot water, folks. I have made quite a play over this power addiction, and I really believe this. And there is one socially approved place where power controlling addicts, beside marriage, can exercise their addiction - that's the pulpit. So we attract a lot of men, and I'm not gonna put a percentage on it who love to beat us up. And they get a lot of needs met, and that's power control. And I think we've got to turn this around someway. I don't think Paul or Peter or John or anybody else ever beat up folks like I have been beat up from the pulpit. I think it's a theological issue as well." (This is not all that brother Napier said, but it is enough. Keep in mind that we may not know how many sessions the Religion News Editor heard or...I quoted from pp. 23-44 of

my transcription, GM).

The only other person that was specifically quoted in the newspaper article was Gary Wilson (remember there was the man who introduced the session and there were four panel members, making five total), therefore, we now note something of what he said (as per the tape).

> *"...various problems they have...I want to begin to explore with the, uh, some of their sexual beliefs...a lot of myths have been created. A lot of misinformation has been presented...I think that if you were to take a look at the scriptures and how we have interpreted those scriptures, you'll find that likewise affects the sexual relationship.*
>
> *"I think that the, especially the concept of submission is so misunderstood. I've gone to several congregations...asked...what does submit mean, and I have not really got that many people to properly discuss the biblical perspective,...*
>
> *"Poor communication is often a block to...Sex is best in a romantic relationship. Uh, sex can be fun. It doesn't have to be in any kind of basic relationship. Uh, we probably don't even know what the word romantic means...One of the other general myths that seems to come out of distortions of biblical teaching is that sex is something that shouldn't be pleasurable ...Uh, sex is for pleasure. There's certain beliefs that certain sexual, uh, ways of relating to one sexually is wrong (and even though I am not going to quote what he said, he did mention oral sex, masturbation, the Bible is*

silent about how to have sex, GM)... Basically, anything that a couple wants to do in terms of relating to one another as long as it's mutually agreed upon is OK...

"I think that there's a lot of negative messages presented to our young people growing up... And I think there are some distortions... some people, especially young men, are so afraid of relating sexually to a woman that they are prone to have sex with a man.

"I'd like to take a moment of time to talk about pornography... I believe that pornography, as far as the people that I work with, is the way that Christians have affairs. You will not believe the number of people that have problems with pornography that are members of the church... It's the same thing in her (the wife's, GM) mind as having an affair.

"I'd like to take a great deal of time now to talk about the role of submission (it seems each panel spoke of this, and one of the two scriptures read at the beginning by James Vandiver, was on this subject, GM)... in our male-female relationships is often distorted. I have before me a list of scriptures... and every one of these scriptures conveys the idea of MUTUAL submission. Not one person submitting... We have the idea of taking the scripture and only taking one part of it - the wife submit to the husband and forget the rest of it. Nor look at the word submission in another context. And then we take that interpretation... what I say goes... I am god in this family... (Just here he gave an example from a

school of preaching. He said "they told her that anything your husband wants - you must do...").

"I have had couples who say there's only one preferred sexual position according to God's teaching. Because any other position connotes domination by woman. And use the scriptures to support that... Mutual submission is a distinctive concept created by Christ. It's a new approach to a functional relationship... We have the idea that man is the head of the household, but forget the rest of the scripture ...distortion of saying that man is not a leader but a dictator, is very prevalent in people's teachings...by taking the submission role to it's ultimate extreme...it's o.k. to promote violence with your wife, and we're going to talk about that tomorrow. That thinking in it's most distorted form says, if she doesn't act the way I want her to I can beat her up. A lot of people in the church doing that.

"I think so often we'll find that we misunderstand the concept of grace and mercy and forget about the Holy Spirit. You see, part of the problems that promote sexual addictions and promotes a lot of the difficulties in our sexual relationships is that we are eat up with guilt... and so since we have not understood the concept of grace and mercy, we simply do not have a way of promoting the kind of relationship that we need" (pp. 6-16 of my transcription, all from first side of the tape, GM).

If you had any doubt as to why *The Tennessean* carried the article it did, I hope the above quotations will eradicate it. I do not have to explain now (if you have read the above quotes from Gayle Napier and Gary Wilson) nor defend our faithful brethren for rising up against such a public display of - YOU NAME IT! Indeed, many of us are offended by this and we wonder why someone did not publicly stand up during the forum and challenge these brethren, take issue with them, or just get up and walk out (at times that may be our only means of protest). One thing we definitely know, the image of the blood-purchased bride of Christ has been tarnished, and it seems that no one knows anything about the scriptures and how to handle problems except "those of us who have been trained to be therapists."

As I write this, brother H. A. (Buster) Dobbs has already penned an article in the *Firm Foundation* (Vol. 106, No. 8, August, 1991, pp. 17-18) with the title, "What Are We Going To Do About This?" and it needs to be read. Even though the September issue is not out at this time, it soon will be (the Lord willing) and it will have an article captioned, "Experts?" (Vol. 106, No. 9, September, 1991, pp. 20-21 by Lindell Mitchell) and people need to study it. I have before me a stack of letters written to men like brother Napier, to the president of David Lipscomb, copy of debate propositions (but we do not have to be concerned about such being accepted, as most of our men today seem "to be above" debating), an article sent to the editor of *The Tennessean,* etc., etc. and all such are far too many for me to list. This shall not pass!

Brethren, let me speak freely and frankly. Our trouble is not so much with our men in the pulpits as it is with these so-called family therapists in their understanding and comprehension of God's eternal message for man today and in their scenario of sadness sessions of counsel-ing. When you hear one of them say (based on Romans

12:1-2, and it is a pure distortion of the passage!), "If you are unhappy in your marriage, leave, as it would be an unreasonable service to stay and God's service is reasonable," or "If you leave, do not return (go back into the marriage)," etc., etc., you can readily see why some counselors are batting zero in helping to unite families. I just wonder how many of them believe that divorce, without fornication, is sinful, tell their "clients" that God hates divorce, that marriage is permanent and only death and "the putting away" of Matthew 19:9 ends it, that the door for reconciliation must always be kept open (cf. 1 Cor. 7:1-11), that there is no forgiveness without repentance, give the biblical definition of true repentance, and let them know that a divorce may occur legally but that does not mean that such is scriptural. Indeed, engrave the fact of the sacred saying of the Master, "What therefore God hath joined together, let not man put asunder" (cf. Matt. 19:6b), into their "clients."

Verily, when a man knows so little of 2 John 9-11 that he will participate with thirty-three religious groups (such as Foursquare Church, The Village On The Rock, Dennis Lee Ministries, Fellowship Bible, Freedom Christian Academy, Bethel Temple, Assembly of God, New Wine Fellowship, Flame Fellowship, Christ For the Nations Institute, Word of Faith, Scofield Memorial Church, Evangelical Lines Missions, Pine Cove Camp, First United Methodist, First Baptist, First Presbyterian Church, Church of God, Grace Bible and Trinity Church, along with 13 others) in the Texas Sunday School Association (TSSA) by being one of the speakers (spoke twice), as brother Napier did (see my book, *A Crucial Study Of A Critical Subject - Fellowship,* p. 55ff as it relates the action of one church, Brown Trail, towards the elders and preachers, Richland Hills, where he was serving, or read my two articles "That The Brethren Might Know"), then I just wonder how much knowledge he has of The Book. If he has no more than this illustrates (TSSA participation), why trust his "therapy sessions" to be true to The Book. I am not so much concerned about "their training to be therapists" as I am about how schooled they are in the divine revelation of God's Word, as it will some day judge us. All of the books in the world that these men have read (and that they often recommend their "clients" to read) will never take the place of the teaching of the Master! I cannot be indifferent, and I am certainly not a puppet whose strings are pulled by someone else. Let's not be like politicians who run for anything and stand for nothing.

7. There is a publication (*The Good News Messenger*) that has caused some "confusion," and so, Julius Lundy (Director of Counseling, Northwest Church of Christ Counseling Center, Loop 1604 and Braun Road, P. O. Box 380275, San Antonio, TX 78230) wrote a "To Whom it May Concern" letter "to clarify a point." Note the following.

> *"'The Good News Messenger' is not funded by the Church of Christ nor does is represent the views of the Elders of the Northwest Church of Christ. The publication is mailed to people in and out of the Church of Christ of varying faiths... It is a publication of various points of views of different people and the different ways that they handle their problems. In love, I refer you to the following scriptures: Philippians 1:15-16 and Mark 9:38-41.*
>
> *"As a counselor my concern is that I reach as many people as possible. Problems of suicide, alcoholism, drug abuse, satanism... are situations that I deal with daily..." (May 27, 1991).*

This did not "clarify confusion" in this mind, but

"created more confusion." You see, in this publication mentioned above (Vol. 2, #5, May, 1991) the label of one article was, BILLY GRAHAM'S COLUMN, and it was "his column" just as he had written it (without any rebuttal of his article). As Billy Graham was writing of "Can you think of...and refuse to accept his gift of salvation?," he said, "By faith ask Christ to come into your life. He accepts you just as you are."

Look again at the above quotes from the "To Whom It May Concern" letter, examine it very carefully and see if it reveals anything relative to WHAT IS HAPPENING among us and to us. Also, since he uses Billy Graham, ask yourself if the author found room for Bill Graham in Mark 9:38-41 as one who is "for us." How many "faiths" do you believe there are (cf. Eph. 4:5; Jude 3)? "Varying faiths," really...?

8. On the day that I had a call informing me of the death of my good brother and friend, Bill Jackson (expired the day before), I had a letter from him in the mail (he was reading the manuscript of this book and had read the first 209 pages and had sent me various statements about it). In addition to what he said about the manuscript, he sent me two ads that had been placed in the paper (The *Austin American-Statesman*) by the University Church of Christ in Austin, Texas. The one that appeared on March 27, 1991, was entitled: "Remembering Easter Is A Right Of Spring. And Summer. And Fall. And Winter." One quote will suffice: "That is why the Holy Communion will be part of our Easter Service."

The other was headed: "If We Said We Had All The Answers, That Would Raise Some Questions." In relation to this article, I will just refer you to the article about it by Kevin Cauley labeled, "We Are Raising Questions: Agnosticism Vs. Arrogance?" (*Biblical Notes,* VOL. XX, No. 3.

May/June, 1991, pp. 14-16). Please read this very excellent material, and once again, you will observe something of WHAT IS HAPPENING among us and to us.

9. **Now That I'm A Christian** is a booklet that we have, for a very long time, given to new converts (copyrighted in 1948). However, let me say that *IT HAS BEEN, AS OF 1991, REVISED;* that, "unless otherwise identified, all Scripture references are from *The Everyday Bible, New Century Version*... 1983, 1986, 1988 by Word Publishing, Dallas, TX 75039. Used by permission" (Sweet Publishing, 3950 Fossil Creek Boulevard, Suite 201, Fort Worth, Texas 76137, p. 1). If I did not say ONE SINGLE WORD EXCEPT THE NAME OF THE VERSION (as it is listed above), THAT WOULD BE ENOUGH!

This is a booklet that is 32 pages long (the former one was some 35 pages), so it is impossible for me to mention all changes as almost every page has some (and every single one is not a concern to me). Let me just categorize a few.

a. *They stem from the Version that is used.*

(1) Ephesians 4:13 has "...in the same faith" instead of "the unity of the faith" (and "the faith" is in the Greek).

(2) Luke 13:3; 24:47; Acts 2:38; 3:19; 17:30-31 have "change your (their) hearts (his heart)" instead of the word "repentance." You can certainly "change your heart" without it being true repentance.

(3) Ephesians 5:19 is, "...Sing and make music..." instead of "singing and making melody." Note that generic term in the words "make music."

(4) Romans 16:16b says, "All of Christ's churches send greetings to you," instead of "All the

churches of Christ..." How many churches did Christ purchase?

(5) Romans 10:10 is given as, "We believe with our hearts, and so we are made right with God. And we use our mouths to say that we believe, and so we are saved." What about the "unto righteousness" and "unto salvation"? Are there two ways to be saved?

(6) Matthew 10:32 is rendered, "If anyone stands before other people and says he believes in me, then I will say that he belongs to me." "Confess me before men" is removed.

(7) 2 Timothy 3:16 has, "All Scripture is given by God and is..." but it leaves out "inspired." It should be "All (or every) scripture inspired of God is..." The Bible is inspired, isn't it?

(8) Ephesians 4:6 is, "There is one God...He is everywhere and in everything," instead of the normal rendering "one God and Father of all, who is over all, and through all, and in all." Pantheism/Animism(?)!

(9) Colossians 1:18, instead of saying "the firstborn from the dead" is, "And he is the first one who was raised from death." What about the widow of Nain's son or Lazareth?

(10) Acts 20:28 states, "This is the church that God bought with his own death," instead of "the church of the Lord which he purchased with his own blood." Did God actually die? (This is only 10 of the 100 or so quotations - some are repeats - all of them need to be read to get the impact of this revision, GM).

b. *They arise from what has been changed or omitted.*

(1) "I will review the steps I have taken which have given me the right to be called a Christian," to "I will review the way I became a Christian." Many today do not like the idea of that found in "the steps..." You know, "the five fingered man."

(2) "To obey Christ's commands,..." is changed to "to show my confidence in Christ...." Note "commands" is removed.

(3) Instead of "With that preparation I was baptized, to gain forgiveness of my sins" was changed to "with that preparation, I was baptized." "Forgiveness of my sins" is omitted. I observed this was done "more than once."

(4) "Those who obeyed the commands of Christ...were called Christians" is changed to "Those who follow Christ as the Son of God and Savior are called 'Christians'." Again "commands" are taken out.

(5) Two complete paragraphs (one dealing with the only rule of faith and practice...Bible authority, and the other referring to human organizations as Baptist, Congregational, Methodist, Christian) are deleted.

(6) "When I became a Christian I became a member of the Church of Christ" is changed to "When I became a Christian I became a part of the body of Christ." (Unless I overlooked, or just missed it, each time "Church of Christ" was used in the older booklet it was "taken out" in the revision. The exception is when it is given as "I am a part

of the church of Christ," GM).

(7) "Those who have obeyed his commands" is changed to "those who have been saved."

(8) "That there is only one church is seen from Ephesians 4:4-6" is changed to "The 'oneness' of the church is seen from Ephesians 4:4-6."

(9) "To ask 'which church?' is like asking which Christ one serves, for Christ is the head of the church," along with the entire next paragraph about this statement is deleted.

(10) "In the New Testament the following five items of worship, and only these five items are revealed to us" is removed completely.

(11) After listing Ephesians 5:19; Colossians 3:16; Hebrews 13:15 and 1 Corinthians 14:15 it is written, "From these passages it is seen that the music which is in worship is singing:..." and is changed to "From these passages it is seen that singing with the spirit and understanding..." The following eight lines that talk about "an instrument," "that instrument," and "any instrument" are completely eradicated.

(12) Beginning on the bottom of page 25 ("Further Important Considerations:"), almost all of the next two pages have been omitted. Note just a few thoughts excluded.

> (a) Adherence strictly to that pattern, not changing, altering the worship or organization to meet modern needs or make the church more efficient in a changed world.

> (b) Two distinct philosophies or views,

doing in religion that which is not specifically forbidden in the scriptures and doing only what we find authority for in the Bible.

(c) Pleasing God comes by doing what God has revealed for us to do. We are not to please ourselves. If a person wants God's approval on his work "he must do it in the way God has told us to do it."

(d) The scriptures themselves are sufficient and there is no need for a creed, confession of faith, manual or...

(e) The omission of verses like 2 Corinthians 10:17-18; 1 Corinthians 4:6; 2 John 9-11; 2 Corinthians 11:3 is so evident.

(13) "It should be my sincerest desire always to 'speak where the scriptures speak and to be silent where the scriptures are silent!'" is changed to "It should be my sincerest desire always to learn the true meaning of a scripture and make the right response to it."

c. *They emanate from a change in emphasis, etc.*

(1) Beginning with the "Certificate Of Baptism," it seems to me the emphasis is upon "grace," with "commands" eliminated.

(a) Original: "I, __________, Became A Christian by Being Baptized, upon Confession of My Faith in Christ on..."

(b) Revision: "By the grace of God I, __________, became a Christian by being baptized as a demonstration and confession of my faith in Jesus Christ, on the...:

(2) An example of this emphasis on (as it seems to me) grace (remember that obedience, commands, commandments, etc., are almost removed, yet I know that "grace alone" is not used) is given in "I have been saved by God's grace," "That grace can save every person," "gratitude for his saving grace" (be it known I fully understand that we are saved by grace, but it is not without man's obedience to and faithfulness to God's salvation plan. Yes, I know no man can earn salvation, and this is not the point herein, GM).

(3) The change in emphasis can be seen in the use that is made of the version from which quotations are given. With the number of verses that I've mentioned as being in the booklet, there is no way I can give them all. *Note:* Hebrews 10:25 has "...the Day coming" (observe the cap. "D" on "day").

(4) Under the organization of the church, in addition to the elders and deacons, a separate heading is given and you have the addition of "Minister."

(5) At times you will read about "his spiritual gift of preaching," "every Christian has a gift to use in the church," and "in many different ways by Christians with many different gifts."

(6) "Disciples" is changed to "followers," "household of faith" is changed to "the family of believers" (this wording is of great interest for today), "in Christ" is changed to "belongs to Christ," etc.

(7) The distinctiveness of one church is lost, such as can be seen in this quote: "To progress toward this unity or 'oneness' (a goal not merely

for the many differing churches, but one to be set within each congregation),..."

(8) Note these questions: "What was the message for the people of his day?" (talking about the Bible writers) and "What message does he have for me today?"

I have not touched the "hem of the garment" in the far reaching implications of the things omitted, the Version used, the changes made, the wording employed, etc., etc., but I have tried to sound forth in all clarity WHAT IS HAPPENING among us and to us as a people of God. Even such a little booklet as this one by Sweet Publishing seems to be making all the changes necessary so it can be sold to and used by all religious groups. It not only removed the word "denominationalism," but took out the "concept" as well.

Many people today do not know about the World Bible Translation Center with Dale Randolph as Translation Center president. There are things that people need to find out, such as who it was that bought Sweet Publishing and whether or not he is an elder at Richland Hills in Fort Worth (I speak about Bill New). People need to know that on the back of the church bulletin (REJOICE) of Richland Hills, under "Brotherhood Ministries" is World Bible Translation Center - 595-1664 (Vol. 15, Num. 36, September 4, 1991, p. 4). People need to know "My invitation to lecture in Moscow came from the World Bible Translation Center" (*Lovelines,* Vol. 17/Num. 15, April 10, 1991, p. 2, given by Rubel Shelly). People need to know about the Bibles sent to Russia, as well as the Version used in "Now That I'm A Christian," so I give this quote:

"World Bible Translation Center is dedicated

to providing accurate, easily-understood Scripture translation in languages throughout the world. The Center has produced the first modern Russian New Testament translation and 475,000 copies have been printed. The Center's English translation, ***The Easy-to-Read Version,*** *serves as the base text for the* ***International Children's Bible*** *and the* ***Everyday Bible****" (World Bible Translation Center, P. O. Box 820648, Fort Worth, Texas 76182, 4/2/91, p. 1. This release also spoke about Rubel's trip, that "W.B.T.C. plants church of Christ in Moscow;...conducted its second series of Bible seminars March 18-21 at its Bible Center in Moscow...", GM).*

When such as I have presented above is clearly observed, it will be no surprise to both observe and understand why the particular version was used, the changes and deletions made and the emphasis given. Maybe the reviser had read what brother Shelly said relative to his own basic beliefs about hermeneutics, when he said:

"The Bible is inspired, hermeneutics is not. Our triparted hermeneutic (command, example, necessary inference) is not inductively Biblical ...We bring our own baggage to the reading of the Bible. Our 'everybody can understand the Bible alike' sermons were a bit arrogant. The Bible wasn't designed for syllogistical argument. It is more complex than we admit...I reject the religious patternism with which I grew up...I can recommend (on the music question) a capella music. Linguistically and historically I think we have a case for a capella music. Do I have a biblical case for it? No"

*(**One Body**, "Restoration Form VIII, by William Pile, article captioned 'They Had A War And Nobody Came,' Winter 1991, p. 10).*

I said the above as the reviser of the booklet took out: "We may do only what we find authority for in the Bible. That authority is to be by: a) direct command; b) approved example, or; c) a necessary inference' (p. 26, older booklet).

As I bring this to a close, rest assured that I haven't even made a start relative to the material that needs to be presented. I only wish that I could have made known other items. Even though (the items I just mentioned) I have these, and one time had permission on some, I will not use that for which permission has been denied. This "mixed bag" part of this closing section, for the alert and astute student of The Book, will also declare how that various pieces of the pattern have been attacked. Beloved, be a man, and always "Behold The Pattern!"

Note these wise words from brother Paul Southern.

> *"One does not have to be a carping critic to recognize that the church is going through a crisis. Only a blind optimist with his head in the sand can deny what is obvious.*
>
> *"**Current Conditions** present an ugly picture. Apostasy has already begun in some congregations. Ecumenical fellowship is replacing church identity more and more.*
>
> *"Individual Christians are crying for the comfort zone. Make things easy and sweet, and try not to upset any one. After all, everybody makes mistakes.*
>
> *"**The Cause** of our present situation has many aspects, but they boil down to one thing in the*

final analysis. The truth of the inspired scriptures is being compromised. How long has it been since you heard a gospel sermon on 'What must I do to be saved?'

"Many sermons that we hear nowadays would be acceptable in almost any denominational pulpit. Denominational error is seldom, if ever, condemned.

"The concept of sin has fallen into disrepute...

"Ministers that refuse to preach the word for fear of losing jobs should get out of the pulpits until they are fully committed to 'the high calling of God in Christ Jesus' (Philippians 3:14). Elders who listen to 'Comfort-zone' sermons without correcting them are also 'parties to the crime.'

*"**The Curse** of our present crisis in the church is obvious: the loss of many precious souls. Many weak members in the church become discouraged and give up.*

"Furthermore, the whole world is still waiting for the sunrise of genuine devotion to the Lord. Christians are expected to 'become... among whom ye are seen as lights in the world, holding forth the word of life' (cf. Philippians 2:15-16)...

*"**The Cure** of the present situation in the church. It is crystal clear from what has been said in this essay that the church must return to the old paths" (**Christian Journal,** Viewpoint, "Crisis in the Church," 2719 Race St., Fort Worth, Texas 76111, VOL. XXXII, NO.*

2, April, 1991, p. 2, all emp. his except those last eight words, GM).